D0084768

THE LOEB CLASSICAL LIBRARY

FOUNDED BY JAMES LOEB, LL.D.

EDITED BY
G. P. GOOLD, PH.D.

THE ATTIC NIGHTS
OF AULUS GELLIUS

THE ATTIC NIGHTS
OF AULUS GELLIUS

WITH AN ENGLISH TRANSLATION BY
JOHN C. ROLFE, Ph.D., Litt.D.
UNIVERSITY OF PENNSYLVANIA

IN THREE VOLUMES

I

CAMBRIDGE, MASSACHUSETTS
HARVARD UNIVERSITY PRESS
LONDON
WILLIAM HEINEMANN LTD
MCMLXXXIV

American SBN 674 99215 6
British SBN 434 99195 3

First printed 1927
Revised and reprinted 1946
Reprinted 1954, 1961, 1970, 1984

Printed in Great Britain

CONTENTS

PREFACE

THIS book was originally assigned to my friend
the late Samuel Ball Platner, of Western Reserve
University. At the time of his death, on August
20, 1921, he had completed a rough draft of the
translation of Books i–x. I have had the benefit of
using this material, and to it I acknowledge my
indebtedness.

The text is independent, being based in general
on that of Hertz and Hosius, but with numerous
changes resulting from the attention which the text
of Gellius has received since 1903. The punctuation,
and the press work generally, have been made to
conform to English and American usage.

J. C. R.

PHILADELPHIA,
    December 26, 1925.

INTRODUCTION

THE LIFE AND WORKS OF AULUS GELLIUS

COMPARATIVELY little is known about Aulus Gellius, the author of the *Noctes Atticae,* and our sources of information are almost entirely his own writings. There is difference of opinion as to the date and the place of his birth and of his death, as to the time and duration of his residence in Athens, and as to the time of his appointment as *iudex* and the beginning of his legal career. Opinions regarding these moot points are based upon his own statements or on the certain dates—also comparatively few in number—in the lives of various personages whom he mentions in the *Noctes*; and the estimates of different scholars vary greatly.

The *gens Gellia* was a clan of Samnite origin, which seems to have taken up its residence in Rome soon after the close of the second Punic war. Two generals of the family, Statius Gellius and Gellius Egnatius, fought against the Romans, the former in the first, the latter in the second Samnite war. The one was defeated and taken prisoner in 305 B.C.,[1] the other lost his life in the battle of Sentinum in 295.[2] At Rome one branch of the

---

[1] Livy, ix. 44. 13.   [2] Livy, x. 18–29.

family attained noble rank, if not earlier, through Lucius Gellius Publicola, who was *praetor peregrinus* in 94 B.C., consul in 72, and censor in 70.[1] It was he who proposed to the senate that the civic crown should be conferred upon Cicero, in recognition of his services in suppressing the conspiracy of Catiline. Aulus Gellius also mentions two other members of the clan : Gnaeus Gellius, a contemporary and opponent of Cato the censor,[2] and another Gnaeus Gellius,[3] of the time of the Gracchi, who wrote a history of Rome, entitled *Annales*, extending at least to the year 145 B.C. Aulus Gellius does not claim kinship with any of these Gellii, and tells us nothing of his own rank and social position. He was evidently of a good family and possessed of considerable means, being also, perhaps, the owner of a country estate at Praeneste.[4] He lived on terms of intimacy with many eminent men of his day, all of whom owed their distinction, at least in part, to their intellectual qualities.

The birthplace of Aulus Gellius, or Agellius, as he was miscalled in the Middle Ages,[5] is unknown. Some have thought that he was of African origin,[6] but this is questioned by others.[7] He is perhaps one of the few Roman writers who were natives of the eternal city; at any rate, he was in Rome at the time when he assumed the gown of manhood, probably at the age of between fifteen and seven-

---

[1] v. 6. 15.   [2] xiv. 2. 21 and 26.
[3] xviii. 12. 6.   [4] Cf. xi. 3. 1.
[5] By joining his praenomen *A.* with the *nomen*; cf. the reverse process in M. Accius for T. Maccius Plautus.
[6] Sittl, *Die lok. Verschiedenheiten* (1882), p 144.
[7] Vogel, *Jahrb. f. klass. Phil.* 127, p. 188.

INTRODUCTION

teen.[1] The year of his birth has been variously
conjectured from the few certain dates of his career
We know that he was in Athens after A.D. 143,
since at the time of his residence there he refers
to Herodes Atticus, who was consul in that year,
as *consularis vir*. At the same time he speaks of
himself as *iuvenis*, from which some have inferred
that he was then thirty years of age; but too much
weight cannot be given to Gellius' use of *iuvenis* and
adulescens (or *adulescentulus*). Not only are *iuvenis*
and *adulescens* used loosely by the Romans in general,
and applied indifferently to men between the ages
of seventeen and thirty or more, but Gellius seems
to use *iuvenis* in a complimentary sense and *adulescens*
with some degree of depreciation or, in speaking of
himself, of modesty. Thus he commonly refers to
his fellow-students at Athens, and to legitimate
students of philosophy in general, as *iuvenes*, while
the ignorant and presuming young men whose
"taking down" he describes ordinarily figure as
adulescentes.[2]

The date of his birth is variously assigned to
A.D. 113,[3] to the early years of the second century,[4]
to 123,[5] and to "about 130."[6] It is certain that
no part of his writing was done until the reign

[1] xviii. 4. 1.
[2] For example, i. 2. 3; i. 10. 1; viii. 3; ix. 15. 2; x. 19.
1; xiii. 20. 3.
[3] Fritz Weiss, *Die Attischen Nächte des Aulus Gellius*,
Leipzig, 1876, p. viii.
[4] B. Romano, *Rivista di Filologia*, xliv. (1916), pp. 547 ff.
[5] *Lectures and Essays*, 1885, p. 249 (from *Amer. Jour. of
Phil.* iv. pp. 4 ff.).
[6] Teuffel, *Römische Literatur*, 6th ed., 1913, iii., p. 95, and
Pauly-Wissowa, *Realencyk. s.v. Aulus Gellius.*

INTRODUCTION

of Antonius Pius (138–161), since he always refers
to Hadrian as *Divus,* and it probably continued
during the first half of the principate of Marcus
Aurelius (161–180). As he says nothing of the
remarkable death of Peregrinus Proteus,[1] whom he
knew and admired, some have assumed that he died
before that event took place, in 165; but Radulfus
de Diceto, writing in the early part of the thirteenth
century, says: " Agellius scribit anno CLXIX." [2] It
seems probable from the Preface to the *Noctes
Atticae,* which was obviously written after the completion of that work, that Gellius died soon after
completing his book, since he has not given
us the continuation which he promises.[3] It seems
evident that at the time of writing the Preface he
was in the prime of life; for his children were still
continuing their education, while he himself was
actively engaged in the practice of his profession,
or of managing his property.[4] On the whole, it
seems probable that he was born about 123, and,
if we accept the statement of de Diceto, that he
died soon after 169.

Gellius pursued in the schools the usual course of
study, consisting of grammar, in the Roman sense
of the term, and rhetoric. Among his instructors
in grammar was the celebrated Carthaginian scholar
Sulpicius Apollinaris,[5] who was also the teacher of

[1] Lucian, *De Morte Peregrini.*

[2] *De Viris Illust.* Radulfus is credited with using good
sources (Teuffel, *Röm. Lit.* ii [6], § 285, 3), but see Schanz-
Hosius, *Röm. Lit.* iii [3], p. 178, and Götz, *Ber. der Sächs. Akad.*
75 (1926). [3] *Praef.* 24.

[4] *Praef.* 23, quantum a tuenda re familiari procurandoque
cultu liberorum meorum dabitur otium.

[5] vii. 6. 12, *etc.*

the emperor Pertinax. He studied rhetoric with
Antonius Julianus,[1] with Titus Castricius,[2] and perhaps with Cornelius Fronto.[3] After completing his
studies in Rome Gellius went to Athens for instruction in philosophy, and, as Nettleship thought,
remained there from the age of nineteen to that of
twenty-three. It is certain that he spent at least
a year in Greece, since he mentions the four seasons
of spring, summer, autumn and winter in that connection. There is nothing, so far as I know, that
indicates a longer residence; his book was merely
begun in Athens,[4] not finished there.

The question of the time of Gellius' stay in
Greece is closely connected with that of his appointment as *iudex*.[5] At the time of his first appointment he must have been at least twenty-five years
old,[6] although he refers to himself as *adulescens,* and
it seems wholly probable that he began his legal
career after returning to Rome;[7] otherwise, since
he continued to practise his profession for some time,[8]
if not to the end of his life, we must infer that his
legal career was interrupted by his sojourn in
Athens, which seems improbable.

Gellius' student life in Athens combined serious
work with agreeable entertainment. With Calvisius
Taurus he studied Plato and Aristotle, but to what

[1] ix. 15. 1; xix. 9. 2.   [2] xi. 13. 1.
[3] ii. 26. 1; xiii. 29. 2; xix. 8. 1.   [4] *Praef.* 4.
[5] xiv. 2. 1; xii. 13. 1; cf. i. 22. 6. Two separate appoint-
ments are mentioned, unless Gellius is inaccurate in referring
one to the praetors and the other to the consuls.
[6] *Digest,* xlii. 1. 57; l. 4. 8.
[7] The writer in Teuffel's *Römische Literatur* thinks it was
after his visit to Athens.
[8] See xi. 3. 1.

extent is uncertain. He seems to have seen a good deal of Peregrinus Proteus, of whom he gives us a very different impression from that conveyed by Lucian, and he was on intimate terms with the famous rhetorician Tiberius Claudius Herodes Atticus, who was afterwards, at Rome, the praeceptor of Lucius Verus and Marcus Aurelius.[1] With his fellow-students he enjoyed the hospitality of Herodes at his villa at Cephisia and elsewhere. He made an excursion to Aegina with his comrades,[2] and with Calvisius Taurus a trip to Delphi.[3] Every week the young philosophers met at dinner, where they indulged in various intellectual diversions.[4]

After his return to Rome Gellius continued his interest in philosophy and other learning, and it was there that he became intimate with Favorinus, the friend of the emperor Hadrian.[5] He speaks with particular admiration of Favorinus, whose Παντοδαπὴ Ἱστορία may have suggested the form of the *Noctes Atticae*, and perhaps have furnished some of its material. He was intimate also with the poets Julius Paulus[6] and Annianus,[7] and with other intellectual men of the time.

The *Noctes Atticae* is a collection of interesting notes on grammar, public and private antiquities, history and biography, philosophy (including natural philosophy), points of law, text criticism, literary criticism, and various other topics. It gives us valuable information in many fields of knowledge,

---

[1] *Scr. Hist. Aug.*, *vita M. Anton.* ii. 4 (*L.C.L.* i. p. 136), *v. Ver.* ii. 5 (*L.C.L.* i. p. 210).
[2] ii. 21. 1.   [3] xii. 5. 1.   [4] xv. 2, 3.
[5] *Scr. Hist. Aug.*, *vita Hadr.* xiv. 12 (i. p. 49 *L.C.L.*).
[6] xix. 7. 1.   [7] xx. 8. 1-2.

and it contains extracts from a great number of Greek and Roman writers (275 are mentioned by name), the works of many of whom are otherwise wholly or in great part lost. While his ability is only moderate, Gellius is in the main accurate and conscientious, although he sometimes gives the impression that he has consulted original authorities when in fact he took his material at second hand. It is believed that he cites from no one whom he does not mention at least once by name, but it is not certain that this applies to the single works of a writer; it does not apply to his contemporaries. He seems to have consulted no authority earlier than Varro (116–28 B.C.), and often to have resorted for his quotations from earlier writers to commentaries and grammatical works. He sometimes tries to pass off the learning of others as his own, particularly in the case of his contemporaries.[1]

The style of Gellius is sometimes obscure, and although he deprecates the use of obsolete words, his own writings are by no means free from unusual and archaic words and expressions.[2] His faults are largely those of the time in which he lived, when the reaction which led to the so-called Silver Latin had come to an end and an archaistic tendency had taken its place. He frequently cites Cicero and Virgil, and always speaks of them with respect, but his authorities for the use of the Latin language are in large part the writers of the ante-classical period.

---

[1] For fuller details see Nettleship, *l.c.* (p. xiii, n. 5) *passim*.
[2] See Knapp, *Archaism in A. Gellius, Class. Stud. in hon. of H. Drisler*, New York and London, 1894 ; Foster, *Studies in Archaism in A. Gellius*, Columbia Univ. Diss., New York, 1912.

His translator Weiss rates him most highly, and he is doubtless right in considering him modest and fond of learning. Augustine[1] calls him "vir elegantissimi eloquii et facundae scientiae," and Erasmus[2] speaks of "Gellii commentariis, quibus nihil fieri potest neque tersius neque eruditius." He was used by many later writers,[3] extensively by Nonius Marcellus and Macrobius.

THE MANUSCRIPTS

Our earliest manuscripts divide the *Noctes Atticae* into two parts, containing respectively Books i–vii and ix–xx. These were not united in a single codex before the fourteenth or fifteenth century. The eighth book is lost except for the chapter headings and some inconsiderable fragments, a loss which must have occurred between the time of Macrobius, who knew the eighth book, and that of the archetype of our oldest manuscripts; that is, between the fifth and the ninth centuries. That the division of the work was sometimes made after the ninth book is indicated by the epigram of Gaius Aurelius Romanus, which is found in some of the manuscripts at the end of that book; but it would be difficult to account for the loss of the eighth book, if that division had been universal. The manuscripts which contain the whole work are all late, with the exception of the *fragmentum Buslidianum*. Those which contain the first part, Books i–vii, are the following:

[1] *De Civ. Dei*, ix. 4.
[2] Adagiorum Chilias I., cent. 4, prov. xxxvii.
[3] For a list see Hertz, ed. maior, ii. (1885), pp. v. ff.

INTRODUCTION

P. Codex Parisinus 5765, of the thirteenth century, in the Bibliothèque Nationale at Paris. It omits i. 1–2. 10 and ends at vii. 4. 3 with the words *ictus solis*.

R. Codex Lugduno-Batavianus Gronovianus 21, formerly Rottendorfianus. This manuscript is written in various hands, for the most part of the twelfth century. It comes to an end at vi. 20. 6, and it lacks the *lemmata*.

V. Codex Vaticanus 3452, of the thirteenth century. It begins with the index of chapters, omitting the Preface.

The descent of these manuscripts from a single archetype is shown by the occurrence of the same lacunae (see i. 4. 3 and i. 22. 5 and other examples in Hertz and Hosius), by the same arbitrary additions (iii. 17. 5; v. 18. 9, etc.), and by the same errors (i. 3. 19, 24, 25, etc.). The nature of some of the errors indicates that the archetype of P, R, and V was written in uncials without word-division.

From a different archetype is our oldest manuscript:

A. Palatino-Vaticanus xxiv, a palimpsest, assigned by Hertz to the fifth, by Teuffel (6th ed.) to the sixth, and by Hosius, with a query, to the seventh century. It contains a Latin version of the books of Tobias, Judith, Job and Esther, written over several earlier works: fragments of Livy xci, Cicero *pro Fonteio* and *pro C. Rabirio*, Seneca, Lucan and others. Beginning with the 80th folio it contains large parts of Books i–iv of the *Noctes Atticae* with the addition of a few chapter headings. All the Greek is omitted and a space left for its insertion by another hand. Although carelessly written in "litteris ex quadrata forma detortis," A supplies lacunae and corrects some errors. It alone contains the end of the second chapter of Book i and the beginning of the third chapter.

β. Besides these extant manuscripts we have some readings from a lost codex of Hieronymus Buslidius, a Belgian cleric and jurist, who died in 1517. These readings are for the most part from Book i, with some from Books ix, x, xvi, xvii, and xviii, and are largely due to L. Carrio. The codex had no connection with A, although it contained the same parts of Books i, ii and iii. The readings are not of great value, although they are occasionally helpful in filling lacunae. Carrio's good faith has been questioned by some, but apparently without sufficient reason.

Of the other manuscripts of the first part of the *Noctes* the earliest, R, is not the best, since it has many indications of corruption and interpolation. Moreover, the writer was unacquainted with Greek except as single words. Nevertheless R sometimes has value (*e.g.* i. 11. 8; 14. 6, etc.). Of the three, V is the most valuable, since it contains all of Book vii, is more accurate in its Greek, and is very little inferior to P in other respects. The readings must, however, be carefully weighed in each case, and no codex has prime authority.

Of Books ix-xx we have seven manuscripts, which on the basis of common readings (correct and incorrect) are divided into two classes. The first of these, γ, contains the following:

O. Codex Reginensis inter Vaticanos 597, of the tenth century. It begins with ix. 14. 2, *grammaticam.*

II. Codex Reginensis inter Vaticanos 1646, written

in the year 1170, as appears from the colophon,
" Willelmus scripsit anno . . . MCLXX."

X. Codex Lugduno-Batavianus Vossianus Lat. F
112, of the tenth century. It contains Books x–xx, and
also ix with the exception of 1–2. 10, *fortissimorum* ;
8. 1, *nasci non*—12. 10, *dicit* ; and 16. 6, *postulantis*,
etc.

N. Codex Magliabecchianus 329, of the fifteenth
century. This codex was written by Nicolai Nicoli,
who was helped with the Greek by Ambrosius
Traversarius. It is the only manuscript, except the
deteriores, which has the words following xx. 10. 7.
It seems to owe to the hand of Nicolai some correct
readings which it offers, either alone or in agreement
with the second family.

The second family, δ, contains the following :

Q. Codex Parisinus 8664, of the thirteenth
century. In the Bibl. Nat. at Paris.

Z. Codex Lugduno-Batavianus Vossianus Lat. F
7, of the fourteenth century.

B. Fragments written in the year 1173, a part of
which are contained in the codex in the library of
Berne which is numbered 404. It gives ix.–xii. 10.
3, *esse potuit*. The rest, as far as xiii. 5 (xiii. 1–4 is
omitted with a mistake in numbering), is supplied
by leaves of a manuscript of the university library at
Utrecht (*codex Ultra-traiectinus*), designated as *Aevum
vetus. Scriptores Graeci. No. 26*.

All these manuscripts of Books ix–xx, with the
exception of Q, sometimes have all or a part of the
Greek written in Latin letters. Neither family is
greatly superior to the other. δ is slightly the
better, especially Q; but all the codices of both
families must be considered.

Codices **O** and **Q** have corrections by a second hand (O², Q²). These sometimes eliminate obvious errors, but at other times introduce new conjectures. O also has corrections by a third hand (O³).

Besides these complete manuscripts there are two *Florilegia* contained in cod. Parisinus 4952 (T) and Vaticanus 3307 (Y), both of the twelfth century. In spite of their age these only occasionally give readings of any value.

Other codices used by Hertz are regarded by Hosius as of no importance.

A number of inferior codices (ς), for the most part later than the fourteenth century, contain the whole of Gellius, including the last part of the last book (otherwise found only in N), as well as the chapter-headings of Book viii. For this reason, and because they occasionally correct errors, they are not wholly to be disregarded.

The value of *testimonia* in text criticism is generally recognized. Of these Hertz has made a thoroughgoing collection. In some *testimonia* Gellius is named (Vopiscus, Lactantius, Servius, Augustinus, Priscian), but in very many instances he is used without mention of his name (as in Apuleius, Nonius, Ammianus, the Glossographers). *Testimonia* later than the ninth century (Einhard, John of Salisbury, etc.) are of no value in restoring the text.

BIBLIOGRAPHICAL NOTE

The *editio princeps* of Gellius was published in Rome in 1469 in one volume. This was followed in 1472 by a second Roman edition in two volumes and a Venetian edition in one volume : the Venetian

xxii

edition appeared in a twelfth reprint in 1500. Other important early editions are the Aldine in 1515, that of J. F. & J. Gronov, Leyden, 4 vols., 1706, and a new edition of the latter by J. L. Conradi, 2 vols., Leipzig, 1762. The standard critical edition is that of Martin Hertz, Leipzig, 1883. An *editio minor* of Hertz appeared in 1886, and the edition of C. Hosius in 1903, both in the series of Teubner texts.

There is an English translation by W. Beloe, London, 3 vols., 1795. It contains numerous errors and omits many words and phrases. A much better version is that into German by Weiss (see note 3, p. xiii). There is a good French translation in the edition of Apuleius, Gellius and Petronius by Nisard. Weiss (p. xvi) mentions four other French translations: one published at Paris in three volumes in 1789; one by Victor Verger with the Latin text, Paris, 3 vols., 1820; one by Jacquinet et Favre; and a fourth by Charpentier et Blanchet (the last two without dates); also a translation into Russian of 1820. Nothing approaching an adequate commentary on the *Noctes Atticae* exists in any language.

A list of the important works dealing with Gellius is given in the edition of Hosius, pp. lxi ff. Besides works already cited the following additions may be made to his list:

W. Heraeus, review of Hosius, *Berl. phil. Woch.* 1904, pp. 1163 ff.

F. Hache, *Quaestiones Archaicae.* I. *De A. Gellio veteris sermonis imitatore,* Breslau, 1907.

A. J. Kronenberg, *ad Gellium, Class. Quart.,* iv. (1910), pp. 23 f.

INTRODUCTION

O. Lauze, *Das synchronistische Kapitel des Gellius* (xvii. 21), *Rh. Mus.* lxvi. (1911), pp. 237–274.

P. Maas, *Varro bei Gellius* (on xviii. 15), *Hermes,* xlviii. (1913), pp. 157–159.

W. Schick, Favorin, Περὶ Παίδων Τροφῆς, Leipzig, 1912.

A. E. Evans, A. Gellius on *Mala prohibita vs Mala in se, Class. Jour.* ix. (1914), pp. 396–398.

P. H. Damsté, *ad A. Gellium, Mnemos.* xlii. (1914), pp. 91–92.

Emendatur locus Gellianus (xi. 21. 8), *Mnemos.* xlvi. (1918), p. 444.

Critical Notes on Gellius i–xx, *Mnemos.* xlvii. (1919), pp. 288–298, and xlviii. pp. 80–89 and 193–204.

E. W. Fay, *Nigidius Grammaticus (casus interrogandi apud Gell.* xx. 6. 7–8), *Amer. Jour. of Phil.* xxxvi. (1915), pp. 76–79.

M. L. De Gubernatis, *Questioncelle Probiane I* (on Gellius xiii. 21), *Rivista di Filologia,* xliv. (1916), pp. 235–245.

J. C. Rolfe, *Prorsus* in Gellius, *Class. Phil.* xvii. (1922), pp. 144–146.[1]

We now have *Noctes Atticus* ed. P. K. Marshall 2 vols.   Oxford Texts 1968, 1969.

Les Nuites Attiques, i–iv ed. with French translation R. Marache Budé, Paris 1967.

---

[1] The total number of examples should be 42; add xiv. 1. 29; 2. 16; 6. 5; xvii. 20. 2; xx. 5. 10.

INTRODUCTION

Sigla

For Books I–VII :

A = Codex palimpsestus Palatino-Vaticanus.
P = Codex Parisinus 5765.
R = Codex Lugduno-Batavianus 21.
V = Codex Vaticanus 3452.
ω = The agreement of (A), P, R, V.
β = Codex Buslidianus.
T = Florilegium codicis Parisini 4952.
Y = Florilegium codicis Vaticani 3307.
ς = The late and inferior codices.
σ = The vulgate reading.

For Books IX–XX :

N = Codex Magliabecchianus 329.
O = Codex Reginensis 597.
Π = Codex Reginensis 1646.
X = Codex Vossianus Lat. F 112.
γ = The archetype of N, O, Π, X.
B = Codex Bernensis 404 and Rheno-traiectinus,
      aevum vetus, Scriptores Graeci 26.
Q = Codex Parisinus 8664.
Z = Codex Vossianus Lat. F 7.
δ = The archetype of (B) Q, Z.
ω = The agreement of the codices of Books
      ix–xx.

Q^2, O^2 = Correctors of codices Q, O.
T, Y, β, ς, σ, as for codices of Books i–vii.

NOTE

A complete Index of Proper Names is given at
the end of vol. iii and, in connection with the names
of the writers, the editions of the fragments of those
whose works are in great part lost are there cited.

PRAEFATIO

1   * * * iucundiora alia reperiri queunt, ad hoc ut liberis quoque meis partae istiusmodi remissiones essent,
quando animus eorum interstitione aliqua negotiorum
2 data laxari indulgerique potuisset.   Usi autem sumus
ordine rerum fortuito, quem antea in excerpendo
feceramus.   Nam proinde ut librum quemque in
manus ceperam seu Graecum seu Latinum vel quid
memoratu dignum audieram, ita quae libitum erat,
cuius generis cumque erant, indistincte atque
promisce annotabam eaque mihi ad subsidium
memoriae quasi quoddam litterarum penus reconde-
bam, ut quando usus venisset aut rei aut verbi, cuius
me repens forte oblivio tenuisset, et libri ex quibus
ea sumpseram non adessent, facile inde nobis inventu
atque depromptu foret.

3   Facta igitur est in his quoque commentariis eadem
rerum disparilitas quae fuit in illis annotationibus
pristinis, quas breviter et indigeste et incondite ex [1]
4 eruditionibus lectionibusque variis feceramus.   Sed
quoniam longinquis per hiemem noctibus in agro,
sicuti dixi, terrae Atticae commentationes hasce
ludere ac facere exorsi sumus, idcirco eas inscripsimus
Noctium esse *Atticarum*, nihil imitati festivitates in-

---

[1] *ex, added by J. F. Gronov.*

PREFACE

* * * other more entertaining writings may be found,[1] in order that like recreation might be provided for my children, when they should have some respite from business affairs and could unbend and divert their minds. But in the arrangement of my material I have adopted the same haphazard order that I had previously followed in collecting it. For whenever I had taken in hand any Greek or Latin book, or had heard anything worth remembering, I used to jot down whatever took my fancy, of any and every kind, without any definite plan or order; and such notes I would lay away as an aid to my memory, like a kind of literary storehouse, so that when the need arose of a word or a subject which I chanced for the moment to have forgotten, and the books from which I had taken it were not at hand, I could readily find and produce it.

It therefore follows, that in these notes there is the same variety of subject that there was in those former brief jottings which I had made without order or arrangement, as the fruit of instruction or reading in various lines. And since, as I have said, I began to amuse myself by assembling these notes during the long winter nights which I spent on a country-place in the land of Attica, I have therefore given them the title of *Attic Nights*, making no at-

---

[1] The beginning of the sentence is lost; the following final clause depends upon some such verb as *scripsi*.

scriptionum quas plerique alii utriusque linguae
5 scriptores in id genus libris fecerunt. Nam quia
variam et miscellam et quasi confusaneam doctrinam
conquisiverant, eo titulos quoque ad eam sententiam
6 exquisitissimos indiderunt. Namque alii *Musarum*
inscripserunt, alii *Silvarum,* ille Πέπλον, hic Ἀμαλθείας
Κέρας, alius Κηρία, partim Λειμῶνας, quidam *Lectionis
Suae,* alius *Antiquarum Lectionum* atque alius Ἀνθηρῶν
7 et item alius Εὐρημάτων. Sunt etiam qui Λύχνους
inscripserint, sunt item qui Στρωματεῖς, sunt adeo
qui Πανδέκτας et Ἑλικῶνα et Προβλήματα et Ἐγχει-
8 ρίδια et Παραξιφίδας. Est qui *Memoriales* titulum
fecerit, est qui Πραγματικὰ et Πάρεργα et Διδασκαλικά,
est item qui *Historiae Naturalis,* et[1] Παντοδαπῆς Ἱστο-
ρίας, est praeterea qui *Pratum,* est itidem qui Πάγκαρ-
πον, est qui Τόπων scripserit[2]; sunt item multi qui
9 *Coniectanea,* neque item non sunt qui indices libris
suis fecerint aut *Epistularum Moralium* aut *Epistoli-
carum Quaestionum* aut *Confusarum* et quaedam alia inscripta nimis lepida multasque prorsum concinnitates
10 redolentia. Nos vero, ut captus noster est, incuriose
et inmeditate ac prope etiam subrustice ex ipso loco
ac tempore hibernarum vigiliarum *Atticas Noctes*

---

[1] et, *Skutsch*; est, ω.
[2] scripserit, *Petschenig*; scripsit, ω.

---

[1] *Silva,* and its Greek equivalent *Hyle* (Suet. *Gramm.* x),
was used metaphorically of material in a rough form, and of
hasty and more or less extempore productions; see Quint.
x. 3. 17.

[2] Of the thirty titles cited by Gellius about one-half can
be assigned to their authors, many of whom Gellius himself
mentions in various parts of his work; see the Index. There
are others which he undoubtedly used, but does not cite,
such as the " Παντοδαπὴ Ἱστορία " of Favorinus. " The
Muses " refers not to Herodotus, the books of whose " His-
xxviii

tempt to imitate the witty captions which many other writers of both languages have devised for works of the kind. For since they had laboriously gathered varied, manifold, and as it were indiscriminate learning, they therefore invented ingenious titles also, to correspond with that idea. Thus some called their books "The Muses," others "Woods"[1] one used the title "Athena's Mantle," another "The Horn of Amaltheia," still another "Honeycomb," several "Meads," one "Fruits of my Reading," another "Gleanings from Early Writers," another "The Nosegay," still another "Discoveries." Some have used the name "Torches," others "Tapestry," others "Repertory," others "Helicon," "Problems," "Handbooks" and "Daggers." One man called his book "Memorabilia," one "Principia," one "Incidentals," another "Instructions." Other titles are "Natural History," "Universal History," "The Field," "The Fruit-basket," or "Topics." Many have termed their notes "Miscellanies," some "Moral Epistles," "Questions in Epistolary Form," or "Miscellaneous Queries," and there are some other titles that are exceedingly witty and redolent of extreme refinement.[2] But I, bearing in mind my limitations, gave my work off-hand, without premeditation, and indeed almost in rustic fashion, the caption of *Attic Nights*, derived merely from the time and place of

tory " the grammarians named from the Muses, but to Aurelius Opilius, cited by Gellius in i. 25. 17. The " Silvae " belong either to Valerius Probus (Suet. *Gramm.* 24) or to Ateius Philologus (id. 10); the " Silvae " of Statius are of a different character. Δειμών was used by Pamphilus, by Gellius himself, and by Cicero of a work of a different kind; the Latin equivalent " Pratum " was used by Suetonius. For further information see the Index.

inscripsimus, tantum ceteris omnibus in ipsius quoque inscriptionis laude cedentes, quantum cessimus in cura et elegantia scriptionis.

11 Sed ne consilium quidem in excerpendis notandisque rebus idem mihi, quod plerisque illis, fuit. Namque illi omnes et eorum maxime Graeci, multa et varia lectitantes, in quas res cumque inciderant, "alba," ut dicitur, "linea" sine cura discriminis solam copiam sectati converrebant, quibus in legendis ante animus senio ac taedio languebit quam unum alterumve reppererit quod sit aut voluptati legere aut cultui

12 legisse aut usui meminisse. Ego vero, cum illud Ephesii viri summe nobilis verbum cordi haberem, quod profecto ita est πολυμαθίη νόον οὐ διδάσκει, ipse quidem volvendis transeundisque multis admodum voluminibus per omnia semper negotiorum intervalla in quibus furari otium potui exercitus defessusque sum, sed modica ex his eaque sola accepi quae aut ingenia prompta expeditaque ad honestae eruditionis cupidinem utiliumque artium contemplationem celeri facilique compendio ducerent aut homines aliis iam vitae negotiis occupatos a turpi certe agrestique rerum atque verborum imperitia vindicarent.

13 Quod erunt autem in his commentariis pauca quaedam scrupulosa et anxia, vel ex grammatica vel ex dialectica vel etiam ex geometrica,[1] quodque erunt

---

[1] geometrica, ω ; geometria, ϛ (A.L.L. x, p. 240).

---

[1] A proverb of Greek origin, found in Sophocles, Frag. 307, Nauck[2] : οὐ μᾶλλον ἢ λευκῷ λίθῳ λευκὴ στάθμη. A builder's chalked line leaves no mark on white substances. The abbreviated form λευκὴ στάθμη (alba linea) in Plato, Charm. p. 154 B, and Lucil. 831, Marx.

my winter's vigils; I thus fall as far short of all
other writers in the dignity too even of my title, as
I do in care and in elegance of style.

Neither had I in making my excerpts and notes
the same purpose as many of those whom I have
mentioned. For all of them, and in particular the
Greeks, after wide and varied reading, with a white
line, as the saying goes,[1] that is with no effort to
discriminate, swept together whatever they had
found, aiming at mere quantity. The perusal of such
collections will exhaust the mind through weariness
or disgust, before it finds one or two notes which it
is a pleasure to read, or inspiring to have read, or
helpful to remember. I myself, on the contrary,
having at heart that well-known saying of the
famous Ephesian,[2] " Much learning does not make
a scholar," did it is true busy and even weary myself
in unrolling and running through many a scroll,
working without cessation in all the intervals of
business whenever I could steal the leisure; but I
took few items from them, confining myself to those
which, by furnishing a quick and easy short-cut,
might lead active and alert minds to a desire for
independent learning and to the study of the useful
arts, or would save those who are already fully
occupied with the other duties of life from an
ignorance of words and things which is assuredly
shameful and boorish.

Now just because there will be found in these
notes some few topics that are knotty and troublesome, either from Grammar or Dialectics or even
from Geometry, and because there will also be some

---

[2] Heracleitus, Frag. 40 Diels. Cf. Aeschylus, Frag. 286 :
ὁ χρήσιμ᾽ εἰδὼς, οὐχ ὁ πολλ᾽ εἰδὼς σοφός.

item paucula remotiora super augurio iure et pontificio,
non oportet ea defugere, quasi aut cognitu non utilia
aut perceptu difficilia.   Non enim fecimus altos nimis
et obscuros in his rebus quaestionum sinus, sed
primitias quasdam et quasi libamenta ingenuarum
artium dedimus, quae virum civiliter eruditum neque
audisse umquam neque attigisse, si non inutile, at
14 quidem certe indecorum est.   Ab his igitur, si cui
forte nonnumquam tempus voluptasque erit lucubra-
tiunculas istas cognoscere, petitum impetratumque
volumus, ut in legendo quae pridem scierint non
15 aspernentur quasi nota invulgataque.   Nam ecquid[1]
tam remotum in litteris est quin id tamen complusculi
sciant?   Et satis hoc blandum est, non esse haec
neque in scholis decantata neque in commentariis
16 protrita.   Quae porro nova sibi ignotaque offenderint,
aequum esse puto ut sine vano obtrectatu considerent
an minutae istae admonitiones et pauxillulae nequaquam tamen sint vel ad alendum studium vescae vel
ad oblectandum fovendumque animum frigidae, sed
eius seminis generisque sint ex quo facile adolescant
aut ingenia hominum vegetiora aut memoria admini-
culatior aut oratio sollertior aut sermo incorruptior
17 aut delectatio in otio atque in ludo liberalior.   Quae
autem parum plana videbuntur aut minus plena in-

---

[1] ecquid, *Madvig*; et quid, ω.

little material of a somewhat recondite character
about augural or pontifical law, one ought not therefore to avoid such topics as useless to know or
difficult to comprehend. For I have not made an
excessively deep and obscure investigation of the
intricacies of these questions, but I have presented
the first fruits, so to say, and a kind of foretaste of
the liberal arts; and never to have heard of these,
or come in contact with them, is at least unbecoming,
if not positively harmful, for a man with even an
ordinary education. Of those then, if such there
be, who may perhaps sometimes have leisure and
inclination to acquaint themselves with these lucu-
brations, I should like to ask and be granted the
favour, that in reading of matters which they have
known for a long time they shall not scorn them as
commonplace and trite; for is there anything in
literature so recondite as not to be known to a
goodish many? In fact, I am sufficiently flattered
if these subjects have not been repeated over and
over again in the schools and become the common
stock of commentaries. Furthermore, if my readers
find anything new and unknown to them, I think
it fair that they should not indulge in useless
criticism, but should ask themselves whether these
observations, slight and trifling though they be,
are after all not without power to inspire study, or
too dull to divert and stimulate the mind; whether
on the contrary they do not contain the germs and
the quality to make men's minds grow more vigorous,
their memory more trustworthy, their eloquence
more effective, their diction purer, or the pleasures
of their hours of leisure and recreation more refined.
But as to matters which seem too obscure, or not

structaque, petimus, inquam, ut ea non docendi magis quam admonendi gratia scripta existiment et, quasi demonstratione vestigiorum contenti, persequantur ea post, si libebit, vel libris repertis vel magistris.

18 Quae vero putaverint reprehendenda, his, si audebunt, succenseant, unde ea nos accepimus; sed enim, si [1] quae aliter apud alium scripta legerint, ne iam statim temere [2] obstrepant, sed et rationes rerum et auctoritates hominum pensitent, quos illi quosque nos secuti sumus.

19   Erit autem id longe optimum, ut qui in lectitando, percontando, [3] scribendo, commentando, numquam voluptates, numquam labores ceperunt, nullas hoc genus vigilias vigilarunt neque ullis inter eiusdem Musae aemulos certationibus disceptationibusque elimati sunt, sed intemperiarum negotiorumque pleni sunt, abeant [4] a "Noctibus" his procul, atque alia sibi oblectamenta quaerant.   Vetus adagium est:

Nil cum fidibus graculost,[5] nihil cum amaracino sui.

20 Atque etiam, quo sit quorundam male doctorum hominum scaevitas et invidentia irritatior, mutuabor ex Aristophanae choro anapaesta pauca et quam ille homo festivissimus fabulae suae spectandae legem dedit, eandem ego commentariis his legendis dabo, ut ea ne attingat neve adeat profestum et profanum

---

[1] si, *added by Skutsch.*
[2] temere, *Carrio*; tempere, ω (tempore *R*).
[3] percontando, *added by J. F. Gronov*; see note 4.
[4] labeant percontando scribendo, ω.   [5] graculos, ω.

---

[1] FPR, p. 56, Bährens. *Amaracinum* (sc. *unguentum*) was a perfumed oil from Cos (Pliny, *N.H.* xiii. 5). Marjoram (*amaracus*) was also used, alone or with other ingredients, in other unguents (Pliny, *N.H.* xiii. 13, 14).

xxxiv

presented in full enough detail, I beg once again that
my readers may consider them written, not so much
to instruct, as to give a hint, and that content with
my, so to speak, pointing out of the path, they may
afterwards follow up those subjects, if they so desire,
with the aid either of books or of teachers.   But if
they find food for criticism, let them, if they have the
courage, blame those from whom I drew my material ;
or if they discover that different statements are made
by someone else, let them not at once give way to
hasty censure, but rather let them weigh the reasons
for the statements and the value of the authorities
which those other writers and which I have followed.

For those, however, who have never found pleasure
nor busied themselves in reading, inquiring, writing
and taking notes, who have never spent wakeful
nights in such employments, who have never im-
proved themselves by discussion and debate with
rival followers of the same Muse, but are absorbed
in the turmoil of business affairs—for such men it
will be by far the best plan to hold wholly aloof
from these "Nights" and seek for themselves other
diversion.   There is an old saying :

The daw knows naught of the lyre, the hog
naught of marjoram ointment.[1]

Moreover, in order that the perversity and envy of
certain half-educated men may be the more aroused,
I shall borrow a few anapaests from a chorus of
Aristophanes, and the conditions which that wittiest
of men imposed for the viewing of his play, I shall
lay down for the reading of these notes of mine :
namely, that the profane and uninitiate throng,
averse to the Muses' play, shall neither touch nor

21 vulgus, a ludo musico diversum.   Versus legis datae
hi sunt :

Εὐφημεῖν χρὴ κἀξίστασθαι τοῖς ἡμετέροισι χοροῖσιν
Ὅστις ἄπειρος τοιῶνδε λόγων ἢ γνώμῃ μὴ καθαρεύει
Ἢ γενναίων ὄργια Μουσῶν μήτ᾽ εἶδεν μήτ᾽ ἐχόρευσεν,
Τούτοις αὐδῶ, καὖθις ἀπαυδῶ, καὖθις τὸ τρίτον μάλ᾽
    ἀπαυδῶ
Ἐξίστασθαι μύσταισι χοροῖς, ὑμεῖς δ᾽ ἀνεγείρετε μολπὴν
Καὶ παννυχίδας τὰς ἡμετέρας, αἳ τῇδε πρέπουσιν ἑορτῇ.

22   Volumina commentariorum ad hunc diem viginti
23 iam facta sunt.   Quantum autem vitae mihi deinceps
deum voluntate erit quantumque a tuenda re familiari
procurandoque cultu liberorum meorum dabitur otium,
ea omnia subsiciva et subsecundaria tempora ad colli-
gendas huiuscemodi memoriarum delectatiunculas
24 conferam.   Progredietur ergo numerus librorum, diis
bene iuvantibus, cum ipsius vitae quantuli quomque [1]
fuerint progressibus, neque longiora mihi dari spatia
vivendi volo quam dum ero ad hanc quoque facultatem
scribendi commentandique idoneus.
25   Capita rerum quae cuique commentario insunt, ex-
posuimus hic universa, ut iam statim declaretur quid
quo in libro quaeri invenirique possit.

[1] quomque, *Skutsch* ; quique, ω.

---

[1] *Frogs*, 354 ff. 359 ff. ; Roger's translation.

PREFACE

approach them. The verses which contain those
conditions run as follows:[1]

> All evil thought and profane be still:
>> far hence, far hence from our choirs depart,
> Who knows not well what the Mystics tell,
>> or is not holy and pure of heart;
> Who ne'er has the noble revelry learned,
>> or danced the dance of the Muses high;

*   *   *   *   *

> I charge them once, I charge them twice,
>> I charge them thrice, that they draw not nigh
> To the sacred dance of the Mystic choir.
>> But YE, my comrades, awake the song,
> The night-long revels of joy and mirth
>> which ever of right to our feast belong.

Up to the present day I have already completed
twenty books of notes. As much longer life as the
Gods' will shall grant me, and as much respite as is
given me from managing my affairs and attending
to the education of my children, every moment of
that remaining and leisure time I shall devote to
collecting similar brief and entertaining memoranda.
Thus the number of books, given the Gods' gracious
help, will keep pace with the years of life itself,
however many or few they may be, nor have I any
desire to be allotted a longer span of existence than
so long as I retain my present ability to write and
take notes.

Summaries of the material to be found in each
book of my Commentaries I have here placed all
together, in order that it may at once be clear what
is to be sought and found in every book.

CAPITULA LIBRI PRIMI[1]

---

[1] *For variants see the chapters to which the headings belong.
The headings are divided among the separate volumes.*

CHAPTER HEADINGS OF BOOK I

CAPITULA

CHAPTER HEADINGS

CAPITULA

xlii

CHAPTER HEADINGS

xliii

CAPITULA

CHAPTER HEADINGS

CAPITULA

xlvi

CHAPTER HEADINGS

CAPITULA

xlviii

CHAPTER HEADINGS

CAPITULA

1

CHAPTER HEADINGS

CAPITULA

CHAPTER HEADINGS

CAPITULA

CHAPTER HEADINGS

CAPITULA

CHAPTER HEADINGS

CAPITULA

lviii

CHAPTER HEADINGS

CAPITULA

lx

CHAPTER HEADINGS

CAPITULA

CHAPTER HEADINGS

THE ATTIC NIGHTS
OF AULUS GELLIUS

BOOK 1

A. GELLII
NOCTIUM ATTICARUM

LIBER PRIMUS

I

Quali proportione quibusque collectionibus Plutarchus ratio-
cinatum esse Pythagoram philosophum dixerit de compre-
hendenda corporis proceritate qua fuit Hercules, cum vitam
inter homines viveret.

1 PLUTARCHUS in libro quem de Herculis quam
diu[1] inter homines fuit animi corporisque ingenio
atque virtutibus conscripsit, scite subtiliterque ratio-
cinatum Pythagoram philosophum dicit in reperienda
modulandaque status longitudinisque eius prae-
2 stantia. Nam cum fere constaret, curriculum stadii
quod est Pisis apud Iovem Olympium Herculem
pedibus suis metatum idque fecisse longum pedes
sescentos, cetera quoque stadia in terra Graecia ab
aliis postea instituta pedum quidem esse numero
sescentum, sed tamen esse aliquantulum breviora,
facile intellexit, modum spatiumque plantae Herculis,
ratione proportionis habita, tanto fuisse quam aliorum
procerius, quanto Olympicum stadium longius esset
3 quam cetera. Comprehensa autem mensura Hercu-

---

[1] quam diu, *Klotz* ; quantum, ω.

THE ATTIC NIGHTS
OF AULUS GELLIUS

BOOK I

I

Plutarch's account of the method of comparison and the
calculations which the philosopher Pythagoras used in
determining the great height of Hercules, while the hero
was living among men.

IN the treatise [1] which he wrote on the mental
and physical endowment and achievements of Hercules while he was among men, Plutarch says that
the philosopher Pythagoras reasoned sagaciously and
acutely in determining and measuring the hero's
superiority in size and stature.   For since it was
generally agreed that Hercules paced off the race-
course of the stadium at Pisae, near the temple of
Olympian Zeus, and made it six hundred feet long,
and since the other courses in the land of Greece, constructed later by other men, were indeed six hundred
feet in length, but yet were somewhat shorter than
that at Olympia, he readily concluded by a process
of comparison that the measured length of Hercules'
foot was greater than that of other men in the same
proportion as the course at Olympia was longer than
the other stadia.   Then, having ascertained the size

[1] This work, probably entitled βίος 'Ηρακλέους, has not
survived.

lani pedis, quanta longinquitas corporis ei mensurae
conveniret secundum naturalem membrorum omnium
inter se competentiam modificatus est atque ita id
collegit, quod erat consequens, tanto fuisse Herculem
corpore excelsiorem quam alios, quanto Olympicum
stadium ceteris pari numero factis anteiret.

II

Ab Herode Attico C. V. tempestive deprompta in quendam
iactantem et gloriosum adulescentem, specie tantum
philosophiae sectatorem, verba Epicteti Stoici, quibus
festiviter a vero Stoico seiunxit vulgus loquacium nebulonum qui se Stoicos nuncuparent.

1 HERODES ATTICUS, vir et Graeca facundia et consulari honore praeditus, accersebat saepe, nos cum
apud magistros Athenis essemus, in villas ei urbi
proximas me et clarissimum virum Servilianum
compluresque alios nostrates qui Roma in Graeciam
2 ad capiendum ingenii cultum concesserant. Atque
ibi tunc, cum essemus apud eum in villa cui nomen
est Cephisia, et aestu anni et sidere autumni flagran-
tissimo, propulsabamus incommoda caloris lucorum
umbra ingentium, longis ambulacris et mollibus,
aedium positu refrigeranti, lavacris nitidis et abundis
et collucentibus totiusque villae venustate, aquis
undique canoris atque avibus personante.

---

[1] The proper height was six times the length of the foot.

[2] According to Apollodorus, II. iv. 9, Hercules was 4 cubits
in height; according to Herodorus, 4 cubits and one foot;
see J. Tzetzes, *Chiliades*, ii. 210. The phrase *ex pede Herculem* has become proverbial, along with *ex ungue leonem* and
ab uno disce omnes (Virg. *Aen.* ii. 65 f.).

[3] *Clarissimus* became a standing title of men of high rank,
especially of the senatorial order.

4

of Hercules' foot, he made a calculation of the bodily
height suited to that measure, based upon the natural
proportion of all parts of the body, and thus arrived
at the logical conclusion that Hercules was as much
taller than other men as the course at Olympia
exceeded the others that had been constructed with
the same number of feet.[2]

II

The apt use made by Herodes Atticus, the ex-consul, in reply
to an arrogant and boastful young fellow, a student of
philosophy in appearance only, of the passage in which
Epictetus the Stoic humorously set apart the true Stoic
from the mob of prating triflers who called themselves
Stoics.

WHILE we were students at Athens, Herodes
Atticus, a man of consular rank and of true Grecian
eloquence, often invited me to his country houses
near that city, in company with the honourable [3] Ser-
vilianus and several others of our countrymen who
had withdrawn from Rome to Greece in quest of
culture. And there at that time, while we were with
him at the villa called Cephisia, both in the heat of
summer and under the burning autumnal sun, we
protected ourselves against the trying temperature
by the shade of its spacious groves, its long, soft [4]
promenades, the cool location of the house, its
elegant baths with their abundance of sparkling
water, and the charm of the villa as a whole, which
was everywhere melodious with plashing waters and
tuneful birds.

[4] Cf. Plin. *Epist.* ii. xvii. 15, vinea . . . nudis etiam pedibus mollis et cedens.

3 Erat ibidem nobiscum simul adulescens philosophiae sectator, "disciplinae," ut ipse dicebat,
4 "stoicae," sed loquacior inpendio et promptior. Is plerumque in convivio sermonibus, qui post epulas haberi solent, multa atque inmodica de [1] philosophiae doctrinis intempestive atque insubide disserebat praeque se uno ceteros omnes linguae Atticae principes gentemque omnem togatam, quodcumque nomen Latinum rudes esse et agrestes praedicabat atque interea vocabulis haut facile cognitis, syllogismorum captionumque dialecticarum laqueis strepebat, κυριεύοντας et ἡσυχάζοντας et σωρείτας aliosque id genus griphos neminem posse dicens nisi se dissolvere. Rem vero ethicam naturamque humani ingenii virtutumque origines officiaque earum et confinia, aut contra morborum vitiorumque fraudes animorumque labes et [2] pestilentias, asseverabat nulli esse ulli magis ea omnia explorata, comperta meditataque.
5 Cruciatibus autem doloribusque corporis et periculis mortem minitantibus habitum statumque vitae beatae, quem se esse adeptum putabat, neque laedi neque inminui existimabat, ac ne oris quoque et vultus serenitatem stoici hominis umquam ulla posse aegritudine obnubilari.

---

[1] de, *Vulg.* ; *omitted by* ω.   [2] et, *R. Klotz*; *omitted by* ω.

---

[1] Where there are three propositions, any two of which are at variance with the third, they may be taken in pairs as true, rejecting the third as false. This is called the "master" argument, from κυριεύω, "to be master over" ; see Epictetus, ii. 18 and 19. The fallacy is due to the fact that all persons do not hold to the truth of the same pair, and it is impossible to maintain all three propositions at once. The "sorites" raised the question, if one grain at a time were taken from a heap, when it would cease to be a heap; and

6

There was with us there at the time a young student of philosophy, of the Stoic school according to his own account, but intolerably loquacious and presuming. In the course of the conversations which are commonly carried on at table after dinner, this fellow often used to prattle unseasonably, absurdly, and at immoderate length, on the principles of philosophy, maintaining that compared with himself all the Greek-speaking authorities, all wearers of the toga, and the Latin race in general were ignorant boors. As he spoke, he rattled off unfamiliar terms, the catchwords of syllogisms and dialectic tricks, declaring that no one but he could unravel the "master," the "resting," and the "heap" arguments,[1] and other riddles of the kind. Furthermore, as to ethics, the nature of the human intellect, and the origin of the virtues with their duties and limits, or on the other hand the ills caused by disease and sin, and the wasting and destruction of the soul, he stoutly maintained that absolutely no one else had investigated, understood and mastered all these more thoroughly than himself. Further, he believed that torture, bodily pain and deadly peril could neither injure nor detract from the happy state and condition of life which, in his opinion, he had attained, and that no sorrow could even cloud the serenity of the Stoic's face and expression.

conversely, if one grain at a time were added, when it would become a heap; see Cic. *Acad.* ii. 49. A variant, called the φαλακρός, inquired whether a man was bald after the loss of one hair, of two, or of how many. Horace, in *Epist.* ii. 1. 45-47, has combined both of these with the story told by Plutarch of Sertorius (*Sert.* 16). The "silent," or "resting" argument consisted in stopping and refusing to answer. It was used to meet the logical fallacy of the "sorites."

6 Has ille inanes glorias cum flaret iamque omnes finem cuperent verbisque eius defetigati pertaeduissent, tum Herodes Graeca, uti plurimus ei mos fuit, oratione utens, " Permitte," inquit, "philosophorum amplissime, quoniam respondere nos tibi, quos vocas idiotas, non quimus, recitari ex libro quid de huiuscemodi magniloquentia vestra senserit dixeritque Epictetus, Stoicorum maximus," iussitque proferri *Dissertationum Epicteti* digestarum ab Arriano primum librum, in quo ille venerandus senex iuvenes qui se " Stoicos " appellabant, neque frugis neque operae probae, sed theorematis tantum nugalibus et puerilium isagogarum commentationibus deblaterantes, obiurgatione iusta incessuit.

7 Lecta igitur sunt ex libro qui prolatus est ea quae addidi ; quibus verbis Epictetus severe simul et festiviter seiunxit atque divisit a vero atque sincero Stoico, qui esset procul dubio ἀκώλυτος, ἀνανάγκαστος, ἀπαραπόδιστος, ἐλεύθερος, εὐπορῶν, εὐδαιμονῶν, vulgus aliud nebulonum hominum qui se " Stoicos " nuncuparent, atraque verborum et argutiarum fuligine ob oculos audientium iacta[1] sanctissimae disciplinae nomen ementirentur : Εἰπέ μοι περὶ ἀγαθῶν καὶ
8 κακῶν. Ἄκουε.

Ἰλιόθεν με φέρων ἄνεμος Κικόνεσσι πέλασσεν.

9 Τῶν ὄντων τὰ μέν ἐστιν ἀγαθά, τὰ δὲ κακά, τὰ δὲ ἀδιάφορα. Ἀγαθὰ μὲν οὖν ἀρεταὶ καὶ τὰ μετέχοντα αὐτῶν, κακὰ δὲ κακία καὶ τὰ μετέχοντα κακίας, ἀδιάφορα δὲ τὰ μεταξὺ

---

[1] atro . . . iacto, ω.

[1] Actually the second book, ii. 19.

[2] Εἰπέ . . . is the request of the pseudo-philosopher, Ἄκουε the answer of Epictetus, who quotes a line of Homer (*Odyss.* ix. 39) which is here meaningless, implying that the pretended Stoics quote both poetry and ethics *glibly*, but without understanding.

Once when he was puffing out these empty boasts, and already all, weary of his prating, were thoroughly disgusted and longing for an end, Herodes, speaking in Greek as was his general custom, said: "Allow me, mightiest of philosophers, since we, whom you call laymen, cannot answer you, to read from a book of Epictetus, greatest of Stoics, what he thought and said about such big talk as that of yours." And he bade them bring the first[1] volume of the *Discourses of Epictetus*, arranged by Arrian, in which that venerable old man with just severity rebukes those young men who, though calling themselves Stoics, showed neither virtue nor honest industry, but merely babbled of trifling propositions and of the fruits of their study of such elements as are taught to children.

Then, when the book was brought, there was read the passage which I have appended, in which Epictetus with equal severity and humour set apart and separated from the true and genuine Stoic, who was beyond question without restraint or constraint, unembarrassed, free, prosperous and happy, that other mob of triflers who styled themselves Stoics, and casting the black soot of their verbiage before the eyes of their hearers, laid false claim to the name of the holiest of sects:

"'Speak to me of good and evil.'—Listen:
      The wind, bearing me from Ilium, drove me to
            the Cicones.[2]

"Of all existing things some are good, some evil, and some indifferent. Now the good things are virtues and what partakes of them, the evil are vice and what partakes of vice, and the indifferent lie

9

τούτων, πλοῦτος, ὑγεία, ζωή, θάνατος, ἡδονή, πόνος.
10 Πόθεν οἶδας; Ἑλλάνικος λέγει ἐν τοῖς Αἰγυπτιακοῖς. Τί
γὰρ διαφέρει τοῦτο εἰπεῖν, ἢ ὅτι Διογένης ἐν τῇ ἠθικῇ ἢ
Χρύσιππος ἢ Κλεάνθης; βεβασάνικας οὖν τι[1] αὐτῶν καὶ
11 δόγμα σαυτοῦ πεποίησαι. Δείκνυε πῶς εἴωθας ἐν πλοίῳ
χειμάζεσθαι·[2] μέμνησαι ταύτης τῆς διαιρέσεως, ὅταν
ψοφήσῃ τὸ ἱστίον καὶ ἀνακραυγάσῃς. Ἄν σοί τις
κακόσχολός πως παραστὰς εἴπῃ, λέγε μοι, τοὺς θεούς σοι,
ἃ πρῴην ἔλεγες, μή τι κακία ἐστὶν τὸ ναυαγῆσαι; μή τι
κακίας μετέχον; οὐκ ἄρα[3] ξύλον ἐνσείσεις αὐτῷ; τί
ἡμῖν καὶ σοί, ἄνθρωπε; ἀπολλύμεθα, καὶ σὺ ἐλθὼν
12 παίζεις. Ἐὰν δέ σε ὁ Καῖσαρ μεταπέμψηται κατηγορού-
μενον * * *

13   His ille auditis insolentissimus adulescens obticuit,
tamquam si ea omnia non ab Epicteto in quosdam
alios, sed ab Herode in eum dicta essent.[4]

III

Quod Chilo Lacedaemonius consilium anceps pro salute amici
cepit ; quodque est circumspecte et anxie considerandum
an pro utilitatibus amicorum delinquendum aliquando sit ;
notataque inibi et relata quae et Theophrastus et M.
Cicero super ea re scripserunt.

1   LACEDAEMONIUM Chilonem, virum ex illo incluto
numero sapientium, scriptum est in libris eorum qui

---

[1] Omitted by ω.   [2] γυμνάζεσθαι, Arrian.
[3] ἄρας, Arrian.   [4] His . . . essent, only in A, β.

---

[1] Some assign this speech—" Of all existing things . . .
pain " to Epictetus, quoting the pseudo-Stoic jargon ; others
to the pseudo-philosopher. The former seems to fit best
with what follows.

[2] The names of these are variously given. They generally
include, in addition to Chilo : Cleobulus of Lindus in Rhodes,
Periander of Corinth, Pittacus of Mitylene, Bias of Priene,

between these : wealth, health, life, death, pleasure, pain.[1]—'How do you know this?'—Hellanicus says so in his *Egyptian History.*   For what difference does it make whether you say that, or that it was Diogenes in his *Ethics* or Chrysippus or Cleanthes? Have you then investigated any of these matters and formed an opinion of your own? Let me see how you are accustomed to act in a storm at sea. Do you recall this classification when the sail cracks and you cry aloud? If some idle fellow should stand beside you and say : 'Tell me, for Heaven's sake, what you told me before.   It isn't a vice to suffer shipwreck, is it?   It doesn't partake of vice, does it?' Would you not hurl a stick of wood at him and cry: 'What have we to do with you, fellow? We perish and you come and crack jokes.' But if Caesar should summon you to answer an accusation . . ."

On hearing these words, that most arrogant of youths was mute, just as if the whole diatribe had been pronounced, not by Epictetus against others, but against himself by Herodes.

III

The difficult decision which the Lacedaemonian Chilo made to save a friend ; and that one should consider scrupulously and anxiously whether one ought ever to do wrong in the interest of friends, with notes and quotations on that subject from the writings of Theophrastus and Marcus Cicero.

Of Chilo the Lacedaemonian, one of that famous group of sages,[2] it is written in the books of those

Thales of Miletus, and Solon of Athens.   Plato, *Protag.* p. 343 A, gives Myson of Chen in place of Periander.

vitas resque gestas clarorum hominum memoriae mandaverunt, eum Chilonem in vitae suae postremo, cum iam inibi mors occuparet, ad circumstantis amicos sic locutum :

2   "Dicta," inquit, "mea factaque in aetate longa pleraque omnia fuisse non paenitenda, fors sit ut vos

3 etiam sciatis.   Ego quidem in hoc certe tempore non fallo me, nihil esse quicquam commissum a me cuius memoria mihi aegritudini sit, ni illud profecto unum sit, quod rectene an perperam fecerim nondum mihi plane liquet.

4   "Super amici capite iudex cum duobus aliis fui. Ita lex fuit uti eum hominem condemnari necessum esset.   Aut amicus igitur capitis perdendus aut ad-

5 hibenda fraus legi fuit.   Multa cum animo meo ad casum tam ancipitem medendum consultavi.   Visum est esse id quod feci praequam erant alia toleratu

6 facilius : ipse tacitus ad condemnandum sententiam tuli, is qui simul iudicabant ut absolverent persuasi.

7 Sic mihi et iudicis et amici officium in re tanta salvum fuit.   Hanc capio ex eo facto molestiam, quod metuo ne a perfidia et culpa non abhorreat, in eadem re eodemque tempore inque communi negotio, quod mihi optimum factu duxerim, diversum eius aliis suasisse."

8   Et hic autem Chilo, praestabilis homo sapientiae, quonam usque debuerit contra legem contraque ius pro amico progredi dubitavit, eaque res in fine quo-

9 que vitae ipso animum eius anxit, et alii deinceps multi philosophiae sectatores, ut in libris eorum

12

who have recorded the lives and deeds of distinguished men, that he, Chilo, at the close of his life, when death was already close upon him, thus addressed the friends about his bedside :

"That very little of what I have said and done in the course of a long life calls for repentance, you yourselves may perhaps know. I, at any rate, at such a time as this do not deceive myself in believing that I have done nothing that it troubles me to remember, except for just one thing ; and as to that it is not even now perfectly clear to me whether I did right or wrong.

"I was judge with two others, and a friend's life was at stake. The law was such that the man must be found guilty. Therefore, either my friend must suffer capital punishment or violence must be done to the law. I considered for a long time how to remedy so difficult a situation. The course which I adopted seemed, in comparison with the alternative, the less objectionable ; I myself secretly voted for conviction, but I persuaded my fellow judges to vote for acquittal. Thus I myself in a matter of such moment did my duty both as a judge and as a friend. But my action torments me with the fear that there may be something of treachery and guilt in having recommended to others, in the same case, at the same time, and in a common duty, a course for them contrary to what I thought best for myself."

This Chilo, then, though a man of surpassing wisdom, was in doubt how far he ought to have gone counter to law and counter to equity for the sake of a friend, and that question distressed him even at the very end of his life. So too many subsequent students of philosophy, as appears in their works,

scriptum est, satis inquisite satisque sollicite quaesiverunt, ut verbis quae scripta sunt ipsis utar, εἰ
δεῖ βοηθεῖν τῷ φίλῳ παρὰ τὸ δίκαιον καὶ μέχρι πόσου
καὶ ποῖα. Ea verba significant, quaesisse eos an nonnumquam contra ius contrave morem faciendum pro
amico sit et in qualibus causis et quemnam usque ad
modum.

10   Super hac quaestione cum ab aliis, sicuti dixi,
multis, tum vel diligentissime a Theophrasto dis-
putatur, viro in philosophia peripatetica modestis-
simo doctissimoque, eaque disputatio scripta est, si
recte meminimus, in libro eius *De Amicitia* primo.

11 Eum librum M. Cicero videtur legisse, cum ipse
quoque librum *De Amicitia* componeret. Et cetera
quidem quae sumenda a Theophrasto existimavit,
ut ingenium facundiaque eius fuit, sumpsit et trans-
12 posuit commodissime aptissimeque; hunc autem
locum de quo satis quaesitum esse dixi, omnium
rerum aliarum difficillimum, strictim atque cursim
transgressus est, neque ea quae a Theophrasto pen-
siculate atque enucleate scripta sunt executus est,
sed anxietate illa et quasi morositate disputationis
praetermissa, genus ipsum rei tantum paucis verbis
13 notavit. Ea verba Ciceronis, si recenseat quis vellet,
apposui : " His igitur finibus utendum esse arbitror,
ut, cum emendati mores amicorum sunt,[1] tum sit inter
eos omnium rerum, consiliorum, voluntatum sine ulla
exceptione communitas, ut etiam, si qua fortuna

[1] sint, *Cicero.*

---

[1] The sentence which follows translates the Greek literally,
except that for τὸ δίκαιον, "what is right," we have in the
Latin *ius moremve*, "law or precedent." The Romans laid

have inquired very carefully and very anxiously, to use their own language, εἰ δεῖ βοηθεῖν τῷ φίλῳ παρὰ τὸ δίκαιον καὶ μέχρι πόσου καὶ ποῖα.[1] That is to say, they inquired "whether one may sometimes act contrary to law or contrary to precedent in a friend's behalf, and under what circumstances and to what extent."

This problem has been discussed, as I have said, not only by many others, but also with extreme thoroughness by Theophrastus, the most conscientious and learned of the Peripatetic school; the discussion is found, if I remember correctly, in the first book of his treatise *On Friendship*. That work Cicero evidently read when he too was composing a work *On Friendship*. Now, the other material that Cicero thought proper to borrow from Theophrastus his talent and command of language enabled him to take and to translate with great taste and pertinence; but this particular topic which, as I have said, has been the object of much inquiry, and is the most difficult one of all, he passed over briefly and hurriedly, not reproducing the thoughtful and detailed argument of Theophrastus, but omitting his involved and as it were over-scrupulous discussion and merely calling attention in a few words to the nature of the problem. I have added Cicero's words, in case anyone should wish to verify my statement:[2] "Therefore these are the limits which I think ought to be observed, namely: when the characters of friends are blameless, then there should be complete harmony of opinions and inclinations in everything without any exception;

great stress on the *mos maiorum*, the precedent set by their forefathers.
[2] *De Amicitia*, 61.

acciderit, ut minus iustae voluntates amicorum adiuvandae sint, in quibus eorum aut caput[1] agatur aut fama, declinandum de via sit, modo ne summa turpitudo sequatur; est enim quatenus amicitiae venia dari possit."

"Cum agetur," inquit, "aut caput amici aut fama, declinandum est de via, ut etiam iniquam 14 voluntatem illius adiutemus." Sed cuiusmodi declinatio esse ista debeat qualisque ad adiuvandum digressio et in quanta voluntatis amici iniquitate, 15 non dicit. Quid autem refert scire me in eiusmodi periculis amicorum, si non magna me turpitudo insecutura est, de via esse recta declinandum, nisi id quoque me docuerit, quam putet magnam turpitudinem, et cum decessero de via, quousque degredi debeam? "Est enim," inquit, "quatenus dari ami-16 citiae venia possit." Hoc immo ipsum est quod maxime discendum est quodque ab his qui docent[2] minime dicitur, quatenus quaque fini dari amicitiae 17 venia debeat. Chilo ille sapiens, de quo paulo ante dixi, conservandi amici causa de via declinavit. Sed video quousque progressus sit; falsum enim pro 18 amici salute consilium dedit. Id ipsum tamen in fine quoque vitae an iure posset reprehendi culpari-que dubitavit.

"Contra patriam," inquit Cicero, "arma pro 19 amico sumenda non sunt." Hoc profecto nemo ignoravit, et "priusquam Theognis," quod[3] Lucilius

---

[1] capitis causa, β; de capite, *codd. of Cic.*
[2] docent, β; doceant, ω.
[3] quomodo, *Marx, l.c. (commentary).*

---

[1] Translation by Falconer, *L.C.L.*

and, even if by some chance the wishes of a friend
are not altogether honourable and require to be
forwarded in matters which involve his life or
reputation, we should turn aside from the straight
path, provided, however, utter disgrace does not
follow. For there are limits to the indulgence which
can be allowed to friendship." [1]

"When it is a question," he says, "either of a
friend's life or good name, we must turn aside from
the straight path, to further even his dishonourable
desire." But he does not tell us what the nature of
that deviation ought to be, how far we may go to help
him, and how dishonourable the nature of the friend's
desire may be. But what does it avail me to know
that I must turn aside from the straight path in the
event of such dangers to my friends, provided I
commit no act of utter disgrace, unless he also in-
forms me what he regards as utter disgrace and,
once having turned from the path of rectitude, how
far I ought to go? "For," he says, "there are limits
to the indulgence which can be allowed to friendship." But that is the very point on which we
most need instruction, but which the teachers make
least clear, namely, how far and to what degree
indulgence must be allowed to friendship. The sage
Chilo, whom I mentioned above, turned from the
path to save a friend. But I can see how far he
went; for he gave unsound advice to save his friend.
Yet even as to that he was in doubt up to his last
hour whether he deserved criticism and censure.

"Against one's fatherland," says Cicero,[2] "one must
not take up arms for a friend." That of course
everybody knew, and "before Theognis was born,"

---

[1] *De Amicitia*, 36 ; Gellius does not quote verbally from Cicero.

ait, "nasceretur." Set id quaero, id desidero : cum
pro amico contra ius, contra quam licet, salva tamen
libertate atque pace, faciendum est et cum de via,
sicut ipse ait, declinandum est, quid et quantum
et in quali causa et quonam usque id fieri debeat.
20 Pericles ille Atheniensis, vir egregio ingenio bonis-
que omnibus disciplinis ornatus, in una quidem
specie, set planius tamen quid existimaret professus
est. Nam cum amicus eum rogaret ut pro re causa-
que eius falsum deiuraret,[1] his ad eum verbis usus
est : "Δεῖ μὲν συμπράττειν τοῖς φίλοις, ἀλλὰ μέχρι τῶν
θεῶν."
21   Theophrastus autem in eo quo dixi libro inqui-
sitius quidem super hac ipsa re et exactius expres-
22 siusque [2] quam Cicero disserit. Set is quoque in
docendo non de unoquoque facto singillatim existimat neque certis exemplorum documentis, set
generibus rerum summatim universimque utitur ad
hunc ferme modum :
23   "Parva," inquit, "et tenuis vel turpitudo vel
infamia subeunda est, si ea re magna utilitas amico
quaeri potest. Rependitur quippe et compensatur
leve damnum delibatae honestatis maiore alia gra-
vioreque in adiuvando amico honestate, minimaque
illa labes et quasi lacuna famae munimentis par-

---

[1] deieraret, *scripsi* ; *cf. Thes. Ling. Lat.* ; deiraret, *A* ;
deiuraret, ω.

[2] expressiusque, *Skutsch* ; pressiusque, ω.

---

[1] 952 Marx, who cites for the proverb Plutarch, *Cum
princip. esse philos.* 2, p. 777, c (C.A.F. iii, p. 495, κ) and
restores Lucilius' line as : *hoc priusquam nasceretur Theognis
omnes noverant.*
[2] That is, so far as one can do so without violating the
laws of the gods or breaking an oath which one has taken in

as Lucilius says.[1]   But what I ask and wish to know
is this : when it is that one must act contrary to law
and contrary to equity in a friend's behalf, albeit
without doing violence to the public liberty and
peace ; and when it is necessary to turn aside from
the path, as he himself puts it, in what way and how
much, under what circumstances, and to what extent
that ought to be done.   Pericles, the great Athenian,
a man of noble character and endowed with all
honourable accomplishments, declared his opinion—
in a single instance, it is true, but yet very clearly.
For when a friend asked him to perjure himself in
court for his sake, he replied in these words : " One
ought to aid one's friends, but only so far as the
gods allow." [2]

Theophrastus, however, in the book that I have
mentioned, discusses this very question more ex-
haustively and with more care and precision than
Cicero.   But even he in his exposition does not
express an opinion about separate and individual
action, nor with the corroborative evidence of
examples, but treats classes of actions briefly and
generally, in about the following terms :

" A small and trifling amount of disgrace or
infamy," he says, " should be incurred, if thereby
great advantage may be gained for a friend ; for the
insignificant loss from impairment of honour is repaid
and made good by the greater and more substantial
honour gained by aiding a friend, and that slight
break or rift, so to speak, in one's reputation is
repaired by the buttress formed by the advantages

the name of a god ; cf. Cic. *Off.* iii. 44, *quae salva fide facere
possit.*

24 tarum amico utilitatium solidatur. Neque nominibus," inquit, "moveri nos oportet, quod paria
genere ipso non sunt honestas meae famae et rei
amici utilitas. Ponderibus haec enim potestatibus-
que praesentibus, non vocabulorum appellationibus
25 neque dignitatibus generum diiudicanda sunt. Nam
cum in rebus aut paribus aut non longe secus utilitas
amici aut honestas nostra consistit, honestas procul
dubio praeponderat; cum vero amici utilitas nimio
est amplior, honestatis autem nostrae in re non
gravi levis iactura est, tunc quod utile amico est,
id prae illo quod honestum nobis est fit plenius,
sicuti est magnum pondus aeris parva lamna auri
pretiosius."

Verba adeo ipsa Theophrasti super ea re ad-
26 scripsi : Οὐκ, εἰ δή που τοῦτο τῷ γένει τιμιώτερον, ἤδη
καὶ ὁτιοῦν ἂν ᾖ μέρος τούτου πρὸς τὸ τηλίκον θατέρου
συγκρινόμενον αἱρετὸν ἔσται. Λέγω δὲ οἷον, οὐκ, εἰ
χρυσίον τιμιώτερον χαλκοῦ, καὶ τηλίκον τοῦ χρυσίου
πρὸς τὸ τηλίκον χαλκοῦ μέγεθος ἀντιπαραβαλλόμενον
πλέον δόξει· ἀλλὰ ποιήσει τινὰ ῥοπὴν καὶ τὸ πλῆθος
καὶ τὸ μέγεθος.

27 Favorinus quoque philosophus huiuscemodi in-
dulgentiam gratiae, tempestive laxato paulum re-
missoque subtili iustitiae examine, his verbis definivit : Ἡ καλουμένη χάρις παρὰ τοῖς ἀνθρώποις, τοῦτο
ἔστιν ὕφεσις ἀκριβείας ἐν δέοντι.

28 Post deinde idem Theophrastus ad hanc ferme
sententiam disseruit : "Has tamen," inquit, "par-
vitates rerum et magnitudines atque has omnes

---

[1] Fr. 81, Wimmer.
[2] Fr. 102, Marres.

gained for one's friend. Nor ought we," says he,
"to be influenced by mere terms, because my fair
fame and the advantage of a friend under accusation
are not of the same class. For such things must be
estimated by their immediate weight and importance,
not by verbal terms and the merits of the classes to
which they belong. For when the interests of a
friend are put into the balance with our own honour
in matters of equal importance, or nearly so, our own
honour unquestionably turns the scale; but when the
advantage of a friend is far greater, but our sacrifice
of reputation in a matter of no great moment is
insignificant, then what is advantageous to a friend
gains in importance in comparison with what is
honourable for us, exactly as a great weight of bronze
is more valuable than a tiny shred of gold."

On this point I append Theophrastus' own words:[1]
"If such and such a thing belongs to a more valuable
class, yet it is not true that some part of it,
compared with a corresponding part of something
else, will be preferable. This is not the case, for
example, if gold is more valuable than bronze, and a
portion of gold, compared with a portion of bronze
of corresponding size, is obviously of more worth;
but the number and size of the portions will have
some influence on our decision."

The philosopher Favorinus too, somewhat loosening
and inclining the delicate balance of justice to suit
the occasion, thus defined such an indulgence in
favour:[2] "That which among men is called favour is
the relaxing of strictness in time of need."

Later on Theophrastus again expressed himself to
about this effect: "The relative importance and
insignificance of things, and all these considerations

officiorum aestimationes alia nonnumquam momenta extrinsecus atque aliae quasi appendices personarum et causarum et temporum et circumstantiae ipsius necessitates, quas includere in praecepta difficilest, moderantur et regunt et quasi gubernant et nunc ratas efficiunt, nunc inritas."

29 Haec taliaque Theophrastus satis caute et sollicite et religiose, cum discernendi magis disceptandique diligentia quam cum decernendi sententia atque fiducia scripsit, quoniam profecto causarum ac temporum varietates discriminumque ac differentiarum tenuitates derectum atque perpetuum distinctumque in rebus singulis praeceptum, quod ego nos in prima tractatus istius parte desiderare dixeram, non capiunt.

30 Eius autem Chilonis, a quo disputatiunculae huius initium fecimus, cum alia quaedam sunt monita utilia atque prudentia, tum id maxime exploratae utilitatis est, quod duas ferocissimas adfectiones amoris atque odii intra modum cautum coercuit. "Hac," inquit, "fini ames, tamquam forte fortuna et osurus; hac itidem tenus oderis, tamquam fortasse post amaturus."

31 Super hoc eodem Chilone Plutarchus philosophus, in libro Περὶ Ψυχῆς primo, verbis his ita scripsit: Χείλων ὁ παλαιός, ἀκούσας τινὸς λέγοντος, μηδένα ἔχειν ἐχθρόν, ἠρώτησεν, εἰ μηδένα φίλον ἔχει, νομίζων ἐξ ἀνάγκης ἐπακολουθεῖν καὶ συνεμπλέκεσθαι ταῖς φιλίαις ἀπεχθείας.

---

[1] Cicero, *De Amicitia*, 59, attributes this saying to Bias, another of the seven sages, as do also Aristotle, Diogenes Laertius and Valerius Maximus. It has appeared in various forms in later times.

of duty, are sometimes directed, controlled, and as it were steered by other external influences and other additional factors, so to say, arising from individuals, conditions and exigencies, as well as by the requirements of existing circumstances; and these influences, which it is difficult to reduce to rules, make them appear now justifiable and now unjustifiable."

On these and similar topics Theophrastus wrote very discreetly, scrupulously and conscientiously, yet with more attention to analysis and discussion than with the intention or hope of arriving at a decision, since undoubtedly the variations in circumstances and exigencies, and the minute distinctions and differences, do not admit of a definite and universal rule that can be applied to individual cases; and it is such a rule, as I said at the beginning of this essay, of which we are in search.

Now this Chilo, with whom I began this little discussion, is the author not only of some other wise and salutary precepts, but also of the following, which has been found particularly helpful, since it confines within due limits those two most ungovernable passions, love and hatred. "So love," said he, "as if you were possibly destined to hate; and in the same way, hate as if you might perhaps afterwards love."[1]

Of this same Chilo the philosopher Plutarch, in the first book of his treatise *On the Soul*, wrote as follows:[2] "Chilo of old, having heard a man say that he had no enemy, asked him if he had no friend, believing that enmities necessarily followed and were involved in friendships."

[2] vii, p. 19, Bern.

IV

Quam tenuiter curioseque exploraverit Antonius Iulianus in oratione M. Tullii verbi ab eo mutati argutiam.

1 ANTONIUS Iulianus rhetor perquam fuit honesti atque amoeni ingeni. Doctrina quoque iste[1] utiliore ac delectabili veterumque elegantiarum cura et memoria multa fuit; ad hoc scripta omnia antiquiora tam curiose spectabat et aut virtutes pensitabat aut vitia rimabatur, ut iudicium esse factum ad amussim[1] diceres.

2 Is Iulianus super eo enthymemate, quod est in
3 oratione M. Tullii, quam *Pro Cn. Plancio* dixit, ita existimavit—sed verba prius, de quibus iudicium ab eo factum est, ipsa ponam : "Quamquam dissimilis est pecuniae debitio et gratiae. Nam qui pecuniam dissolvit, statim non habet id quod reddidit, qui autem debet, is retinet alienum; gratiam autem et qui refert habet, et qui habet in eo ipso quod habet refert. Neque ego nunc Plancio desinam debere, si hoc solvero, nec minus ei redderem[4] voluntate ipsa, si hoc molestiae non accidisset"—
4 "Crispum sane," inquit, "agmen orationis rotundumque ac modulo ipso numerorum venustum, sed quod cum venia legendum sit verbi paulum ideo

---

[1] iste, *Falster* ; ista, ω.

---

[1] Lit., "according to a rule or level."
[2] § 68.
[3] The point of this passage depends on the meaning of *referre gratiam*, "requite" ("pay" a debt of gratitude), and *habere gratiam*, "feel gratitude." I have followed to some extent the rendering of Watts (*L.C.L.*), but with some changes.
[4] That is, the prosecution of Plancius, which enabled Cicero to pay his debt by defending his friend.

IV

The care and fine taste with which Antonius Julianus examined the artful substitution of one word for another by Marcus Cicero in one of his orations.

THE rhetorician Antonius Julianus had an exceedingly noble and winning personality. He also possessed learning of a delightful and helpful sort, devoting great attention to the refinements of the writers of old and readily recalling them. Moreover, he inspected all the earlier literature with such care, weighing its merits and ferreting out its defects, that you might say that his judgment was perfect.[1]

This Julianus expressed the following opinion of the syllogism which is found in the speech of Marcus Tullius spoken *In Defence of Gnaeus Plancius*[2]—but first I will quote the exact words on which he passed judgment: "And yet, a debt of money is a different thing from a debt of gratitude. For he who discharges a debt in money ceases forthwith to have that which he has paid, while one who continues in debt keeps what belongs to another. But in the case of a debt of gratitude, he who returns it has it; and he who has it returns it by the mere fact of having it.[3] In the present instance I shall not cease to be Plancius' debtor if I pay this debt, nor should I be paying him any the less simply by feeling goodwill, if the present unfortunate situation had not occurred."[4] "Here," said Julianus, "is to be sure a fine artistry in the way the words are marshalled, something well-rounded that charms the ear by its mere music; but it must be read with the privilege of a slight change in the meaning of one word in order to

25

5 inmutati, ut sententiae fides salva esset. Namque
debitio gratiae et pecuniae conlata verbum utrubi-
que servari postulat. Ita enim recte opposita inter
sese gratiae pecuniaeque debitio videbitur, si et
pecunia quidem deberi dicatur et gratia, sed quid
eveniat in pecunia debita solutave, quid contra in
gratia debita redditave, debitionis verbo utrimque
6 servato disseratur. Cicero autem," inquit, "cum
gratiae pecuniaeque debitionem dissimilem esse
dixisset eiusque sententiae rationem redderet, verbum 'debet' in pecunia ponit, in gratia 'habet' subicit
pro debet; ita enim dicit: 'gratiam autem et qui
refert habet, et qui habet in eo ipso quod habet
7 refert.' Sed id verbum 'habet' cum proposita com-
paratione non satis convenit. Debitio enim gratiae,
non habitio, cum pecunia confertur, atque ideo consequens quidem fuerat sic dicere: 'et qui debet
in eo ipso quod debet refert'; sed absurdum et
nimis coactum foret, si nondum redditam gratiam
8 eo ipso redditam diceret, quia debetur. Inmutavit
ergo," inquit, "et[1] subdidit verbum ei verbo, quod
omiserat, finitimum, ut videretur et sensum debitionis conlatae non reliquisse et concinnitatem
sententiae retinuisse." Ad hunc modum Iulianus
enodabat diiudicabatque veterum scriptorum sententias, quae aput eum adulescentes delecti lecti-
tabant.[2]

---

[1] *A omits* et; verbum, subdidit, *Vogel.*
[2] adulescentes delectitabant, ω.

preserve the truth of the proposition. Now the comparison of a debt of gratitude with a pecuniary debt demands the use of the word 'debt' in both instances. For a debt of money and a debt of gratitude will seem to be properly compared, if we may say that both money and gratitude are owed; but let us consider what happens in the owing or paying of money, and on the other hand in the owing and paying of a debt of gratitude, if we retain the word 'debt' in both instances. Now Cicero," continued Julianus, "having said that a debt of money was a different thing from a debt of gratitude, in giving his reason for that statement applies the word 'owe' to money, but in the case of gratitude substitutes 'has' (*i.e.* 'feels') for 'owes'; for this is what he says : 'But in the case of a debt of gratitude, he who returns it has it; and he who has it returns it by the mere fact of having it.' But that word 'has' does not exactly fit the proposed comparison. For it is the owing, and not the having, of gratitude that is compared with money, and therefore it would have been more consistent to say : 'He who owes pays by the mere fact of owing.' But it would be absurd and quite too forced if a debt of gratitude that was not yet paid should be said to be paid by the mere fact that it was owed. Therefore," said Julianus, "Cicero made a change and substituted a similar word for one which he had dropped, in order to seem to have kept the idea of a comparison of debts, and at the same time retained the careful balance of his period." Thus it was that Julianus elucidated and criticized passages in the earlier literature, which a select group of young men read under his guidance.

V

Quod Demosthenes rhetor cultu corporis atque vestitu
probris obnoxio infamique munditia fuit; quodque item
Hortensius orator, ob eiusmodi munditias gestumque in
agendo histrionicum, Dionysiae saltatriculae cognomento
compellatus est.

1 DEMOSTHENEN traditum est vestitu ceteroque
cultu corporis nitido venustoque nimisque accurato
fuisse. Et hinc ei τὰ κομψὰ illa χλανίσκια et
μαλακοὶ χιτωνίσκοι ab aemulis adversariisque probro
data, hinc etiam turpibus indignisque in eum verbis
non temperatum, quin parum vir et ore quoque
polluto diceretur.

2 Ad eundem modum Q. Hortensius omnibus ferme
oratoribus aetatis suae, nisi M. Tullio, clarior, quod
multa munditia et circumspecte compositeque in-
dutus et amictus esset manusque eius inter agendum
forent argutae admodum et gestuosae, maledictis
compellationibusque probris iactatus est multaque
in eum, quasi in histrionem, in ipsis causis atque
3 iudiciis dicta sunt. Sed cum L. Torquatus, suba-
gresti homo ingenio et infestivo, gravius acerbi-
usque apud consilium iudicum, cum de causa Sullae
quaereretur, non iam histrionem eum esse diceret,
sed gesticulariam Dionysiamque eum notissimae
saltatriculae nomine appellaret, tum voce molli atque
demissa Hortensius "Dionysia," inquit, "Dionysia
malo equidem esse quam quod tu, Torquate, ἄμουσος,
ἀναφρόδιτος, ἀπροσδιόνυσος."

---

[1] Aeschines, *in Tir*). 131.
[2] Cf. "Wer nicht liebt Wein, Weib und Sang, Der bleibt
ein Narr sein Leben lang", falsely attributed to Luther.

V

That the orator Demosthenes was criticized because of his
care for his person and attire, and taunted with foppishness; and that the orator Hortensius also, because of
similar foppishness and the use of theatrical gestures when
he spoke, was nicknamed Dionysia the dancing-girl.

It is said that Demosthenes in his dress and other
personal habits was excessively spruce, elegant and
studied. It was for that reason that he was taunted
by his rivals and opponents with his "exquisite,
pretty mantles" and " soft, pretty tunics";[1] for that
reason, too, that they did not refrain from applying
to him foul and shameful epithets, alleging that he
was no man and was even guilty of unnatural vice.

In like manner Quintus Hortensius, quite the
most renowned orator of his time with the exception
of Marcus Tullius, because he dressed with extreme
foppishness, arranged the folds of his toga with
great care and exactness, and in speaking used his
hands to excess in lively gestures, was assailed with
gibes and shameful charges; and many taunts were
hurled at him, even while he was pleading in court,
for appearing like an actor. But when Sulla was on
trial, and Lucius Torquatus, a man of somewhat
boorish and uncouth nature, with great violence and
bitterness did not stop with calling Hortensius an
actor in the presence of the assembled jurors, but
said that he was a posturer and a Dionysia—which
was the name of a notorious dancing-girl—then
Hortensius replied in a soft and gentle tone: "I
would rather be a Dionysia, Torquatus, yes, a
Dionysia, than like you, a stranger to the Muses, to
Venus and to Dionysus."[2]

VI

Verba ex oratione Metelli Numidici quam dixit in censura
ad populum, cum eum ad uxores ducendas adhortaretur;
eaque oratio quam ob causam reprehensa et quo contra
modo defensa sit.

1   MULTIS et eruditis viris audientibus legebatur
oratio Metelli Numidici, gravis ac diserti viri, quam
in censura dixit ad populum de ducendis uxoribus,
cum eum ad matrimonia capessenda hortaretur.   In
2 ea oratione ita scriptum fuit: "Si sine uxore pati[1]
possemus, Quirites, omnes[2] ea molestia careremus;
set quoniam ita natura tradidit, ut nec cum illis
satis commode, nec sine illis ullo modo vivi possit,
saluti perpetuae potius quam brevi voluptati con-
sulendum est."

3   Videbatur quibusdam, Q. Metellum censorem, cui
consilium esset ad uxores ducendas populum hortari,
non oportuisse de molestia incommodisque perpetuis
rei uxoriae confiteri, neque id hortari magis esse
quam dissuadere absterrereque; set contra in id
potius orationem debuisse sumi dicebant, ut et
nullas plerumque esse in matrimoniis molestias
adseveraret et, si quae tamen accidere nonnumquam
viderentur, parvas et leves facilesque esse toleratu
diceret maioribusque eas emolumentis et volupta-

---

[1] pati *suggested by Hosius;* vivere, *Hertz;* esse, ς.
[2] omnes, ω; omni, *apparently, A.*

---

[1] Metellus Numidicus was censor in 102 B.C.   Livy
(Periocha 59) attributes a speech on this subject to Q.
Caecilius Metellus Macedonicus, censor in 131 B.C., which
he says was read to the people by Augustus; cf. Suet. *Aug.*
lxxxix.   Since Suetonius, who gives the name simply as
Q. Metellus, cites the speech under the title *De Prole*

30

VI

An extract from the speech delivered to the people by
Metellus Numidicus when he was censor, urging them to
marry ; why that speech has been criticized and how on
the contrary it has been defended.

A number of learned men were listening to the
reading of the speech which Metellus Numidicus,[1]
an earnest and eloquent man, delivered to the
people when he was censor, *On Marriage,* urging
them to be ready to undertake its obligations. In
that speech these words were written : " If we
could get on without a wife, Romans, we would all
avoid that annoyance ; but since nature has ordained
that we can neither live very comfortably with
them nor at all without them, we must take thought
for our lasting well-being rather than for the
pleasure of the moment."

It seemed to some of the company that Quintus
Metellus, whose purpose as censor was to encourage
the people to take wives, ought not to have
admitted the annoyance and constant inconveniences
of the married state ; that to do this was not so
much to encourage, as to dissuade and deter them.
But they said that his speech ought rather to have
taken just the opposite tone, insisting that as a rule
there were no annoyances in matrimony, and if after
all they seemed sometimes to arise, they were
slight, insignificant and easily endured, and were
completely forgotten in its greater pleasures and

Augenda and the Periocha says that it was delivered *ut
cogerentur omnes ducere uxores liberorum creandorum causa,*
it seems probable that it was not identical with this address
of Metellus Numidicus.

tibus oblitterari easdemque ipsas neque omnibus
neque naturae vitio, set quorundam maritorum
4 culpa et iniustitia evenire. Titus autem Castricius
recte atque condigne Metellum esse locutum existimabat. "Aliter," inquit, "censor loqui debet, aliter
rhetor. Rhetori concessum est, sententiis uti falsis,
audacibus, versutis, subdolis, captiosis, si veri modo
similes sint et possint movendos hominum animos
qualicumque astu inrepere." Praeterea turpe esse
ait rhetori, si quid in mala causa destitutum atque
5 inpropugnatum relinquat. "Sed enim Metellum,"
inquit, "sanctum virum, illa gravitate et fide praeditum cum tanta honorum atque vitae dignitate
aput populum Romanum loquentem, nihil decuit
aliud dicere quam quod verum esse sibi atque
omnibus videbatur, praesertim cum super ea re
diceret quae cotidiana intellegentia et communi
6 pervolgatoque vitae usu comprenderetur. De molestia igitur cunctis hominibus notissima confessus,
fidem sedulitatis[1] veritatisque commeritus, tum
denique facile et procliviter, quod fuit rerum
omnium validissimum atque verissimum, persuasit
civitatem salvam esse sine matrimoniorum frequentia
non posse."
7 Hoc quoque aliut ex eadem oratione Q. Metelli
dignum esse existimavimus adsidua lectione non
hercle minus quam quae a gravissimis philosophis

---

[1] *Damsté compares* Cic. *Cluent.* 58, quamquam *sedulo*
faciebat, *praevaricari* (videbatur).

advantages; furthermore, that even these annoyances did not fall to the lot of all or from any
fault natural to matrimony, but as the result of
the misconduct and injustice of some husbands
and wives. Titus Castricius, however, thought that
Metellus had spoken properly and as was altogether
worthy of his position. "A censor," said he,
"ought to speak in one way, an advocate in
another. It is the orator's privilege to make statements that are untrue, daring, crafty, deceptive and
sophistical, provided they have some semblance of
truth and can by any artifice be made to insinuate
themselves into the minds of the persons who are
to be influenced. Furthermore," he said, "it is
disgraceful for an advocate, even though his case
be a bad one, to leave anything unnoticed or
undefended. But for a Metellus, a blameless man,
with a reputation for dignity and sense of honour,
addressing the Roman people with the prestige of
such a life and course of honours, it was not
becoming to say anything which was not accepted
as true by himself and by all men, especially when
speaking on a subject which was a matter of every-
day knowledge and formed a part of the common
and habitual experience of life. Accordingly, having
admitted the existence of annoyances notorious with
all men, and having thus established confidence in
his sincerity and truthfulness, he then found it no
difficult or uphill work to convince them of what
was the soundest and truest of principles, that the
State cannot survive without numerous marriages."

This other passage also from the same address of
Metellus in my opinion deserves constant reading,
not less by Heaven! than the writings of the

8 scripta sunt. Verba Metelli haec sunt : " Di immortales plurimum possunt ; sed non plus velle nobis debent quam parentes. At parentes, si pergunt liberi errare, bonis exheredant. Quid ergo nos ab immortalibus dissimile ius[1] expectemus, nisi malis rationibus finem faciamus? Is demum deos propitios esse aecum est, qui sibi adversarii non sunt. Dii immortales virtutem adprobare, non adhibere debent."

VII

In hisce verbis Ciceronis ex oratione quinta in Verrem "hanc sibi rem praesidio sperant futurum," neque mendum esse neque vitium, errareque istos qui bonos libros violant et " futuram " scribunt ; atque ibi de quodam alio Ciceronis verbo dictum, quod probe scriptum perperam mutatur ; et aspersa pauca de modulis numerisque orationis, quos Cicero avide sectatus est.

1 IN oratione Ciceronis quinta *In Verrem,* libro spectatae fidei, Tironiana cura atque disciplina facto,
2 ita[2] scriptum fuit : " Homines tenues, obscuro loco nati, navigant ; adeunt ad ea loca quae numquam antea adierant.[3] Neque noti esse iis quo venerunt neque semper cum cognitoribus esse possunt, hac una tamen fiducia civitatis, non modo apud nostros magistratus, qui et legum et existimationis periculo con-

---

[1] dissimile ius, *Damsté;* nos . . . diutius, *ω;* ab immortalibus dis divinitus, *Hertz;* nos immortalibus dissimilius, *Hosius, comparing A.*
[2] ita facto ita, *ω* ; facto, *A.*
[3] viderunt, ubi neque, *Cic.*

---

[1] *Sibi* is taken by some as referring to *dii,* but see Lane, *Lat. Gr.* 2343.
[2] ii. 5. 167.

greatest philosophers. His words are these: "The immortal gods have mighty power, but they are not expected to be more indulgent to us than our parents. But parents, if their children persist in wrong-doing, disinherit them. What different application of justice then are we to look for from the immortal gods, unless we put an end to our evil ways? Those alone may fairly claim the favour of the gods who are not their own worst enemies.[1] The immortal gods ought to support, not supply, virtue."

VII

In these words of Cicero, from his fifth oration *Against Verres*, *hanc sibi rem praesidio sperant futurum*, there is no error in writing or grammar but those are wrong who do violence to good copies by writing *futuram*; and in that connection mention is also made of another word of Cicero's which, though correct, is wrongly changed; with a few incidental remarks on the melody and cadence of periods for which Cicero earnestly strove.

IN the fifth oration of Cicero *Against Verres*,[2] in a copy of unimpeachable fidelity, since it was the result of Tiro's[3] careful scholarship, is this passage: "Men of low degree and humble birth sail the seas; they come to places which they had never before visited. They are neither known to those to whom they have come nor can they always find acquaintances to vouch for them, yet because of this mere faith in their citizenship they believe that they will be safe, not only before our magistrates, who are constrained by fear of the

[3] Cicero's favourite freedman, who not only aided him in his literary work, but also, after the orator's death, collected, arranged, and published his patron's writings, in particular his correspondence.

tinentur, neque apud cives solum Romanos, qui et
sermonis et iuris et multarum rerum societate iuncti
sunt, fore se tutos arbitrantur, sed quocumque
venerint, hanc sibi rem praesidio sperant futurum.[1]

3   Videbatur compluribus in extremo verbo menda
esse.   Debuisse enim scribi putabant non " futurum,"
sed "futuram," neque dubitabant quin liber emen-
dandus esset, ne, ut in Plauti comoedia moechus, sic
enim mendae suae inludiabant, ita in Ciceronis
oratione soloecismus esset "manifestarius."

4   Aderat forte ibi amicus noster, homo lectione
multa exercitus, cui pleraque omnia veterum littera-
5 rum quaesita, meditata evigilataque erant.   Is, libro
inspecto, ait nullum esse in eo verbo neque mendum
neque vitium et Ciceronem probe ac vetuste locutum.

6 " Nam futurum," inquit, " non refertur ad rem, sicut
legentibus temere et incuriose videtur, neque pro
participio positum est, set verbum est indefinitum,
quod Graeci appellant ἀπαρέμφατον, neque numeris
7 neque generibus praeserviens, set liberum undique
et impromiscum, quali C. Gracchus verbo usus est in
oratione cuius titulus est De P. Popilio circum
Conciliabula, in qua ita scriptum est : ' Credo ego
inimicos meos hoc dicturum.' ' Inimicos dicturum,'
inquit, non 'dicturos ' ; videturne ea ratione posi-
8 tum esse aput Gracchum 'dicturum,' qua est aput

---

[1] futuram, *MSS. of Cic.*

---

[1] *Bacch.* 918.
[2] Gracchus delivered two speeches against Popilius, one in
the Forum at Rome (*pro rostris*), the other *circum concilia-*

laws and public opinion, and not only among Roman citizens, who are united by the common bond of language, rights, and many interests, but wherever they may come, they hope that this possession will protect them."

It seemed to many that there was an error in the last word. For they thought that *futuram* should be written instead of *futurum*, and they were sure that the book ought to be corrected, lest like the adulterer in the comedy of Plautus[1]—for so they jested about the error which they thought they had found—this solecism in an oration of Cicero's should be "caught in the act."

There chanced to be present there a friend of mine, who had become an expert from wide reading and to whom almost all the older literature had been the object of study, meditation and wakeful nights. He, on examining the book, declared that there was no mistake in writing or grammar in that word, but that Cicero had written correctly and in accordance with early usage. "For *futurum* is not," said he, "to be taken with *rem*, as hasty and careless readers think, nor is it used as a participle. It is an infinitive, the kind of word which the Greeks call ἀπαρέμφατος or 'indeterminate,' affected neither by number nor gender, but altogether free and independent, such a word as Gaius Gracchus used in the speech entitled *On Publius Popilius, delivered in the places of assembly,*[2] in which we read: 'I suppose that my enemies will say this.' He said *dicturum,* not *dicturos*; and is it not clear that *dicturum* in Gracchus is used according to the same principle

bula, in the market-places of various towns of Latium ; see Meyer, *O. R. F,*[2] p. 239.

Ciceronem 'futurum'? Sicut in Graeca oratione
sine ulla vitii suspicione omnibus numeris generi-
busque sine discrimine tribuuntur huiuscemodi
9 verba: ἐρεῖν, ποιήσειν, ἔσεσθαι et similia." In Claudi
quoque Quadrigarii tertio *Annali* verba haec esse
dixit: " I[1] dum conciderentur, hostium copias ibi
occupatas futurum"; in duodevicesimo *Annali* eiusdem Quadrigarii principium libri sic scriptum: "Si
pro tua bonitate et nostra voluntate tibi valitudo subpetit, est quod speremus deos bonis benefacturum";
10 item in Valerii Antiatis libro quarto vicesimo simili
modo scriptum esse: "Si eae res divinae factae
recteque perlitatae essent, haruspices dixerunt omnia
ex sententia processurum esse." "Plautus etiam
11 in *Casina*, cum de puella loqueretur, 'occisurum'
dixit, non 'occisuram,' his verbis:

> Etiamne habet[2] Casina gladium?
> Habét, sed duós.—Quid duós?[3]—Alteró te
> Occísurum aít, alteró vilicum.

12 Item Laberius in *Gemellis*:

> Nón putavi (inquit) hoc eám facturum.

13 Non ergo isti omnes soloecismus quid esset ignora-
runt, sed et Gracchus 'dicturum' et Quadrigarius
'futurum' et 'facturum' et Antias 'processurum' et
Plautus 'occisurum' et Laberius 'facturum' indefinito
14 modo dixerunt, qui modus neque in numeros neque
in personas neque in tempora neque in genera dis-

---

[1] I = ei, ii.   [2] sed etiamne habet nunc, *Plaut.*
[3] quid duos, *Plaut.*; quibus, ω.

---

[1] Fr. 43, Peter.   [2] Fr. 79, Peter.
[3] Fr. 59, Peter.   [4] v. 691.

as *futurum* in Cicero? Just as in the Greek language, without any suspicion of error, words such as ἐρεῖν, ποιήσειν, ἔσεσθαι, and the like, are used in all genders and all numbers without distinction." He added that in the third book of the *Annals* of Claudius Quadrigarius are these words :[1] "While they were being cut to pieces, the forces of the enemy would be busy there (*copias . . . futurum*)"; and at the beginning of the eighteenth book of the same Quadrigarius :[2] "If you enjoy health proportionate to your own merit and our good-will, we have reason to hope that the gods will bless the good (*deos . . . facturum*)"; that similarly Valerius Antias also in his twenty-fourth book wrote : "If those religious rites should be performed, and the omens should be wholly favourable, the soothsayers declared that everything would proceed as they desired (*omnia . . . processurum esse*)."[3] "Plautus also in the *Casina*,[4] speaking of a girl, used *occisurum*, not *occisuram* in the following passage :

Has Casina a sword ?—Yes, two of them.—
Why two ?—With one she'd fain the bailiff slay,
With t'other you.

So too Laberius in *The Twins* wrote :[5]

I thought not she would do (*facturum*) it.

Now, all those men were not unaware of the nature of a solecism, but Gracchus used *dicturum*, Quadrigarius *futurum* and *facturum*, Antias *processurum*, Plautus *occisurum* and Laberius *facturum*, in the infinitive mood, a mood which is not inflected for mood or number or person or tense or gender,

[5] v. 51, Ribbeck.[8]

trahitur, sed omnia istaec una eademque declinatione
15 complectitur, sicuti M. Cicero 'futurum' dixit non
virili genere neque neutro, soloecismus enim plane
foret, sed verbo usus est ab omni necessitate generum
absoluto."

16   Idem autem ille amicus noster in eiusdem M. Tullii
oratione, quae est *De imperio Cn. Pompei*, ita
scriptum esse a Cicerone dicebat atque ipse ita lecti-
tabat : " Cum vestros portus, atque eos portus
quibus vitam ac spiritum ducitis, in praedonum fuisse
17 potestatem sciatis," neque soloecismum esse aiebat
" in potestatem fuisse," ut vulgus semidoctum putat,
sed ratione dictum certa et proba contendebat,
qua et Graeci ita uterentur ; et Plautus, verborum
Latinorum elegantissimus, in *Amphitruone* dixit :

Número[1] mihi in mentém fuit,

non, ut dici solitum est, "in mente."
18   Sed enim praeter Plautum, cuius ille in praesens
exemplo usus est, multam nos quoque⋅ apud veteres
scriptores locutionum talium copiam offendimus atque
19 his vulgo adnotamentis inspersimus.   Ut et rationem
autem istam missam facias et auctoritates, sonus
tamen et positura ipsa verborum satis declarat id
potius ἐπιμελείᾳ τῶν λέξεων modulamentisque orationis
M. Tullii convenisse, ut, quoniam utrumvis dici

---

[1] nunc vero, *codd. Plaut.* ; numero, β, *Nonius, 352.*

---

[1] Gellius' friend was partly right.   Such forms as *dicturum*
were derived from the second supine *dictu* + **erom* (earlier
*esom), the infinitive of *sum.*   Later, the resulting form
dicturum was looked upon as a participle and declined.   In
the early writers such infinitives did not change their form,
and did not add the tautological *esse.*

but expresses them all by one and the same form, just as Marcus Cicero did not use *futurum* in the masculine or neuter gender—for that would clearly be a solecism—but employed a form which is independent of any influence of gender." [1]

Furthermore, that same friend of mine used to say that in the oration of that same Marcus Tullius *On Pompey's Military Command* [2] Cicero wrote the following, and so my friend always read it: " Since you know that your harbours, and those harbours from which you draw the breath of life, were in the power of the pirates." And he declared that *in potestatem fuisse* [3] was not a solecism, as the half-educated vulgar think, but he maintained that it was used in accordance with a definite and correct principle, one which the Greeks also followed; and Plautus, who is most choice in his Latinity, said in the *Amphitruo :* [4]

Número mihi in mentém fuit,

not *in mente*, as we commonly say.

But besides Plautus, whom my friend used as an example in this instance, I myself have come upon a great abundance of such expressions in the early writers, and I have jotted them down here and there in these notes of mine. But quite apart from that rule and those authorities, the very sound and order of the words make it quite clear that it is more in accordance with the careful attention to diction and the rhythmical style of Marcus Tullius that, either

---

[2] § 33.
[3] That is, for *in potestate*.
[4] v. 180. Leo reads *num número mi in mentém fuit* "it hasn't just occurred to me, has it?"

Latine posset, "potestatem" dicere mallet, non
20 "potestate." Illud enim sic compositum iucundius
ad aurem completiusque, insuavius hoc imperfecti-
usque est, si modo ita explorata aure homo sit, non
surda nec iacenti ; sicuti est hercle quod "explicavit"
dicere maluit quam "explicuit," quod esse iam usi-
tatius coeperat.

Verba sunt haec ipsius ex oratione, quam *De
imperio Cn. Pompei* habuit : "Testis est Sicilia,
quam, multis undique cinctam periculis, non terrore
belli, sed consilii celeritate explicavit." At si
"explicuit" diceret, inperfecto et debili numero
verborum sonus clauderet.

VIII

Historia in libris Sotionis philosophi reperta super Laide
meretrice et Demosthene rhetore.

1 Sotion ex peripatetica disciplina haut sane ignobilis vir fuit. Is librum multae variaeque historiae
refertum composuit eumque inscripsit Κέρας ᾿Αμαλ-
2 θείας. Ea vox hoc ferme valet, tamquam si dicas
"Cornum Copiae."
3 In eo libro super Demosthene rhetore et Laide
meretrice historia haec scripta est : "Lais," inquit,
"Corinthia ob elegantiam venustatemque formae
grandem pecuniam demerebat conventusque ad eam
ditiorum hominum ex omni Graecia celebres erant,
neque admittebatur nisi qui dabat quod poposcerat ;

---

[1] § 30.
[2] The cadence $-\cup-\cup$ was a favourite one with Cicero at
the end of a sentence.

being good Latin, he should prefer to say *potestatem*
rather than *potestate*. For the former construction
is more agreeable to the ear and better rounded,
the latter harsher and less finished, provided always
that a man has an ear attuned to such distinctions,
not one that is dull and sluggish; it is for the same
reason indeed that he preferred to say *explicavit*
rather than *explicuit*, which was already coming to
be the commoner form.

These are his own words from the speech which
he delivered *On Pompey's Military Command*:[1]
"Sicily is a witness, which, begirt on all sides by
many dangers, he freed (*explicavit*), not by the
threat of war, but by his promptness in decision."
But if he had said *explicuit*, the sentence would halt
with weak and imperfect rhythm.[2]

VIII

An anecdote found in the works of the philosopher Sotion
about the courtesan Lais and the orator Demosthenes.

Sotion was a man of the Peripatetic school, far
from unknown. He wrote a book filled with wide
and varied information and called it Κέρας ’Αμαλθείας,[3]
which is about equivalent to *The Horn of Plenty*.

In that book is found the following anecdote
about the orator Demosthenes and the courtesan
Lais: "Lais of Corinth," he says, "used to gain a
great deal of money by the grace and charm of
her beauty, and was frequently visited by wealthy
men from all over Greece; but no one was received
who did not give what she demanded, and her

---

[3] *The Horn of Amaltheia*; see Greek Index.

4 poscebat autem illa nimium quantum." Hinc ait
natum esse illud frequens apud Graecos adagium :

Οὐ παντὸς ἀνδρὸς ἐς Κόρινθον ἔσθ' ὁ πλοῦς,

quod frustra iret Corinthum ad Laidem qui non
5 quiret dare quod posceretur. " Ad hanc ille Demosthenes clanculum adit et ut sibi copiam sui faceret
petit. At Lais μυρίας δραχμὰς poposcit—" hoc facit
6 nummi nostratis denarium decem milia. " Tali petu-
lantia mulieris atque pecuniae magnitudine ictus
expavidusque Demosthenes avertitur et discedens
' ego,' inquit, ' paenitere tanti non emo.' " Sed
Graeca ipsa, quae fertur dixisse, lepidiora sunt : οὐκ
ὠνοῦμαι, inquit, μυρίων δραχμῶν μεταμέλειαν.

IX

Quis modus fuerit, quis ordo disciplinae Pythagoricae, quantumque temporis imperatum observatumque sit discendi
simul ac tacendi.

1   ORDO atque ratio Pythagorae, ac deinceps familiae
et [1] successionis eius, recipiendi instituendique dis-
2 cipulos huiuscemodi fuisse traditur : Iam a principio
adulescentes qui sese ad discendum obtulerant ἐφυ-
σιογνωμόνει. Id verbum significat, mores natur-
asque hominum coniectatione quadam de oris et

[1] et added by Bongars.

---

[1] Cf. Horace, Epist. i. 17. 36.
[2] The drachma and the denarius (about 8d. or 16 cents)
was the average wage of a day-labourer.

demands were extravagant enough." He says that this was the origin of the proverb common among the Greeks:

Not every man may fare to Corinth town,[1]

for in vain would any man go to Corinth to visit Lais who could not pay her price. "The great Demosthenes approached her secretly and asked for her favours. But Lais demanded ten thousand drachmas"—a sum equivalent in our money to ten thousand denarii.[2] "Amazed and shocked at the woman's great impudence and the vast sum of money demanded, Demosthenes turned away, remarking as he left her: 'I will not buy regret at such a price.'" But the Greek words which he is said to have used are neater; he said: Οὐκ ὠνοῦμαι μυρίων δραχμῶν μεταμέλειαν.[3]

IX

What the method and what the order of the Pythagorean training was, and the amount of time which was prescribed and accepted as the period for learning and at the same time keeping silence.

IT is said that the order and method followed by Pythagoras, and afterwards by his school and his successors, in admitting and training their pupils were as follows: At the very outset he "physiognomized" the young men who presented themselves for instruction. That word means to inquire into the character and dispositions of men by an inference drawn from their facial appearance and

[3] I will not buy regret for ten thousand drachmas.

vultus ingenio deque totius corporis filo atque habitu
3 sciscitari. Tum qui exploratus ab eo idoneusque
inventus [1] fuerat recipi in disciplinam statim
iubebat et tempus certum tacere; non omnes idem,
sed alios [2] aliud tempus pro aestimato captu soller-
4 tiae. Is autem qui tacebat quae dicebantur ab aliis
audiebat, neque percontari, si parum intellexerat,
commentari quae audierat fas erat; sed non minus
quisquam tacuit quam biennium : hi prorsus appella-
bantur intra tempus tacendi audiendique ἀκουστι-
5 κοί. Ast ubi res didicerant rerum omnium difficil-
limas, tacere audireque, atque esse iam coeperant
silentio eruditi cui erat nomen ἐχεμυθία, tun
verba facere et quaerere, quaeque audissent scribere,
6 et quae ipsi opinarentur expromere potestas erat;
hi dicebantur in eo tempore μαθηματικοί, ab his
scilicet artibus quas iam discere atque meditari in-
ceptaverant : quoniam geometriam, gnomonicam,
musicam ceterasque item disciplinas altiores μαθήματα veteres Graeci appellabant; vulgus autem,
quos gentilicio vocabulo "Chaldaeos" dicere oportet,
7 "mathematicos" dicit. Exinde, his scientiae studiis
ornati, ad perspicienda mundi opera et principia

---

[1] inventus *added by Vahlen.*
[2] alios, *J. F. Gronov ;* alius, ω.

---

[1] The science of dialling, concerned with the making and
testing of sun-dials (γνώμονες).

expression, and from the form and bearing of their whole body. Then, when he had thus examined a man and found him suitable, he at once gave orders that he should be admitted to the school and should keep silence for a fixed period of time; this was not the same for all, but differed according to his estimate of the man's capacity for learning quickly. But the one who kept silent listened to what was said by others; he was, however, religiously forbidden to ask questions, if he had not fully understood, or to remark upon what he had heard. Now, no one kept silence for less than two years, and during the entire period of silent listening they were called ἀκουστικοί or "auditors." But when they had learned what is of all things the most difficult, to keep quiet and listen, and had finally begun to be adepts in that silence which is called ἐχεμυθία or "continence in words," they were then allowed to speak, to ask questions, and to write down what they had heard, and to express their own opinions. During this stage they were called μαθηματικοί or "students of science," evidently from those branches of knowledge which they had now begun to learn and practise; for the ancient Greeks called geometry, gnomonics,[1] music and other higher studies μαθήματα or "sciences"; but the common people apply the term *mathematici* to those who ought to be called by their ethnic name, Chaldaeans.[2] Finally, equipped with this scientific training, they advanced to the investigation of the phenomena of the universe and the laws of nature,

[2] *Chaldaei* and *mathematici* were general terms for astrologers at Rome; see *e.g.* Suet. *Dom.* xiv. 1, xv. 3; *Tib.* lxix; *etc.*

naturae procedebant ac tunc denique nominabantur φυσικοί.

8   Haec eadem super Pythagora noster Taurus cum dixisset: "Nunc autem," inquit, "isti qui repente pedibus inlotis ad philosophos devertunt, non est hoc satis quod sunt omnino ἀθεώρητοι, ἄμουσοι, ἀγεωμέ-τρητοι, sed legem etiam dant qua philosophari dis-

9   cant.   Alius ait 'hoc me primum doce,' item alius 'hoc volo,' inquit, 'discere, istud nolo'; hic a *Symposio* Platonis incipere gestit propter Alcibiadae comisationem, ille a *Phaedro* propter Lysiae ora-

10   tionem.   Est etiam," inquit, "pro Iuppiter! qui Platonem legere postulet non vitae ornandae, sed linguae orationisque comendae gratia, nec ut modes-

11   tior fiat, sed ut lepidior."   Haec Taurus dicere solitus, novicios philosophorum sectatores cum veteribus Pythagoricis pensitans.

12   Sed id quoque non praetereundum est, quod omnes, simul atque a[1] Pythagora in cohortem illam disciplinarum recepti erant, quod quisque familiae, pecuniae habebat in medium dabat et coibatur societas inseparabilis, tamquam[2] illud fuit anticum consortium, quod iure atque verbo Romano appellabatur "ercto non cito."

---

[1] atque a, *J. Gronov;* at quia, *P* ; qui a, ω.
[2] tam, quam, *Mommsen.*

and then, and not till then, they were called φυσικοί or " natural philosophers."

Having thus expressed himself about Pythagoras, my friend Taurus continued: " But nowadays these fellows who turn to philosophy on a sudden with unwashed feet,[1] not content with being wholly ' without purpose, without learning, and without scientific training,' even lay down the law as to how they are to be taught philosophy. One says, ' first teach me this,' another chimes in, ' I want to learn this, I don't want to learn that '; one is eager to begin with the *Symposium* of Plato because of the revel of Alcibiades,[2] another with the *Phaedrus* on account of the speech of Lysias.[3] By Jupiter !" said he, " one man actually asks to read Plato, not in order to better his life, but to deck out his diction and style, not to gain in discretion, but in prettiness." That is what Taurus used to say, in comparing the modern students of philosophy with the Pythagoreans of old.

But I must not omit this fact either—that all of them, as soon as they had been admitted by Pythagoras into that band of disciples, at once devoted to the common use whatever estate and property they had, and an inseparable fellowship was formed, like the old-time association which in Roman legal parlance was termed an " undivided inheritance." [4]

[1] Proverbial for " without preparation."
[2] Ch. 30.
[3] Ch. 6.
[4] See Servius on *Aen.* viii. 642, " *ercto non cito*," *id est, hereditate non divisa; nam citus divisus significat.*

X

Quibus verbis compellaverit Favorinus philosophus adulescentem casce nimis et prisce loquentem.

1   FAVORINUS philosophus adulescenti veterum verborum cupidissimo et plerasque voces nimis priscas
et ignotas in cotidianis communibusque sermonibus expromenti : " Curius," inquit, "et Fabricius
et Coruncanius, antiquissimi viri, et his antiquiores Horatii illi trigemini, plane ac dilucide
cum suis fabulati sunt neque Auruncorum aut Sica-
norum aut Pelasgorum, qui primi coluisse Italiam [1]
2 dicuntur, sed aetatis suae verbis locuti sunt ; tu
autem, proinde quasi cum matre Euandri nunc
loquare, sermone abhinc multis annis iam desito
uteris, quod scire atque intellegere neminem vis
quae dicas. Nonne, homo inepte, ut quod vis
3 abunde consequaris, taces? Sed antiquitatem tibi
placere ais, quod honesta et bona et sobria et
4 modesta sit. Vive ergo moribus praeteritis, loquere
verbis praesentibus atque id, quod a C. Caesare,
excellentis ingenii ac prudentiae viro, in primo *De
Analogia* libro scriptum est, habe semper in memoria
atque in pectore, ut tamquam scopulum, sic fugias
inauditum [2] atque insolens verbum."

[1] in Italia, *Macrobius*, i. 5. 1.
[2] infrequens, *Macrob.*

---

[1] Evander, a Greek from Pallanteum in Arcadia, migrated
to Italy and settled on the Palatine hill before the coming
of Aeneas.
[2] A work on grammar in two books, mentioned among the
writings of Caesar by Suet. *Jul.* lvi. 5 ; Fronto, p. 221,

X

In what terms the philosopher Favorinus rebuked a young
man who used language that was too old-fashioned and
archaic.

THE philosopher Favorinus thus addressed a
young man who was very fond of old words and
made a display in his ordinary, everyday conversation
of many expressions that were quite too unfamiliar
and archaic: "Curius," said he, "and Fabricius and
Coruncanius, men of the olden days, and of a still
earlier time than these those famous triplets, the
Horatii, talked clearly and intelligibly with their
fellows, using the language of their own day, not that
of the Aurunci, the Sicani, or the Pelasgi, who are said
to have been the earliest inhabitants of Italy. You,
on the contrary, just as if you were talking to-day
with Evander's mother,[1] use words that have
already been obsolete for many years, because you
want no one to know and comprehend what you are
saying. Why not accomplish your purpose more
fully, foolish fellow, and say nothing at all? But
you assert that you love the olden time, because it
is honest, sterling, sober and temperate. Live by
all means according to the manners of the past, but
speak in the language of the present, and always
remember and take to heart what Gaius Caesar, a
man of surpassing talent and wisdom, wrote in the
first book of his treatise *On Analogy*:[2] 'Avoid, as
you would a rock, a strange and unfamiliar word.'"

Naber (*L.C.L.* ii, pp. 29 and 255 ff.); described by Cic.
Brut. 253 as *de ratione Latine loquendi*.

ATTIC NIGHTS OF AULUS GELLIUS

XI

Quod Thucydides, scriptor inclitus, Lacedaemonios in acie
non tuba, sed tibiis esse usos dicit verbaque eius super ea
re posita; quodque Herodotus Alyattem regem fidicinas
in procinctu habuisse tradit; atque inibi quaedam notata
de Gracchi fistula contionaria.

1 Auctor historiae Graecae gravissimus Thucydides,
Lacedaemonios, summos bellatores, non cornuum
tubarumve signis, sed tibiarum modulis in proeliis
esse usos refert, non prorsus ex aliquo ritu religionum
neque rei divinae gratia neque autem ut excitarentur
atque evibrarentur animi, quod cornua et litui moli-
untur; sed contra, ut moderatiores modulatioresque
2 fierent, quod tibicinis numeris vis[1] temperatur.
Nihil adeo in congrediendis hostibus atque in prin-
cipiis proeliorum ad salutem virtutemque aptius rati,
quam si permulcti sonis mitioribus non inmodice
3 ferocirent. Cum procinctae igitur classes erant et
instructa acies coeptumque in hostem progredi
tibicines inter exercitum positi canere inceptabant.
4 Ea ibi praecentione tranquilla et delectabili atque
adeo[2] venerabili ad quandam quasi militaris musicae
disciplinam vis et impetus militum, ne sparsi dispala-
tique proruerent, cohibebatur.
5 Sed ipsius illius egregii scriptoris uti verbis libet,
quae et dignitate et fide graviora sunt: Καὶ μετὰ

[1] vis, *inserted by Nettleship.*
[2] delectabili . . . adeo, β; *omitted by* ω.

[1] v. 70.

XI

THUCYDIDES, the most authoritative of Greek historians, tells us [1] that the Lacedaemonians, greatest
of warriors, made use in battle, not of signals by
horns or trumpets, but of the music of pipes,
certainly not in conformity with any religious usage
or from any ceremonial reason, nor yet that their
courage might be roused and stimulated, which is
the purpose of horns and trumpets; but on the
contrary that they might be calmer and advance in
better order, because the effect of the flute-player's
notes is to restrain impetuosity.   So firmly were they
convinced that in meeting the enemy and beginning
battle nothing contibuted more to valour and confidence than to be soothed by gentler sounds and
keep their feelings under control.   Accordingly,
when the army was drawn up, and began to advance
in battle-array against the foe, pipers stationed
in the ranks began to play.   Thereupon, by this
quiet, pleasant, and even solemn prelude the fierce
impetuosity of the soldiers was checked, in conformity with a kind of discipline of military music,
so to speak, so that they might not rush forth in
straggling disorder.

But I should like to quote the very words of that
outstanding writer, which have greater distinction
and credibility than my own: "And after this the

53

ταῦτα ἡ ξύνοδος ἦν· Ἀργεῖοι μὲν καὶ οἱ σύμμαχοι ἐντόνως
καὶ ὀργῇ χωροῦντες, Λακεδαιμόνιοι δὲ βραδέως καὶ ὑπὸ
αὐλητῶν πολλῶν, νόμου [1] ἐγκαθεστώτων, οὐ τοῦ θείου
χάριν, ἀλλ' ἵνα ὁμαλῶς μετὰ ῥυθμοῦ βαίνοντες προσέλθοιεν
καὶ μὴ διασπασθείη αὐτοῖς ἡ τάξις, ὅπερ φιλεῖ τὰ μεγάλα
στρατόπεδα ἐν ταῖς προσόδοις ποιεῖν.

6   Cretenses quoque proelia ingredi solitos memoriae
datum est praecinente ac praemoderante cithara
7 gressibus; Alyattes autem, rex terrae Lydiae, more
atque luxu barbarico praeditus, cum bellum Milesiis
faceret, ut Herodotus in *Historiis* tradit, concinentes
habuit fistulatores et fidicines atque feminas etiam
tibicinas in exercitu atque in procinctu habuit, lasci-
8 vientium delicias conviviorum.   Sed enim Achaeos
Homerus   pugnam   indipisci   ait   non   fidicularum
tibiarumque, sed mentium animorumque [2] concentu
conspiratuque tacito nitibundos:

Οἱ δ' ἄρ' ἴσαν σιγῇ μένεα πνείοντες Ἀχαιοί,
Ἐν θυμῷ μεμαῶτες ἀλεξέμεν ἀλλήλοισιν.

9   Quid ille vult ardentissimus clamor militum Romanorum, quem in congressibus proeliorum fieri
solitum scriptores annalium memoravere?   Contrane
institutum fiebat antiquae disciplinae tam probabile?
An tum et gradu clementi et silentio est opus, cum
ad hostem itur in conspectu longinquo procul dis-
tantem, cum vero prope ad manus ventum est, tum
iam e propinquo hostis et impetu propulsandus et
clamore terrendus est?

---

[1] νόμου, ὁμοῦ, νόμῳ, codd. *Thuc.*
[2] sed . . . -que β; *omitted by* ω.

---

[1] i. 17.   [2] *Iliad*, iii. 8.
[3] This is approved by Julius Caesar, *Bell. Civ.* iii. 92. 5.

attack began. The Argives and their allies rushed
forward eagerly and in a rage, but the Lacedaemonians advanced slowly to the music of many flute-
players stationed at regular intervals; this not
for any religious reason, but in order that they
might make the attack while marching together
rhythmically, and that their ranks might not be
broken, which commonly happens to great armies
when they advance to the attack."

Tradition has it that the Cretans also commonly
entered battle with the lyre playing before them
and regulating their step. Futhermore, Alyattes,
king of the land of Lydia, a man of barbaric
manners and luxury, when he made war on the
Milesians, as Herodotus tells us in his *History*,[1] had
in his army and his battle-array orchestras of pipe-
and lyre-players, and even female flute-players, such
as are the delight of wanton banqueters. Homer,
however, says[2] that the Achaeans entered battle,
relying, not on the music of lyres and pipes, but on
silent harmony and unanimity of spirit:

> In silence came the Achaeans, breathing rage,
> Resolved in mind on one another's aid.

What then is the meaning of that soul-stirring
shout of the Roman soldiers which, as the annalists
have told us, was regularly raised when charging
the foe?[3] Was that done contrary to so generally
accepted a rule of old-time discipline? Or are a
quiet advance and silence needful when an army is
marching against an enemy that is far off and visible
from a distance, but when they have almost come to
blows, then must the foe, already at close quarters,
be driven back by a violent assault and terrified by
shouting?

10 Ecce autem per tibicinia Laconica tibiae quoque
illius contionariae in mentem venit, quam C. Graccho
cum populo agente praeisse ac praeministrasse modu-
11 los ferunt. Sed nequaquam sic est, ut a vulgo
dicitur, canere tibia solitum qui pone eum loquentem
staret, et variis modis tum demulcere animum
12 actionemque eius, tum intendere. Quid enim foret
ista re ineptius, si, ut planipedi saltanti, ita Graccho
contionanti numeros et modos et frequentamenta [1]
13 quaedam varia tibicen incineret? Sed qui hoc
compertius memoriae tradiderunt, stetisse in circum-
stantibus dicunt occultius, qui fistula brevi sensim
graviusculum sonum inspiraret ad reprimendum
sedandumque inpetus vocis eius effervescentes ; [2]
14 namque inpulsu et instinctu extraneo naturalis illa
Gracchi vehementia indiguisse, non, opinor, existi-
15 manda est. M. tamen Cicero fistulatorem istum
utrique rei adhibitum esse a Graccho putat, ut sonis
tum placidis tum citatis aut demissam iacentemque
orationem eius erigeret aut ferocientem saevientem-
que cohiberet. Verba ipsius Ciceronis apposui :
16 " Itaque idem Gracchus, quod potes audire, Catule,
ex Licinio cliente tuo, litterato homine, quem servum
sibi habuit ad manum, cum eburnea [3] solitus est
habere fistula, qui staret occulte post ipsum cum
contionaretur, peritum hominem, qui inflaret cele-
riter eum sonum, qui [4] illum aut remissum excitaret
aut a contentione revocaret."

[1] fritamenta, *W. Heraeus, Berl. phil. Woch. 1904*, comparing v. 1. 1 and Corp. Gloss. Lat. ii. 580. 42 ; see note on
v. 1. 1.
[2] effervescente namque, ω ; *corr. by Mommsen.*
[3] eburneola, *Cic.*   [4] quo, *Cic.*

[1] *De Orat.* iii. 225.

But, look you, the Laconian pipe-playing reminds me also of that oratorical pipe, which they say was played for Gaius Gracchus when he addressed the people, and gave him the proper pitch. But it is not at all true, as is commonly stated, that a musician always stood behind him as he spoke, playing the pipe, and by varying the pitch now restrained and now animated his feelings and his delivery. For what could be more absurd than that a piper should play measures, notes, and a kind of series of changing melodies for Gracchus when addressing an assembly, as if for a dancing mountebank? But more reliable authorities declare that the musician took his place unobserved in the audience and at intervals sounded on a short pipe a deeper note, to restrain and calm the exuberant energy of the orator's delivery. And that in my opinion is the correct view, for it is unthinkable that Gracchus' well-known natural vehemence needed any incitement or impulse from without. Yet Marcus Cicero thinks that the piper was employed by Gracchus for both purposes, in order that with notes now soft, now shrill, he might animate his oratory when it was becoming weak and feeble, or check it when too violent and passionate. I quote Cicero's own words:[1] "And so this same Gracchus, Catulus, as you may hear from your client Licinius, an educated man, who was at that time Gracchus' slave and amanuensis,[2] used to have a skilful musician stand behind him in concealment when he addressed an audience, who could quickly breathe a note to arouse the speaker if languid, or recall him from undue vehemence."

[2] The more usual expression for "amanuensis" is (*servus*) *a manu*, but *ad manum* also occurs.

17 Morem autem illum ingrediendi ad tibicinum modulos proelii institutum esse a Lacedaemonis, Aristoteles in libris *Problematon*[1] scripsit, quo manifestior fieret exploratiorque militum securitas et alacritas. 18 " Nam diffidentiae," inquit, " et timori cum ingressione huiuscemodi minime convenit et maesti atque formidantes ab hac tam intrepida ac tam decora 19 incedendi modulatione alieni sunt." Verba pauca Aristotelis super ea re apposui : Διὰ τί, ἐπειδὰν κινδυνεύειν μέλλωσιν, πρὸς αὐλὸν ἐμβαίνουσιν ; ἵνα τοὺς δειλοὺς ἀσχημονοῦντας γινώσκωσιν. ✳ ✳ ✳

XII

Virgo Vestae quid aetatis et ex quali familia et quo ritu quibusque caerimoniis et religionibus ac quo nomine a pontifice maximo capiatur, et quo statim iure esse incipiat simul atque capta est ; quodque, ut Labeo dicit, nec intestato cuiquam nec eius intestatae quisquam iure heres est.

1 Qui de virgine capienda scripserunt, quorum diligentissime scripsit Labeo Antistius, minorem quam annos sex, maiorem quam annos decem natam, nega-
2 verunt capi fas esse ; item quae non sit patrima et
3 matrima ; item quae lingua debili sensuve aurium
4 deminuta aliave qua corporis labe insignita sit ; item

---

[1] The work discusses thirty-eight problems, or questions, dealing for the most part with Natural History, but also with Music and Poetry. The collection as it has come down to us is only in part the work of Aristotle. Frag. 244, V. Rose.

Finally, Aristotle wrote in his volume of *Problems* [1] that the custom of the Lacedaemonians which I have mentioned, of entering battle to the music of pipers, was adopted in order to make the fearlessness and ardour of the soldiers more evident and indubitable. "For," said he, "distrust and fear are not at all consistent with an advance of that kind, and such an intrepid and rhythmical advance cannot be made by the faint-hearted and despondent." I have added a few of Aristotle's own words on the subject: "Why, when on the point of encountering danger, did they advance to music of the pipe? In order to detect the cowards by their failure to keep time." ∗∗∗[2]

XII

At what age, from what kind of family, by what rites, ceremonies and observances, and under what title a Vestal virgin is "taken" by the chief pontiff; what legal privileges she has immediately upon being chosen; also that, according to Labeo, she is lawfully neither heir of an intestate person, nor is anyone her heir, in case she dies without a will.

Those who have written about "taking" a Vestal virgin, of whom the most painstaking is Antistius Labeo,[3] have stated that it is unlawful for a girl to be chosen who is less than six, or more than ten, years old; she must also have both father and mother living; she must be free too from any impediment in her speech, must not have impaired hearing, or be marked by any other bodily defect;

[1] The marching of the cowards, because of their fear, would not be in time with the music.
[2] Some comment on the quotation should follow. Hertz indicated a lacuna.
[3] *De Iure Pontificali*, fr. 21, Huschke; 3, Bremer.

quae ipsa aut cuius pater emancipatus sit, etiamsi
5 vivo patre in avi potestate sit ; item cuius parentes
alter ambove servitutem servierunt aut in negotiis
6 sordidis versantur.   Set et[1] eam cuius soror ad id
sacerdotium lecta est excusationem mereri aiunt ;
item cuius pater flamen aut augur aut quindecim-
virum sacris faciundis aut[2] septemvirum epulonum
7 aut Salius est.   Sponsae quoque pontificis et tubicinis
sacrorum filiae vacatio a sacerdotio isto tribui solet.
8 Praeterea Capito Ateius scriptum reliquit, neque
eius legendam filiam qui domicilium in Italia non
haberet, et excusandam eius qui liberos tres haberet.
9   Virgo autem Vestalis simul est capta atque in
atrium Vestae deducta et pontificibus tradita est, eo
statim tempore sine emancipatione ac sine capitis
minutione e patris potestate exit et ius testamenti
faciundi adipiscitur.
10   De more autem rituque capiundae virginis litterae
quidem antiquiores non extant, nisi quae capta prima

---

[1] *added by Cramer.*
[2] aut, *Cramer* ; autem, *A*; aut qui, *ω.*

---

[1] The Roman father had control over his children (*patria potestas*) until he died, or lost his civic rights through some misconduct, or voluntarily "emancipated" them ; for a striking example see Suet. *Tib.* xv. 2.

[2] If a man was emancipated after having children born to him, the latter remained under the control of their grand-father (cf. Gaius, i. 133) and were legally orphans, hence not *patrima et matrima ;* Pruner, *Hestia-Vesta,* p. 273, N. 1.

[3] Cf. Cic. *De Off.* i. 150.

[4] The *XVviri sacris faciundis,* who had charge of the Sibylline Books.   Tarquin appointed *IIviri sacris faciundis* for the purpose (Livy, v. 13. 6), but by the Licinian laws of 367 B.C. the number was increased to ten, five patricians and five plebeians.   The Fifteen are first mentioned by Cicero

she must not herself have been freed from paternal control,[1] nor her father before her, even if her father is still living and she is under the control of her grandfather;[2] neither one nor both of her parents may have been slaves or engaged in mean occupations.[3] But they say that one whose sister has been chosen to that priesthood acquires exemption, as well as one whose father is a flamen or an augur, one of the Fifteen in charge of the Sibylline Books,[4] one of the Seven who oversee the banquets of the gods, or a dancing priest of Mars. Exemption from that priesthood is regularly allowed also to the betrothed of a pontiff and to the daughter of a priest of the tubilustrium.[5] Furthermore the writings of Ateius Capito inform us [6] that the daughter of a man without residence in Italy must not be chosen, and that the daughter of one who has three children must be excused.

Now, as soon as the Vestal virgin is chosen, escorted to the House of Vesta and delivered to the pontiffs, she immediately passes from the control of her father without the ceremony of emancipation or loss of civil rights, and acquires the right to make a will.

But as to the method and ritual for choosing a Vestal, there are, it is true, no ancient written records,

(*Epist.* viii. 4. 1) in 51 B.C. They were ex-praetors or ex-consuls until a late period, and the priesthood continued to exist until the books were burned by Stilicho in the fourth century.

[5] At the *tubilustrium*, on March 23, the trumpets used in sacred rites were purified by the *tibicines sacrorum populi Romani;* at the same time the Salii had their third procession in honour of Mars and Nerio; cf. Festus, 482. 27, Lindsay.

[6] *De Iure Pontificali*, fr. 11, Huschke; 7, Bremer.

11 est a Numa rege esse captam. Sed Papiam legem
invenimus, qua cavetur ut pontificis maximi arbitratu
virgines e populo viginti legantur sortitioque in contione ex eo numero fiat et[1] cuius sors[2] virginis
ducta erit, ut eam pontifex maximus capiat eaque

12 Vestae fiat. Sed ea sortitio ex lege Papia non
necessaria nunc videri solet. Nam si quis honesto
loco natus adeat pontificem maximum atque offerat
ad sacerdotium filiam suam, cuius dumtaxat salvis
religionum observationibus ratio haberi possit, gratia
Papiae[3] legis per senatum fit.

13 "Capi" autem virgo propterea dici videtur, quia
pontificis maximi manu prensa ab eo parente in cuius

14 potestate est, veluti bello capta, abducitur. In
libro primo Fabii Pictoris, quae verba pontificem
maximum dicere oporteat, cum virginem capiat,
scriptum est. Ea verba haec sunt : "Sacerdotem
Vestalem, quae sacra faciat quae ius siet sacerdotem
Vestalem facere pro populo Romano Quiritibus, uti
quae[4] optima lege fuit, ita te, Amata, capio."

15 Plerique autem "capi" virginem solam debere
dici putant. Sed flamines quoque Diales, item

16 pontifices et augures "capi" dicebantur. L. Sulla
Rerum Gestarum libro secundo ita scripsit : "P.
Cornelius, cui primum cognomen Sullae impositum

17 est, flamen Dialis captus." M. Cato de Lusitanis,

---

[1] et . . . fiat, β; *omitted by* ω.
[2] sors *added by Mommsen.*
[3] Papiae, *Carrio* ; Popiliae, ω ; Papiae illae, *Hertz.*
[4] utique, ω.

---

[1] The date of this law is unknown ; it is not identical with
the lex Papia-Poppaea of 250 B.C.
[2] The *comitia calata ;* see xv. 27. 1 ff.
[3] Fr. 4, Huschke ; 1, Bremer.

except that the first to be appointed was chosen by
Numa.   There is, however, a Papian law,[1] which
provides that twenty maidens be selected from the
people at the discretion of the chief pontiff, that
a choice by lot be made from that number in the
assembly,[2] and that the girl whose lot is drawn be
"taken" by the chief pontiff and become Vesta's.
But that allotment in accordance with the Papian
law is usually unnecessary at present.   For if any
man of respectable birth goes to the chief pontiff
and offers his daughter for the priesthood, provided
consideration may be given to her candidacy without
violating any religious requirement, the senate grants
him exemption from the Papian law.

Now the Vestal is said to be "taken," it appears,
because she is grasped by the hand of the chief
pontiff and led away from the parent under whose
control she is, as if she had been taken in war.   In
the first book of Fabius Pictor's *History* [3] the formula
is given which the chief pontiff should use in choosing
a Vestal.   It is this : " I take thee, Amata, as one who
has fulfilled all the legal requirements, to be priestess
of Vesta, to perform the rites which it is lawful
for a Vestal to perform for the Roman people, the
Quirites."

Now, many think that the term " taken " ought to
be used only of a Vestal.   But, as a matter of fact,
the flamens of Jupiter also, as well as the augurs,
were said to be " taken."   Lucius Sulla, in the second
book of his *Autobiography*,[4] wrote as follows :
" Publius Cornelius, the first to receive the surname
Sulla, was taken to be flamen of Jupiter."   Marcus

[4] Fr. 2, Peter.

cum Servium Galbam accusavit[1]: "Tamen dicunt
deficere voluisse. Ego me nunc volo ius pontificium
optime scire; iamne ea causa pontifex capiar? Si
volo augurium optime tenere, ecquis me ob eam
rem [1] augurem capiat?"

18 Praeterea in *Commentariis* Labeonis, quae *ad Duodecim Tabulas* composuit, ita scriptum est: "Virgo
Vestalis neque heres est cuiquam intestato, neque
intestatae quisquam, sed bona eius in [2] publicum
redigi aiunt. Id quo iure fiat, quaeritur."

19 "Amata" inter capiendum a pontifice maximo
appellatur, quoniam quae prima capta est hoc fuisse
nomen traditum est.

XIII

Quaesitum esse in philosophia, quidnam foret in recepto man-
dato rectius, idne omnino facere quod mandatum est, an
nonnumquam etiam contra, si id speres ei qui mandavit
utilius fore; superque ea quaestione expositae diversae
sententiae.

1 IN officiis capiendis, censendis iudicandisque, quae
καθήκοντα philosophi appellant, quaeri solet an
negotio tibi dato et quid omnino faceres definito,
contra quid facere debeas, si eo facto videri possit

[1] ob eam rem, σ; ob meam, ω.
[2] in, ς; *omitted by* ω.

---

[1] The title of the oration is variously given as *Contra
Servium Galbam* and *Pro Direptis Lusitanis;* perhaps the two
titles were combined in one. See Jordan's *Cato*, p. 27.

[2] Fr. 24, Huschke; 2, Bremer. The comment quoted by
Gellius is on *Twelve Tables* V. 1.

[3] Various other reasons have been given, of which perhaps
the most attractive is that it is from an original ἀδαμάτα,

Cato, in his accusation of Servius Galba, says of the Lusitanians:[1] "Yet they say that they wished to revolt. I myself at the present moment wish a thorough knowledge of the pontifical law; shall I therefore be taken as chief pontiff? If I wish to understand the science of augury thoroughly, shall anyone for that reason take me as augur?"

Furthermore, in the *Commentaries on the Twelve Tables* compiled by Labeo[2] we find this passage: "A Vestal virgin is not heir to any intestate person, nor is anyone her heir, should she die without making a will, but her property, they say, reverts to the public treasury. The legal principle involved is an unsettled question."

The Vestal is called "Amata" when taken by the chief pontiff, because there is a tradition that the first one who was chosen bore that name.[3]

XIII

On the philosophical question, what would be more proper on receipt of an order—to do scrupulously what was commanded, or sometimes even to disobey, in the hope that it would be more advantageous to the giver of the order; and an exposition of varying views on that subject.

In interpreting, evaluating and weighing the obligations which the philosophers call καθήκοντα, or "duties," the question is often asked, when some task has been assigned to you and exactly what was to be done has been defined, whether you ought to do anything contrary to instructions, if by so doing

unwedded. According to Pruner, *Hestia-Vesta*, p. 276, followed by Rossbach in Pauly-Wissowa, *s.v., amata* is not a proper name, but means "beloved."

res eventura prosperius exque utilitate eius qui id
2 tibi negotium mandavit. Anceps quaestio et in
utramque partem a prudentibus viris arbitrata est.
3 Sunt enim non pauci qui sententiam suam una in
parte defixerint et re semel statuta deliberataque ab
eo cuius id negotium pontificiumque esset, nequaquam
putaverint contra dictum eius esse faciendum, etiamsi
repentinus aliqui casus rem commodius agi posse
polliceretur; ne, si spes fefellisset, culpa inpatientiae
4 et poena indeprecabilis subeunda esset; si res forte
melius vertisset, dis quidem gratia habenda, sed
exemplum tamen intromissum videretur, quo bene
consulta consilia religione mandati soluta corrum-
5 perentur. Alii existimaverunt incommoda prius
quae metuenda essent, si res gesta aliter foret quam
imperatum est, cum emolumento spei pensitanda
esse et, si ea leviora minoraque, utilitas autem contra
gravior et amplior spe quantum potest firma osten-
deretur, tum posse adversum mandata fieri censuerunt, ne oblata divinitus rei bene gerendae occasio
6 amitteretur; neque timendum exemplum non parendi
crediderunt, si rationes dumtaxat huiuscemodi non
7 abessent. Cumprimis autem respiciendum putaverunt ingenium naturamque illius cuia[1] res praecep-
tumque esset: ne ferox, durus, indomitus inexora-

---

[1] cuia, *Carrio*; cui ea, *ω*.

it might seem that the outcome would be more successful and more advantageous to the one who imposed the task upon you. It is a difficult question which has been answered both ways by wise men. For several have taken a position on the one side and expressed the decided belief that when a matter has once for all been determined, after due deliberation, by the one whose business and right are concerned, nothing should be done contrary to his order, even if some unlooked for occurrence should promise a better way of accomplishing the end in view; for fear that, if the expectation were not realized, the offender would be liable to blame and inexorable punishment for his insubordination. If, on the other hand, the affair chanced to result more favourably, thanks would indeed be due the gods, but nevertheless a precedent would seem to have been established, which might ruin well-laid plans by weakening the binding force of a command. Others have thought that the disadvantages to be feared, in case the order was not strictly obeyed, should carefully be weighed in advance against the advantage hoped for, and if the former were comparatively light and trivial, while on the contrary a greater and more substantial advantage was confidently to be expected, then they judged that one might go counter to instructions, to avoid losing a providential opportunity for successful action; and they did not believe that a precedent for disobedience was to be feared, provided always that considerations of such a kind could be urged. But they thought that particular regard should be paid to the temperament and disposition of the person whose business and command were involved: he must not be stern,

67

bilisque sit, qualia fuerunt Postumiana imperia et
8 Manliana. Nam si tali praeceptori ratio reddenda
sit, nihil faciendum esse monuerunt aliter quam
praeceptum est.

9 Instructius deliberatiusque fore arbitramur theore-
matium hoc de mandatis huiuscemodi obsequendis, si
exemplum quoque P. Crassi Muciani, clari atque in-
10 cluti viri, apposuerimus. Is Crassus a Sempronio
Asellione et plerisque aliis historiae Romanae scrip-
toribus traditur habuisse quinque rerum bonarum
maxima et praecipua : quod esset ditissimus, quod
nobilissimus, quod eloquentissimus, quod iuriscon-
11 sultissimus, quod pontifex maximus. Is cum in
consulatu obtineret Asiam provinciam et circumsedere
oppugnareque Leucas pararet opusque esset firma
atque procera trabe, qui arietem faceret quo muros
eius oppidi quateret, scripsit ad magistrum ἀρχιτεκτόνων Mylattensium,[1] sociorum amicorumque populi
Romani, ut ex malis duobus, quos apud eos vidisset,
12 uter maior esset eum mittendum curaret. Tum
magister ἀρχιτεκτόνων,[2] comperto quamobrem malum
desideraret, non, uti iussus erat, maiorem, sed quem
esse magis idoneum aptioremque faciendo arieti

---

[1] magistrum ἀρχιτεκτόνων, *Capps* ; magistrum architectona
Moleatensium, β ; mag. (māg., *V*) G. mole (more, *P*)
Atheniensium (attenisium, *V*), ω ; magistratus (-tum, ς)
Mylasensium *or* Mylattensium, *Mommsen* ; ἀρχιτέκτονα Myl.,
Hertz ; magistrum Myl., *Hosius*.
[2] magister ἀρχιτεκτόνων, *Capps* ; ma g (mag, *P*) G., ω ;
magister ἀρχιτέκτων, ς.

---

[1] Titus Manlius Torquatus had his own son executed for
disobedience to his father's command ; see ix. 1̣3̣. 29. A
similar story is told of Postumius ; see xvii. 21. 17 ; cf. Otto,
Sprichw. p. 209. [2] Fr. 8, Peter.
[3] In the year of his consulship (131 B.C.) he was sent with

hard, autocratic and implacable, as in the case of the orders of a Postumius and a Manlius.[1] For if an account must be rendered to such a commander, they recommended that nothing be done contrary to the letter of his order.

I think that this question of obedience to commands of such a nature will be more clearly defined, if I add the example set by Publius Crassus Mucianus, a distinguished and eminent man. This Crassus is said by Sempronius Asellio[2] and several other writers of Roman history to have had the five greatest and chiefest of blessings; for he was very rich, of the highest birth, exceedingly eloquent, most learned in the law, and chief pontiff. When he, in his consulship, was in command in[3] the province of Asia, and was making preparations to beset and assault Leucae, he needed a long, stout beam from which to make a battering-ram, to breach the walls of that city. Accordingly, he wrote to the chief engineer of the people of Mylatta,[4] allies and friends of the Romans, to have the larger of two masts which he had seen in their city sent him. Then the chief engineer on learning the purpose for which Crassus wanted the mast, did not send him the larger, as had been ordered, but the smaller, which he thought was more suitable, and better adapted for

an army against Aristonicus, who laid claim to the kingdom of Pergamum, which Attalus III had bequeathed to the Romans.

[4] The text seems hopelessly corrupt. We perhaps have a fusion of ἐπάρχων ἀρχιτεκτόνων (Dittenberger[3], 804. 5) and its equivalent *magister* (= *praefectus*) *fabrum*. With ἀρχιτέκτονα (Hertz), the meaning would be "builder." With *magistrum* (Hosius), "the chief magistrate," or perhaps "a ship-captain" (sc. *navis*). For the town, Bergk proposed Mytilene ; Hosius, Myrina. The MSS. suggest Mylasa (Mylassa, Mylatta).

facilioremque portatu existimabat, minorem misit.
13 Crassus eum vocari iussit et, cum interrogasset cur
non quem iusserat misisset, causis rationibusque quas
dictitabat spretis, vestimenta detrahi imperavit
virgisque multum cecidit, corrumpi atque dissolvi
officium omne imperantis ratus. si quis ad id quod
facere iussus est non obsequio debito, sed consilio
non desiderato respondeat.

XIV

Quid dixerit feceritque C. Fabricius, magna vir gloria
magnisque rebus gestis, sed familiae pecuniaeque inops,
cum ei Samnites tamquam indigenti grave aurum donarent.

1 IULIUS Hyginus, in libro *De Vita Rebusque Inlustrium Virorum* sexto, legatos dicit a Samnitibus ad
C. Fabricium, imperatorem populi Romani, venisse
et memoratis multis magnisque rebus quae bene ac
benivole post redditam pacem Samnitibus fecisset,
obtulisse dono grandem pecuniam orasseque uti
acciperet uteretturque, atque id facere Samnites
dixisse, quod viderent multa ad splendorem domus
atque victus defieri neque pro amplitudine dignitate-
2 que lautum paratum esse. Tum Fabricium planas
manus ab auribus ad oculos et infra deinceps ad nares
et ad os et ad gulam atque inde porro ad ventrem
imum deduxisse et legatis ita respondisse : dum illis
omnibus membris quae attigisset obsistere atque
imperare posset, numquam quicquam defuturum ;

---

[1] Fr. 3, Peter.

making a ram, besides being easier to transport. Crassus ordered him to be summoned, asked why he had not sent the mast which had been ordered, and ignoring the excuses and reasons which the man urged, caused him to be stripped and soundly beaten with rods; for he thought that all the authority of a commander was weakened and made of no effect, if one might reply to orders which he received, not with due obedience, but with an unsolicited plan of his own.

XIV

What was said and done by Gaius Fabricius, a man of great renown and great deeds, but of simple establishment and little money, when the Samnites offered him a great amount of gold, in the belief that he was a poor man.

JULIUS HYGINUS, in the sixth book of his work *On the Lives and Deeds of Famous Men*,[1] says that a deputation from the Samnites came to Gaius Fabricius, the Roman general, and after mentioning his many important acts of kindness and generosity to the Samnites since peace was restored, offered him a present of a large sum of money, begging that he would accept and use it. And they said that they did this because they saw that his house and mode of life were far from magnificent, and that he was not so well provided for as his high rank demanded. Thereupon Fabricius passed his open hands from his ears to his eyes, then down to his nose, his mouth, his throat, and finally to the lower part of his belly; then he replied to the envoys: "So long as I can restrain and control all those members which I have touched, I shall never lack

propterea se pecuniam qua nihil sibi esset usus ab his quibus eam sciret usui esse non accipere.

XV

Quam inportunum vitium plenumque odii sit futilis inanis-que loquacitas, et quam multis in locis a principibus utrius-que linguae viris detestatione iusta culpata sit.

1 Qui sunt leves et futiles et importuni locutores quique nullo rerum pondere innixi verbis uvidis [1] et lapsantibus diffluunt, eorum orationem bene existima-tum est in ore nasci, non in pectore, linguam autem debere aiunt non esse liberam nec vagam, sed vinclis de pectore imo ac de corde aptis moveri et quasi gu-
2 bernari. Sed enim videas quosdam scatere verbis sine ullo iudicii negotio cum securitate multa et pro-funda, ut loquentes plerumque videantur loqui sese
3 nescire. Ulixen contra Homerus, virum sapienti facundia praeditum, vocem mittere ait non ex ore, sed ex pectore, quod [2] scilicet non ad sonum magis habitumque vocis quam ad sententiarum penitus conceptarum altitudinem pertineret, petulantiaeque verborum coercendae vallum esse oppositum dentium luculente dixit, ut loquendi temeritas non cordis tantum custodia atque vigilia cohibeatur, sed et quibusdam quasi excubiis in ore positis saepiatur.

[1] uvidis, *Salmasius*; ubi dis (diis *P²*) *P*; (h)umidis, *ω*; tumidis, *Falster*.
[2] quod, *J. E. Gronov*; quos (quo, *P*) scilicet (licet, *R*), *ω*.

anything; therefore I cannot accept money, for which I have no use, from those who, I am sure, do have use for it."

XV

What a tiresome and utterly hateful fault is vain and empty loquacity, and how often it has been censured in deservedly strong language by the greatest Greek and Latin writers.

THE talk of empty-headed, vain and tiresome babblers, who with no foundation of solid matter let out a stream of tipsy, tottering words, has justly been thought to come from the lips and not from the heart. Moreover, men say that the tongue ought not to be unrestrained and rambling, but guided and, so to speak, steered by cords connected with the heart and inmost breast. Yet you may see some men spouting forth words with no exercise of judgment, but with such great and profound assurance that many of them in the very act of speaking are evidently unaware that they are talking. Ulysses, on the contrary, a man gifted with sagacious eloquence, spoke, not from his lips but from his heart, as Homer says—a remark which applies less to the sound and quality of his utterance than to the depth of the thoughts inwardly conceived; and the poet went on to say, with great aptness, that the teeth form a rampart to check wanton words, in order that reckless speech may not only be restrained by that watchful sentry the heart, but also hedged in by a kind of outpost, so to speak, stationed at the lips.

4   Homerica, de quibus supra dixi, haec sunt:

'Αλλ' ὅτε δὴ ὄπα τε μεγάλην ἐκ στήθεος εἴη,

et:

Ποῖόν σε ἔπος φύγεν ἕρκος ὀδόντων.

5 M. Tullii quoque verba posui, quibus stultam et ina-
nem dicendi copiam graviter et vere detestatus est:
6 " Dummodo," inquit, " hoc constet, neque infantiam
eius, qui rem norit, sed eam explicare dicendo non
queat, neque inscientiam illius, cui res non subpetat,
verba non desint, esse laudandam ; quorum si alterum
sit optandum, malim equidem indisertam prudent-
7 iam quam stultam loquacitatem." [1] Item in libro De
Oratore primo verba haec posuit: " Quid enim est
tam furiosum quam verborum vel optimorum atque
ornatissimorum sonitus inanis, nulla subiecta sen-
8 tentia nec scientia?" Cumprimis autem M. Cato
9 atrocissimus huiusce vitii insectator est. Namque
in oratione, quae inscripta est Si se Caelius tribunus
plebis appellasset, " Numquam," inquit, " tacet, quem
morbus tenet loquendi tamquam veternosum bibendi
atque dormiendi. Quod si non conveniatis, cum
convocari iubet, ita cupidus orationis conducat, qui
auscultet. Itaque auditis, non auscultatis, tamquam
pharmacopolam. Nam eius verba audiuntur, verum

---

[1] stultitiam loquacem, Cic.

---

[1] Iliad, iii. 221.   [2] Iliad, iv. 350, etc.
[3] De Orat. iii. 142.   [4] i. 51.
[5] See Jordan's Cato, xl. 1. The meaning of the title, which
is uncertain, is discussed in his Prolegomena, p. lxix f. Se
refers to Cato himself. By some the speech is regarded as
identical with the one mentioned by Fronto, vol. i, p. 117,
L.C.L., and by Plutarch, Cato ix. 7, vol. ii, p. 329, L.C.L.

The words of Homer which I mentioned above are these : [1]

When from his breast his mighty voice went forth

and : [2]

What a word has passed the barrier of your teeth.

I have added also a passage from Marcus Tullius, in which he expresses his strong and just hatred of silly and unmeaning volubility. He says : [3] " Provided this fact be recognized, that neither should one commend the dumbness of a man who knows a subject, but is unable to give it expression in speech, nor the ignorance of one who lacks knowledge of his subject, but abounds in words ; yet if one must choose one or the other alternative, I for my part would prefer tongue-tied knowledge to ignorant loquacity." Also in the first book of the *De Oratore* [4] he wrote as follows : "For what is so insane as the empty sound of words, however well-chosen and elegant, if there be no foundation of sense or sagacity ? " But Marcus Cato in particular is a relentless assailant of this fault. For in the speech entitled *If Caelius, tribune of the commons, should have summoned him,* [5] he says : " That man is never silent who is afflicted with the disease of talking, as one in a lethargy is afflicted with that of drinking and sleeping. For if you should not come together when he calls an assembly, so eager is he to talk that he would hire someone to listen. And so you hear him, but you do not listen, just as if he were a quack. For a quack's words are heard, but no one trusts himself

10 se ei[1] nemo committit, si aeger est." Idem Cato in
eadem oratione eidem M. Caelio tribuno plebi vilit-
atem obprobrans non loquendi tantum, verum etiam
tacendi : " Frusto," inquit, " panis conduci potest,

11 vel uti taceat vel uti loquatur." Neque non merito
Homerus unum ex omnibus Thersitam ἀμετροεπῆ et
ἀκριτόμυθον appellat verbaque illius multa et ἄκοσμα
strepentium sine modo graculorum similia esse dicit.

12 Quid enim est aliud ἐκολώα? Eupolidis quoque
versus de id genus hominibus consignatissime factus
est :

Λαλεῖν ἄριστος, ἀδυνατώτατος λέγειν,

13 quod Sallustius noster imitari volens[2] sic scribit :

14 " Loquax," inquit, " magis quam facundus." Quapropter Hesiodus, poetarum prudentissimus, linguam
non vulgandam, sed recondendam esse dicit proinde
ut thesaurum, eiusque esse in promendo gratiam
plurimam, si modesta et parca et modulata sit :

Γλώσσης τοι θησαυρὸς ἐν ἀνθρώποισιν ἄριστος,
Φειδωλῆς πλείστη δὲ χάρις κατὰ μέτρον ἰούσης,

15 Epicharmium quoque illud non inscite se habet :

Οὐ λέγειν τύγ' ἐσσὶ δεινός, ἀλλὰ σιγᾶν ἀδύνατος,

16 ex quo hoc profecto sumptum est : " Qui cum loqui
non posset, tacere non potuit."

---

[1] ei, *added by* σ.   [2] sic, *added by Hertz.*

---

[1] xl. 2, Jordan.   [2] *Iliad.* ii. 212, 246.
[3] *Iliad,* ii. 213.   [4] Fr. 95, Koch.
[5] *Hist.* iv. 43, Maur.   [6] *Works and Days,* 719.
[7] Fr. 272, Kaib.

to him when he is sick." Again Cato, in the same speech,[1] upbraiding the same Marcus Caelius, tribune of the commons, for the cheapness at which not only his speech but also his silence could be bought, says: "For a crust of bread he can be hired either to keep silence or to speak." Most deservedly too does Homer call Thersites alone of all the Greeks ἀμετροεπής, "of measureless speech," and ἀκριτόμυθος,[2] "a reckless babbler," declaring that his words are many and ἄκοσμα, or "disordered," like the endless chatter of daws;[3] for what else does ἐκολώα ("he chattered") mean? There is also a line of Eupolis most pointedly aimed at men of that kind:[4]

In chatter excellent, unable quite to speak,

and our countryman Sallust, wishing to imitate this, writes:[5] "Talkative rather than eloquent." It is for the same reason that Hesiod, wisest of poets, says[6] that the tongue should not be vulgarly exposed but hidden like a treasure, and that it is exhibited with best effect when it is modest, restrained and musical. His own words are:

The greatest of man's treasures is the tongue,
Which wins most favour when it spares its words
And measured is of movement.

The following verse of Epicharmus is also to the point:[7]

Thou art not skilled in speech, yet silence cannot keep,

and it is from this line surely that the saying arose: "Who, though he could not speak, could not be silent."

17   Favorinum ego audivi dicere versus istos Euripidi :

> Ἀχαλίνων στομάτων
> Ἀνόμου τ' ἀφροσύνας
> Τὸ τέλος δυστυχία,

non de his tantum factos accipi debere, qui impia aut inlicita dicerent, sed vel maxime de hominibus quoque posse dici stulta et inmodica blaterantibus, quorum lingua tam prodiga infrenisque sit, ut fluat semper et aestuet conluvione verborum taeterrima, quod genus homines a Graecis significantissimo 18 vocabulo κατάγλωσσοι appellantur. Valerium Probum, grammaticum inlustrem, ex familiari eius, docto viro, comperi, Sallustianum illud, "satis eloquentiae, sapientiae parum," brevi antequam vita decederet, sic legere coepisse et sic a Sallustio relictum affirmavisse : "satis loquentiae, sapientiae parum," quod "loquentia" novatori verborum Sallustio maxime congrueret, "eloquentia" cum insipientia minime conveniret.

19   Huiuscemodi autem loquacitatem verborumque turbam magnitudine inani vastam facetissimus poeta Aristophanes insignibus vocabulis denotavit in his versibus :

> Ἄνθρωπον ἀγριοποιόν, αὐθαδόστομον,
> Ἔχοντ' ἀχάλινον, ἀκρατές, ἀπύλωτον στόμα,
> Ἀπεριλάλητον, κομποφακελορρήμονα,

---

[1] *Bacch.* 386.   [2] *Cat.* v. 4.

[3] It is true that Sallust was fond of new words, but the best MSS. of Sallust are unanimous for *eloquentiae*. Besides this passage of Gellius, L. and S. cite *loquentia* only in Plin. *Epist.* v. 20. 5, *Iulius Cordus . . . solet dicere aliud esse eloquentiam, aliud loquentiam.*

I once heard Favorinus say that the familiar lines of Euripides:[1]

> Of unrestrained mouth
> And of lawless folly
> Is disaster the end,

ought not to be understood as directed only at those who spoke impiously or lawlessly, but might even with special propriety be used also of men who prate foolishly and immoderately, whose tongues are so extravagant and unbridled that they ceaselessly flow and seethe with the foulest dregs of language, the sort of persons to whom the Greeks apply the highly significant term κατάγλωσσοι, or "given to talk." I learned from a friend of his, a man of learning, that the famous grammarian Valerius Probus, shortly before his death, began to read Sallust's well-known saying,[2] "a certain amount of eloquence but little discretion," as "abundant talkativeness, too little discretion," and that he insisted that Sallust left it in that form, since the word *loquentia* was very characteristic of Sallust, an innovator in diction,[3] while *eloquentia* was not at all consistent with lack of discretion.

Finally, loquacity of this kind and a disorderly mass of empty grandiloquence is scored with striking epithets by Aristophanes, wittiest of poets, in the following lines:[4]

> A stubborn-creating, stubborn-pulling fellow,
> Uncurbed, unfettered, uncontrolled of speech,
> Unperiphrastic, bombastiloquent.

[4] *Frogs*, 837 ff., Rogers (*L.C.L.*). The epithets are applied to Aeschylus!

20 neque minus insigniter veteres quoque nostri hoc genus homines in verba proiectos "locutuleios" et
"blaterones" et "linguaces" dixerunt.

XVI

Quod verba istaec Quadrigari ex *Annali* tertio, "ibi mille
hominum occiditur," non licenter neque de poetarum
figura, sed ratione certa et proba grammaticae disciplinae
dicta sunt.

1 QUADRIGARIUS in tertio *Annalium* ita scripsit : " Ibi
occiditur mille hominum." " Occiditur," inquit, non
2 " occiduntur." Item Lucilius in tertio *Satirarum :*

Ad portam mille a porta est, sex inde Salernum,

3 mille, inquit, est, non "mille sunt." Varro in
XVII. *Humanarum :* " Ad Romuli initium plus mille
4 et centum annorum est." M. Cato in primo *Originum :*
5 " Inde est ferme mille passum." M. Cicero in sexta
in Antonium : "Itane Ianus medius in L. Antonii
clientela est ? Quis umquam in illo Iano inventus est,
qui L. Antonio mille nummum ferret expensum ? "
6   In his atque in multis aliis "mille" numero sin-
7 gulari dictum est ; neque hoc, ut quidam putant,
vetustati concessum est aut per figurarum concinnitatem admissum est, sed sic videtur ratio poscere.

___

¹ Fr. 44, Peter.
² v. 124, Marx, who has *exinde* for *sex inde* and supplies
sumus profecti.
³ xviii, fr. 2, Mirsch.
⁴ Fr. 26, Peter.
⁵ *Phil.* vi. 15.
⁶ The "middle Janus" was the seat of money-lenders and
bankers. As a district it extended along the northern side

And no less pointedly did our forefathers also call
men of that kind, who were drowned in words,
"babblers, gabblers and chatterboxes."

XVI

*That those words of Quadrigarius in the third book of his
Annals, "there a thousand of men is killed," are not used
arbitrarily or by a poetic figure, but in accordance with a
definite and approved rule of the science of grammar.*

QUADRIGARIUS in the third book of his *Annals*[1]
wrote the following: "There a thousand of men is
killed," using *occiditur*, not *occiduntur*.   So too Lucilius
in the third book of his *Satires*,

> From gate to gate a thousand of paces is.
> Thence to Salernum six,[2]

has *mille est*, not *mille sunt*.   Varro in the seven-
teenth book of his *Antiquities of Man* writes:[3]
"To the beginning of Romulus' reign is more than
a thousand and one hundred years," Marcus Cato
in the first book of his *Origins*,[4] "From there it
is nearly a thousand of paces."   Marcus Cicero has
in his sixth *Oration against Antony*,[5] "Is the middle
Janus[6] so subject to the patronage of Lucius
Antonius?   Who has ever been found in that Janus
who would lend Lucius Antonius a thousand of
sesterces?"

In these and many other passages *mille* is used
in the singular number, and that is not, as some
think, a concession to early usage or admitted as a
neat figure of speech, but it is obviously demanded

of the Forum Romanum. The "Janus" itself was near the
basilica Aemilia, perhaps at the entrance to the Argiletum.

81

8 "Mille" enim non pro eo ponitur, quod Graece
χίλιοι dicitur, sed quod χιλιάς et sicuti una χιλιάς
et duae χιλιάδες, ita "unum mille" et "duo milia"
9 certa atque directa ratione dicitur. Quamobrem id
quoque recte et probabiliter dici solitum "mille
denarium in arca est" et "mille equitum in exer-
10 citu est." Lucilius autem, praeterquam supra posui,
11 alio quoque in loco id manifestius demonstrat, nam
in libro XV. ita dicit:

> Hunc, milli passum qui vicerit atque duobus,
> Campanus sonipes succussor nullus sequetur
> Maiore in spatio ac diversus videbitur ire;

12 item libro nono:[1]

> Tu milli nummum potes uno quaerere centum;

13 milli passum dixit pro "mille passibus" et "uno
milli nummum" pro "unis mille nummis" aper-
teque ostendit "mille" et vocabulum esse et singulari numero dici eiusque plurativum esse "milia"
14 et casum etiam capere ablativum. Neque ceteros
casus requiri oportet, cum sint alia pleraque vocabula,
quae in singulos tantum casus, quaedam etiam, quae
15 in nullum inclinentur. Quapropter nihil iam dubium
est, quin M. Cicero in oratione, quam scripsit *pro
Milone*, ita scriptum reliquerit: "Ante fundum Clodi,
quo in fundo propter insanas illas substructiones facile

---

[1] alio libro ix mille, ω.

---

[1] 506 ff., Marx, who punctuates with a comma after
succussor, with a slight change in the meaning, taking *nullus
sequetur* in the sense of *non sequetur*. On the Campanian
horses see Livy, viii.11.5 and xxvi.4.3, 6; Val. Max. ii.3.3.
[2] 327, Marx.

by rule. For the word *mille* does not stand for the Greek χίλιοι, "thousand," but for χιλιάς, "a thousand"; and just as they say one χιλιάς, or two χιλιάδες, so we say one thousand and two thousands according to a definite and regular rule. Therefore these common expressions are correct and good usage, "There is a thousand of denarii in the chest," and "There is a thousand of horsemen in the army." Furthermore Lucilius, in addition to the example cited above, makes this point still clearer in another place also: for in his fifteenth book he says:[1]

> This horse no jolting fine Campanian steed,
> Though he has passed him by one thousand, aye
> And twain, of paces, can in a longer course
> Compete with, but he will in fact appear
> To run the other way.

So too in the ninth book:[2]

> With sesterces a thousand you can gain
> A hundred thousand.

Lucilius wrote *milli passum* instead of *mille passibus* and *uno milli nummum* for *unis mille nummis,* thus showing clearly that *mille* is a noun, used in the singular number, that its plural is *milia,* and that it also forms an ablative case. Nor ought we to expect the rest of the cases; for there are many other words which are declined only in single cases, and even some which are not declined at all. Therefore we can no longer doubt that Cicero, in the speech which he wrote *In Defence of Milo,*[3] used these words: "Before the estate of Clodius, where fully a thousand of able-

[3] § 53.

mille hominum versabatur valentium," non "versabantur," quod in libris minus accuratis scriptum est; alia enim ratione "mille homines," alia [1] "mille hominum" dicendum est.

XVII

Quanta cum animi aequitate toleraverit Socrates uxoris ingenium intractabile; atque inibi, quid M. Varro in quadam satura de officio mariti scripserit.

1 XANTHIPPE, Socratis philosophi uxor, morosa admodum fuisse fertur et iurgiosa, irarumque et molestiarum muliebrium per diem perque noctem
2 scatebat. Has eius intemperies in maritum Alcibiades demiratus, interrogavit Socraten quaenam ratio esset cur mulierem tam acerbam domo non
3 exigeret. "Quoniam," inquit Socrates, "cum illam domi talem perpetior, insuesco et exerceor, ut ceterorum quoque foris petulantiam et iniuriam facilius feram."
4 Secundum hanc sententiam quoque Varro in *Satura Menippea*, quam *De Officio Mariti* inscripsit : [2] "Vitium," inquit, "uxoris aut tollendum aut ferendum est. Qui tollit vitium, uxorem commodiorem
5 praestat, qui fert, sese meliorem facit." Haec verba Varronis "tollere " et " ferre " lepide quidem com-

---

[1] homines . . . alia, *supplied by Klotz*.
[2] inscripsit, *Vahlen*; scripsit, *MSS.*

---

[1] Varro's Menippean Satires, in 150 books, based to some extent on the Σπευδογέλοιον of Menippus, a Cynic philosopher of the third century B.C., treated in a mixture of prose and verse a great variety of moral and serious topics in a playful

bodied men was employed on those crazy substructures," not "were employed," as we find it in less accurate copies; for one rule requires us to say "a thousand men," but another, "a thousand of men."

XVII

The patience with which Socrates endured his wife's shrewish disposition; and in that connection what Marcus Varro says in one of his satires about the duty of a husband.

XANTHIPPE, the wife of the philosopher Socrates, is said to have been ill-tempered and quarrelsome to a degree, with a constant flood of feminine tantrums and annoyances day and night. Alcibiades, amazed at this outrageous conduct of hers towards her husband, asked Socrates what earthly reason he had for not showing so shrewish a woman the door. "Because," replied Socrates, "it is by enduring such a person at home that I accustom and train myself to bear more easily away from home the impudence and injustice of other persons."

In the same vein Varro also said in the *Menippean Satire*[1] which he entitled *On the Duty of a Husband* :[2] "A wife's faults must be either put down or put up with. He who puts down her faults, makes his wife more agreeable; he who puts up with them, improves himself." Varro contrasted the two words *tollere* and *ferre* very cleverly,[3] to be sure,

and sometimes jocose manner. For other titles see Index under (M.) Terentius Varro, and for the fragments, Bücheler's *Petronius*, 3d. ed., Berlin, 1882, pp. 161 ff.

[2] Fr. 83, Bücheler.

[3] For a similar play on two meanings of *tollere*, cf. Suet. *Aug.* xii.

posita sunt, sed "tollere" apparet dictum pro
6 "corrigere." Id etiam apparet, eiusmodi vitium
uxoris, si corrigi non possit, ferendum esse Varronem
censuisse, quod ferri scilicet a viro honeste potest;
vitia enim flagitiis leviora sunt.

XVIII

Quod M. Varro in quarto decimo *Humanarum* L. Aelium
magistrum suum in[1] ἐτυμολογίᾳ falsa reprehendit; quodque
idem Varro in eodem libro falsum furis ἔτυμον dicit.

1 In XIV. *Rerum Divinarum* libro M. Varro doc-
tissimum tunc civitatis hominem L. Aelium errasse
ostendit, quod vocabulum Graecum vetus traductum
in linguam Romanam, proinde atque si primitus
Latine fictum esset, resolverit in voces Latinas
ratione etymologica falsa.
2 Verba ipsa super ea re Varronis posuimus: "In
quo L. Aelius noster, litteris ornatissimus memoria
nostra, erravit aliquotiens. Nam aliquot verborum
Graecorum antiquiorum, proinde atque essent propria
nostra, reddidit causas falsas. Non 'leporem'
dicimus, ut ait, quod est levipes, sed quod est
vocabulum anticum Graecum. Multa vetera illorum
ignorantur, quod pro his aliis nunc vocabulis utuntur;
et illorum esse plerique ignorent 'Graecum,' quod
nunc nominant Ἕλληνα, 'puteum,' quod vocant

---

[1] in, *Hertz,* et in, ω.

---

[1] Fr. 99, Agahd. In the *lemma,* or chapter heading,
Varro's statement is wrongly referred to the *Antiquities of
Man,* the other division of his great work *Antiquitatum*

but he obviously uses *tollere* in the sense of "correct." It is evident too that Varro thought that if a fault of that kind in a wife cannot be corrected, it should be tolerated, in so far of course as a man may endure it honourably; for faults are less serious than crimes.

XVIII

How Marcus Varro, in the fourteenth book of his *Antiquities of Man*,[1] criticizes his master Lucius Aelius for a false etymology; and how Varro in his turn, in the same book, gives a false origin for *fur*.

In the fourteenth book of his *Divine Antiquities*[1] Marcus Varro shows that Lucius Aelius, the most learned Roman of his time, went astray and followed a false etymological principle in separating an old Greek word which had been taken over into the Roman language into two Latin words, just as if it were of Latin origin.

I quote Varro's own words on the subject: "In this regard our countryman Lucius Aelius, the most gifted man of letters within my memory, was sometimes misled. For he gave false derivations of several early Greek words, under the impression that they were native to our tongue. We do not use the word *lepus* ('hare') because the animal is *levipes* ('light-footed'), as he asserts, but because it is an old Greek word. Many of the early words of that people are unfamiliar, because to-day the Greeks use other words in their place; and it may not be generally known that among these are *Graecus*, for which they now use Ἕλλην, *puteus* ('well') which

Libri XLI, treating the political and religious institutions of the Romans. Only scanty fragments have survived.

φρέαρ, 'leporem,' quod λαγωὸν dicunt. In quo non modo Aelii ingenium non reprehendo, sed industriam laudo; successum enim fert [1] fortuna, experientiam laus sequitur."

3 Haec Varro in primore libro scripsit, de ratione vocabulorum scitissime, de usu utriusque linguae 4 peritissime, de ipso Aelio clementissime. Sed in posteriore eiusdem libri parte "furem" dicit ex eo dictum, quod veteres Romani "furvum" atrum appellaverint et fures per noctem, quae atra sit, facilius 5 furentur. Nonne sic videtur Varro de fure,[2] tamquam Aelius de lepore? Nam quod a Graecis nunc κλέπτης dicitur, antiquiore Graeca lingua φὼρ dictum est. Hinc per adfinitatem litterarum, qui φὼρ Graece, 6 est Latine "fur." Sed ea res fugeritne tunc Varronis memoriam, an contra aptius et cohaerentius putarit, "furem" a "furvo," id est nigro,[3] appellari, in hac re de viro tam excellentis doctrinae non meum iudicium est.

XIX

Historia super libris Sibyllinis ac de Tarquinio Superbo rege.

1 In antiquis annalibus memoria super libris Si-
2 byllinis haec prodita est: Anus hospita atque incognita ad Tarquinium Superbum regem adiit, novem libros ferens, quos esse dicebat divina oracula; 3 eos velle venundare. Tarquinius pretium per-
4 contatus est. Mulier nimium atque inmensum

----

[1] fert, *added by Hirschfeld*; fortuna dat, *Mommsen*; fortuna fundat, *Hertz* (from Amm. xvii. 5. 8).

[2] *The Aldine ed. added* errasse.

[3] id est nigro *is probably a gloss*.

they call φρέαρ, and *lepus*, which they call λαγωός. But as to this, far from disparaging Aelius' ability, I commend his diligence; for it is good fortune that brings success, endeavour that deserves praise."

This is what Varro wrote in the first part of his book, with great skill in the explanation of words, with wide knowledge of the usage of both languages, and marked kindliness towards Aelius himself. But in the latter part of the same book he says that *fur* is so called because the early Romans used *furvus* for *ater* ("black"), and thieves steal most easily in the night, which is black. Is it not clear that Varro made the same mistake about *fur* that Aelius did about *lepus*. For what the Greeks now call κλέπτης, or "thief," in the earlier Greek language was called φώρ. Hence, owing to the similarity in sound, he who in Greek is φώρ, in Latin is *fur*. But whether that fact escaped Varro's memory at the time, or on the other hand he thought that *fur* was more appropriately and consistently named from *furvus*, that is, "black," as to that question it is not for me to pass judgment on a man of such surpassing learning.

XIX

The story of king Tarquin the Proud and the Sibylline Books.

In ancient annals we find this tradition about the Sibylline Books. An old woman, a perfect stranger, came to king Tarquin the Proud, bringing nine books; she declared that they were oracles of the gods and that she wished to sell them. Tarquin inquired the price; the woman demanded an im-

poposcit ; rex, quasi anus aetate desiperet, derisit.
5 Tum illa foculum coram cum igni apponit, tris libros
ex novem deurit et ecquid reliquos sex eodem
6 pretio emere vellet regem interrogavit. Sed enim
Tarquinius id multo risit magis dixitque anum iam
7 procul dubio delirare. Mulier ibidem statim tris
alios libros exussit atque id ipsum denuo placide
rogat, ut tris reliquos eodem illo pretio emat.
8 Tarquinius ore iam serio atque attentiore animo fit,
eam constantiam confidentiamque non insuper habendam intellegit, libros tris reliquos mercatur nihilo
minore pretio quam quod erat petitum pro omnibus.
9 Sed eam mulierem tunc a Tarquinio digressam
10 postea nusquam loci visam constitit. Libri tres, in
11 sacrarium conditi, " Sibyllini " appellati ; ad eos
quasi ad oraculum quindecimviri adeunt, cum di
immortales publice consulendi sunt.

XX

Quid geometrae dicant ἐπίπεδον, quid στερεόν, quid κύβον
quid γραμμήν ; quibusque ista omnia Latinis vocabulis
appellentur.

1 FIGURARUM quae σχήματα geometrae appellant,
2 genera sunt duo, " planum " et " solidum." Haec
ipsi vocant ἐπίπεδον καὶ στερεόν. " Planum " est quod
in duas partis solum lineas habet, qua latum est et

---

[1] In the temple of Jupiter on the Capitol. Augustus
transferred them to the temple of Apollo on the Palatine ;
see Suet. Aug. xxxi. 1.
[2] Because the old woman was regarded as a Sibyl. Although
the books came to Tarquin by way of Cumae, the origin of the
Sibylline books was probably Asia Minor. There were

mense and exorbitant sum : the king laughed her to
scorn, believing her to be in her dotage. Then she
placed a lighted brazier before him, burned three of
the books to ashes, and asked whether he would buy
the remaining six at the same price. But at this
Tarquin laughed all the more and said that there
was now no doubt that the old woman was crazy.
Upon that the woman at once burned up three more
books and again calmly made the same request, that
he would buy the remaining three at the original
figure. Tarquin now became serious and more
thoughtful, and realising that such persistence and
confidence were not to be treated lightly, he bought
the three books that were left at as high a price as
had been asked for all nine. Now it is a fact that
after then leaving Tarquin, that woman was never
seen again anywhere. The three books were deposited in a shrine[1] and called " Sibylline " ;[2] to
them the Fifteen[3] resort whenever the immortal
gods are to be consulted as to the welfare of the
State.

XX

On what the geometers call ἐπίπεδος, στερεός, κύβος and γραμμή,
with the Latin equivalents for all these terms.

Of the figures which the geometers call σχήματα
there are two kinds, " plane " and " solid." These
the Greeks themselves call respectively ἐπίπεδος and
στερεός. A " plane " figure is one that has all its lines
in two dimensions only, breadth and length ; for

several Sibyls (Varro enumerates ten), of whom the Ery-
thraean, from whom the books apparently came, was the
most important ; see Marquardt, *Staatsverw.* iii². 350 ff.
    [3] See note 4, page 61.

qua longum ; qualia sunt triquetra et quadrata, quae
3 in area fiunt, sine altitudine. "Solidum" est quando
non longitudines modo et latitudines planas numeri
linearum efficiunt, sed etiam extollunt altitudines,
quales sunt ferme metae triangulae quas "pyramidas"
appellant, vel qualia sunt quadrata undique, quae κύ-
4 βους illi, nos "quadrantalia" dicimus. Κύβος enim
est figura ex omni latere quadrata, "quales sunt,"
inquit M. Varro, "tesserae quibus in alveolo luditur,
5 ex quo ipsae quoque appellatae κύβοι." In numeris
etiam similiter κύβος dicitur, cum omne latus
eiusdem numeri aequabiliter in sese solvitur, sicuti
fit cum ter terna ducuntur atque ipse numerus
terplicatur.
6 Huius numeri cubum Pythagoras vim habere
lunaris circuli dixit, quod et luna orbem suum
lustret septem et viginti diebus et numerus ternio,[1]
qui τριὰς Graece dicitur, tantundem efficiat in cubo.
7 "Linea" autem a nostris dicitur, quam γραμμὴν
8 Graeci nominant. Eam [2] M. Varro ita definit :
"Linea est," inquit, "longitudo quaedam sine latitu-
9 dine et altitudine." Εὐκλείδης autem brevius, praetermissa altitudine : γραμμή, inquit, est μῆκος ἀπλατές, quod exprimere uno Latino verbo non queas,
nisi audeas dicere "inlatabile."

---

[1] ternio, ϛ ; triennio, ω.   [2] ea M., ω ; corr. in ϛ.

---

[1] See Euclid, *Elementa* I, *Definitions*, 20, cubus autem est
aequaliter aequalis aequalis, sive qui tribus aequalibus
numeris comprehenditur.

[2] Fr. p. 350, Bipont.

[3] Euclid, *l.c.*, 17, ubi autem tres numeri inter se multiplicantes numerum aliquem efficiunt, numerus inde ortus
"solidus" (= κύβος) est, *latera* autem eius numeri inter se
multiplicantes.

example, triangles and squares, which are drawn on a
flat surface without height. We have a " solid " figure,
when its several lines do not produce merely length
and breadth in a plane, but are raised so as to produce height also ; such are in general the triangular
columns which they call " pyramids," or those which
are bounded on all sides by squares, such as the
Greeks call κύβοι,[1] and we *quadrantalia*. For the
κύβος is a figure which is square on all its sides,
" like the dice," says Marcus Varro,[2] " with which we
play on a gaming-board, for which reason the dice
themselves are called κύβοι." Similarly in numbers
too the term κύβος is used, when every factor[3] consisting of the same number is equally resolved into
the cube number itself,[4] as is the case when three is
taken three times and the resulting number itself
is then trebled.

Pythagoras declared that the cube of the number
three controls the course of the moon, since the
moon passes through its orbit in twenty-seven days,
and the *ternio*, or " triad," which the Greeks call
τριάς, when cubed makes twenty-seven.

Furthermore, our geometers apply the term *linea*,
or " line," to what the Greeks call γραμμή. This is
defined by Marcus Varro as follows :[5] " A line," says
he, " is length without breadth or height." But
Euclid says more tersely, omitting " height " :[6]
" A line is μῆκος ἀπλατές, or ' breadthless length.' "
Ἀπλατές cannot be expressed in Latin by a single
word, unless you should venture to coin the term
inlatabile.

[4] That is, is an equal factor in the cube number.
[5] Fr. p. 337, Bipont.
[6] *l.c.* 2, γραμμὴ δὲ μῆκος ἀπλατές.

93

XXI

Quod Iulius Hyginus affirmatissime contendit, legisse se
librum P. Vergilii domesticum, ubi[1] scriptum esset " et
ora Tristia temptantum sensus torquebit amaror," non
quod vulgus legeret " sensu torquebit amaro."

1 VERSUS istos ex *Georgicis* Vergilii plerique omnes
sic legunt :

At sapor indicium faciet manifestus et ora
Tristia temptantum sensu torquebit amaro.

2 Hyginus autem, non hercle ignobilis grammaticus,
in *Commentariis* quae in Vergilium fecit, confirmat et
perseverat, non hoc a Vergilio relictum, sed quod
ipse invenerit in libro qui fuerit ex domo atque ex
familia Vergilii :

et ora
Tristia temptantum sensus torquebit amaror,

3 neque id soli Hygino, sed doctis quibusdam etiam
viris complacitum, quoniam videtur absurde dici
" sapor sensu amaro torquet." " Cum ipse," inquiunt, " sapor sensus sit, non alium in semet ipso
sensum habeat ac proinde sit quasi dicatur ' sensus
4 sensu amaro torquet.' " Sed enim cum Favorino
Hygini commentarium legissem atque ei statim
displicita esset insolentia et insuavitas illius " sensu
torquebit amaro," risit et[2] : " Iovem lapidem,"[3]

---

[1] ubi *added by Hertz* ; in quo, σ.
[2] illius . . . risit et, β ; amaror is, ω.
[3] lapidem, β ; lapideum, ω.

---

[1] ii. 246 f.
[2] But the taste will tell its tale full plainly, and with its
bitter flavour will distort the testers' soured mouths.

XXI

The positive assertion of Julius Hyginus that he had read a
manuscript of Virgil from the poet's own household, in
which there was written *et ora tristia temptantum sensus
torquebit amaror* and not the usual reading, *sensu torquebit
amaro.*

NEARLY everyone reads these lines from the
Georgics of Virgil [1] in this way :

> At sapor indicium faciet manifestus et ora
> Tristia temptantum sensu torquebit amaro. [2]

Hyginus, however, on my word no obscure grammarian, in the *Commentaries* [3] which he wrote on
Virgil, declares and insists that it was not this that
Virgil left, but what he himself found in a copy
which had come from the home and family of the
poet :

> et ora
> Tristia temptantum sensus torquebit amaror, [4]

and this reading has commended itself, not to
Hyginus alone, but also to some other learned men,
because it seems absurd to say " the taste will distort
with its bitter sensation." " Since," they say, " taste
itself is a sensation, it cannot have another sensation
in itself, but it is exactly as if one should say, ' the
sensation will distort with a bitter sensation.' " Moreover, when I had read Hyginus' note to Favorinus,
and the strangeness and harshness of the phrase
" sensu torquebit amaro " at once had displeased him,

[3] Fr. 4, p. 528, Fun.
[4] But the bitterness of the sensation will distort the testers'
soured mouths.

inquit, "quod sanctissimum iusiurandum habitum
est, paratus ego iurare sum Vergilium hoc numquam
scripsisse, sed Hyginum ego verum dicere arbitror.
5 Non enim primus finxit hoc verbum Vergilius insolenter, sed in carminibus Lucreti invento usus est,
non[1] aspernatus auctoritatem poetae ingenio et
6 facundia praecellentis." Verba ex IV. Lucreti haec
sunt :

dilutaque contra
Cum tuimur misceri absinthia, tangit amaror.

7 Non verba autem sola, sed versus prope totos et
locos quoque Lucreti plurimos sectatum esse Vergilium videmus.

XXII

An qui causas defendit recte Latineque dicat "superesse
se"[2] is[3] quos[4] defendit ; et "superesse" proprie quid sit.

1 INROBORAVIT inveteravitque falsa atque aliena
verbi significatio, quod dicitur "hic illi superest,"
cum dicendum est advocatum esse quem cuipiam
2 causamque eius defendere. Atque id dicitur non in
compitis tantum neque in plebe vulgaria, sed in foro,
3 in comitio, apud tribunalia. Qui integre autem

---

[1] inventus est non, *ω* ; *corr. by Ehrenthal.*
[2] se *added by Carrio.*
[3] is = eis, iis.
[4] id quod, *ω* ; *corr. by Hertz.*

---

[1] This much discussed oath is best taken as equivalent to
per Iovem et lapidem ; see Fowler, *Roman Festivals*, p. 231 ;
Nettleship, *Essays*, p. 35, and others. The *locus classicus* on
the process is Polybius, iii. 25 ; cf. Plutarch, *Sulla*, 10.

he said with a laugh: "I am ready to swear by Jupiter and the stone,[1] which is considered the most sacred of oaths, that Virgil never wrote that, but I believe that Hyginus is right. For Virgil was not the first to coin that word arbitrarily, but he found it in the poems of Lucretius and made use of it, not disdaining to follow the authority of a poet who excelled in talent and power of expression." The passage, from the fourth book of Lucretius, reads as follows: [2]

> dilutaque contra
> Cum tuimur misceri absinthia, tangit amaror.[3]

And in fact we see that Virgil imitated, not only single words of Lucretius, but often almost whole lines and passages.

XXII

Whether it is correct Latin for counsel for the defence to say *superesse se*, "that he is appearing for" those whom he is defending; and the proper meaning of *superesse*.

An incorrect and improper meaning of a word has been established by long usage, in that we use the expression *hic illi superest* when we wish to say that anyone appears as another's advocate and pleads his cause. And this is not merely the language of the streets and of the common people, but is used in the forum, the comitium and the courts. Those, however, who have spoken language undefiled have

[2] iv. 221 f.
[3] When we look on at the mixing of a decoction of wormwood in our presence, its bitterness affects us.

locuti sunt magnam partem "superesse" ita dixerunt, ut eo verbo significarent superfluere et supervacare

4 atque esse supra necessarium modum. Itaque M. Varro, in satura quae inscripta est *Nescis Quid Vesper Vehat,* "superfuisse" dicit immodice et in-

5 tempestive fuisse. Verba ex eo libro haec sunt: "In convivio legi nec omnia debent et ea potissimum, quae simul sint βιωφελῆ et delectent, potius ut id quoque videatur non defuisse quam superfuisse." [1]

6 Memini ego praetoris, docti hominis, tribunali me forte assistere atque ibi advocatum non incelebrem sic postulare, ut extra causam diceret remque quae agebatur non attingeret. Tunc praetorem ei cuia res erat dixisse advocatum eum non habere, et cum is qui verba faciebat reclamasset "ego illi V. C. supersum," respondisse praetorem festiviter "tu plane superes, non ades."

7 M. autem Cicero, in libro qui inscriptus est *De Iure Civili in Artem Redigendo,* verba haec posuit: "Nec vero scientia iuris maioribus suis Q. Aelius Tubero defuit, doctrina etiam superfuit." In quo loco "superfuit" significare videtur "supra fuit et praestitit superavitque maiores suos doctrina sua, superfluenti tamen et nimis abundanti," disciplinas

8 enim Tubero stoicas et dialecticas percalluerat. In

---

[1] quod superfuisse, β; *omitted by* ω; non videatur magis defuisse quam superfuisse, *codd. Carrionis*; *Vogel put* potius *after* defuisse.

---

[1] Fr 340, Bücheler.

[2] It is difficult to reproduce the word-play on *superesse,* "be present for" and "be superfluous." There is a pun also on *adesse,* "be present" and "help, assist."

for the most part used *superesse* in the sense of "to overflow, be superfluous, or exceed the required amount." Thus Marcus Varro, in the satire entitled " *You know not what evening may bring,*" [1] uses *superfuisse* in the sense of having exceeded the amount proper for the occasion. These are his words : " Not everything should be read at a dinner party, but preferably such works as are at the same time improving and diverting, so that this feature of the entertainment also may seem not to have been neglected, rather than overdone."

I remember happening to be present in the court of a praetor who was a man of learning, and that on that occasion an advocate of some repute pleaded in such fashion that he wandered from the subject and did not touch upon the point at issue. Thereupon the praetor said to the man whose case was before him : " You have no counsel." And when the pleader protested, saying " I am present (*supersum*) for the honourable gentleman," the praetor wittily retorted : " You surely present too much, but you do not represent your client." [2]

Marcus Cicero, too, in his book entitled *On Reducing the Civil Law to a System* [3] wrote these words : " Indeed Quintus Aelius Tubero did not fall short of his predecessors in knowledge of the law, in learning he even outstripped them." In this passage *superfuit* seems to mean " he went beyond, surpassed and excelled his predecessors in his learning, which, however, was excessive and overabundant " ; [4] for Tubero was thoroughly versed in Stoic dialectics.

---

[3] Fr. 2, p. 980, Orelli [2] ; Fr. 1, Huschke, and Bremer.
[4] It was superfluous in being more than he needed for the practice of his profession.

libro quoque *De Republica* secundo id ipsum verbum
Cicero ponit non temere transeundum. Verba ex
eo libro haec sunt : " Non gravarer, Laeli, nisi et hos
velle putarem et ipse cuperem te quoque aliquam
partem huius nostri sermonis attingere, praesertim
cum heri ipse dixeris te nobis etiam superfuturum.
Verum id quidem fieri non potest ; ne desis omnes
te rogamus."

9   Exquisite igitur et comperte Iulius Paulus dicebat, homo in nostra memoria doctissimus, "superesse" non simplici ratione dici tam Latine quam
Graece ; Graecos enim περισσὸν in utramque partem
ponere, vel quod supervacaneum esset ac non
10 necessarium, vel quod abundans nimis et afluens et
exuberans [1] ; sic nostros quoque veteres " superesse "
alias dixisse pro superfluenti et vacivo neque admodum necessario, ita ut supra posuimus Varronem
dicere, alias ita ut Cicero dixit, pro eo quod copia
quidem et facultate ceteris anteiret, super modum
tamen et largius prolixiusque flueret quam esset
11 satis. Qui dicit ergo " superesse se " ei quem defendit, nihil istorum vult dicere sed nescio quid
12 aliud indictum inscitumque dicit ac ne Vergilii
quidem poterit auctoritate uti, qui in *Georgicis* ita
scripsit ·

Primus ego in patriam mecum, modo vita supersit . . .

[1] exuperans, ω ; *corr. by Hertz.*

---

[1] An error of Gellius ; the reference is iii. 32.
[2] iii. 10.

Cicero's use of the word in the second book [1] of the *Republic* also deserves attention. This is the passage in question : " I should not object, Laelius, if I did not think that these friends wished, and if I myself did not desire, that you should take some part in this discussion of ours, especially since you yourself said yesterday that you would give us even more than enough (*te superfuturum*). But that indeed is impossible : we all ask you not to give us less than enough (*ne desis*)."

Now Julius Paulus, the most learned man within my recollection, used to say with keenness and understanding that *superesse* and its Greek equivalent had more than one meaning : for he declared that the Greeks used περισσόν both ways, either of what was superfluous and unnecessary or of what was too abundant, overflowing and excessive ; that in the same way our earlier writers also employed *superesse* sometimes of what was superfluous, idle and not wholly necessary, a sense which we have just cited from Varro, and sometimes, as in Cicero, of that which indeed surpassed other things in copiousness and plentifulness, yet was immoderate and too extensive, and gushed forth more abundantly than was sufficient. Therefore one who says *superesse se* with reference to a man whom he is defending tries to convey none of these meanings, but uses *superesse* in a sense that is unknown and not in use. And he will not be able to appeal even to the authority of Virgil, who in his *Georgics* wrote as follows : [2]

I will be first to bear, so but my life still last (*supersit*),
Home to my native land . . .

Hoc enim in loco Vergilius ἀκυρότερον eo verbo usus
videtur, quod "supersit" dixit pro "longinquius
13 diutiusque adsit," illudque contra eiusdem Vergili
aliquanto est probabilius :

> Florentisque secant herbas fluviosque ministrant
> Farraque, ne blando nequeat superesse labori ;

significat enim supra laborem esse neque opprimi a
labore.
14 An autem "superesse" dixerint veteres pro
"restare et perficiendae rei deesse," quaerebamus.
15 Nam Sallustius in significatione ista non "superesse,"
sed "superare" dicit. Verba eius in *Iugurtha* haec
sunt : "Is[1] plerumque seorsum a rege exercitum
ductare et omnis res exequi solitus erat, quae
Iugurthae fesso aut maioribus astricto superaverant."
16 Sed invenimus in tertio Enni *Annalium* in hoc
versu :

> Inde sibi memorat unum super esse laborem,

id est relicum esse et restare, quod, quia id est, divise
pronuntiandum est, ut non una pars orationis esse
17 videatur, sed duae. Cicero autem in secunda *An-
tonianarum*,[2] quod est relicum, non "superesse," sed
"restare" dicit.
18 Praeter haec "superesse" invenimus dictum pro
19 "superstitem esse." Ita enim scriptum est in libro
epistularum M. Ciceronis ad L. Plancum, et in

---

[1] is, ⸔ ; his, ω ; qui, *Sall.*　　　[2] Antoniarum, ω.

---

[1] iii. 126.　　　[2] lxx. 2.
[3] v. 158, Vahlen[2].
[4] *Phil.* ii. 71, cum praesertim belli pars tanta restaret.
[5] The tenth book of the *Epist. ad Fam.* contains numerous
letters of Cicero to Plancus and of Plancus to Cicero.

For in this place Virgil seems to have used that word somewhat irregularly in giving *supersit* the sense of "be present for a longer or more extended period," but on the contrary his use of the word in the following line is more nearly the accepted one : [1]

> They cut him tender grass,
> Give corn and much fresh water, that his strength
> Be more than equal to (*superesse*) the pleasing toil.

for here *superesse* means to be more than equal to the task and not to be crushed by it.

I also used to raise the question whether the ancients used *superesse* in the sense of "to be left and be lacking for the completion of an act." For to express that idea Sallust says, not *superesse*, but *superare*. These are his words in the *Jugurtha* : [2] "This man was in the habit of exercising a command independently of the king, and of attending to all business which had been left undone (*superaverant*) by Jugurtha when he was weary or engaged in more important affairs." But we find in the third book of Ennius' *Annals* : [3]

> Then he declares one task's left over (*super esse*)
>   for him,

that is, is left and remains undone ; but there *superesse* must be divided and read as if it were not one part of speech, but two, as in fact it is. Cicero, however, in his second *Oration against Antony* [4] expresses "what is left" by *restare*, not by *superesse*.

Besides these uses we find *superesse* with the meaning "survive." For it is so employed in the book of letters of Marcus Cicero to Lucius Plancus, [5] as

epistula M. Asini Pollionis ad Ciceronem, verbis his:
"Nam neque deesse reipublicae volo neque superesse," per quod significat, si respublica emoriatur et
20 pereat, nolle se vivere. In Plauti autem *Asinaria*
manifestius id ipsum scriptum est in his versibus, qui
sunt eius comoediae primi:

> Sicút tuum vis únicum gnatúm tuae
> Superésse vitae sóspitem et supérstitem.

21 Cavenda igitur est non improprietas sola verbi,
sed etiam pravitas ominis,[1] si quis senior advocatus
adulescenti "superesse se" dicat.

XXIII

Quis fuerit Papirius Praetextatus; quae istius causa cogno-
menti sit; historiaque ista omnis super eodem Papirio
cognitu iucunda.

1 HISTORIA de Papirio Praetextato dicta scriptaque
est a M. Catone in oratione qua usus est *Ad Milites
contra Galbam,* cum multa quidem venustate atque
2 luce atque munditia verborum. Ea Catonis verba
huic prorsus commentario indidissem, si libri copia
3 fuisset id temporis, cum haec dictavi. Quod si non
virtutes dignitatesque verborum, sed rem ipsam
4 scire quaeris, res ferme ad hunc modum est: Mos
antea senatoribus Romae fuit in curiam cum prae-
5 textatis filiis introire. Tum, cum in senatu res

---

[1] omnis, ω.

---

[1] *Ad Fam.* x. 33.5. It should be Gaius Asinius Pollio.
[2] v. 16.   [3] xxxix, Jordan.

well as in a letter of Marcus Asinius Pollio to Cicero,[1] as follows: "For I wish neither to fail the commonwealth nor to survive it (*superesse*)," meaning that if the commonwealth should be destroyed and perish, he does not wish to live. Again in the *Asinaria* of Plautus that same force is still more evident in these, the first verses of that comedy:[2]

> As you would hope to have your only son
> Survive (*superesse*) you and be ever sound and
> hale.

Thus we have to avoid, not merely an improper use of the word, but also the evil omen, in case an older man, acting as advocate for a youth, should say that he "survives" him.

XXIII

Who Papirius Praetextatus was; the reason for that surname; and the whole of the entertaining story about that same Papirius.

The story of Papirius Praetextatus was told and committed to writing in the speech which Marcus Cato made *To the soldiers against Galba*,[3] with great charm, brilliance and elegance of diction. I should have included Cato's own words in this very commentary, if I had had access to the book at the time when I dictated this extract. But if you would like to hear the bare tale, without the noble and dignified language, the incident was about as follows: It was formerly the custom at Rome for senators to enter the House with their sons under age.[4] In those days, when a matter of considerable importance

[4] The *toga praetexta*, with a purple border, was worn by senators and also by boys of free birth until they assumed the *toga virilis*.

maior quaepiam consultata eaque in diem posterum
prolata est placuitque ut eam rem super qua tracta-
vissent ne quis enuntiaret priusquam decreta esset,
mater Papirii pueri, qui cum parente suo in curia
fuerat, percontata est filium quidnam in senatu
6 patres egissent. Puer respondit tacendum esse
7 neque id dici licere. Mulier fit audiendi cupidior;
secretum rei et silentium pueri animum eius ad
inquirendum everberat; quaerit igitur compressius
8 violentiusque. Tum puer, matre urgente, lepidi
atque festivi mendacii consilium capit. Actum in
senatu dixit, utrum videretur utilius exque republica
esse unusne ut duas uxores haberet, an ut una apud
9 duos nupta esset. Hoc illa ubi audivit, animus
10 compavescit, domo trepidans egreditur, ad ceteras
matronas perfert. Venit[1] ad senatum postridie
matrum familias caterva. Lacrimantes atque ob-
secrantes orant una potius ut duobus nupta fieret
11 quam ut uni duae. Senatores, ingredientes in
curiam, quae illa mulierum intemperies et quid sibi
12 postulatio istaec vellet, mirabantur. Puer Papirius
in medium curiae progressus, quid mater audire
institisset, quid ipse matri dixisset, rem, sicut fuerat,
13 denarrat. Senatus fidem atque ingenium pueri
exosculatur, consultum facit uti posthac pueri cum
patribus in curiam ne introeant, praeter ille unus
Papirius, atque puero postea cognomentum honoris

---

[1] perfert. Venit, *Klotz*; pervenit, *ω*; pervenit. It,
Mommsen.

had been discussed and was postponed to the following day, it was voted that no one should mention the subject of the debate until the matter was decided. The mother of the young Papirius, who had been in the House with his father, asked her son what the Fathers had taken up in the senate. The boy replied that it was a secret and that he could not tell. The woman became all the more eager to hear about it; the secrecy of the matter and the boy's silence piqued her curiosity; she therefore questioned him more pressingly and urgently. Then the boy, because of his mother's insistence, resorted to a witty and amusing falsehood. He said that the senate had discussed the question whether it seemed more expedient, and to the advantage of the State, for one man to have two wives or one woman to have two husbands. On hearing this, she is panic-stricken, rushes excitedly from the house, and carries the news to the other matrons. Next day a crowd of matrons came to the senate, imploring with tears and entreaties that one woman might have two husbands rather than one man two wives. The senators, as they entered the House, were wondering at this strange madness of the women and the meaning of such a demand, when young Papirius, stepping forward to the middle of the House, told in detail what his mother had insisted on hearing, what he himself had said to her, in fact, the whole story exactly as it had happened. The senate paid homage to the boy's cleverness and loyalty, but voted that thereafter boys should not enter the House with their fathers, save only this Papirius; and the boy was henceforth honoured with the

gratia inditum " Praetextatus " ob tacendi loquen-
dique in aetate praetextae prudentiam.

XXIV

Tria epigrammata trium veterum poetarum, Naevii, Plauti,
Pacuvii, quae facta ab ipsis sepulcris eorum incisa sunt.

1   TRIUM poetarum inlustrium epigrammata, Cn.
Naevii, Plauti, M. Pacuvii, quae ipsi fecerunt et
incidenda sepulcro suo reliquerunt, nobilitatis eorum
gratia et venustatis scribenda in his commentariis
esse duxi.

2   Epigramma Naevi plenum superbiae Campanae,
quod testimonium esse iustum potuisset, nisi ab ipso
dictum esset :

   Inmórtalés mortáles sí forét fas flére,
   Flerént divaé Caménae Naéviúm poétam.
   Itáque póstquam est Órcho [1] tráditús thesaúro,
   Oblíti súnt Romaé loquiér linguá Latína.[2]

3   Epigramma Plauti, quod dubitassemus an Plauti
foret, nisi a M. Varrone positum esset in libro *De
Poetis* primo :

   [1] Orcho, ω ; Orchi, β ; *cf. alicui dono dare.*
   [2] The scansion is quantitative.   Saturnian verse is also
scanned as accentual.

---

   [1] This has been regarded as evidence that Naevius was a
native of Campania ; but Campanian arrogance was proverbial.

surname Praetextatus, because of his discretion in keeping silent and in speaking, while he was still young enough to wear the purple-bordered gown.

XXIV

Three epitaphs of three early poets, Naevius, Plautus and Pacuvius, composed by themselves and inscribed upon their tombs.

THERE are three epitaphs of famous poets, Gnaeus Naevius, Plautus and Marcus Pacuvius, composed by themselves and left to be inscribed upon their tombs, which I have thought ought to be included among these notes, because of their distinction and charm.

The epitaph of Naevius, although full of Campanian[1] arrogance, might have been regarded as a just estimate, if he had not written it himself:[2]

If that immortals might for mortals weep,
Then would divine Camenae[3] weep for Naevius.
For after he to Orcus as treasure was consigned,
The Romans straight forgot to speak the Latin
      tongue.

We should be inclined to doubt whether the epitaph of Plautus was really by his own hand, if it had not been quoted by Marcus Varro in the first book of his work *On Poets*:[4]

[2] The authorship of all these epitaphs is questioned: Gudeman thought they came from Varro's *Imagines*; see *Trans. Amer Phil. Assoc.* xxv, 150 ff.; cf p. 296. 3, Bährens.
[3] The Latin equivalent of the Greek Muses.
[4] p. 296. 4, Bährens.

Postquam est mortem aptus Plautus, Comoedia
  luget,
Scaena est deserta, dein Risus, Ludus Iocusque
Et Numeri innumeri simul omnes conlacrimarunt.

4   Epigramma Pacuvii verecundissimum et purissi-
mum dignumque eius elegantissima gravitate:

Aduléscens, tametsi[1] próperas, hoc te saxúlum[2]
  rogat,
Ut sése aspicias, deínde quod scriptum ést legas.
Hic súnt poetae Pácuvi[3] Marcí sita
Ossa. Hóc volebam néscius ne essés. Vale.

XXV

Quibus verbis M. Varro indutias definierit; quaesitumque
inibi curiosius, quaenam ratio sit vocabuli indutiarum.

1   Duobus modis M. Varro in libro *Humanarum,* qui
est *De Bello et Pace,* "indutiae" quid sint, definit.
"Indutiae sunt," inquit, "pax castrensis paucorum
2 dierum"; item alio in loco, "indutiae sunt,"
3 inquit, "belli feriae." Sed lepidae magis atque
iucundae brevitatis utraque definitio quam plana aut
4 proba esse videtur. Nam neque pax est indutiae—
bellum enim manet, pugna cessat—neque in solis
castris neque paucorum tantum dierum indutiae
5 sunt. Quid enim dicemus, si indutiis mensum

    [1] tamen etsi, *ω.*
    [2] te saxulum, *Bücheler and Bormann*; te saxum, *P, V*;
thesaurum, *R.*
    [3] Pacuvii, *ω.*

---

    [1] *Numeri innumeri* was formerly rendered "unrhythmic
measures" and applied to Plautus' supposed irregularities in
scansion; it rather refers to the variety of his metres.

Since Plautus has met death, Comedy mourns,
Deserted is the stage; then Laughter, Sport and
    Wit,
And Music's countless numbers[1] all together
    wept.[2]

Pacuvius' epitaph is the most modest and simple,
worthy of his dignity and good taste:[3]

Young man, although you haste, this little stone
Entreats thee to regard it, then to read its
    tale.
Here lie the bones of Marcus, hight Pacuvius.
Of this I would not have you unaware. Good-
    bye.

XXV

Marcus Varro's definition of the word "indutiae"; to which
    is added a somewhat careful investigation of the derivation
    of that word.

MARCUS VARRO, in that book of his *Antiquities of
Man* which treats *Of War and Peace*,[4] defines
indutiae (a truce) in two ways. "A truce," he says,
"is peace for a few days in camp;" and again
in another place, "A truce is a holiday in war."
But each of these definitions seems to be wittily
and happily concise rather than clear or satisfactory.
For a truce is not a peace—since war continues,
although fighting ceases—nor is it restricted to a
camp or to a few days only. For what are we to
say if a truce is made for some months, and the

---

[2] The metre of the Latin is dactylic hexameter; final *a* in
deserta is lengthened, and *s* in *ludus* is suppressed.
[3] p. 296, 5, Bährens.
[4] xxii, fr. 1, 2, Mirsch.

aliquot factis in oppida castris concedatur? Nonne
6 tum quoque indutiae sunt? Aut rursus quid esse
id dicemus quod in primo *Annalium* Quadrigarii
scriptum est, C. Pontium Samnitem a dictatore
Romano sex horarum indutias postulasse, si indutiae
7 paucorum tantum dierum appellandae sunt? "Belli"
autem "ferias" festive magis dixit quam aperte
atque definite.

8   Graeci autem significantius consignatiusque cessa-
tionem istam pugnae pacticiam ἐκεχειρίαν dixerunt,
exempta littera una sonitus vastioris et subdita[1]
9 lenioris. Nam quod eo tempore non pugnetur
10 et manus cohibeantur, ἐκεχειρίαν appellarunt. Sed
profecto non id fuit Varroni negotium, ut indutias
superstitiose definiret et legibus rationibusque omni-
11 bus definitionum inserviret. Satis enim visum est,
eiusmodi facere demonstrationem, quod genus
Graeci τύπους magis et ὑπογραφὰς quam ὁρισμοὺς
vocant.

12   "Indutiarum" autem vocabulum qua sit ratione
13 factum, iam diu est, cum quaerimus. Sed ex multis,
quae vel audimus vel legimus, probabilius id, quod
14 dicam, videtur. "Indutias" sic dictas arbitramur,
15 quasi tu dicas "inde uti iam." Pactum indutiarum
eiusmodi est, ut in diem certum non pugnetur
nihilque incommodetur, sed ex eo die postea uti iam
16 omnia belli iure agantur. Quod igitur[2] dies certus

---

[1] subdita, *J. F. Gronov*; sub vita (vitae, *R*), ω.
[2] igitur, *J. F. Gronov*; dicitur, ω.

---

[1] Fr. 21, Peter.

troops withdraw from camp into the towns? Have we not then also a truce? Again, if a truce is to be defined as only lasting for a few days, what are we to say of the fact, recorded by Quadrigarius in the first book of his *Annals*, that Gaius Pontius the Samnite asked the Roman dictator for a truce of six hours?[1] The definition "a holiday in war," too, is rather happy than clear or precise.

Now the Greeks, more significantly and more pointedly, have called such an agreement to cease from fighting ἐκεχειρία, or "a staying of hands," substituting for one letter of harsher sound a smoother one.[2] For since there is no fighting at such a time and their hands are withheld, they called it ἐκεχειρία. But it surely was not Varro's task to define a truce too scrupulously, and to observe all the laws and canons of definition; for he thought it sufficient to give an explanation of the kind which the Greeks call τύποι ("typical") and ὑπογραφαί ("outline"), rather than ὁρισμοί ("exact definition").

I have for a long time been inquiring into the derivation of *indutiae*, but of the many explanations which I have either heard or read this which I am going to mention seems most reasonable. I believe that *indutiae* is made up of *inde uti iam* ("that from then on"). The stipulation of a truce is to this effect, that there shall be no fighting and no trouble up to a fixed time, but that after that time all the laws of war shall again be in force. Therefore, since a definite date is set and an agreement is

---

[2] That is, ἐκεχειρία instead of an original ἐχεχειρία, from ἔχω and χείρ, the first χ, an aspirate, being reduced to the smooth mute κ, since in Greek an aspirate may not begin two successive syllables.

praefinitur pactumque fit, ut ante eum diem ne
pugnetur atque is dies ubi venit[1] " inde uti iam "
pugnetur, idcirco ex his quibus dixi vocibus, quasi
per quendam coitum et copulam nomen indutiarum
conexum est.

17 Aurelius autem Opilius in primo librorum, quos
Musarum inscripsit, "indutiae," inquit, " dicuntur,
cum hostes inter sese utrimque utroque alteri ad
alteros impune et sine pugna ineunt ; inde adeo
inquit nomen factum videtur, quasi initiae,[2] hoc est
18 initus atque introitus." Hoc ab Aurelio scriptum
propterea non praeterii, ne cui harum *Noctium*
aemulo eo tantum nomine elegantius id videretur,
tamquam id nos originem verbi requirentes fugisset.

XXVI

Quem in modum mihi Taurus philosophus responderit per-
contanti an sapiens irasceretur.

1 INTERROGAVI in diatriba Taurum, an sapiens irasce-
2 retur. Dabat enim saepe post cotidianas lectiones
3 quaerendi quod quis vellet potestatem. Is cum
graviter, copiose de morbo affectuve irae disseruisset,
quae et in veterum libris et in ipsius commentariis
exposita sunt, convertit ad me, qui interrogaveram,

---

[1] ubi venit, *omitted by R.*
[2] initiae, *Lambecius* ; induitiae, *Fleckeisen* ; inviae, *ω.*

---

[1] The correct derivation seems to be from * *in-du-tus*
(cf. *duellum* for *bellum*), ''not in a state of war.''

made that before that date there shall be no fighting but when that time comes, "that from then on," fighting shall be resumed: by uniting (as it were) and combining those words which I have mentioned the term *indutiae* is formed.[1]

But Aurelius Opilius, in the first book of his work entitled *The Muses*, says:[2] "It is called a truce when enemies pass back and forth from one side to another safely and without strife; from this the name seems to be formed, as if it were *initiae*,[3] that is, an approach and entrance." I have not omitted this note of Aurelius, for fear that it might appear to some rival of these *Nights* a more elegant etymology, merely because he thought that it had escaped my notice when I was investigating the origin of the word.

XXVI

The answer of the philosopher Taurus, when I asked him whether a wise man ever got angry.

I ONCE asked Taurus in his lecture-room whether a wise man got angry. For after his daily discourses he often gave everyone the opportunity of asking whatever questions he wished. On this occasion he first discussed the disease or passion of anger seriously and at length, setting forth what is to be found in the books of the ancients and in his own commentaries; then, turning to me who had asked

---

[2] p. 88, Fun.
[3] This derivation is clearer from the older form *induitiae*; see the critical note.

et "haec ego," inquit, "super irascendo sentio;
4 sed, quid et Plutarchus noster, vir doctissimus ac
prudentissimus, senserit, non ab re est ut id quoque
5 audias. Plutarchus," inquit, "servo suo, nequam
homini et contumaci, sed libris disputationibusque
philosophiae aures inbutas habenti, tunicam detrahi
ob nescio quod delictum caedique eum loro iussit.
6 Coeperat verberari et obloquebatur non meruisse
ut vapulet,[1] nihil mali, nihil sceleris admisisse.
7 Postremo vociferari inter vapulandum incipit, neque
iam querimonias aut gemitus eiulatusque facere,[2]
sed verba seria et obiurgatoria : non ita esse
Plutarchum, ut philosophum deceret; irasci turpe
esse : saepe eum de malo irae dissertavisse, librum
quoque Περὶ Ἀοργησίας pulcherrimum conscripsisse ;
his omnibus quae in eo libro scripta sint nequaquam
convenire, quod provolutus effususque in iram pluri-
8 mis se plagis multaret. Tum Plutarchus lente et
leniter 'quid autem,' inquit, 'verbero, nunc ego
tibi irasci videor ? Ex vultune meo an ex voce an
ex colore an etiam ex verbis correptum esse me ira
intellegis ? Mihi quidem neque oculi, opinor, truces
sunt neque os turbidum neque inmaniter clamo
neque in spumam ruboremve effervesco neque
pudenda dico aut paenitenda neque omnino trepido
9 ira et gestio. Haec enim omnia, si ignoras, signa
esse irarum solent.' Et simul ad eum qui caedebat

---

[1] vapularet, *Veen* ; *Damsté regards as a gloss.*
[2] iacere, *Falster.*

---

[1] *On Freedom from Anger* ; the work has not survived.

the question, he said: "This is what I think about
getting angry, but it will not be out of place for you
to hear also the opinion of my master Plutarch, a man
of great learning and wisdom. Plutarch," said he,
"once gave orders that one of his slaves, a worthless
and insolent fellow, but one whose ears had been filled
with the teachings and arguments of philosophy,
should be stripped of his tunic for some offence or
other and flogged. They had begun to beat him,
and the slave kept protesting that he did not deserve
the flogging; that he was guilty of no wrong, no
crime. Finally, while the lashing still went on,
he began to shout, no longer uttering complaints
or shrieks and groans, but serious reproaches.
Plutarch's conduct, he said, was unworthy of a
philosopher; to be angry was shameful: his master
had often descanted on the evil of anger and had
even written an excellent treatise Περὶ Ἀοργησίας;[1]
it was in no way consistent with all that was written
in that book that its author should fall into a fit of
violent rage and punish his slave with many stripes.
Then Plutarch calmly and mildly made answer:
'What makes you think, scoundrel, that I am now
angry with you. Is it from my expression, my voice,
my colour, or even my words, that you believe me to
be in the grasp of anger? In my opinion my eyes
are not fierce, my expression is not disturbed, I am
neither shouting madly nor foaming at the mouth
and getting red in the face; I am saying nothing
to cause me shame or regret; I am not trembling
at all from anger or making violent gestures. For
all these actions, if you did but know it, are the
usual signs of angry passions.' And with these
words, turning to the man who was plying the lash,

conversus, 'interim,' inquit, 'dum ego atque hic disputamus, tu hoc age.'

10 Summa autem totius sententiae Tauri haec fuit: Non idem esse existimavit ἀοργησίαν et ἀναλγησίαν aliudque esse non iracundum animum, aliud ἀνάλγητον et ἀναίσθητον, id est hebetem et stupentem.

11 Nam sicut aliorum omnium, quos Latini philosophi "affectus" vel "affectiones," Graeci πάθη appellant, ita huius quoque motus animi, qui cum est ulciscendi causa saevior "ira" dicitur, non privationem esse utilem censuit, quam Graeci στέρησιν dicunt, sed mediocritatem, quam μετριότητα illi appellant.

he said : ' In the meantime, while this fellow and
I are arguing, do you keep at it.' "

Now the sum and substance of Taurus' whole dis-
quisition was this : he did not believe that ἀοργησία
or "freedom from anger," and ἀναλγησία, or "lack
of sensibility," were identical ; but that a mind not
prone to anger was one thing, a spirit ἀνάλγητος and
ἀναίσθητος, that is, callous and unfeeling, quite
another. For as of all the rest of the emotions which
the Latin philosophers call *affectus* or *affectiones,* and
the Greeks πάθη, so of the one which, when it becomes a cruel desire for vengeance, is called " anger,"
he did not recommend as expedient a total lack,
στέρησις as the Greeks say, but a moderate amount,
which they call μετριότης.

BOOK II

LIBER SECUNDUS

I

Quo genere solitus sit philosophus Socrates exercere patientiam corporis ; deque eiusdem viri temperantia.[1]

1 INTER labores voluntarios et exercitia corporis ad fortuitas patientiae vices firmandi id quoque accepi-
2 mus Socraten facere insuevisse : stare solitus Socrates dicitur pertinaci statu perdius atque pernox a summo lucis ortu ad solem alterum orientem inconivens, immobilis, isdem in vestigiis et ore atque oculis eundem in locum directis cogitabundus, tamquam quodam secessu mentis atque animi facto a
3 corpore. Quam rem cum Favorinus de fortitudine eius viri ut pleraque disserens attigisset, πολλάκις, inquit, ἐξ ἡλίου εἰς ἥλιον εἰστήκει ἀστραβέστερος τῶν πρέμνων.
4 Temperantia quoque fuisse eum tanta traditum est, ut omnia fere vitae suae tempora valitudine in-
5 offensa vixerit. In illius etiam pestilentiae vastitate quae in belli Peloponnensiaci principis Atheniensium civitatem internecivo genere morbi depopulata est, is parcendi moderandique rationibus dicitur et a voluptatum labe cavisse et salubritates corporis retinuisse, ut nequaquam fuerit communi omnium cladi obnoxius.

[1] temperantia, ς ; pacientia, ω ; parcimonia, *J. F. Gronov.*

BOOK II

I

How Socrates used to train himself in physical endurance; and of the temperate habits of that philosopher.

AMONG voluntary tasks and exercises for strengthening his body for any chance demands upon its endurance we are told that Socrates habitually practised this one: he would stand, so the story goes, in one fixed position, all day and all night, from early dawn until the next sunrise, open-eyed, motionless, in his very tracks and with face and eyes riveted to the same spot in deep meditation, as if his mind and soul had been, as it were, withdrawn from his body. When Favorinus in his discussion of the man's fortitude and his many other virtues had reached this point, he said: "He often stood from sun to sun, more rigid than the tree trunks." [1]

His temperance also is said to have been so great, that he lived almost the whole period of his life with health unimpaired. Even amid the havoc of that plague which, at the beginning of the Peloponnesian war, devastated Athens with a deadly species of disease, by temperate and abstemious habits he is said to have avoided the ill-effects of indulgence and retained his physical vigour so completely, that he was not at all affected by the calamity common to all.

[1] Fr. 66. Marres.

II

Quae ratio observatioque officiorum esse debeat inter patres
filiosque in discumbendo sedendoque atque id genus rebus
domi forisque, si filii magistratus sunt et patres privati;
superque ea re Tauri philosophi dissertatio et exemplum
ex historia Romana petitum.

1 Ad philosophum Taurum Athenas visendi cogno-
scendique eius gratia venerat V. C., praeses Cretae
provinciae, et cum eo simul eiusdem praesidis pater.
2 Taurus, sectatoribus commodum dimissis, sedebat pro
cubiculi sui foribus et cum assistentibus nobis sermo-
3 cinabatur. Introivit provinciae praeses et cum eo
4 pater; assurrexit placide Taurus et post mutuam sa-
5 lutationem resedit. Allata mox una sella est, quae
in promptu erat, atque dum aliae promebantur, apposita est. Invitavit Taurus patrem praesidis uti sede-
6 ret. Ad quae [1] ille ait: "Sedeat hic potius qui
7 populi Romani magistratus est." "Absque prae-
iudicio," inquit Taurus, "tu interea sede, dum [2]
inspicimus quaerimusque utrum conveniat, tene
potius sedere, qui pater es, an filium, qui magis-
8 tratus est." Et cum pater assedisset appositumque
esset aliud filio quoque eius sedile, verba super ea
re Taurus facit cum summa, dii boni, honorum atque
officiorum perpensatione.

9 Eorum verborum sententia haec fuit: In publicis
locis atque muneribus atque actionibus patrum iura,

---

[1] Ad quae, *Cramer*; atque (adque, *P*), ω.
[2] dum, *Aldine ed.*; cum, *RV*; dum cum, *P*; dum
circumspicimus, *Madvig.*

II

What rules of courtesy should be observed by fathers and
sons in taking their places at table, keeping their seats,
and similar matters at home and elsewhere, when the sons
are magistrates and the fathers private citizens ; and a
discourse of the philosopher Taurus on this subject, with
an illustration taken from Roman history.

THE governor of the province of Crete, a man of
senatorial rank, had come to Athens for the purpose
of visiting and becoming acquainted with the
philosopher Taurus, and in company with this same
governor was his father. Taurus, having just dis-
missed his pupils, was sitting before the door of his
room, and we stood by his side conversing with him.
In came the governor of the province and with him
his father. Taurus arose quietly, and after saluta-
tions had been exchanged, sat down again. Presently the single chair that was at hand was brought
and placed near them, while others were being
fetched. Taurus invited the governor's father to
be seated ; to which he replied : " Rather let this
man take the seat, since he is a magistrate of the
Roman people." " Without prejudicing the case,"
said Taurus, " do you meanwhile sit down, while we
look into the matter and inquire whether it is more
proper for you, who are the father, to sit, or your
son, who is a magistrate." And when the father
had seated himself, and another chair had been
placed near by for his son also, Taurus discussed
the question with what, by the gods ! was a most
excellent valuation of honours and duties.

The substance of the discussions was this : In
public places, functions and acts the rights of fathers,

cum filiorum qui in magistratu sunt potestatibus
collata, interquiescere paululum et conivere; sed
cum extra rempublicam in domestica re atque vita
sedeatur, ambuletur, in convivio quoque familiari
discumbatur, tum inter filium magistratum et patrem
privatum publicos honores cessare, naturales et
10 genuinos exoriri. "Hoc igitur," inquit, "quod ad
me venistis, quod colloquimur nunc, quod de officiis
disceptamus, privata actio est. Itaque utere apud
me his honoribus prius, quibus domi quoque vestrae
te uti priorem decet."

11 Haec atque alia in eandem sententiam Taurus
12 graviter simul et comiter disseruit. Quid autem
super huiuscemodi patris atque filii officio apud
Claudium legerimus, non esse ab re visum est ut
13 adscriberemus. Posuimus igitur verba ipsa Quadrigarii ex *Annali* eius sexto transscripta: "Deinde
facti consules Ti.[1] Sempronius Gracchus iterum,[2]
Q. Fabius Maximus, filius eius qui priore anno erat
consul. Ei consuli pater proconsul obviam in equo
vehens venit neque descendere voluit, quod pater
erat, et quod inter eos sciebant maxima concordia
convenire, lictores non ausi sunt descendere iubere.
Ubi iuxta venit, tum consul ait: "Quid postea?";
lictor ille qui apparebat cito intellexit, Maximum
proconsulem descendere iussit. Fabius imperio
paret et filium collaudavit, cum imperium, quod
populi esset, retineret.

---

[1] Ti *added by Skutsch.*   [2] iterumque, ω.

[1] Fr. 57. Peter.

compared with the authority of sons who are
magistrates, give way somewhat and are eclipsed;
but when they are sitting together unofficially in
the intimacy of home life, or walking about, or even
reclining at a dinner party of intimate friends, then
the official distinctions between a son who is a
magistrate and a father who is a private citizen are
at an end, while those that are natural and inherent
come into play. "Now, your visit to me," said he,
"our present conversation, and this discussion of
duties are private actions. Therefore enjoy the same
priority of honours at my house which it is proper
for you to enjoy in your own home as the older man."

These remarks and others to the same purport
were made by Taurus at once seriously and plea-
santly. Moreover, it has seemed not out of place
to add what I have read in Claudius about the
etiquette of father and son under such circumstances.
I therefore quote Quadrigarius' actual words, tran-
scribed from the sixth book of his *Annals*:[1] "The
consuls then elected were Tiberius Sempronius
Gracchus for the second time and Quintus Fabius
Maximus, son of the Maximus who had been consul
the year before. The father, at the time proconsul,
mounted upon a horse met his son the consul, and
because he was his father, would not dismount, nor
did the lictors, who knew that the two men lived
in the most perfect harmony, presume to order him
to do so. As the father drew near, the consul said:
"What next?" The lictor in attendance quickly
understood and ordered Maximus the proconsul to
dismount. Fabius obeyed the order and warmly
commended his son for asserting the authority
which he had as the gift of the people.

ATTIC NIGHTS OF AULUS GELLIUS

III

Qua ratione verbis quibusdam vocabulisque veteres immiserint
h litterae spiritum.

1 H LITTERAM, sive illam spiritum magis quam litteram dici oportet, inserebant eam veteres nostri
plerisque vocibus verborum firmandis roborandisque,
ut sonus earum esset viridior vegetiorque ; atque id
videntur fecisse studio et exemplo linguae Atticae.
2 Satis notum est Atticos ἰχθὺν et ἵππον¹ et multa
itidem alia contra morem gentium Graeciae cetera-
3 rum inspirantis primae litterae dixisse. Sic "lach-
rumas," sic "sepulchrum," sic "ahenum," sic
"vehemens," sic "incohare," sic "helluari," sic
"halucinari," sic "honera," sic "honustum" dixe-
4 runt. In his enim verbis omnibus litterae seu
spiritus istius nulla ratio visa est, nisi ut firmitas
et vigor vocis quasi quibusdam nervis additis inten-
deretur.
5 Sed quoniam "aheni" quoque exemplo usi sumus,
venit nobis in memoriam Fidum Optatum, multi
nominis Romae grammaticum, ostendisse mihi librum
Aeneidos secundum mirandae vetustatis, emptum in
Sigillariis viginti aureis, quem ipsius Vergili fuisse

---

¹ ἵππον, Skutsch (cf. Meyer, Gr. Gram.³ p. 108) ; ippon,
VP ; ippō, *R* ; ἵ pronomen, *Hertz.*

---

¹ I find no authority for this. Brugmann in Müller's
Handbuch, II², 61 (end) cites ἵππος as a word which originally
had a smooth breathing and acquired the rough from the
combination ὁ ἵππος. Since the ι in ἰχθύς is prosthetic, ἰχθύς,
if it existed must have had the same origin, but Brugmann
does not cite it. See also *Indoger. Forsch.* xxii, p. 197 (gives
some additional information).
² A street or quarter in Rome where the little images were

III

For what reason our forefathers inserted the aspirate h in certain verbs and nouns.

THE letter *h* (or perhaps it should be called a breathing rather than a letter) was added by our forefathers to give strength and vigour to the pronunciation of many words, in order that they might have a fresher and livelier sound; and this they seem to have done from their devotion to the Attic language, and under its influence. It is well known that the people of Attica, contrary to the usage of the other Greek races, pronounced ἰχθύς (fish), ἵππος (horse), and many other words besides, with a rough breathing on the first letter.[1] In the same way our ancestors said *lachrumae* (tears), *sepulchrum* (burial-place), *ahenum* (of bronze), *vehemens* (violent), *incohare* (begin), *helluari* (gormandize), *hallucinari* (dream), *honera* (burdens), *honustum* (burdened). For in all these words there seems to be no reason for that letter, or breathing, except to increase the force and vigour of the sound by adding certain sinews, so to speak.

But apropos of the inclusion of *ahenum* among my examples, I recall that Fidus Optatus, a grammarian of considerable repute in Rome, showed me a remarkably old copy of the second book of the *Aeneid*, bought in the Sigillaria[2] for twenty pieces of gold, which was believed to have belonged to

sold which were given as presents at the festival of the Sigillaria; this was on Dec. 21 and 22, an extension of the Saturnalia, although not a religious holiday. The *aureus* was the standard gold coin of the Romans, of the value of 100 sesterces; its weight varied at different periods.

credebatur.   In quo duo isti versus cum ita scripti
forent:

> Vestibulum ante ipsum primoque in limine Pyrrus
> Exultat, telis et luce coruscus aena,

additam supra vidimus *h* litteram et "ahena"
6 factum.   Sic in illo quoque Vergili versu in optimis
libris scriptum invenimus:

> Aut[1] foliis undam trepidi despumat aheni.

IV

*Quam ob causam Gavius Bassus genus quoddam iudicii
"divinationem" appellari scripserit; et quam alii causam
esse eiusdem vocabuli dixerint.[2]*

1   CUM de constituendo accusatore quaeritur iudi-
ciumque super ea re redditur cuinam potissimum ex
duobus pluribusque accusatio subscriptiove in reum
permittatur, ea res atque iudicum cognitio "divi-
2 natio" appellatur.   Id vocabulum quam ob causam
ita factum sit, quaeri solet.
3   Gavius Bassus in tertio librorum, quos *De Origine
Vocabulorum* composuit, "Divinatio," inquit, "iudicium appellatur, quoniam divinet quodammodo iudex
4 oportet quam sententiam sese ferre par sit."   Nimis
quidem est in verbis Gavi Bassi ratio inperfecta vel
5 magis inops et ieiuna.   Sed videtur tamen significare
velle idcirco dici "divinationem," quod in aliis

----

[1] aut, ω ; et, *Virg.*   [2] dixerunt, ω.

----

[1] ii. 469 f.   [2] *Georg.* i. 296.

Virgil himself. In that book, although the following two lines were written thus : [1]

> Before the entrance-court, hard by the gate,
> With sheen of brazen (*aena*) arms proud Pyrrhus
>   gleams,

we observed that the letter *h* had been added above
the line, changing *aena* to *ahena*. So too in
the best manuscripts we find this verse of Virgil's
written as follows : [2]

> Or skims with leaves the bubbling brass's (*aheni*)
>   wave.

IV

*The reason given by Gavius Bassus for calling a certain kind
of judicial inquiry* divinatio; *and the explanation that
others have given of the same term.*

WHEN inquiry is made about the choice of a
prosecutor, and judgment is rendered on the question
to which of two or more persons the prosecution
of a defendant, or a share in the prosecution, is to
be entrusted, this process and examination by jurors
is called *divinatio*.[3] The reason for the use of this
term is a matter of frequent inquiry.

Gavius Bassus, in the third book of his work *On
the Origin of Terms*, says:[4] "This kind of trial is
called *divinatio* because the juror ought in a sense
to divine what verdict it is proper for him to give."
The explanation offered in these words of Gavius
Bassus is far from complete, or rather, it is inadequate and meagre. But at least he seems to be
trying to show that *divinatio* is used because in

---

[3] Cf. Cicero's *Divinatio in Caecilium*, preliminary to the
prosecution of Verres.

[4] Fr. I. Fun.

quidem causis iudex ea quae [1] didicit quaeque argumentis vel testibus demonstrata sunt sequi solet, in
hac autem re, cum eligendus accusator est, parva
admodum et exilia sunt quibus moveri iudex possit,
et propterea quinam magis ad accusandum idoneus
sit quasi divinandum est.

6   Haec Bassus. Sed alii quidam " divinationem "
esse appellatam putant quoniam, cum accusator et
reus duae res quasi cognatae [2] coniunctaeque sint
neque utra sine altera constare possit, in hoc
tamen genere causae reus quidem iam est, sed
accusator nondum est, et idcirco quod adhuc usque
deest et latet divinatione supplendum est, quisnam
sit accusator futurus.

V

Quam lepide signateque [3] dixerit Favorinus philosophus quid
intersit inter Platonis et Lysiae orationem.

1   FAVORINUS de Lysia et Platone solitus dicere est :
" Si ex Platonis," inquit, " oratione verbum aliquod
demas mutesve atque id commodatissime facias,
de elegantia tamen detraxeris ; si ex Lysiae, de
sententia."

VI

Quibus verbis ignaviter et abiecte Vergilius usus esse dicatur ;
et quid his qui improbe id [4] dicunt respondeatur.

1   NONNULLI grammatici aetatis superioris, in quibus
est Cornutus Annaeus, haut sane indocti neque

---

[1] quae, *added in σ.*   [2] cognitae, *ω ; corr. in σ.*
[3] designate, *ω ; corr. by Falster.*

other trials it is the habit of the juror to be influenced by what he has heard and by what has been shown by evidence or by witnesses; but in this instance, when a prosecutor is to be selected, the considerations which can influence a juror are very few and slight, and therefore he must, so to speak, "divine" what man is the better fitted to make the accusation.

Thus Bassus. But some others think that the *divinatio* is so called because, while prosecutor and defendant are two things that are, as it were, related and connected, so that neither can exist without the other, yet in this form of trial, while there is already a defendant, there is as yet no prosecutor, and therefore the factor which is still lacking and unknown—namely, what man is to be the prosecutor—must be supplied by divination.

V

How elegantly and clearly the philosopher Favorinus described the difference between the style of Plato and that of Lysias.

FAVORINUS used to say of Plato and Lysias: "If you take a single word from a discourse of Plato or change it, and do it with the utmost skill, you will nevertheless mar the elegance of his style; if you do the same to Lysias, you will obscure his meaning."

VI

On some words which Virgil is asserted to have used carelessly and negligently; and the answer to be made to those who bring this false charge.

SOME grammarians of an earlier time, men by no means without learning and repute, who wrote com-

---

⁴ id *added by Hertz (Stephanus).*

ignobiles, qui commentaria in Vergilium compo-
suerunt, reprehendunt quasi incuriose et abiecte
verbum positum in his versibus:

> Candida succinctam latrantibus inguina monstris
> Dulichias vexasse rates et gurgite in alto
> A! timidos nautas canibus lacerasse marinis;

2 "vexasse" enim putant verbum esse leve et tenuis
ac parvi incommodi, nec tantae atrocitati congruere,
cum homines repente a belua immanissima rapti
laniatique sint.

3 Item aliud huiuscemodi reprehendunt:

> Quis aut Eurysthea durum
> Aut inlaudati nescit Busiridis aras?

"Inlaudati" parum idoneum verbum esse dicunt, neque
id satis esse ad faciendam scelerati hominis detesta-
tionem, qui, quod hospites omnium gentium immolare solitus fuit, non laude indignus, sed detestatione[1]
execrationeque totius generis humani dignus esset.

4 Item aliud verbum culpaverunt:

> Per tunicam squalentem auro latus haurit apertum,

tamquam si non convenerit dicere "auro squalentem,"
quoniam nitoribus splendoribusque auri squaloris
inluvies sit contraria.

5 Sed de verbo "vexasse" ita responderi posse credo:
"Vexasse" grave verbum est factumque ab eo videtur,

---

[1] detestatione, *Macr. vi. 7, and iii. 5. 9*; de retractacione
(retractione, *P*), *ω*; detract(at)ione, *T Y*; deprecatione, *Mdg.*

---

[1] *Ecl.* vi. 75. ff.   [2] *Georg.* iii. 4
[3] *Aen.* x. 314.

mentaries on Virgil, and among them Annaeus
Cornutus, criticize the poet's use of a word in the
following verses [1] as careless and negligent:

> That, her white waist with howling monsters girt,
> Dread Scylla knocked about (*vexasse*) Ulysses' ships
> Amid the swirling depths, and, piteous sight!
> The trembling sailors with her sea-dogs rent.

They think, namely, that *vexasse* is a weak word,
indicating a slight and trivial annoyance, and not
adapted to such a horror as the sudden seizing and
rending of human beings by a ruthless monster.

They also criticize another word in the following: [2]

> Who has not heard
> Of king Eurystheus' pitiless commands
> And altars of Busiris, the unpraised (*inlaudati*)?

Inlaudati, they say, is not at all a suitable word,
but is quite inadequate to express abhorrence of a
wretch who, because he used to sacrifice guests from
all over the world, was not merely "undeserving of
praise," but rather deserving of the abhorrence and
execration of the whole human race.

They have criticized still another word in the
verse: [3]

> Through tunic rough (*squalentem*) with gold the
>   sword drank from his pierced side,

on the ground that it is out of place to say *auro
squalentem*, since the filth of squalor is quite opposed
to the brilliance and splendour of gold.

Now as to the word *vexasse*, I believe the
following answer may be made: *vexasse* is an
intensive verb, and is obviously derived from *ve-*

135

quod est "vehere," in quo inest vis iam quaedam
alieni arbitrii ; non enim sui potens est, qui vehitur.
"Vexare" autem, quod ex eo inclinatum est, vi
atque motu procul dubio vastiorest. Nam qui fertur
et rapsatur atque huc atque illuc distrahitur, is
"vexari" proprie dicitur, sicuti "taxare" pressius cre-
briusque est quam "tangere," unde id procul dubio
inclinatum est, et "iactare" multo fusius largiusque
est quam "iacere," unde id verbum traductum est,
et "quassare" quam "quatere" gravius violentiusque
6 est. Non igitur, quia vulgo dici solet "vexatum
esse" quem fumo aut vento aut pulvere, propterea debet vis vera atque natura verbi deperire,
quae a veteribus, qui proprie atque signate locuti
sunt, ita ut decuit, conservata est.

7 M. Catonis verba sunt ex oratione quam *De
Achaeis* scripsit : "Cumque Hannibal terram Italiam
laceraret atque vexaret " ; "vexatam" Italiam dixit
Cato ab Hannibale, quando nullum calamitatis aut
saevitiae aut immanitatis genus reperiri queat quod
8 in eo tempore Italia non perpessa sit ; M. Tullius *IV.
In Verrem :* "Quae ab isto sic spoliata atque direpta
est, non ut ab hoste aliquo, qui tamen in bello
religionem et consuetudinis iura retineret, sed ut a
barbaris praedonibus vexata esse videatur."

9 De "inlaudato" autem duo videntur responderi
posse. Unum est eiusmodi : Nemo quisquam tam

---

[1] xxxv. Jordan.
[2] The temple of Artemis at Syracuse ; § 122.

here, in which there is already some notion of
compulsion by another; for a man who is carried is
not his own master. But *vexare,* which is derived
from *vehere,* unquestionably implies greater force
and impulse. For *vexare* is properly used of one
who is seized and carried away, and dragged about
hither and yon; just as *taxare* denotes more
forcible and repeated action than *tangere,* from
which it is undoubtedly derived; and *iactare* a
much fuller and more vigorous action than *iacere,*
from which it comes; and *quassare* something
severer and more violent than *quatere.* Therefore, merely because *vexare* is commonly used of
the annoyance of smoke or wind or dust is no reason
why the original force and meaning of the word
should be lost; and that meaning was preserved by
the earlier writers who, as became them, spoke
correctly and clearly.

Marcus Cato, in the speech which he wrote *On the
Achaeans,*[1] has these words: "And when Hannibal
was rending and harrying (*vexaret*) the land of Italy."
That is to say, Cato used *vexare* of the effect on Italy
of Hannibal's conduct, at a time when no species of
disaster, cruelty or savagery could be imagined which
Italy did not suffer from his hands. Marcus Tullius,
in his fourth *Oration against Verres,* wrote: "This[2]
was so pillaged and ravaged by that wretch, that it
did not seem to have been laid waste (*vexata*) by an
enemy who in the heat of war still felt some religious
scruple and some respect for customary law, but by
barbarous pirates."

But concerning *inlaudatus* it seems possible to
give two answers. One is of this kind: There is
absolutely no one who is of so perverted a character

efflictis[1] est moribus quin faciat aut dicat nonnumquam aliquid quod laudari queat. Unde hic antiquissimus versus vice proverbii celebratus est:

Πολλάκι τοι[2] καὶ μωρὸς ἀνὴρ μάλα καίριον εἶπεν.

10 Sed enim qui omni in re atque omni tempore laude
omni vacat, is " inlaudatus " est isque omnium pes-
simus deterrimusque est, sicuti omnis culpae privatio
" inculpatum " facit. " Inculpatus " autem instar
est absolutae virtutis; " inlaudatus " quoque igitur
11 finis est extremae malitiae. Itaque Homerus non
virtutibus appellandis, sed vitiis detrahendis laudare
ampliter solet. Hoc enim est: τὼ δ᾽ οὐκ ἄκοντε πετέσθην,
et item illud:

*Ενθ᾽ οὐκ ἂν βρίζοντα ἴδοις Ἀγαμέμνονα δῖον
Οὐδὲ καταπτώσσοντ᾽, οὐδ᾽ οὐκ ἐθέλοντα μάχεσθαι.

12 Epicurus quoque simili modo maximam voluptatem
privationem detractionemque omnis doloris definivit
his verbis: Ὅρος τοῦ μεγέθους τῶν ἡδονῶν ἡ παντὸς[3]
13 τοῦ ἀλγοῦντος ὑπεξαίρεσις. Eadem ratione idem Ver-
14 gilius " inamabilem " dixit Stygiam paludem. Nam
sicut " inlaudatum " κατὰ στέρησιν laudis, ita " in-
15 amabilem " κατὰ amoris στέρησιν detestatus est.
16 Altero modo " inlaudatus " ita defenditur: " Laudare " significat prisca lingua nominare appellareque.
Sic in actionibus civilibus auctor[4] " laudari " dicitur,
17 quod est nominari. Is " inlaudatus " autem[5] est,

---

[1] efflictis. *Macr. vi 7 12.*; effi(c)tis, ω; efferis, σ.
[2] τοι, Stobaeus, Diog., Apost.; γὰρ, *Macr.*
[3] τοῦ . . . παντός, *Macr.*; *omitted by* ω.
[4] auctor, *Macr.*; autem, ω.   [5] ergo, *Macr.*

---

[1] *Iliad* iv. 366, 768, etc.   [2] *Iliad* iv. 223.

as not sometimes to do or say something that can be commended (*laudari*). And therefore this very ancient line has become a familiar proverb :

> Oft-times even a fool expresses himself to the purpose.

But one who, on the contrary, in his every act and at all times, deserves no praise (*laude*) at all is *inlaudatus*, and such a man is the very worst and most despicable of all mortals, just as freedom from all reproach makes one *inculpatus* (blameless). Now *inculpatus* is the synonym for perfect goodness; therefore conversely *inlaudatus* represents the limit of extreme wickedness. It is for that reason that Homer usually bestows high praise, not by enumerating virtues, but by denying faults; for example :[1] " And not unwillingly they charged," and again :[2]

> Not then would you divine Atrides see
> Confused, inactive, nor yet loath to fight.

Epicurus too in a similar way defined the greatest pleasure as the removal and absence of all pain, in these words :[3] "The utmost height of pleasure is the removal of all that pains." Again Virgil on the same principle called the Stygian pool "unlovely."[4] For just as he expressed abhorrence of the "unpraised" man by the denial of praise, so he abhorred the "unlovable " by the denial of love. Another defence of *inlaudatus* is this : *laudare* in early Latin means "to name" and "cite." Thus in civil actions they use *laudare* of an authority, when he is cited. Conversely, the *inlaudatus* is the same as

[3] *Sent.* iii. p. 72, Ussing.
[4] *Georg.* iv. 479 ; *Aen.* vi. 438.

quasi inlaudabilis, qui neque mentione aut memoria
18 ulla dignus neque umquam nominandus est, sicuti
quondam a communi consilio Asiae decretum est uti
nomen eius qui templum Dianae Ephesi incenderat
ne quis ullo in tempore nominaret.

19   Tertium restat ex is quae reprehensa sunt, quod
20 "tunicam squalentem auro" dixit.   Id autem significat copiam densitatemque auri in squamarum speciem intexti.   "Squalere" enim dictum a squamarum
crebritate asperitateque, quae in serpentium pisci-
21 umve coriis visuntur.   Quam rem et alii et hic
quidem poeta locis aliquot demonstrat :

> Quem pellis (inquit) ahenis
> In plumam squamis auro conserta tegebat,

22 et alio loco :

> Iamque adeo rutilum thoraca indutus ahenis
> Horrebat squamis.

23 Accius in *Pelopidis* ita scribit :

> Éius serpentis squámae squalido aúro et purpurá
> pertextae.

24 Quicquid igitur nimis inculcatum obsitumque aliqua
re erat, ut[1] incuteret visentibus facie nova horrorem,
25 id "squalere" dicebatur.   Sic in corporibus incultis
squamosisque alta congeries sordium "squalor"
appellabatur.   Cuius significationis multo assiduoque
usu totum id verbum ita contaminatum est, ut iam
"squalor" de re alia nulla quam de solis inquina-
mentis dici coeperit.

[1] ut, *Macr.* ; et, *ω.*

---

[1] He is said to have set fire to the temple in order to make
himself notorious for all time ; see Val. Max. viii. 14. *Exb.* 5.
His name, Herostratus, was preserved by Theopompus.

the *inlaudabilis,* namely, one who is worthy neither of mention nor remembrance, and is never to be named; as, for example, in days gone by the common council of Asia decreed that no one should ever mention the name of the man who had burned the temple of Diana at Ephesus.[1]

There remains the third criticism, his use of the expression "a tunic rough with gold." But *squalentem* signifies a quantity or thick layer of gold, laid on so as to resemble scales. For *squalere* is used of the thick, rough scales (*squamae*) which are to be seen on the skins of fish or snakes. This is made clear both by others and indeed by this same poet in several passages; thus:[2]

> A skin his covering was, plumed with brazen scales (*squamis*)
> And clasped with gold.

and again:[3]

> And now has he his flashing breastplate donned,
> Bristling with brazen scales (*squamis*).

Accius too in the *Pelopidae* writes thus:[4]

> This serpent's scales (*squamae*) rough gold and purple wrought.

Thus we see that *squalere* was applied to whatever was overloaded and excessively crowded with anything, in order that its strange appearance might strike terror into those who looked upon it. So too on neglected and scaly bodies the deep layer of dirt was called *squalor,* and by long and continued use in that sense the entire word has become so corrupted, that finally *squalor* has come to be used of nothing but filth.

[2] *Aen.* xi. 770.   [3] *Aen.* xi. 487.   [4] v. 517, Ribbeck[3].

VII

De officio erga patres liberorum ; deque ea re ex philosophiae
   libris, in quibus scriptum quaesitumque est an omnibus
   patris iussis obsequendum sit.

1   QUAERI solitum est in philosophorum disceptatio-
nibus, an semper inque omnibus iussis patri paren-
2 dum sit.   Super ea re Graeci nostrique, qui *De
Officiis* scripserunt, tres sententias esse quae spectandae considerandaeque sint tradiderunt easque
3 subtilissime diiudicarunt.   Earum una est : omnia
4 quae pater imperat parendum ; altera est : in[1]
5 quibusdam parendum, quibusdam non obsequendum ;
tertia est : nihil necesse esse patri obsequi et parere.
6   Haec sententia quoniam primore aspectu nimis
infamis est, super ea prius quae dicta sunt dicemus.
7 " Aut recte," inquiunt, " imperat pater aut perperam.
Si recte imperat, non quia imperat parendum, sed
quoniam id fieri ius est ; si perperam, nequaquam sci-
8 licet faciendum quod fieri non oportet."   Deinde ita
concludunt : " Numquam igitur est patri parendum
9 quae imperat."   Set neque istam sententiam probari
accepimus—argutiola   quippe   haec,   sicuti   mox
10 ostendemus, frivola et inanis est—neque autem illa
quam primo in loco diximus vera et proba videri
potest, omnia esse quae pater iusserit parendum.
11 Quid enim ? si proditionem patriae, si matris necem,
12 si alia quaedam imperabit[2] turpia aut impia ? Media

---

[1] in, *T* ; *omitted by* ω.   [2] imperabi, *A* ; imperavit, ω.

142

VII

Of the obedience of children to their parents ; and quotations
on this subject from the writings of the philosophers,
in which it is inquired whether all a father's commands
should be obeyed.

IT is a frequent subject of discussion with philosophers, whether a father should always be obeyed,
whatever the nature of his commands. As to this
question writers *On Duty*, both Greeks and our
own countrymen, have stated that there are three
opinions to be noticed and considered, and these
they have differentiated with great acuteness. The
first is, that all a father's commands must be obeyed ;
the second, that in some he is to be obeyed, in
others not ; the third, that it is not necessary to yield
to and obey one's father in anything.

Since at first sight this last opinion is altogether
shameful, I shall begin by stating what has been
said on that point. " A father's command," they
say, " is either right or wrong. If it is right, it is
not to be obeyed because it is his order, but the
thing must be done because it is right that it be
done. If his command is wrong, surely that should
on no account be done which ought not to be done."
Thus they arrive at the conclusion that a father's
command should never be obeyed. But I have
neither heard that this view has met with approval
—for it is a mere quibble, both silly and foolish, as
I shall presently show—nor can the opinion which
we stated first, that all a father's commands are to be
obeyed, be regarded as true and acceptable. For
what if he shall command treason to one's country,
a mother's murder, or some other base or impious

igitur sententia optima atque tutissima visa est,
quaedam esse parendum, quaedam non obsequendum.

13 Sed ea tamen, quae obsequi non oportet, leniter et
verecunde ac sine detestatione nimia sineque obpro-
bratione acerba reprehensionis declinanda sensim et
relinquenda esse dicunt quam respuenda.

14 Conclusio vero illa qua colligitur, sicuti supra
dictum est, nihil patri parendum, inperfecta est

15 refutarique ac dilui sic potest : Omnia, quae in rebus
humanis fiunt, ita ut docti censuerunt, aut honesta

16 sunt aut turpia. Quae sua vi recta aut honesta
sunt, ut fidem colere, patriam defendere, ut amicos
diligere, ea fieri oportet, sive imperet pater sive non

17 imperet; sed quae his contraria quaeque turpia,

18 omnino iniqua sunt, ea ne si imperet quidem. Quae
vero in medio sunt et a Graecis tum μέσα, tum
ἀδιάφορα appellantur, ut in militiam ire, rus colere,
honores capessere, causas defendere, uxorem ducere,
ut iussum proficisci, ut accersitum venire, quoniam et
haec et his similia per sese ipsa neque honesta sunt
neque turpia, sed proinde ut a nobis aguntur, ita ipsis
actionibus aut probanda fiunt aut reprehendenda :
propterea in eiusmodi omnium rerum generibus patri
parendum esse censent, veluti si uxorem ducere im-

19 peret aut causas pro reis dicere. Quod enim utrumque in genere ipso per sese neque honestum neque
turpe est, idcirco, si pater iubeat, obsequendum est.

20 Sed enim si imperet uxorem ducere infamem, propu-

deed? The intermediate view, therefore, has seemed best and safest, that some commands are to be obeyed and others not. But yet they say that commands which ought not to be obeyed must nevertheless be declined gently and respectfully, without excessive aversion or bitter recrimination, and rather left undone than spurned.

But that conclusion from which it is inferred, as has been said above, that a father is never to be obeyed, is faulty, and may be refuted and disposed of as follows: All human actions are, as learned men have decided, either honourable or base. Whatever is inherently right or honourable, such as keeping faith, defending one's country, loving one's friend's, ought to be done whether a father commands it or not; but whatever is of the opposite nature, and is base and altogether evil, should not be done even at a father's order. Actions, however, which lie between these, and are called by the Greeks now μέσα, or "neutral," and now ἀδιάφορα, or "indifferent," such as going to war, tilling the fields, seeking office, pleading causes, marrying a wife, going when ordered, coming when called; since these and similar actions are in themselves neither honourable nor base, but are to be approved or disapproved exactly according to the manner in which we perform them: for this reason they believe that in every kind of action of this description a father should be obeyed; as for instance, if he should order his son to marry a wife or to plead for the accused. For since each of these acts, in its actual nature and of itself, is neither honourable nor base, if a father should command it, he ought to be obeyed. But if he should order his son to

diosam, criminosam, aut pro reo Catilina aliquo aut
Tubulo aut P. Clodio causam dicere, non scilicet
parendum, quoniam accedente aliquo turpitudinis
numero desinunt esse per sese haec media atque
21 indifferentia. Non ergo integra est propositio di-
centium " aut honesta sunt, quae imperat pater, aut
turpia," neque ὑγιὲς et νόμιμον διεζευγμένον videri
potest. Deest enim diiunctioni isti tertium : " aut
neque honesta sunt neque turpia." Quod si additur,
non potest ita concludi : "numquam est igitur patri
parendum."

VIII

Quod parum aequa reprehensio Epicuri a Plutarcho facta [1]
sit in synlogismi disciplina.

1 PLUTARCHUS, secundo librorum quos *De Homero*
composuit, inperfecte atque praepostere atque inscite synlogismo esse usum Epicurum dicit verbaque
ipsa Epicuri ponit : Ὁ θάνατος οὐδὲν πρὸς ἡμᾶς· τὸ
γὰρ διαλυθὲν [2] ἀναισθητεῖ· τὸ δὲ ἀναισθητοῦν οὐδὲν πρὸς
2 ἡμᾶς. " Nam praetermisit," inquit, " quod in prima
parte sumere debuit, τὸν θάνατον εἶναι ψυχῆς καὶ
3 σώματος διάλυσιν, tum deinde eodem ipso, quod
omiserat, quasi posito concessoque ad confirmandum
4 aliud utitur. Progredi autem hic," inquit, " synlo-
gismus, nisi illo prius posito, non potest."

[1] pacta, ω.; *corr. by J. F. Gronov;* peracta, ϛ.
[2] λυθέν, *Plut. contra Epic. Beat.* 27.

---

[1] Catiline and Clodius are too notorious to require comment.
L. Hostilius Tubulus, praetor in 142 B.C., accepted bribes

marry a woman of ill repute, infamous and criminal, or to speak in defence of a Catiline, a Tubulus,[1] or a Publius Clodius, of course he ought not to be obeyed, since by the addition of a certain degree of evil these acts cease to be inherently neutral and indifferent. Hence the premise of those who say that "the commands of a father are either honourable or base" is incomplete, and it cannot be considered what the Greeks call "a sound and regular disjunctive proposition." For that disjunctive premise lacks the third member, "or are neither honourable nor base." If this be added, the conclusion cannot be drawn that a father's command must never be obeyed.

VIII

The unfairness of Plutarch's criticism of Epicurus' knowledge of the syllogism.

PLUTARCH, in the second book of his essay *On Homer*,[2] asserts that Epicurus made use of an incomplete, perverted and faulty syllogism, and he quotes Epicurus' own words:[3] "Death is nothing to us, for what is dissolved is without perception, and what is without perception is nothing to us." "Now Epicurus," says Plutarch, "omitted what he ought to have stated as his major premise, that death is a dissolution of body and soul, and then, to prove something else, he goes on to use the very premise that he had omitted, as if it had been stated and conceded. But this syllogism," says Plutarch, "cannot advance, unless that premise be first presented."

when presiding at a trial for murder. Cic., *De Nat. Deorum* i. 63 and elsewhere, cites him as an example of iniquity.
[2] vii, p. 100, Bern.   [3] *Sent.* II, p. 71, Ussing.

5 Vere hoc quidem Plutarchus de forma atque
ordine synlogismi scripsit. Nam si, ut[1] in disciplinis traditur, ita colligere et ratiocinari velis, sic
dici oportet : Ὁ θάνατος ψυχῆς καὶ σώματος διάλυσις·
τὸ δὲ διαλυθὲν ἀναισθητεῖ· τὸ δὲ ἀναισθητοῦν οὐδὲν πρὸς
6 ἡμᾶς. Sed Epicurus, cuiusmodi homost, non in-
7 scitia videtur partem istam synlogismi praeter-
misisse, neque id ei negotium fuit, synlogismum
tamquam in scholis philosophorum cum suis numeris
omnibus et cum suis finibus dicere, sed profecto,
quia separatio animi et corporis in morte evidens
est, non est ratus necessariam esse eius admoni-
8 tionem, quod omnibus prosus erat[2] obvium. Sicuti
etiam, quod coniunctionem synlogismi non in fine
posuit, set in principio ; nam id quoque non inperite
factum, quis non videt ?
9 Aput Platonem quoque multis in locis reperias
synlogismos, repudiato conversoque ordine isto qui
in docendo traditur, cum eleganti quadam reprehensionis contemptione positos esse.

IX

Quod idem Plutarchus evidenti calumnia verbum ab Epicuro
dictum insectatus sit.

1 In eodem libro idem Plutarchus eundem Epicurum
reprehendit, quod verbo usus sit parum proprio et
2 alienae significationis. Ita enim scripsit Epicurus :
Ὅρος τοῦ μεγέθους τῶν ἡδονῶν ἡ παντὸς τοῦ ἀλγοῦντος
ὑπεξαίρεσις. " Non," inquit, " παντὸς τοῦ ἀλγοῦντος,

---

[1] sicut, ω.   [2] prosumserat. A ; prorsus erat, ω.

What Plutarch wrote as to the form and sequence of a syllogism is true enough; for if you wish to argue and reason according to the teaching of the schools, you ought to say: "Death is the dissolution of soul and body; but what is dissolved is without perception; and what is without perception is nothing to us." But we cannot suppose that Epicurus, being the man he was, omitted that part of the syllogism through ignorance, or that it was his intention to state a syllogism complete in all its members and limitations, as is done in the schools of the logicians; but since the separation of body and soul by death is self-evident, he of course did not think it necessary to call attention to what was perfectly obvious to everyone. For the same reason, too, he put the conclusion of the syllogism, not at the end, but at the beginning; for who does not see that this also was not due to inadvertence?

In Plato too you will often find syllogisms in which the order prescribed in the schools is disregarded and inverted, with a kind of lofty disdain of criticism.

IX

How the same Plutarch, with obvious captiousness, criticized the use of a word by Epicurus.

In the same book,[1] Plutarch also finds fault a second time with Epicurus for using an inappropriate word and giving it an incorrect meaning. Now Epicurus wrote as follows:[2] "The utmost height of pleasure is the removal of everything that pains." Plutarch declares that he ought not to have said

---

[1] vii, p. 101, Bern.   [2] *Sect.* iii, p. 72, Ussing.

3 sed παντὸς τοῦ ἀλγεινοῦ dicere oportuit; detractio
enim significandi est doloris, non," inquit, "dolentis."

4 Nimis minute ac prope etiam subfrigide Plutarchus
5 in Epicuro accusando λεξιθηρεῖ. Has enim curas
vocum verborumque elegantias non modo non sectatur Epicurus, sed etiam insectatur.

X

Quid sint favisae Capitolinae; et quid super eo verbo M.
Varro Servio Sulpicio quaerenti rescripserit.

1 SERVIUS SULPICIUS, iuris civilis auctor, vir bene
litteratus, scripsit ad M. Varronem rogavitque ut
rescriberet quid significaret verbum quod in censoriis
libris scriptum esset. Id erat verbum "favisae
2 Capitolinae." Varro rescripsit in memoria sibi esse
quod Q. Catulus curator restituendi Capitolii dixisset, voluisse se aream Capitolinam deprimere, ut
pluribus gradibus in aedem[1] conscenderetur sug-
gestusque pro fastigii magnitudine altior fieret, sed
facere id non quisse, quoniam "favisae" impedissent.
3 Id esse cellas quasdam et cisternas quae in area sub

---

[1] aedem, *Mercier*; eadem, ω; eandem, σ.

---

[1] There is an obvious word-play on *sectatur* and *in-sectatur*.

[2] p. 140, Bremer.　　　　[3] p. 199, Bipont.

[4] After the destruction of the temple by fire in 83 B.C.
In spite of Caesar's opposition (Suet. *Jul.* xv), Catulus
dedicated the new temple in 69 B.C.

[5] The open space in front of and around the temple of
Jupiter.

[6] Sulla and Catulus in their restorations of the Capitoline

"of everything that pains," but "of everything that is painful"; for it is the removal of pain, he explains, that should be indicated, not of that which causes pain.

In bringing this charge against Epicurus Plutarch is "word-chasing" with excessive minuteness and almost with frigidity; for far from hunting up such verbal meticulousness and such refinements of diction, Epicurus hunts them down.[1]

X

The meaning of *favisae Capitolinae*; and what Marcus Varro replied to Servius Sulpicius, who asked him about that term.

SERVIUS SULPICIUS, an authority on civil law and a man well versed in letters, wrote[2] to Marcus Varro and asked him to explain the meaning of a term which was used in the records of the censors; the term in question was *favisae Capitolinae*. Varro wrote in reply[3] that he recalled that Quintus Catulus, when in charge of the restoration of the Capitol,[4] had said that it had been his desire to lower the area Capitolina,[5] in order that the ascent to the temple might have more steps and that the podium might be higher, to correspond with the elevation and size of the pediment[6]; but that he had been unable to carry out his plan because the *favisae* had prevented. These, he said, were certain underground chambers and cisterns in the area, in which

temple used columns that were taller than those of the earlier building. Catulus wished to make the podium (or elevated platform) higher, to correspond with the greater elevation and size of the pediment (or gable). This he could have done most easily by lowering the area about the temple.

terra essent, ubi reponi solerent signa vetera quae
ex eo templo collapsa essent, et alia[1] quaedam
religiosa e donis consecratis. Ac deinde eadem
epistula negat quidem se in litteris invenisse cur
" favisae " dictae sint, sed Q. Valerium Soranum
solitum dicere ait, quos " thesauros " Graeco nomine
appellaremus, priscos Latinos " flavisas " dixisse,
quod in eos non rude aes argentumque, sed flata
4 signataque pecunia conderetur. Coniectare igitur
se detractam esse ex eo verbo secundam litteram et
" favisas " esse dictas cellas quasdam et specus,
quibus aeditui Capitolii uterentur ad custodiendas
res veteres religiosas.

XI

De Sicinio Dentato egregio bellatore multa memoratu digna.

1 L. Sicinium Dentatum, qui tribunus plebi fuit Sp.
Tarpeio, A. Aternio consulibus, scriptum est in libris
annalibus plus quam credi debeat strenuum bellato-
rem fuisse nomenque ei factum ob ingentem fortitu-
2 dinem appellatumque esse Achillem Romanum. Is
pugnasse in hostem dicitur centum et viginti proeliis, cicatricem aversam nullam, adversas quinque
et quadraginta tulisse, coronis donatus esse aureis

---

[1] et alia, ς ; talia, ω ; aliaque, *Hertz.*

---

[1] For original *flavisae*, from *flare.* Minted or coined money
had to be softened or melted before being cast or struck, and
for this process the word is *flare* ; hence the directors of the

it was the custom to store ancient statues that had
fallen from the temple, and some other conse-
crated objects from among the votive offerings.
And then Varro goes on to say in the same letter,
that he had never found any explanation of the
term *favisae* in literature, but that Quintus
Valerius Soranus used to assert that what we called
by their Greek name *thesauri* (treasuries) the early
Latins termed *flavisae*, their reason being that there
was deposited in them, not uncoined copper and
silver, but stamped and minted money. His theory
therefore was, he said, that the second letter had
dropped out of the word *flavisae*, and that certain
chambers and pits, which the attendants of the
Capitol used for the preservation of old and sacred
objects, were called *favisae*.[1]

XI

Numerous important details about Sicinius Dentatus, the distinguished warrior.

WE read in the annals that Lucius Sicinius
Dentatus, who was tribune of the commons in the
consulship of Spurius Tarpeius and Aulus Aternius,[2]
was a warrior of incredible energy; that he won a
name for his exceeding great valour, and was called
the Roman Achilles. It is said that he fought
with the enemy in one hundred and twenty battles,
and had not a scar on his back, but forty-five in
front; that golden crowns were given him eight

mint were called Triumviri Auro Argento Aere Flando
Feriundo. where *aere* is of course an old dative. *Favisa* is
apparently for *fovisa and cognate with *fovea*, " pit."
[2] 454 B.C.

octo, obsidionali una, muralibus tribus, civicis quattuordecim, torquibus tribus et octoginta, armillis plus centum sexaginta, hastis duodeviginti ; phaleris
3 item donatus est quinquies viciesque ; spolia [1] militaria habuit multiiuga, in his provocatoria pleraque ;
4 triumphavit cum imperatoribus suis triumphos novem.

XII

Considerata perpensaque lex quaedam Solonis, speciem habens primorem iniquae iniustaeque legis, sed ad usum et emolumentum salubritatis penitus reperta.

1   In legibus Solonis illis antiquissimis quae Athenis axibus ligneis incisae sunt quasque latas ab eo Athenienses, ut sempiternae manerent, poenis et religionibus sanxerunt, legem esse Aristoteles refert scriptam ad hanc sententiam : "Si ob discordiam dissensionemque seditio atque discessio populi in duas partes fiet et ob eam causam irritatis animis utrimque arma capientur pugnabiturque, tum qui in eo tempore in eoque casu civilis discordiae non alterutrae parti sese adiunxerit, sed solitarius separatusque a communi malo civitatis secesserit, is domo, patria fortunisque omnibus careto, exul extorrisque esto."

[1] spolia, σ ; populi, ω.

---

[1] The Romans awarded a great variety of military prizes, which are here enumerated, for the most part, in descending order of importance.   *Phalerae* were discs of metal worn on the breast like medals, or sometimes on the harness of horses ; the spears were *hastae purae*, unused (hence "bloodless") and perhaps sometimes headless weapons, although they are represented with heads on two tombstones (Cagnat et

times, the siege crown once, mural crowns three
times, and civic crowns fourteen times; that eighty-
three neck-chains were awarded him, more than one
hundred and sixty armlets, and eighteen spears; he
was presented besides with twenty-five decorations[1];
he had a number of spoils of war,[2] many of which
were won in single combat; he took part with his
generals in nine triumphal processions.

XII

A law of Solon, the result of careful thought and consideration, which at first sight seems unfair and unjust, but on
close examination is found to be altogether helpful and
salutary.

AMONG those very early laws of Solon which were
inscribed upon wooden tablets at Athens, and which,
promulgated by him, the Athenians ratified by
penalties and oaths, to ensure their permanence,
Aristotle says[3] that there was one to this effect:
" If because of strife and disagreement civil dissension shall ensue and a division of the people into
two parties, and if for that reason each side, led by
their angry feelings, shall take up arms and fight,
then if anyone at that time, and in such a condition
of civil discord, shall not ally himself with one or the
other faction, but by himself and apart shall hold
aloof from the common calamity of the State, let him
be deprived of his home, his country, and all his
property, and be an exile and an outlaw."

Chapot, *Arch. Rom.* ii, p. 359, and *Bonner Jahrbücher*, 114
(1905), Plate 1, Fig. 4). Besides golden crowns without a
particular designation, there were others which are enumerated and described in v. 6.
    [2] The armour of the defeated antagonist; cf. Livy xxii.
6. 5. etc.   [3] Cf. Πολ. 'Αθην. 8.

2   Cum hanc legem Solonis, singulari sapientia prae-
diti, legissemus, tenuit nos gravis quaedam in principio admiratio, requirens quam ob causam dignos
esse poena existimaverit, qui se procul a seditione et
3 civili pugna removissent.   Tum, qui penitus atque
alte usum ac sententiam legis introspexerant, non
ad augendam, sed ad desinendam seditionem legem
4 hanc esse dicebant.   Et res prorsum se sic habent.
Nam si boni omnes, qui in principio coercendae
seditioni impares fuerint, populum percitum et
amentem non deseruerint, ad alterutram partem
dividi[1] sese adiunxerint, tum eveniet, ut cum socii
partis seorsum utriusque fuerint eaeque partes ab
his, ut maioris auctoritatis viris, temperari ac regi
coeperint, concordia per eos potissimum restitui
conciliarique possit, dum et suos, apud quos sunt,
regunt atque mitificant et adversarios sanatos magis
cupiunt quam perditos.

5   Hoc idem Favorinus philosophus inter fratres
quoque aut amicos dissidentis oportere fieri censebat,
ut qui in medio sunt utriusque partis benivoli, si in
concordia adnitenda parum auctoritatis quasi ambigui
amici habuerint, tum alteri in alteram partem disce-
dant ac per id meritum viam sibi ad utriusque con-
6 cordiam muniant.   " Nunc autem plerique," inquit,
" partis utriusque amici, quasi probe faciant, duos
litigantes destituunt et relinquunt deduntque eos

---

[1] dividi, ς; dividui, *J. F. Gronov*; dividiae, *Landgraf*.
156

When I read this law of Solon, who was a man of extraordinary wisdom, I was at first filled with something like great amazement, and I asked myself why it was that those who had held themselves aloof from dissension and civil strife were thought to be deserving of punishment. Then those who had profoundly and thoroughly studied the purpose and meaning of the law declared that it was designed, not to increase, but to terminate, dissension. And that is exactly so. For if all good men, who have been unequal to checking the dissension at the outset, do not abandon the aroused and frenzied people, but divide and ally themselves with one or the other faction, then the result will be, that when they have become members of the two opposing parties, and, being men of more than ordinary influence, have begun to guide and direct those parties, harmony can best be restored and established through the efforts of such men, controlling and soothing as they will the members of their respective factions, and desiring to reconcile rather than destroy their opponents.

The philosopher Favorinus thought that this same course ought to be adopted also with brothers, or with friends, who are at odds ; that is, that those who are neutral and kindly disposed towards both parties, if they have had little influence in bringing about a reconciliation because they have not made their friendly feelings evident, should then take sides, some one and some the other, and through this manifestation of devotion pave the way for restoring harmony. "But as it is," said he, "most of the friends of both parties make a merit of abandoning the two disputants, leaving them to the tender

advocatis malivolis aut avaris, qui lites animasque
eorum inflamment aut odii studio aut lucri."

XIII

Liberos in multitudinis numero etiam unum filium filiamve
veteres dixisse.

1 Antiqui oratores historiaeque aut carminum scriptores etiam unum filium filiamve " liberos " multitu-
2 dinis numero appellarunt.   Idque nos, cum in complurium   veterum   libris   scriptum   aliquotiens
adverterimus, nunc quoque in libro Sempronii Asellionis   *Rerum   Gestarum*   quinto   ita   esse   positum
3 offendimus.   Is Asellio sub P. Scipione Africano tribunus militum ad Numantiam fuit resque eas quibus
gerendis ipse interfuit conscripsit.
4   Eius verba de Tiberio Graccho, tribuno pl., quo
in tempore interfectus in Capitolio est, haec sunt :
" Nam Gracchus domo cum proficiscebatur, numquam minus terna aut quaterna milia hominum
5 sequebantur."   Atque inde infra de eodem Graccho
ita   scripsit: " Orare   coepit   id   quidem,   ut   se
defenderent liberosque suos, eumque [1] quem virile
secus tum [2] in eo tempore habebat produci iussit
populoque commendavit prope flens."

XIV

Quod M. Cato, in libro qui inscriptus est *Contra Tiberium
Exulem*, " stitisses vadimonium " per i litteram dicit, non
" stetisses " ; eiusque verbi ratio reddita.

1   In libro vetere M. Catonis, qui inscribitur *Contra
Tiberium Exulem*, scriptum sic [3] erat : " Quid si va-

---

[1] -que *added by Cramer.*   [2] unum, *J. F. Gronov.*
[3] sic, *J. F. Gronov* ; quid sic, *ω* ; quidem sic, *ς.*

mercies of ill-disposed or greedy advisers, who, animated by hatred or by avarice, add fuel to their strife and inflame their passions."

XIII

That the early writers used *liberi* in the plural number even of a single son or daughter.

THE early orators and writers of history or of poetry called even one son or daughter *liberi*, using the plural. And I have not only noticed this usage at various times in the works of several other of the older writers, but I just now ran across it in the fifth book of Sempronius Asellio's *History*.[1] This Asellio was military tribune under Publius Scipio Africanus at Numantia and wrote a detailed account of the events in whose action he himself took part.

His words about Tiberius Gracchus, tribune of the commons, at the time when he was killed on the Capitol, are as follows: "For whenever Gracchus left home, he was never accompanied by less than three or four thousand men." And farther on he wrote thus of the same Gracchus: "He began to beg that they would at least defend him and his children (*liberi*); and then he ordered that the one male child which he had at that time should be brought out, and almost in tears commended him to the protection of the people."

XIV

That Marcus Cato, in the speech entitled *Against the Exile Tiberius*, says *stitisses vadimonium* with an *i*, and not *stetisses*; and the explanation of that word.

IN an old copy of the speech of Marcus Cato, which is entitled *Against the Exile Tiberius*,[2] we find

[1] Fr. 6, Peter.   [2] xliii. Jordan.

2 dimonium capite obvoluto stitisses?" Recte quidem
ille "stitisses" scripsit; sed falsa et audaci emendatione editores [1] "e" scripto per [2] libros "stetisses"
fecerunt, tamquam "stitisses" vanum et nihili ver-
3 bum esset. Quin potius ipsi nequam et nihili sunt,
qui ignorant "stitisses" dictum a Catone, quoniam
"sisteretur" vadimonium, non "staretur."

XV

Quod antiquitus aetati senectae potissimum habiti sint ampli
honores; et cur postea ad maritos et ad patres idem isti
honores delati sint; atque ibi de capite quaedam legis
Iuliae septimo.

1 APUD antiquissimos Romanorum neque generi neque pecuniae praestantior honos tribui quam aetati
solitus, maioresque natu a minoribus colebantur ad
deum prope et parentum vicem atque omni in loco
inque omni specie honoris priores potioresque habiti.
2 A convivio quoque, ut scriptum in antiquitatibus est,
seniores a iunioribus domum deducebantur, eumque
morem accepisse Romanos a Lacedaemoniis traditum
est, apud quos Lycurgi legibus maior omnium rerum honos aetati maiori habebatur.
3 Sed postquam suboles civitati necessaria visa est
et ad prolem populi frequentandam praemiis atque
invitamentis usus fuit, tum antelati quibusdam in rebus qui uxorem quique liberos haberent senioribus

---

[1] audaci emendatione editores, *H. J. Müller*; falsa et
audax . . . emendatores, *MSS.*
[2] et per, *MSS.*

the following words: " What if with veiled head you
had kept your recognizance?" Cato indeed wrote
stitisses, correctly; but revisers have boldly and
falsely written an *e* and put *stetisses* in all the
editions, on the ground that *stitisses* is an unmeaning and worthless reading. Nay, it is rather
they themselves that are ignorant and worthless,
in not knowing that Cato wrote *stitisses* because
sisteretur is used of recognizance, not *staretur*.

XV

To what extent in ancient days it was to old age in particular
that high honours were paid; and why it was that later
those same honours were extended to husbands and fathers;
and in that connection some provisions of the seventh
section of the Julian law.

AMONG the earliest Romans, as a rule, neither birth
nor wealth was more highly honoured than age, but
older men were reverenced by their juniors almost
like gods and like their own parents, and everywhere
and in every kind of honour they were regarded as
first and of prior right. From a dinner-party, too,
older men were escorted home by younger men, as
we read in the records of the past, a custom which,
as tradition has it, the Romans took over from the
Lacedaemonians, by whom, in accordance with the
laws of Lycurgus, greater honour on all occasions was
paid to greater age.

But after it came to be realised that progeny were
a necessity for the State, and there was occasion to
add to the productivity of the people by premiums
and other inducements, then in certain respects
greater deference was shown to men who had a
wife, and to those who had children, than to older

4 neque liberos neque uxores habentibus. Sicuti kapite
VII. legis Iuliae priori ex consulibus fasces sumendi
potestas fit, non qui pluris annos natus est, sed qui
pluris liberos quam collega aut in sua potestate habet
5 aut bello amisit.   Sed si par utrique numerus liberorum est, maritus aut qui in numero maritorum est
6 praefertur; si vero ambo et mariti et patres totidem
liberorum sunt, tum ille pristinus honos instauratur
7 et qui maior natu est prior fasces sumit.   Super his
autem, qui aut caelibes ambo sunt et parem numerum
filiorum habent aut mariti sunt et liberos non habent,
8 nihil scriptum in ea lege de [1] aetate est.   Solitos
tamen audio, qui lege potiores essent fasces primi
mensis collegis concedere aut longe aetate prioribus
aut nobilioribus multo aut secundum consulatum
ineuntibus.

XVI

Quod Caesellius Vindex a Sulpicio Apollinari reprehensus est
in sensus Vergiliani enarratione.

1   Vergilii versus sunt e libro sexto:

Ille, vides, pura iuvenis qui nititur hasta,
Proxima sorte tenet lucis loca.   Primus ad auras
Aetherias Italo commixtus sanguine surget,
Silvius, Albanum nomen, tua postuma proles,

---

[1] ea lege de, *Vogel*; lege de ea, *ω*; lege de aetate, *Carrio.*

[1] In 18 B.C. Augustus proposed a law *de maritandis ordini-
bus,* imposing liabilities on the unmarried and offering rewards
to those who married and reared children.   It was violently
opposed, but was finally passed in a modified form.   See
Suet. *Aug.* xxxiv.   In A.D. 9 the lex Papia Poppaea, called
from the consules suffecti of the year, was added.   The

men who had neither wives nor children. Thus in chapter seven of the Julian law [1] priority in assuming the emblems of power is given, not to the elder of the consuls, but to him who either has more children under his control than his colleague, or has lost them in war. But if both have an equal number of children, the one who has a wife, or is eligible for marriage, is preferred. If, however, both are married and are fathers of the same number of children, then the standard of honour of early times is restored, and the elder is first to assume the rods. But when both consuls are without wives and have the same number of sons, or are husbands but have no children, there is no provision in that law as to age. However, I hear that it was usual for those who had legal priority to yield the rods for the first month to colleagues who were either considerably older than they, or of much higher rank, or who were entering upon a second consulship.

XVI

Sulpicius Apollinaris' criticism of Caesellius Vindex for his explanation of a passage in Virgil.

Virgil has the following lines in the sixth book : [2]

Yon princeling, thou beholdest leaning there
Upon a bloodless [3] lance, shall next emerge
Into the realms of day. He is the first
Of half-Italian strain, thy last-born heir,
To thine old age by fair Lavinia given,

combined *Lex Iulia et Papia Poppaea* contained at least 35 chapters (*Dig.* 23. 2. 19).
[2] 760 ff.   [3] See note 1, p. 155.

> Quem tibi longaevo serum Lavinia coniunx
> Educet silvis regem regumque parentem,
> Unde genus Longa nostrum dominabitur Alba,

2   Videbantur haec nequaquam convenire:

> tua postuma proles,

et:

> Quem tibi longaevo serum Lavinia coniunx
> Educet silvis.

3 Nam si hic Silvius, ita ut in omnium ferme annalium monumentis scriptum est, post mortem Aeneae [1]
natus est ob eamque causam praenomen ei Postumo
fuit, qua ratione subiectum est:

> Quem tibi longaevo serum Lavinia coniunx
> Educet silvis?

4 Haec enim verba significare videri possunt, Aenea
vivo ac iam sene, natum ei Silvium et educatum.
5 Itaque hanc sententiam esse verborum istorum
Caesellius opinatus in *Commentario Lectionum Antiquarum*: "Postuma," inquit, "proles non eum
significat qui patre mortuo, sed qui postremo loco
natus est, sicuti Silvius, qui Aenea iam sene tardo
6 seroque partu est editus." Sed huius historiae
7 auctorem idoneum nullum nominat; Silvium autem
post Aeneae mortem, sicuti diximus, natum esse
multi tradiderunt.
8   Idcirco Apollinaris Sulpicius, inter cetera in quis
Caesellium reprehendit, hoc quoque eius quasi

---

[1] Aeneae, *added by Hertz.*

Called Silvius, a royal Alban name
(Of sylvan birth and sylvan nurture he),
A king himself and sire of kings to come,
By whom our race in Alba Longa reign.

It appeared to Caesellius that there was utter
inconsistency between

thy last-born heir

and

To thine old age by fair Lavinia given,
Of sylvan birth.

For if, as is shown by the testimony of almost all
the annals, this Silvius was born after the death of
Aeneas, and for that reason was given the forename Postumus, with what propriety does Virgil
add :

To thine old age by fair Lavinia given,
Of sylvan birth ?

For these words would seem to imply that while
Aeneas was still living, but was already an old man, a
son Silvius was born to him and was reared.   Therefore Caesellius, in his *Notes on Early Readings,*
expressed the opinion that the meaning of the
words was as follows: *" Postuma proles,"* said he,
" does not mean a child born after the death of his
father, but the one who was born last; this applies
to Silvius, who was born late and after the usual time,
when Aeneas was already an old man." But Caesellius names no adequate authority for this version,
while that Silvius was born, as I have said, after
Aeneas' death, has ample testimony.

Therefore Sulpicius Apollinaris, among other
criticisms of Caesellius, notes this statement of his as

erratum animadvertit errorisque istius hanc esse
causam dixit, quod scriptum ita sit ' quem tibi
longaevo.' 'Longaevo' " [1] inquit, " non seni significat, hoc enim[2] est contra historiae fidem, sed in longum
9 iam aevum et perpetuum recepto immortalique facto.
Anchises enim, qui haec ad filium dicit, sciebat
eum, cum hominum vita discessisset, immortalem
atque indigetem futurum et longo perpetuoque aevo
10 potiturum." Hoc sane Apollinaris argute. Sed aliud
tamen est " longum aevum," aliud " perpetuum,"
neque dii " longaevi " appellantur, sed " inmortales."

XVII

Cuiusmodi esse naturam quarundam praepositionum M.
Cicero animadverterit; disceptatumque ibi super eo ipso
quod Cicero observaverat.

1 OBSERVATE curioseque animadvertit M. Tullius
"in" et "con" praepositiones verbis aut vocabulis
praepositas tunc produci atque protendi, cum litterae sequerentur quae primae sunt in "sapiente"
atque "felice," in aliis autem omnibus correpte
pronuntiari.
2 Verba Ciceronis haec sunt: "Quid vero hoc
elegantius, quod non fit natura, sed quodam
instituto? 'Indoctus' dicimus brevi prima littera,
'insanus' producta, 'immanis'[3] brevi, 'infelix'
longa et, ne multis, quibus in verbis hae primae
litterae sunt quae in 'sapiente' atque 'felice,'
producte dicuntur, in ceteris omnibus breviter;
itemque 'conposuit,' 'consuevit,' 'concrepuit,' 'con-

---

[1] longaevo, *added by Carrio.* [2] significato (-tio, *P*) enim, *ω.*
[3] immanis, *L. Müller*; inhumanus, *ω.*

an error, and says that the cause of the error is the phrase *quem tibi longaevo.* "*Longaevo*," he says, "does not mean 'when old,' for that is contrary to historical truth, but rather 'admitted into a life that is now long and unending, and made immortal.' For Anchises, who says this to his son, knew that after Aeneas had ended his life among men he would be immortal and a local deity, and enjoy a long and everlasting existence." Thus Apollinaris, ingeniously enough. But yet a "long life" is one thing, and an "unending life" another, and the gods are not called "of great age," but "immortal."

XVII

Marcus Cicero's observations on the nature of certain prepositions ; to which is added a discussion of the particular matter which Cicero had observed.

AFTER careful observation Marcus Tullius noted that the prepositions *in* and *con*, when prefixed to nouns and verbs, are lengthened and prolonged when they are followed by the initial letters of *sapiens* and *felix ;* but that in all other instances they are pronounced short.

Cicero's words are : [1] " Indeed, what can be more elegant than this, which does not come about from a natural law, but in accordance with a kind of usage? We pronounce the first vowel in *indoctus* short, in *insanus* long; in *immanis* short, in *infelix* long; in brief, in compound words in which the first letters are those which begin *sapiens* and *felix* the prefix is pronounced long, in all others short; thus we have *cŏnposuit* but *cōnsuevit*, *cŏncrepuit*

[1] *Orator*, § 159.

fecit.' Consule veritatem, reprehendet; refer ad
auris, probabunt; quaere cur ita sit? dicent iuvare.[1]
Voluptati autem aurium morigerari debet oratio."

3 Manifesta quidem ratio suavitatis est in his vocibus de quibus Cicero locutus est. Sed quid dicemus
de praepositione " pro," quae, cum produci et corripi
soleat, observationem hanc tamen M. Tullii aspernata

4 est ? Non enim semper producitur, cum sequitur ea
littera quae prima est in verbo "fecit," quam Cicero
hanc habere vim significat ut propter eam rem "in"

5 et "con" praepositiones producantur. Nam "proficisci " et "profugere " et "profundere " et "profanum" et "profestum " correpte dicimus, "pro-
ferre " autem et "profligare " et "proficere "

6 producte. Cur igitur ea littera, quam Cicero
productionis causam facere observavit, non in
omnibus consimilibus eandem vim aut rationis
aut suavitatis tenet, sed aliam vocem produci facit,
aliam corripi?

Neque vero "con" particula tum solum producitur, cum ea littera, de qua Cicero dixit, insequitur.

7 Nam et Cato et Sallustius : "faenoribus," inquiunt,

8 "copertus est." Praeterea "coligatus " et "conexus "
producte dicitur.

9 Sed tamen videri potest in his quae posui, ob eam
causam particula haec produci, quoniam eliditur ex
ea *n* littera ; nam detrimentum litterae productione

10 syllabae compensatur. Quod quidem etiam in eo

11 servatur, quod est "cogo "; neque repugnat quod

---

[1] cur ? ita se dicent iuvari, Cic.

---

[1] That is beginning with *f*.
[2] He is loaded with debt; Fr. 50, Jordan ; Sall *Hist.* iv.
52, Maurenbrecher.

but *cōnficit.* Consult the rules of grammar and
they will censure your usage; refer the matter
to your ears and they will approve. Ask why
it is so; they will say that it pleases them. And
language ought to gratify the pleasure of the
ear."

In these words of which Cicero spoke it is clear
that the principle is one of euphony, but what are we
to say of the preposition *pro?* For although it is
often shortened or lengthened, yet it does not conform to this rule of Marcus Tullius. For it is not
always lengthened when it is followed by the
first letter of the word *fecit,* which Cicero says
has the effect of lengthening the prepositions *in*
and *con.* For we pronounce *prŏficisci, prŏfugere,*
prŏfundere, prŏfanum and *prŏfestum* with the first
vowel short, but *prōferre, prōfligare* and *prōficere*
with that syllable long. Why is it then that this
letter, which, according to Cicero's observation, has
the effect of lengthening, does not have the same
effect by reason of rule or of euphony in all words
of the same kind,[1] but lengthens the vowel in one
word and shortens it in another.

Nor, as a matter of fact, is the particle *con*
lengthened only when followed by that letter which
Cicero mentioned: for both Cato and Sallust say
" *faenoribus copertus est.*" [2] Moreover *cōligatus* and
cōnexus are pronounced long.

But after all, in these cases which I have cited one
can see that this particle is lengthened because the
letter *n* is dropped; for the loss of a letter is com-
pensated by the lengthening of the syllable. This
principle is observed also in the word *cōgo;* and
it is no contradiction that we pronounce *cŏegi*

"coegi" correpte dicimus; non enim salva id ἀναλογίᾳ dicitur a verbo, quod est "cogo."

XVIII

Quod Phaedon Socraticus servus fuit ; quodque item alii[1] complusculi servitutem servierunt.

PHAEDON Elidensis ex cohorte illa Socratica fuit 2 Socratique et Platoni per fuit familiaris. Eius nomini Plato librum illum divinum de immortalitate 3 animae dedit. Is Phaedon servus fuit forma atque ingenio liberali et, ut quidam scripserunt, a lenone 4 domino puer ad merendum coactus. Eum Cebes Socraticus hortante Socrate emisse dicitur habuis- 5 seque in philosophiae disciplinis. Atque is postea philosophus inlustris fuit sermonesque eius de Socrate admodum elegantes leguntur.

6 Alii quoque non pauci servi fuerunt qui post philo- 7 sophi clari extiterunt. Ex quibus ille Menippus fuit cuius libros M. Varro in satiris aemulatus est, quas alii "Cynicas," ipse appellat "Menippeas."

---

[1] alii philosophi, *Carrio.*

---

[1] For "analogy" in this sense of "regularity," see ii. 25. Gellius thought that *coegi* was an irregular form because *oē* did not contract, as *oi* did in *cogo* ; but contraction of unlike vowels did not take place when the second was long ; cf. *coāctus.* Cicero's rule is correct, because a vowel is naturally long before *ns* and *nf.* The case of *pro* is quite different. The *ō* in *cōpertus* is due to contraction from *co-opertus.* *Cōligatus* is a very rare form; Skutsch, quoted by Hosius, thought it might come from *co-alligatus.* The *ō* in *cogo* is also due to contraction (*co-ago, co-igo*), which does not apply to the perfect *coegi.* Compensatory lengthening takes place usually when an *s* is lost, as in *cōnecto* for *co-snecto,* or *n* before *s* and *f;* less commonly when *nc* is lost before *n.*

short; for this form cannot be derived from *cōgo* without violation of the principle of analogy.[1]

XVIII

That Phaedo the Socratic was a slave; and that several others also were of that condition.

PHAEDO of Elis belonged to that famous Socratic band and was on terms of close intimacy with Socrates and Plato. His name was given by Plato to that inspired dialogue of his on the immortality of the soul. This Phaedo, though a slave, was of noble person and intellect,[2] and according to some writers, in his boyhood was driven to prostitution by his master, who was a pander. We are told that Cebes the Socratic, at Socrates' earnest request, bought Phaedo and gave him the opportunity of studying philosophy. And he afterwards became a distinguished philosopher, whose very tasteful discourses on Socrates are in circulation.

There were not a few other slaves too who afterwards became famous philosophers, among them that Menippus whose works Marcus Varro emulated [3] in those satires which others call "Cynic," but he himself, "Menippean." [4]

---

[2] It must be remembered that the slaves of the Greeks and Romans were often freeborn children, who had been cast off by their parents, or free men, who had been taken prisoner in war. Phaedo belonged to the latter class, and the details of his life are very uncertain.

[3] The word implies, not merely imitation, but rivalry, a recognized principle in classic literature; see *Revue des Études Latines*, II. (1924), pp. 46 ff.

[4] See note 1, p. 85.

8   Sed et Theophrasti Peripatetici servus Pompylus et Zenonis Stoici servus, qui Persaeus vocatus est, et Epicuri, cui Mys nomen fuit, philosophi non incelebres vixerunt.

9   Diogenes etiam Cynicus servitutem servivit. Sed is ex libertate in servitutem venum ierat. Quem cum emere vellet Ξενιάδης Κορίνθιος et ecquid artificii novisset esset [1] percontatus : " Novi," inquit Diogenes,

10   " hominibus liberis imperare." Tum Ξενιάδης responsum eius demiratus emit et manu emisit filiosque suos ei tradens : " Accipe," inquit, " liberos meos quibus imperes."

    De Epicteto autem philosopho nobili, quod is quoque servus fuit recentior est memoria quam ut scribi quasi oblitteratum debuerit.

XIX

" Rescire " verbum quid sit ; et quam habeat veram atque propriam significationem.

1   VERBUM " rescire " observavimus vim habere propriam quandam, non ex communi significatione ceterorum verborum quibus eadem praepositio imponitur ; neque ut " rescribere," " relegere," " restituere " *** substituere dicimus, itidem dicimus

2   " rescire " ; nam qui factum aliquod occultius aut inopinatum insperatumque cognoscit, is dicitur proprie " rescire."

---

[1] esset *added by Hertz.*

---

[1] I. 438, Arn.
[2] The word for free men and children is the same (*liberi*), but it seems impossible to reproduce the word play in English.

Besides these, Pompylus, the slave of the Peripatetic Theophrastus, and the slave of the Stoic Zeno who was called Persaeus, and the slave of Epicurus whose name was Mys, were philosophers of repute. [1]

Diogenes the Cynic also served as a slave, but he was a freeborn man, who was sold into slavery. When Xeniades of Corinth wished to buy him and asked whether he knew any trade, Diogenes replied : " I know how to govern free men." [2] Then Xeniades, in admiration of his answer, bought him, set him free, and entrusting to him his own children, said : " Take my children to govern."

But as to the well-known philosopher Epictetus, the fact that he too was a slave is too fresh in our memory to need to be committed to writing, as if it had been forgotten.

XIX

On the nature of the verb *rescire*; and its true and distinctive meaning.

I HAVE observed that the verb *rescire* has a peculiar force, which is not in accord with the general meaning of other words compounded with that same preposition; for we do not use *rescire* in the same way that we do *rescribere* (write in reply), *relegere* (reread), *restituere* (restore), . . . and *substituere* (put in the place of); [3] but *rescire* is properly said of one who learns of something that is hidden, or unlooked for and unexpected.

[3] As *substituere* does not contain *re-*, it seems clear that there is a lacuna before that word, but it seems impossible to fill the gap.

3 Cur autem in hoc uno verbo "re" particula huius sententiae vim habeat, equidem[1] adhuc quaero.
4 Aliter enim dictum esse "rescivi" aut "rescire" apud eos qui diligenter locuti sunt, nondum invenimus quam super is rebus quae aut consulto consilio latuerint aut contra spem opinionemve usu
5 venerint; quamquam ipsum "scire" de omnibus communiter rebus dicatur vel adversis vel prosperis
6 vel insperatis vel expectatis. Naevius in *Triphallo* ita scripsit:

Sive[2] úmquam quicquam fílium rescívero,
Argéntum amoris caúsa sumpse mútuum,
Extémplo illo te dúcam ubi non déspuas.

7 Claudius Quadrigarius in primo *Annali*: "Ea Lucani ubi resciverunt, sibi per fallacias verba data
8 esse." Item Quadrigarius in eodem libro in re tristi et inopinata verbo isto ita utitur: "Id ubi rescierunt propinqui obsidum, quos Pontio traditos supra demonstravimus, eorum parentes cum pro-
9 pinquis capillo passo in viam provolarunt." M. Cato in quarto *Originum*: "Deinde dictator iubet postridie magistrum equitum arcessi: 'mittam te, si vis, cum equitibus.' 'Sero est,' inquit magister equitum, 'iam rescivere.'"

---

[1] et quidem, ω.
[2] sive, *Skutsch*; si umquam, MSS.

---

[1] v. 96, Ribbeck[3].

But why the particle *re* has this special force in this one word alone, I for my part am still inquiring. For I have never yet found that *rescivi* or *rescire* was used by those who were careful in their diction, otherwise than of things which were purposely concealed, or happened contrary to anticipation and expectation; although *scire* itself is used of everything alike, whether favourable or unfavourable, unexpected or expected. Thus Naevius in the *Triphallus* wrote:[1]

If ever I discover (*rescivero*) that my son
Has borrowed money for a love affair,
Straightway I'll put you where you'll spit no
  more.[2]

Claudius Quadrigarius in the first book of his *Annals* says:[3] "When the Lucanians discovered (*resciverunt*) that they had been deceived and tricked." And again in the same book Quadrigarius uses that word of something sad and unexpected:[4] "When this became known to the relatives (*rescierunt propinqui*) of the hostages, who, as I have pointed out above, had been delivered to Pontius, their parents and relatives rushed into the street with hair in disarray." Marcus Cato writes in the fourth book of the *Origins*:[5] "Then next day the dictator orders the master of the horse to be summoned: 'I will send you, if you wish, with the cavalry.' 'It is too late,' said the master of the horse, 'they have found it out already (*rescivere*).'"

[2] Literally, "spit down" into one's bosom, referring to the wooden fork about the slave's neck which would prevent this, and to spitting as a charm for averting evil.
[3] Fr. 16, Peter.   [4] Fr. 19, Peter.   [5] Fr. 87, Peter.

XX

Quae volgo dicuntur "vivaria," id vocabulum veteres non dixisse; et quid pro eo P. Scipio in oratione ad populum, quid postea M. Varro in libris *De Re Rustica* dixerit.

1 "VIVARIA," quae nunc dicuntur saepta quaedam loca, in quibus ferae vivae pascuntur, M. Varro in libro *De Re Rustica* III. dicit "leporaria" appellari.

2 Verba Varronis subieci: "Villaticae pastionis genera sunt tria, ornithones, leporaria, piscinae.[1] Nunc ornithonas dico omnium alitum quae intra parietes villae solent pasci. Leporaria te accipere volo, non ea quae tritavi nostri dicebant, ubi soli[2] lepores sint, sed omnia saepta adficta[3] villae quae sunt et

3 habent inclusa animalia quae pascuntur." Is item infra eodem in libro ita scribit: "Cum emisti fundum Tusculanum a M. Pisone, in leporario apri multi fuere."

4 "Vivaria" autem quae nunc vulgus dicit—quos παραδείσους Graeci appellant, quae "leporaria" Varro dicit—haut usquam memini apud vetustiores

5 scriptum. Sed quod apud Scipionem, omnium aetatis suae purissime locutum, legimus "roboraria," aliquot Romae doctos viros dicere audivi id significare, quod nos "vivaria" dicimus, appellataque esse a tabulis roboreis, quibus saepta essent; quod genus saeptorum

6 vidimus in Italia locis plerisque. Verba ex oratione

---

[1] piscinae . . . leporaria, *Varro*; *omitted by* ω.
[2] soliti, *Varro*.   [3] adficta, *Varro*; aedificia, ω.

---

[1] iii. 3. 1.   [2] iii. 3. 8.
[3] The word means an enclosed park, handsomely laid out and stocked with game; also, a garden, and in Septuagint, *Gen.* 2. 8, the garden of Eden, Paradise.

XX

That for what we commonly call *vivaria* the earlier
  writers did not use that term ; and what Publius Scipio
  used for this word in his speech to the people, and
  afterwards Marcus Varro in his work *On Farming*.

In the third book of his treatise *On Farming*,[1]
Marcus Varro says that the name *leporaria* is
given to certain enclosures, now called *vivaria*,
in which wild animals are kept alive and fed. I
have appended Varro's own words: "There are
three means of keeping animals on the farm—bird
houses, *leporaria* (warrens), and fish-ponds. I am
now using the term *ornithones* of all kinds of birds
that are ordinarily kept within the walls of the farmhouse. *Leporaria* I wish you to understand, not
in the sense in which our remote ancestors used the
word, of places in which only hares are kept, but of
all enclosures which are connected with a farmhouse
and contain live animals that are fed." Farther on
in the same book Varro writes:[2] "When you bought
the farm at Tusculum from Marcus Piso, there were
many wild boars in the *leporarium*."

But the word *vivaria*, which the common people
now use—the Greek παράδεισοι[3] and Varro's *leporaria*—I do not recall meeting anywhere in the
older literature. But as to the word *roboraria*,
which we find in the writings of Scipio, who used
the purest diction of any man of his time, I have
heard several learned men at Rome assert that
this means what we call *vivaria* and that the name
came from the "oaken" planks of which the enclosures were made, a kind of enclosure which we
see in many places in Italy. This is the passage

177

eius *Contra Claudium Asellum* quinta haec sunt:
"Ubi agros optime cultos atque villas expolitissimas
vidisset, in his regionibus excelsissimo loco grumam[1]
statuere aiebat; inde corrigere viam, aliis per vineas
medias, aliis per roborarium atque piscinam, aliis per
villam."

7   Lacus vero aut stagna quae[2] piscibus vivis coer-
centur clausa, suo atque proprio nomine "piscinas"
nominaverunt.

8   "Apiaria" quoque vulgus dicit loca in quibus siti
sunt alvei apum; sed neminem ferme qui incorrupte
9 locuti sunt aut scripsisse memini aut dixisse.   M.
autem Varro in libro *De Re Rustica* tertio: "Μελισ-
σῶνας," inquit, "ita facere oportet, quae quidam 'mellaria' appellant."   Sed hoc verbum quo Varro usus
est Graecum est; nam μελισσῶνες ita dicuntur, ut
ἀμπελῶνες et δαφνῶνες.

XXI

Super eo sidere quod Graeci ἄμαξαν, nos "septentriones"
vocamus; ac de utriusque vocabuli ratione et origine.

1   AB Aegina in Piraeum complusculi earundem
disciplinarum sectatores Graeci Romanique homines
2 eadem in navi transmittebamus.   Nox fuit et clemens

---

[1] grumam, *Madvig*; locorum mu (*P omits* mu), ω.
[2] quae, *supplied in* σ.

from Scipio's fifth oration *Against Claudius Asellus* :[1]
"When he had seen the highly-cultivated fields
and well-kept farmhouses, he ordered them to set
up a measuring rod on the highest spot in that
district; and from there to build a straight road,
in some places through the midst of vineyards, in
others through the *roborarium* and the fish-pond,
in still others through the farm buildings."

Thus we see that to pools or ponds of water in
which live fish are kept in confinement, they gave
their own appropriate name of *piscinae,* or "fish-
ponds."

Apiaria too is the word commonly used of
places in which bee-hives are set; but I recall
almost no one of those who have spoken correctly
who has used that word either in writing or speaking. But Marcus Varro, in the third book of his
treatise *On Farming,* remarks :[2] "This is the way
to make μελισσῶνες, which some call *mellaria,* or
'places for storing honey.'" But this word which
Varro used is Greek; for they say μελισσῶνες, just
as they do ἀμπελῶνες (vineyards) and δαφνῶνες (laurel
groves).

XXI

About the constellation which the Greeks call ἅμαξα and
the Romans *septentriones* ; and as to the origin and
meaning of both those words.

SEVERAL of us, Greeks and Romans, who were
pursuing the same studies, were crossing in the
same boat from Aegina to the Piraeus. It was night,
the sea was calm, the time summer, and the sky

[1] *Orat. Rom. Frag.* p. 184, Myer[2].   [2] iii. 16. 12.

mare et anni aestas caelumque liquide serenum.
Sedebamus ergo in puppi simul universi et lucentia
3 sidera considerabamus. Tum, qui eodem in numero
Graecas res eruditi erant, quid ἄμαξα esset, quid
βοώτης, et quaenam maior¹ et quae minor, cur ita
appellata et quam in partem procedentis noctis
spatio moveretur et quamobrem Homerus solam eam
non occidere dicat, cum et quaedam alia non occidant²
astra,³ scite ista omnia ac perite disserebant.
4   Hic ego ad nostros iuvenes convertor et "quin,"⁴
inquam, "vos opici dicitis mihi quare quod ἄμαξαν
5 Graeci vocant nos 'septentriones' vocamus? Non
enim satis est quod septem stellas videmus, sed quid
hoc totum quod 'septentriones' dicimus significet
scire," inquam, "id prolixius volo."
6   Tum quispiam ex his, qui se ad litteras memorias-
que veteres dediderat: "Vulgus," inquit, "grammaticorum 'septentriones' a solo numero stellarum
7 dictum putat. 'Triones' enim per sese nihil significare aiunt, sed vocabuli esse supplementum; sicut
in eo, quod 'quinquatrus' dicamus, quod quinque
8 ab Idibus dierum numerus sit, 'atrus' nihil. Sed
ego quidem cum L. Aelio et M. Varrone sentio, qui
'triones' rustico cetera⁵ vocabulo boves appellatos
scribunt, quasi quosdam 'terriones,' hoc est arandae

---

¹ maior ἄρκτος, σ.   ² non occidant, added by Carrio.
³ astra, added by Hosius.   ⁴ quin, Markland; quid, ω.
⁵ caetero, MSS.; probably a gloss. (sc. e tero), Damsté.

---

¹ Iliad, xviii. 489; Odyss. v. 275 Ἄρκτον . . . οἴη δ'
ἄμμορός ἐστι λοετρῶν Ὠκεανοῖο.
² The quinquatrus, or festival of Minerva, was so called
because it came on the fifth day after the Ides (fifteenth) of
March.
³ Fr. 42, Fun.   ⁴ De Ling. Lat. vii. 4. 74.

bright and clear. So we all sat together in the
stern and watched the brilliant stars. Then those
of our company who were acquainted with Grecian
lore discussed with learning and acumen such
questions as these: what the ἄμαξα, or "Wain,"
was, and what Boötes, which was the Great, and
which the Little Bear and why they were so called;
in what direction that constellation moved in the
course of the advancing night, and why Homer
says [1] that this is the only constellation that does
not set, in view of the fact that there are some
other stars that do not set.

Thereupon I turned to our compatriots and said:
"Why don't you barbarians tell me why we give
the name of *septentriones* to what the Greeks
call ἄμαξα. Now 'because we see seven stars' is
not a sufficient answer, but I desire to be informed
at some length," said I, "of the meaning of the whole
idea which we express by the word *septentriones*."

Then one of them, who had devoted himself to
ancient literature and antiquities, replied: "The
common run of grammarians think that the word
septentriones is derived solely from the number of
stars. For they declare that *triones* of itself has
no meaning, but is a mere addition to the word;
just as in our word *quinquatrus*, so called because
five is the number of days after the Ides,[2] *atrus*
means nothing. But for my part, I agree with
Lucius Aelius [3] and Marcus Varro,[4] who wrote that
oxen were called *triones*, a rustic term it is true, as
if they were *terriones*,[5] that is to say, adapted to

---

[5] A word made up from *terra*, "earth"; the derivation
is a fanciful one. *Triones* is connected with *tero*, "rub,
tread," etc.

9 colendaeque terrae idoneos. Itaque hoc sidus, quod
a figura posituraque ipsa, quia simile plaustri videtur,
antiqui Graecorum ἅμαξαν dixerunt, nostri quoque
veteres a bubus iunctis 'septentriones' appellarunt,
id est septem stellas,[1] ex quibus quasi iuncti 'triones'
10 figurantur. Praeter hanc," inquit, "opinionem id
quoque Varro addit, dubitare sese an propterea
magis hae septem stellae 'triones' appellatae sint,
quia ita sunt sitae ut ternae stellae proximae quaeque
inter sese faciant 'trigona,' id est triquetras figuras."
11 Ex his duabus rationibus quas ille dixit, quod
posterius est subtilius elegantiusque est[2] visum.
Intuentibus enim nobis in illud, ita propemodum
res erat, ut forma esse[3] triquetra viderentur.

XXII

De vento "Iapyge" deque aliorum ventorum vocabulis
regionibusque accepta ex Favorini sermonibus.

1 APUD mensam Favorini in convivio familari legi
solitum erat aut vetus carmen melici poetae aut
historia partim Graecae linguae, alias Latinae.
2 Legebatur ergo ibi tunc in carmine Latino "Iapyx"
ventus quaesitumque est quis hic ventus et quibus
ex locis spiraret et quae tam infrequentis vocabuli
ratio esset; atque etiam petebamus, ut super ceterorum nominibus regionibusque docere nos ipse vellet,

---

[1] stellas, *Skutsch*; stellis, *MSS*.
[2] est, *Lion*; esse, ω.　　　[3] esse, *Carrio*; esset ut, ω.

---

[1] This is true, whatever the origin of the name.

ploughing and cultivating the earth. Therefore this
constellation, which the early Greeks called ἄμαξα
merely from its form and position, because it seemed
to resemble a wagon, the early men also of our
country called *septentriones*, from oxen yoked together, that is, seven stars by which yoked oxen
(*triones*) seem to be represented. After giving this
opinion, Varro further added," said he, "that he suspected that these seven stars were called *triones*
rather for the reason that they are so situated that
every group of three neighbouring stars forms a
triangle, that is to say, a three-sided figure."

Of these two reasons which he gave, the latter
seemed the neater and the more ingenious; for as
we looked at that constellation, it actually appeared
to consist of triangles.[1]

XXII

Information about the wind called Iapyx and about the
names and quarters of other winds, derived from the
discourses of Favorinus.

At Favorinus' table, when he dined with friends,
there was usually read either an old song of one
of the lyric poets, or something from history, now
in Greek and now in Latin. Thus one day there
was read there, in a Latin poem,[2] the word *Iapyx*,
the name of a wind, and the question was asked
what wind this was, from what quarter it blew,
and what was the origin of so rare a term; and we
also asked Favorinus to be so good as to inform us
about the names and quarters of the other winds,

[2] Perhaps Horace, *Odes*, i. 3. 4 or iii. 27. 20. Gellius
mentions Horace by name only once, in § 25, below.

ATTIC NIGHTS OF AULUS GELLIUS

quia vulgo neque de appellationibus eorum neque de
finibus neque de numero conveniret.

3 Tum Favorinus ita fabulatus est: "Satis," inquit,
"notum est, limites regionesque esse caeli quattuor:
'exortum,' 'occasum,' 'meridiem,' 'septentriones.'

4 Exortus et occasus mobilia et varia sunt, meridies
septentrionesque statu perpetuo stant et manent.

5 Oritur enim sol non indidem semper, sed aut
'aequinoctialis' oriens dicitur, cum in circulo currit
qui appellatur ἰσημερινός, aut 'solstitialis,' quae
sunt θεριναὶ τροπαί, aut 'brumalis,' quae sunt

6 χειμεριναὶ τροπαί. Item cadit sol non in eundem
semper locum. Fit enim similiter occasus eius aut

7 'aequinoctialis' aut 'solstitialis' aut 'brumalis.' Qui
ventus igitur ab oriente verno, id est aequinoctiali,
venit, nominatur 'eurus,' ficto vocabulo, ut isti

8 ἐτυμολογικοὶ aiunt, ὁ ἀπὸ τῆς ἠοῦς ῥέων. Is alio
quoque a Graecis nomine ἀφηλιώτης, Romanis

9 nauticis 'subsolanus' cognominatur. Sed qui ab
aestiva et solstitiali orientis meta venit, Latine
'aquilo,' βορέας Graece dicitur, eumque propterea
quidam dicunt ab Homero αἰθρηγενέτην appellatum;
boream autem putant dictum ἀπὸ τῆς βοῆς, quoniam

10 sit violenti flatus et sonori. Tertius ventus, qui ab
oriente hiberno spirat—'volturnum' Romani vocant—, eum plerique Graeci mixto nomine, quod
inter notum et eurum sit, εὐρόνοτον appellant.

---

[1] Since the Latin terms for "east" and "west" mean the
sun's "rising" and "setting."

[2] This at the summer solstice would be far to the north.

[3] *Odyss.* v. 296.

[4] That is, from the clear, bright sky, often attending the
sunrise.

since there was no general agreement as to their designations, positions or number.

Then Favorinus ran on as follows: "It is well known," said he, "that there are four quarters and regions of the heavens—east, west, south and north. East and west are movable and variable points[1]; south and north are permanently fixed and unalterable. For the sun does not always rise in exactly the same place, but its rising is called either *equinoctial* when it runs the course which is called ἰσημερινός (with equal days and nights), or *solsticial*, which is equivalent to θεριναὶ τροπαί (summer turnings), or *brumal*, which is the same as χειμεριναὶ τροπαί, or 'winter turnings.' So too the sun does not always set in the same place; for in the same way its setting is called *equinoctial, solstitial*, or *brumal*. Therefore the wind which blows from the sun's spring, or *equinoctial*, rising is called *eurus*, a word derived, as your etymologists say, from the Greek which means 'that which flows from the east.' This wind is called by the Greeks by still another name, ἀφηλιώτης, or 'in the direction of the sun'; and by the Roman sailors, *subsolanus* (lying beneath the sun). But the wind that comes from the summer and solstitial point of rising[2] is called in Latin *aquilo*, in Greek βορέας, and some say it was for that reason that Homer called[3] it αἰθρηγενέτης, or 'ether-born'[4]; but *boreas*, they think, is so named ἀπὸ τῆς βοῆς, 'from the loud shout,' since its blast is violent and noisy. To the third wind, which blows from the point of the winter rising—the Romans call it *volturnus*—many of the Greeks give a compound name, εὐρόνοτος, because it is between *eurus* and *notus*. These

11 Hi sunt igitur tres venti orientales: 'aquilo,' 'vol-
12 turnus,' 'eurus,' quorum medius eurus est. His
oppositi et contrarii sunt alii tres occidui: 'caurus,'
quem solent Graeci appellare[1] ἀργεστήν: is adversus aquilonem flat; item alter 'favonius,' qui
Graece ζέφυρος vocatur: is adversus eurum flat;
tertius 'Africus,' qui Graece λίψ: is[2] adversus
13 volturnum facit. Hae duae regiones caeli orientis
occidentisque inter sese adversae sex habere ventos
14 videntur. Meridies autem, quoniam certo atque
fixo limite est, unum meridialem ventum habet: is
Latine 'auster,' Graece νότος nominatur, quoniam
est nebulosus atque umectus; νοτίς enim Graece
15 umor nominatur. Septentriones autem habent ob
eandem causam unum. Is obiectus derectusque in
austrum, Latine 'septentrionarius,' Graece ἀπαρ-
16 κτίας appellatus. Ex his octo ventis alii quattuor
ventos detrahunt atque id facere se dicunt Homero
auctore, qui solos quattuor ventos noverit: eurum,
17 austrum, aquilonem, favonium, a quattuor caeli partibus, quas quasi primas nominavimus, oriente scilicet
atque occidente latioribus atque simplicibus, non
18 tripertitis. Partim autem sunt qui pro octo duodecim faciant, tertios quattuor in media loca in-

---

[1] appellare, *added by Hertz.*   [2] is, *added in σ.*

---

[1] From ἀργής, "white, brilliant." The Latin equivalent
was *argestis*, which, according to Isidor (*Orig.* xiii. 11. 10), the
common people corrupted into *agrestis*.

[2] Perhaps connected with *foveo*, as a mild, pleasant wind;
see *Thes. Ling. Lat.*, *s.v.* Or with *faveo, Faunus*, Walde,
Etym. Lat. Dict.

[3] From λείβω, Lat. *libo*, "pour, pour out."

[4] The derivation of *auster* is uncertain; see *Thes. Ling.
Lat.*, *s.v.* Walde connects it with words meaning "east"
and "eastern," adding "Merkwürdig ist die Bedeutung

then are the three east winds: *aquilo, vollurnus*
and *eurus*, and *eurus* lies between the other two.
Opposite to and facing these are three other
winds from the west: *caurus*, which the Greeks
commonly call ὀργεστής[1] or 'clearing'; this blows
from the quarter opposite *aquilo*. There is a second,
favonius,[2] which in Greek is called ζέφυρος, blowing from the point opposite to *eurus*; and a third,
Africus, which in Greek is λίψ,[3] or 'wet-bringing,'
blows in opposition to *vollurnus*. These two opposite
quarters of the sky, east and west, have, as we see,
six winds opposite to one another. But the south,
since it is a fixed and invariable point, has but
one single south wind; this in Latin is termed
auster, in Greek νότος, because it is cloudy and
wet, for νοτίς is the Greek for 'moisture.'[4] The
north too, for the same reason, has but one wind.
This, called in Latin *septentrionarius*, in Greek
ἀπαρκτίας, or ' from the region of the Bear,' is directly
opposite to *auster*. From this list of eight winds
some subtract four, and they declare that they do so
on the authority of Homer,[5] who knows only four
winds: *eurus, auster, aquilo* and *favonius*, blowing
from the four quarters of the heaven which we have
named primary, so to speak ; for they regard the
east and west as broader, to be sure, but nevertheless single and not divided into three parts.
There are others, on the contrary, who make twelve
winds instead of eight, by inserting a third group

'Sudwind,' nicht 'Ostwind'; doch ist auch in der Vogel-
schau die Richtung gegen Osten teilweise durch die Richtung
nach Süden abgelost." But Thurneysen (*T. L. L.*) remarks :
" Sed ab his Latini nominis significatus nimium distat."
    [5] *Odyss.* v. 295, 331.

serentes circum meridiem et septentriones eadem
ratione qua secundi quattuor intersiti sunt inter
primores duos apud orientem occidentemque.

19 "Sunt porro alia quaedem nomina quasi peculiarum
ventorum, quae incolae in suis quisque regionibus
fecerunt aut ex locorum vocabulis in quibus colunt,
aut[1] ex alia qua causa quae ad faciendum vocabulum

20 acciderat. Nostri namque Galli ventum ex sua terra
flantem, quem saevissimum patiuntur, 'circium' ap-

21 pellant a turbine, opinor, eius ac vertigine; ex
Ἰαπυγίας ipsius ore proficiscentem, quasi sinibus,
Apuli eodem quo ipsi sunt nomine 'Iapygem' dicunt.

22 Eum esse propemodum caurum existimo; nam et
est occidentalis et videtur exadversum eurum flare.

23 Itaque Vergilius Cleopatram e navali proelio in
Aegyptum fugientem vento iapyge ferri ait, ecum
quoque Apulum eodem quo ventum vocabulo 'iapy-

24 gem' appellavit. Est etiam ventus nomine 'caecias.'
quem Aristotoles ita flare dicit, ut nubes non procul
propellat, sed ut ad sese vocet, ex quo versum istum
proverbialem factum ait:

Ἕλκων ἐφ' αὑτὸν ὥστε καικίας νέφος.

25 Praeter hos autem, quos dixi, sunt alii plurifariam
venti commenticii et suae quisque regionis indigenae,

---

[1] aut, *added by J. F. Gronov.*

---

[1] That is, the Gauls of Gallia Narbonensis. Favorinus
was a native of Arelate, the modern Arles.
[2] Text and meaning are very uncertain. No satisfactory
explanation of *ore* or *sinibus* has been offered, so far as I
know. Apuleius, *De Mundo* 14, says : Apuli "Iapagem"
eum (ventum) ex Iapygae sinu, id est ex ipso Gargano
venientem (appellant).

of four in the intervening space about the south
and north, in the same way that the second four are
placed between the original two at east and west.

" There are also some other names of what might
be called special winds, which the natives have
coined each in their own districts, either from the
designations of the places in which they live or
from some other reason which has led to the
formation of the word. Thus our Gauls [1] call the
wind which blows from their land, the most violent
wind to which they are exposed, *circius*, doubtless
from its whirling and stormy character; the Apulians
give the name *Iapyx*—the name by which they
themselves are known (*Iapyges*)—to the wind that
blows from the mouth of Ἰαπυγία itself, from its
inmost recesses, as it were.[2] This is, I think, about
the same as *caurus*; for it is a west wind and seems
to blow from the quarter opposite *eurus*. Therefore
Virgil says [3] that Cleopatra, when fleeing to Egypt
after the sea-fight, was borne onward by Iapyx, and
he called [4] an Apulian horse by the same name as
the wind, that is, Iapyx. There is also a wind
named *caecias*, which, according to Aristotle [5] blows
in such a way as not to drive away clouds, but to
attract them. This, he says, is the origin of the
proverbial line: [6]

Attracting to oneself, as *caecias* does the clouds.

Moreover, besides these which I have mentioned
there are in various places other names of winds,
of new coinage and each peculiar to its own region,

[3] *Aen.* viii. 709.   [4] *Aen.* xi. 678.
[5] *Meteor.* ii. 6; *Prob.* xxvi. 29.
[6] Trag. fr. adesp. 75, Nauck.[2]

ut est Horatianus quoque ille 'atabulus,' quos ipsos quoque exsecuturus fui; addidissemque eos qui 'etesiae' et 'prodromi' appellitantur, qui certo tempore anni, cum canis oritur, ex alia atque alia parte caeli spirant; rationesque omnium vocabulorum, quoniam plus paulo adbibi, effutissem, nisi multa iam prosus omnibus vobis reticentibus verba fecissem,

26 quasi fieret a me ἀκρόασις ἐπιδεικτική. In convivio autem frequenti loqui solum unum neque honestum est," inquit, "neque commodum."

27 Haec nobis Favorinus in eo, quod dixi, tempore apud mensam suam summa cum elegantia verborum totiusque sermonis comitate atque gratia denarravit.

28 Sed, quod ait ventum qui ex terra Gallia flaret "circium" appellari, M. Cato in libris *Originum*

29 eum ventum "cercium" dicit, non "circium." Nam cum de Hispanis scriberet, qui citra Hiberum colunt, verba haec posuit: "Set in his regionibus ferrareae, argentifodinae pulcherrimae, mons ex sale mero magnus; quantum demas, tantum adcrescit. Ventus cercius, cum loquare, buccam implet, armatum hominem, plaustrum oneratum percellit."

30 Quod supra autem dixi, ἐτησίας ex alia atque alia caeli parte flare, haut scio an secutus opinionem

31 multorum temere dixerim. P. enim Nigidii, in

---

[1] *Serm.* i. 5. 78. The wind corresponds to the sirocco. Porphyrio, *ad loc.* gives the fanciful derivation, ἀπὸ τοῦ ἐs τὴν ἄτην βάλλειν πάντα. The *Thes. Ling. Lat.* connects it with *Atabuli*, the name of an Aethiopian tribe.

[2] "Periodic," or "trade" winds, referring especially to the Egyptian monsoon, which blow from the north-west during the whole summer (Herodotus, ii, 20); used also of winds which blow from the north in the Aegean for forty days after the rising of the Dog-star.

for example the *Atabulus* of Horace;[1] these too I intended to discuss; I would also have added those which are called *etesiae*[2] and *prodromi*,[3] which at a fixed time of year, namely when the dog-star rises, blow from one or another quarter of the heavens; and since I have drunk a good bit, I would have prated on about the meaning of all these terms, had I not already done a deal of talking while all of you have been silent, as if I were delivering 'an exhibition speech.' But for one to do all the talking at a large dinner-party," said he, "is neither decent nor becoming."

This is what Favorinus recounted to us at his own table at the time I mentioned, with extreme elegance of diction and in a delightful and graceful style throughout. But as to his statement that the wind which blows from the land of Gaul is called *circius*, Marcus Cato in his *Origins*[4] calls that wind, not *circius*, but *cercius*. For writing about the Spaniards who dwell on this side the Ebro, he set down these words: "But in this district are the finest iron and silver mines, also a great mountain of pure salt; the more you take from it, the more it grows. The *cercius* wind, when you speak, fills your mouth; it overturns an armed man or a loaded wagon."

In saying above that the ἐτησίαι blow from one or another quarter of the heavens, although following the opinion of many, I rather think I spoke hastily.[5]

---

[1] "Preceding" the *etesiae*, and blowing north-north-east for eight days before the rising of the Dog-star.

[4] Fr. 93, Peter.

[5] Gellius, as he sometimes does elsewhere, refers to Favorinus' statement as if it were his own. Gronovius' proposed change to *dixit* and *dixerit* is unnecessary.

secundo librorum quos *De Vento* composuit, verba
haec sunt: " Et ἐτησίαι et austri anniversarii secundo sole flant." Considerandum igitur est, quid
sit secundo sole.

XXIII

Consultatio diiudicatioque locorum facta ex comoedia Menandri et Caecilii, quae *Plocium* inscripta est.

1   Comoedias lectitamus nostrorum poetarum sump-
tas ac versas de Graecis Menandro aut Posidippo
aut Apollodoro aut Alexide et quibusdam item aliis
2 comicis.   Neque, cum legimus eas, nimium sane
displicent, quin lepide quoque et venuste scriptae
videntur,[1] prorsus ut melius posse fieri nihil cen-
3 seas.   Set enim[2] si conferas et compoaas Graeca
ipsa, unde illa venerunt, ac singula considerate atque
apte iunctis et alternis lectionibus committas, oppido
quam iacere atque sordere incipiunt quae Latina
sunt ; ita Graecarum, quas aemulari nequiverunt,
facetiis atque luminibus obsolescunt.
4.5   Nuper adeo usus huius rei nobis venit.   Caecili
Plocium legebamus ; hautquaquam mihi et qui
6 aderant displicebat.   Libitum et Menandri quoque
Plocium legere, a quo istam comoediam verterat.
7 Sed enim postquam in manus Menander venit, a
principio statim, di boni, quantum stupere atque
frigere quantumque mutare a Menandro Caecilius

---

[1] videntur, *Skutsch ;* videantur, ω.
[2] Set enim, *Hertz ;* etenim, ω.

---

[1] Fr. 104, Swoboda.

For in the second book of Publius Nigidius' treatise *On Wind* are these words:[1] "Both the ἐτησίαι and the annual south winds follow the sun." We ought therefore to inquire into the meaning of "follow the sun."

XXIII

A discussion and comparison of passages taken from the comedy of Menander and that of Caecilius, entitled *Plocium*.

I often read comedies which our poets have adapted and translated from the Greeks—Menander or Posidippus, Apollodorus or Alexis, and also some other comic writers. And while I am reading them, they do not seem at all bad; on the contrary, they appear to be written with a wit and charm which you would say absolutely could not be surpassed. But if you compare and place beside them the Greek originals from which they came, and if you match individual passages, reading them together alternately with care and attention, the Latin versions at once begin to appear exceedingly commonplace and mean; so dimmed are they by the wit and brilliance of the Greek comedies, which they were unable to rival.

Only recently I had an experience of this kind. I was reading the *Plocium* or *Necklace* of Caecilius, much to the delight of myself and those who were present. The fancy took us to read also the *Plocium* of Menander, from which Caecilius had translated the said comedy. But after we took Menander in hand, good Heavens! how dull and lifeless, and how different from Menander did Caecilius appear!

visus est! Diomedis hercle arma[1] et Glauci non
8 dispari magis pretio existimata sunt. Accesserat
dehinc lectio ad eum locum, in quo maritus senex
super uxore divite atque deformi querebatur, quod
ancillam suam, non inscito puellam ministerio et
facie haut inliberali, coactus erat venundare, sus-
pectam uxori quasi paelicem. Nihil dicam ego,
quantum differat; versus utrimque eximi iussi et
9 aliis ad iudicium faciundum exponi. Menander sic:

> Ἐπ' ἀμφότερα νῦν ἠπίκληρος ἡ καλή
> Μέλλει καθευδήσειν. Κατείργασται μέγα
> Καὶ περιβόητον ἔργον· ἐκ τῆς οἰκίας
> Ἐξέβαλε τὴν λυποῦσαν, ἣν ἐβούλετο,
> ῞Ιν' ἀποβλέπωσι πάντες εἰς τὸ Κρωβύλης
> Πρόσωπον ᾖ τ' εὔγνωστος οὖσ' ἐμὴ γυνή
> Δέσποινα. Καὶ τὴν ὄψιν, ἣν ἐκτήσατο,
> ῎Ονος ἐν πιθήκοις, τοῦτο δὴ τὸ λεγόμενον
> ῎Εστιν. Σιωπᾶν βούλομαι τὴν νύκτα τήν
> Πολλῶν κακῶν ἀρχηγόν. Οἴμοι Κρωβύλην
> Λαβεῖν ἔμ', ἐκκαίδεκα τάλαντα προῖκα καί[2]
> Τὴν ῥῖν' ἔχουσαν πηχέως· εἶτ' ἐστὶ τό
> Φρύαγμά πως ὑπόστατον; μὰ τὸν Δία
> Τὸν Ὀλύμπιον καὶ τὴν Ἀθηνᾶν, οὐδαμῶς.
> Παιδισκάριον θεραπευτικὸν δὲ καὶ λόγου
> † Τάχιον ἀπαγέσθω δέ τις ἄρ' ἀντεισαγάγοι.

10 Caecilius autem sic:

> Is démum miser est, qui aérumnam suám néscit
> occultáre.

[1] arma, ς, *Vulg.*; amerca, ω; munera, *Lion.*
[2] προῖκα καί, *Allison.*

---

[1] Homer (*Iliad* vi. 234 ff) tells us that Diomedes proposed
to exchange armour with Glaucus in token of friendship.
Diomedes' arms of bronze cost nine oxen; those of Glaucus,

Upon my word, the armour of Diomedes and of Glaucus were not more different in value.[1]   Our reading had reached the passage where the aged husband was complaining of his rich and ugly wife, because he had been forced to sell his maid-servant, a girl skilled at her work and very good looking, since his wife suspected her of being his mistress. I shall say nothing of the great difference; but I have had the lines of both poets copied and submitted to others for their decision.   This is Menander:[2]

> Now may our heiress fair on both ears sleep.
> A great and memorable feat is hers;
> For she has driven forth, as she had planned,
> The wench that worried her, that all henceforth
> Of Crobyle alone the face may see,
> And that the famous woman, she my wife,
> May also be my tyrant.   From the face
> Dame Nature gave her, she's an ass 'mong apes,
> As says the adage.   I would silent be
> About that night, the first of many woes.
> Alas that I took Crobyle to wife,
> With sixteen talents and a foot of nose.
> Then too can one her haughtiness endure?
> By Zeus Olympius and Athena, no!
> She has dismissed a maid who did her work
> More quickly than the word was given her,
> More quickly far than one will bring her back!

But Caecilius renders it thus:[3]

> In very truth is he a wretched man,
> Who cannot hide his woe away from home;

inlaid with gold, a hundred.   Hence "gold for bronze" became proverbial.
    [2] Fr. 402, Kock; p. 428, *L.C.L.*   [3] vv. 142 ff., Ribbeck[2].

Foris :[1] íta me uxor forma ét factís facit, sí taceam,
   tamen íudicium.
Quae nísi dotem, ómnia quaé nolis habet; quí
   sapiet, de mé discet,
Qui quási ad hostis captús liber servío salva urbe
   atque árce.
Quaen[2] míhi quidquid placet éo privatum id me
   servatam velim?
Dum ego éius mortem inhio, égomet vivo mórtuus
   inter vivos.
Éa me clam se cúm mea ancilla aít consuetum,
   id me árguit;
Íta plorando, orándo, instando atque óbiurgando
   me óbtudit
      Eam utí venderém; nunc credo ínter suás
      Aequális et cognátas sermoném serit:
         "Quís vestrarúm fuit íntegra aetátula,
            Quae hóc idem a viro
         Ímpetrarít suo, quód ego anus modo
      Efféci, paelice út meum privarém virum?
   Haéc erunt concília hodie, dífferor sermóne miser."

11   Praeter venustatem autem rerum atque verborum,
   in duobus libris nequaquam parem, in hoc equidem
   soleo animum attendere, quod quae Menander prae-
   clare et apposite et facete scripsit, ea Caecilius, ne
12   qua potuit quidem, conatus est enarrare, sed quasi
   minime probanda praetermisit et alia nescio quae
   mimica inculcavit et illud Menandri de vita hominum media sumptum, simplex et verum et delecta-
   bile, nescio quo pacto omisit.   Idem enim ille
   maritus senex cum altero sene vicino colloquens
   et uxoris locupletis superbiam deprecans, haec ait:

---

[1] foris, *Ribbeck.*   [2] quaen, *Ribbeck;* quae, ω.

And that my wife makes me by looks and acts:
If I kept still, I should betray myself
No less.   And she has all that you would wish
She had not, save the dowry that she brought.
Let him who's wise a lesson take from me,
Who, like a free man captive to the foe,
Am slave, though town and citadel are safe.
What! wish her safe who steals whate'er I prize?
While longing for her death, a living corpse am I.
She says I've secret converse with our maid—
That's what she said, and so belaboured me
With tears, with prayers, with importunities,
That I did sell the wench. Now, I suppose,
She blabs like this to neighbours and to friends:
" Which one of you, when in the bloom of youth,
Could from her husband win what I from mine
Have gained, who've robbed him of his concubine."
Thus they, while I, poor wretch, am torn to
    shreds.

Now, not to mention the charm of subject matter
and diction, which is by no means the same in
the two books, I notice this general fact—that
some of Menander's lines, brilliant, apt and witty,
Caecilius has not attempted to reproduce, even
where he might have done so; but he has passed
them by as if they were of no value, and has dragged
in some other farcical stuff; and what Menander
took from actual life, simple, realistic and delightful,
this for some reason or other Caecilius has missed.
For example, that same old husband, talking with
another old man, a neighbour of his, and cursing the
arrogance of his rich wife, says:[1]

[1] Fr. 403, Kock ; p. 428, *L.C.L.*

Ἔχω δ' ἐπίκληρον Λάμιαν· οὐκ εἴρηκά σοι
Τοῦτ'; εἶτ' ἄρ' οὐχί; κυρίαν τῆς οἰκίας
Καὶ τῶν ἀγρῶν καὶ † πάντων ἀντ' ἐκείνης
Ἔχομεν, Ἄπολλον, ὡς χαλεπῶν χαλεπώτατον·
Ἅπασι δ' ἀργαλέα 'στίν, οὐκ ἐμοὶ μόνῳ,
Υἱῷ, πολὺ μᾶλλον θυγατρί—Πρᾶγμ' ἄμαχον λέγεις.
—Εὖ οἶδα.

13 Caecilius vero hoc in loco ridiculus magis quam
personae isti quam tractabat aptus atque conveniens
videri maluit. Sic enim haec corrupit:

Sed túa morosane úxor, quaeso, est?—Quám
rogas?
Qui tándem?—Taedet méntionis, quáe mihi,
Ubí domum advení, adsédi, extemplo sávium
Dat iéiuna anima.—Níl peccat de sávio.
Ut dévomas vult, quod foris potáveris.

14   Quid de illo quoque loco, in utraque comoedia
posito, existimari debeat, manifestum est, cuius loci
15 haec ferme sententia: Filia hominis pauperis in
16 pervigilio vitiata est. Ea res clam patrem fuit, et
17 habebatur pro virgine. Ex eo vitio gravida men-
18 sibus exactis parturit. Servus bonae frugi, cum pro
foribus domus staret et propinquare partum erili
filiae atque omnino vitium esse oblatum ignoraret,
gemitum et ploratum audit puellae in puerperio
enitentis; timet, irascitur, suspicatur, miseretur,
19 dolet. Hi omnes motus eius affectionesque animi

I have to wife an heiress ogress, man !
I did not tell you that ?   What, really ? no ?
She is the mistress of my house and lands,
Of all that's hereabout.   And in return
I have by Zeus ! the hardest of hard things.
She scolds not only me, but her son too,
Her daughter most of all.—You tell a thing
There's no contending with.—I know it well.

But in this passage Caecilius chose rather to play
the buffoon than to be appropriate and suitable
to the character that he was representing.   For this
is the way he spoiled the passage : [1]

But tell me, sir ; is your wife captious, pray ?—
How can you ask ?—But in what manner, then?—
I am ashamed to tell.   When I come home
And sit beside her, she with fasting [2] breath
Straight kisses me.—There's no mistake in that.
She'd have you spew up what you've drunk
    abroad.

It is clear what your judgment ought to be about
that scene also, found in both comedies, which is
about of the following purport : The daughter of a
poor man was violated during a religious vigil.   This
was unknown to her father, and she was looked
upon as a virgin.   Being with child as the result
of that assault, at the proper time she is in labour.
An honest slave, standing before the door of the
house, knowing nothing of the approaching delivery
of his master's daughter, and quite unaware that
violence had been offered her, hears the groans and
prayers of the girl labouring in childbirth ; he gives
expression to his fear, anger, suspicion, pity and
grief.   In the Greek comedy all these emotions and

in Graeca quidem comoedia mirabiliter acres et
illustres, apud Caecilium autem pigra istaec omnia
20 et a rerum dignitate atque gratia vacua sunt. Post,
ubi idem servus percontando quod acciderat rep-
perit, has apud Menandrum voces facit:

> Ὦ τρὶς κακοδαίμων, ὅστις ὢν πένης γαμεῖ
> Καὶ παιδοποιεῖ. Ὡς ἀλόγιστός ἐστ' ἀνήρ,
> Ὃς μήτε φυλακὴν τῶν ἀναγκαίων ἔχει,
> Μήτ', ἂν ἀτυχήσῃ εἰς τὰ κοινὰ τοῦ βίου,
> Ἐπαμφιέσαι δύναιτο τοῦτο χρήμασιν,
> Ἀλλ' ἐν ἀκαλύπτῳ καὶ ταλαιπώρῳ βίῳ
> Χειμαζόμενος ζῇ, τῶν μὲν ἀνιαρῶν ἔχων
> Τὸ μέρος ἁπάντων, τῶν δ' ἀγαθῶν οὐδὲν μέρος.
> Ὑπὲρ γὰρ ἑνὸς ἀλγῶν ἅπαντας νουθετῶ.

21 Ad horum autem sinceritatem veritatemque verborum an adspiraverit Caecilius, consideremus.
Versus sunt hi Caecili trunca quaedam ex Menandro
dicentis et consarcinantis verba tragici tumoris:

> Is demum infórtunatus ést homo,
> Paupér qui educit ín egestatem líberos,
> Cuí fortuna et rés ut est continuó patet.
> Nam opuléntó famam fácile occultat fáctio:

22 Itaque, ut supra dixi, cum haec Caecilii seorsum
lego, neutiquam videntur ingrata ignavaque, cum
autem Graeca comparo et contendo, non puto
Caecilium sequi debuisse quod assequi nequiret.[1]

---

[1] assequi nequiret, σ; assequiret, ω.

feelings of his are wonderfully vivid and clear, but in Caecilius they are all dull and without any grace and dignity of expression. Afterwards, when the same slave by questioning has found out what has happened, in Menander he utters this lament : [1]

> Alas! thrice wretched he who weds, though poor,
> And children gets. How foolish is the man
> Who keeps no watch o'er his necessities,
> And if he luckless be in life's routine,
> Can't use his wealth as cloak, but buffeted
> By ev'ry storm, lives helpless and in grief.
> All wretchedness he shares, of blessings none,
> Thus sorrowing for one I'd all men warn.

Let us consider whether Caecilius was sufficiently inspired to approach the sincerity and realism of these words. These are the lines of Caecilius, in which he gives some mangled fragments from Menander, patching them with the language of tragic bombast : [2]

> Unfortunate in truth the man, who poor,
> Yet children gets, to share his poverty.
> His fortune and his state at once are clear ;
> The ill fame of the rich their set conceals.

Accordingly, as I said above, when I read these passages of Caecilius by themselves, they seem by no means lacking in grace and spirit, but when I compare and match them with the Greek version, I feel that Caecilius should not have followed a guide with whom he could not keep pace.

[1] Fr. 404, Kock ; p. 430, *L.C.L.*   [2] vv. 169 ff., Ribbeck.[3]

XXIV

De vetere parsimonia ; deque antiquis legibus sumptuariis.

1 Parsimonia apud veteres Romanos et victus atque cenarum tenuitas non domestica solum observatione ac disciplina, sed publica quoque animadversione legumque complurium sanctionibus custodita est. 2 Legi adeo nuper in Capitonis Atei *Coniectaneis* senatus decretum vetus C. Fannio et M. Valerio Messalla consulibus factum, in quo iubentur principes civitatis, qui ludis Megalensibus antiquo ritu "mutitarent," id est mutua inter sese dominia agitarent, iurare apud consules verbis conceptis, non amplius in singulas cenas sumptus se[1] esse facturos quam centenos vicenosque aeris praeter olus et far et vinum, neque vino alienigena, sed patriae usuros, neque argenti in convivio plus pondo quam[2] libras centum inlaturos.

3 Sed post id senatus consultum lex Fannia lata est, quae ludis Romanis, item ludis plebeis et Saturnalibus et aliis quibusdam diebus, in singulos dies centenos aeris insumi concessit decemque aliis diebus in singulis mensibus tricenos, ceteris autem 4 diebus omnibus denos. Hanc Lucilius poeta legem significat, cum dicit :

Fanni centussis misellus.

[1] se, *added by Hertz.*
[2] quam, *omitted by J. F. Gronov;* quam libras, *omitted by Mommsen.*

---

[1] Fr. 5, Huschke ; 6, Bremer.   [2] 161 B.C.
[3] The Megalensian or Megalesian festival, on April 4. The games eventually extended from the 4th to the 10th inclusive. Only the nobles gave dinner parties on the 4th ; the plebeians celebrated at the Cerealia, April 19.

XXIV

On the ancient frugality ; and on early sumptuary laws.

FRUGALITY among the early Romans, and moderation in food and entertainments were secured not only by observance and training at home, but also by public penalties and the inviolable provisions of numerous laws. Only recently I read in the *Miscellanies*[1] of Ateius Capito an old decree of the senate, passed in the consulship of Gaius Fannius and Marcus Valerius Messala,[2] which provides that the leading citizens, who according to ancient usage "interchanged" at the Melagesian games[3] (that is, acted as host to one another in rotation), should take oath before the consuls in set terms, that they would not spend on each dinner more than one hundred and twenty asses in addition to vegetables, bread and wine ; that they would not serve foreign, but only native, wine, nor use at table more than one hundred pounds' weight of silverware.

But subsequent to that decree of the senate the law of Fannius was passed, which allowed the expenditure of one hundred asses a day at the Roman and the plebeian games,[4] at the Saturnalia,[5] and on certain other days ; of thirty asses on ten additional days each month ; but on all other days of only ten. This is the law to which the poet Lucilius alludes when he says :[6]

The paltry hundred pence of Fannius.

[4] The *ludi Romani* in Cicero's time extended from Sept. 5 to 19 ; the *ludi plebei*, at first probably held on one day, finally lasted from Nov. 4 to 17.

[5] Originally on Dec. 17 ; extended to seven days, of which five (under Augustus, three) were legal holidays.

[6] 1172, Marx.

5 In quo erraverunt quidam commentariorum in Lucilium scriptores, quod putaverunt Fannia lege perpetuos in omne dierum genus centenos aeris 6 statutos. Centum enim aeris Fannius constituit, sicuti supra dixi, festis quibusdam diebus eosque ipsos dies nominavit, aliorum autem dierum omnium in singulos dies sumptum inclusit intra aeris alias tricenos, alias denos.

7 Lex deinde Licinia rogata est, quae cum certis diebus, sicuti Fannia, centenos aeris inpendi permisisset, nuptiis ducenos indulsit ceterisque diebus statuit aeris tricenos; cum et carnis aridae[1] et salsamenti certa pondera in singulos dies constituisset, quidquid esset natum[2] e terra, vite, arbore, 8 promisce atque indefinite largita est. Huius legis 9 Laevius poeta meminit in *Erotopaegniis*. Verba Laevii haec sunt, quibus significat haedum, qui ad epulas fuerat adlatus, dimissum cenamque ita ut lex Licinia sanxisset, pomis oleribusque instructam;

> Lex Licinia (inquit) introducitur,
> Lux liquida haedo redditur.

10 Lucilius quoque legis istius meminit in his verbis:

> Legem vitemus Licini.

11 Postea L. Sulla dictator, cum, legibus istis situ atque senio oblitteratis, plerique in patrimoniis

---

[1] aridae, ς, *Macr.* iii., 17. 9; autem, ω.
[2] natum, ς, *Macr.* ; tamen, ω.

---

[1] Probably in 103 B.C.
[2] Fr. 23, Bährens, *Frag. Poet. Rom.*, p. 292. *Erotopaegnia* means " Playful Verses about Love " ; a sixth book is cited by Charisius (i. 204 K). One fragment indicates that Laevius

In regard to this some of the commentators on
Lucilius have been mistaken in thinking that
Fannius' law authorized a regular expenditure of a
hundred asses on every kind of day. For, as I have
stated above, Fannius authorized one hundred asses
on certain holidays which he expressly named, but
for all other days he limited the daily outlay to
thirty asses for some days and to ten for others.

Next the Licinian law was passed [1] which, while
allowing the outlay of one hundred asses on designated days, as did the law of Fannius, conceded two
hundred asses for weddings and set a limit of thirty
for other days ; however, after naming a fixed weight
of dried meat and salted provisions for each day, it
granted the indiscriminate and unlimited use of the
products of the earth, vine and orchard. This law
the poet Laevius mentions in his *Erotopaegnia*.[2]
These are the words of Laevius, by which he means
that a kid that had been brought for a feast was
sent away and the dinner served with fruit and
vegetables, as the Licinian law had provided :

> The Licinian law is introduced,
> The liquid light to the kid restored.

Lucilius also has the said law in mind in these
words :

> Let us evade the law of Licinius. [3]

Afterwards, when these laws were illegible from
the rust of age and forgotten, when many men of
abundant means were gormandizing, and recklessly

was a contemporary of Varro. His brief and scanty fragments show great variety in metre (cf. Prisc. ii. 258 K), and
innovations in diction (Gell. xix. 7.)

[3] 1200, Marx.

amplis elluarentur et familiam pecuniamque suam prandiorum conviviorumque[1] gurgitibus proluissent, legem ad populum tulit qua cautum est ut Kalendis, Idibus, Nonis diebusque ludorum et feriis quibusdam sollemnibus sestertios trecenos in cenam insumere ius potestasque esset, ceteris autem diebus omnibus non amplius tricenos.

12 Praeter has leges Aemiliam quoque legem invenimus, qua lege non sumptus cenarum, sed ciborum genus et modus praefinitus est.

13 Lex deinde Antia praeter sumptum aeris id etiam sanxit, ut qui magistratus esset magistratumve capturus esset, ne quo ad cenam, nisi ad certas personas, itaret.

14 Postrema lex Iulia ad populum pervenit Caesare Augusto imperante, qua profestis quidem diebus ducenti finiuntur, Kalendis, Idibus, Nonis et aliis quibusdam festis trecenti, nuptiis autem et repotiis sestertii mille.

15 Esse etiam dicit Capito Ateius edictum—divine vero[2] Augusti an Tiberii Caesaris non satis commemini—quo edicto per dierum varias sollemnitates a trecentis sestertiis adusque duo sestertia sumptus cenarum propagatus est, ut his saltem finibus luxuriae effervescentis aestus coerceretur.

pouring their family and fortune into an abyss of
dinners and banquets, Lucius Sulla in his dictatorship
proposed a law to the people, which provided that
on the Kalends, Ides and Nones, on days of games,
and on certain regular festivals, it should be proper
and lawful to spend three hundred sesterces on a
dinner, but on all other days no more than thirty.

Besides these laws we find also an Aemilian law,[1]
setting a limit not on the expense of dinners, but on
the kind and quantity of food.

Then the law of Antius,[2] besides curtailing outlay,
contained the additional provision, that no magistrate or magistrate elect should dine out anywhere,
except at the house of stipulated persons.

Lastly, the Julian law came before the people
during the principate of Caesar Augustus,[3] by which
on working days two hundred sesterces is the limit,
on the Kalends, Ides and Nones and some other
holidays, three hundred, but at weddings and the
banquets following them, a thousand.

Ateius Capito says [4] that there is still another
edict—but whether of the deified Augustus or of
Tiberius Caesar I do not exactly remember—by
which the outlay for dinners on various festal days
was increased from three hundred sesterces to two
thousand, to the end that the rising tide of luxury
might be restrained at least within those limits.

---

[1] 78 B.C.   Another Aemilian sumptuary law was passed
in 115 B.C.
[2] Passed a few years after the Aemilian law.
[3] Cf. Suet. *Aug.* xxxiv, 1.   [4] Fr, 6, Huschke ; 7, Bremer.

---

[1] conviviorum, *added by Hertz. ;* cenarum, *Salmasius.*
[2] vero, *added by Skutsch* ; rue, nerve, *MSS.*

XXV

Quid Graeci ἀναλογίαν, quid contra ἀνωμαλίαν vocent.

1 In Latino sermone, sicut in Graeco, alii ἀνα-
2 λογίαν sequendam putaverunt, alii ἀνωμαλίαν.
'Αναλογία est similium similis declinatio, quam
3 quidam Latine " proportionem " vocant. 'Ανωμαλία
est inaequalitas declinationum, consuetudinem se-
4 quens. Duo autem Graeci grammatici illustres,
Aristarchus et Crates, summa ope ille ἀναλογίαν,
5 hic ἀνωμαλίαν defensitavit. M. Varronis liber ad
Ciceronem *De Lingua Latina* octavus nullam esse
observationem similium docet inque omnibus paene
6 verbis consuetudinem dominari ostendit : " Sicuti
cum dicimus," inquit, " ' lupus lupi,' ' probus probi '
et ' lepus leporis,' item ' paro paravi ' et ' lavo lavi,'
' pungo pupugi,' ' tundo tutudi ' et ' pingo pinxi.'
7 Cumque," inquit, " a ' ceno ' et ' prandeo ' et ' poto,'
et ' cenatus sum ' et ' pransus sum ' et ' potus sum '
dicamus, a ' destringor ' tamen et ' extergeor ' et
' lavor,' ' destrinxi ' et ' extersi ' et ' lavi ' dicimus.
8 Item cum dicamus ab ' Osco,' ' Tusco,' ' Graeco,'
' Osce,' ' Tusce,' ' Graece,' a ' Gallo ' tamen et
' Mauro ' ' Gallice ' et ' Maurice ' dicimus ; item a
' probus ' ' probe,' a[1] ' doctus ' ' docte,' sed a[1] ' rarus '
non dicitur ' rare,' sed alii ' raro ' dicunt, alii
9 ' rarenter.' " Idem M. Varro[2] in eodem libro :

---

[1] a, ς ; *omitted by* ω.
[2] idem M. *Skutsch* ; inde mauro, ω ; eodem Varro, *A.*

---

[1] viii, p. 146, G. & S.
[2] That is, *pransus, potus* and *cenatus* are used in an active
sense ; see Cic. *pro Mil.* 56, adde inscitiam pransi, poti,
oscitantis ducis, and Priscian (ii. 565. 17, Keil) ut " cenatus
sum " . . . pro " cenavi."

XXV

What the Greeks understand by ἀναλογία, and, on the
contrary, by ἀνωμαλία.

In the Latin language, just as in Greek, some
have thought that the principle of ἀναλογία should
be followed, others that of ἀνωμαλία. Ἀναλογία is
the similar inflection of similar words, which some
call in Latin *proportio*, or "regularity." Ἀνωμαλία
is irregularity in inflection, following usage. Now
two distinguished Greek grammarians, Aristarchus
and Crates, defended with the utmost vigour, the
one analogy, the other anomaly. The eighth book
of Marcus Varro's treatise *On the Latin Language*,
dedicated to Cicero, maintains[1] that no regard is
paid to regularity, and points out that in almost all
words usage rules. "As when we decline," says
he, "*lupus lupi*, *probus probi*, but *lepus leporis*;
again, *paro paravi* and *lavo lavi*, *pungo pupugi*,
tundo tutudi and *pingo pinxi*. And although,"
he continues, "from *ceno* and *prandeo* and *poto*
we form *cenatus sum*, *pransus sum* and *potus
sum*,[2] yet from *destringor* and *extergeor* and *lavor*
we make *destrinxi* and *extersi* and *lavi*. Furthermore, although from *Oscus*, *Tuscus* and *Graecus*
we derive the adverbs *Osce*, *Tusce* and *Graece*,
yet from *Gallus* and *Maurus* we have *Gallice*
and *Maurice*; also from *probus probe*, from *doctus
docte*, but from *rarus* there is no adverb *rare*,
but some say *raro*, others *rarenter*.[3]" In the
same book Varro goes on to say: "No one uses

---

[3] Charisius (i. 217. 8, Keil), cites *rare* from Cicero, Cato
and Plautus, but the modern texts do not admit the form.

"Sentior," inquit, "nemo dicit et id per se nihil est, 'adsentior' tamen fere omnes dicunt. Sisenna unus 'adsentio' in senatu dicebat et eum postea multi secuti, neque tamen vincere consuetudinem
10 potuerunt." Sed idem Varro in aliis libris multa
11 pro ἀναλογίᾳ tuenda scribit. Sunt igitur ii tamquam loci quidam communes, contra ἀναλογίαν dicere et item rursum pro ἀναλογίᾳ.

XXVI

Sermones[1] M. Frontonis et Favorini philosophi de generibus colorum vocabulisque eorum Graecis et Latinis ; atque inibi color spadix cuiusmodi sit.

1 Favorinus philosophus cum ad M. Frontonem consularem pedibus aegrum visum iret, voluit me
2 quoque ad eum secum ire. Ac deinde, cum ibi aput Frontonem plerisque viris doctis praesentibus sermones de coloribus vocabulisque eorum agitarentur, quod multiplex colorum facies, appellationes
3 autem incertae et exiguae forent, "plura," inquit "sunt" Favorinus, "in sensibus oculorum quam in
4 verbis vocibusque colorum discrimina. Nam, ut alias eorum inconcinnitates[2] omittamus, simplices isti rufus et viridis colores singula quidem vocabula,
5 multas autem species differentis habent. Atque eam vocum inopiam in lingua magis Latina video quam in Graeca. Quippe qui 'rufus' color a rubore quidem appellatus est, sed cum aliter rubeat ignis, aliter

[1] sermonem, ω.
[2] inconcinnitates, *Mommsen* ; concinnitates, ω.

[1] Haec argumenta quae transferri in multas causas possunt

sentior and that form by itself is naught, but almost everyone says *adsentior*. Sisenna alone used to say *adsentio* (I agree) in the senate, but later many followed his example, yet could not prevail over usage." But Varro himself in other books wrote a good deal in defence of analogy. Therefore his utterances on the subject are, as it were, commonplaces,[1] to cite now against analogy and again also in its favour.

XXVI

Discourses of Marcus Fronto and the philosopher Favorinus on the varieties of colours and their Greek and Latin names: and incidentally, the nature of the colour *spadix*.

WHEN the philosopher Favorinus was on his way to visit the exconsul Marcus Fronto, who was ill with the gout, he wished me also to go with him. And when there at Fronto's, where a number of learned men were present, a discussion took place about colours and their names, to the effect that the shades of colours are manifold, but the names for them are few and indefinite, Favorinus said : " More distinctions of colour are detected by the eye than are expressed by words and terms. For leaving out of account other incongruities, your simple colours, red (*rufus*) and green (*viridis*), have single names, but many different shades. And that poverty in names I find more pronounced in Latin than in Greek. For the colour red (*rufus*) does in fact get its name from redness, but although fire is one kind of red, blood

locos communes nominamus. Cic. *De Inv.* ii. 48 ; cf. *Brut.* 46. and Quintilian *passim*.

sanguis, aliter ostrum, aliter crocum, aliter aurum,[1]
has singulas rufi varietates Latina oratio singulis pro-
priisque vocabulis non demonstrat omniaque ista
significat una ' ruboris' appellatione, nisi[2] cum ex
ipsis rebus vocabula colorum mutuatur et ' igneum'
aliquid dicit et ' flammeum' et 'sanguineum' et
6 ' croceum' et ' ostrinum' et 'aureum.' ' Russus'[3]
enim color et ' ruber' nimirum[4] a vocabulo ' rufi'
dicuntur neque proprietates eius omnes declarant,
ξανθός autem et ἐρυθρός et πυρρός et κιρρός
et φοῖνιξ habere quasdam distantias coloris rufi
videntur, vel augentes eum vel remittentes vel
mixta quadam specie temperantes."
7   Tum Fronto ad Favorinum, " Non infitias," inquit,
"imus quin lingua Graeca, quam tu videre elegisse,
prolixior fusiorque sit quam nostra ; sed in his tamen
coloribus quibus modo dixisti denominandis, non
8 proinde inopes sumus ut tibi videmur.   Non enim
haec sunt sola vocabula rufum colorem demonstran-
tia, quae tu modo dixisti, ' russus' et 'ruber,' sed
alia quoque habemus plura quam quae dicta abs te
Graeca sunt ; ' fulvus' enim et 'flavus' et 'rubidus'
et ' poeniceus' et ' rutilus' et 'luteus' et 'spadix'
appellationes sunt rufi coloris, aut acuentes eum,
quasi incendentes, aut cum colore viridi miscentes
aut nigro infuscantes aut virenti sensim albo
9 illuminantes.   Nam ' poeniceus,' quem tu Graece
φοίνικα dixisti, noster est et ' rutilus' et 'spadix,'
poenicei συνώνυμος, qui factus e Graeco[5] noster

---

[1] aliter aurum, *added by J. F. Gronov.*
[2] nisi, *added by Skutsch.*
[3] russus, *Carrio;* rufus, ω.
[4] nimirum, *suggested by Hosius;* nihil, ω ; nihil . . . dinos-
cuntur, *Hertz.*
[5] e Graeco, *J. F. Gronov*; Graece, ω.

another, purple another, saffron another, and gold still
another, yet the Latin tongue does not indicate
these special varieties of red by separate and
individual words, but includes them all under the
one term *rubor*, except in so far as it borrows names
from the things themselves, and calls anything 'fiery,'
'flaming,' 'blood-red,' 'saffron' 'purple' and 'golden.'
For *russus* and *ruber* are no doubt derived from
rufus, and do not indicate all its special varieties,
but ξανθός and ἐρυθρός and πυρρός and κιρρός¹ and
φοῖνιξ seem to mark certain differences in the colour
red, either intensifying it or making it lighter, or
qualifying it by the admixture of some shade."

Then Fronto, replying to Favorinus, said : "I do
not deny that the Greek language, which you seem
to prefer, is richer and more copious than ours; but
nevertheless in naming these colours of which you
have just spoken we are not quite so badly off as
you think. For *russus* and *ruber*, which you have
just mentioned, are not the only words that denote
the colour red, but we have others also, more
numerous than those which you have quoted from
the Greek. For *fulvus, flavus, rubidus, poeniceus,
rutilus, luteus* and *spadix* are names of the colour
red, which either brighten it (making it fiery, as
it were), or combine it with green, or darken it
with black, or make it luminous by a slight addition
of gleaming white. For *poeniceus*, which you
call φοῖνιξ in Greek, belongs to our language, and
rutilus and *spadix*, a synonym of *poeniceus* which
is taken over into Latin from the Greek, in-

¹ κιρρός "tawny, orange-tawny" designates a shade between ξανθός, "yellow," and πυρρός, "flame-coloured."

est, exuberantiam splendoremque significant ruboris,
quales sunt fructus palmae arboris non admodum
sole incocti, unde spadici et poeniceo nomen est;
10 σπάδικα enim Dorice[1] vocant avulsum e palma
11 termitem cum fructu. 'Fulvus' autem videtur de
rufo atque viridi mixtus in aliis plus viridis, in aliis
plus rufi habere. Sic poeta verborum diligentissimus
'fulvam' aquilam dicit et iaspidem, 'fulvos' galeros
et 'fulvum' aurum et arenam 'fulvam' et 'fulvum'
leonem, sicque Ennius in *Annalibus* 'aere fulvo'[2] dixit.
12 'Flavus' contra videtur e viridi et rufo et albo con-
cretus; sic 'flaventes comae' et, quod mirari quosdam
video, frondes olearum a Vergilio 'flavae' dicuntur,
13 sic multo ante Pacuvius aquam 'flavam' dixit et
'fulvum' pulverem. Cuius versus, quoniam sunt iu-
cundissimi, libens commemini:

Cédo tuum[3] pedém mi,[4] lymphis flávis fulvum ut
púlverem
Mánibus isdem, quíbus Ulixi sáepe permulsi,[5]
ábluam,
Lássitudinémque minuam mánuum[6] mollitúdine.

14 "Rubidus' autem est rufus atrior et nigrore multo
15 inustus, 'luteus' contra rufus color est dilutior;
16 inde ei nomen quoque esse factum videtur. Non
igitur," inquit, "mi Favorine, species rufi coloris
plures aput Graecos quam aput nos nominantur.

[1] Dorice, *suggested by Hosius* ; Dorici, ω.
[2] fulva, *Gell.* xiii. 21. 14.
[3] tuum, *Fleckeisen* ; tum, ω.
[4] *added by Peerlkamp.*
[5] permulsis, ω.   [6] manum, ω.

[1] Virg. *Aen.* xi. 751.   [2] *id.* iv. 261.   [3] *id.* vii. 688.
[4] *id.* vii. 279, *etc.*   [5] *id.* v. 374, *etc.*   [6] ii. 722, *etc.*

214

dicate a rich, gleaming shade of red like that of
the fruit of the palm-tree when it is not fully
ripened by the sun. And from this *spadix* and
poeniceus get their name; for *spadix* in Doric
is applied to a branch torn from a palm-tree along
with its fruit. But the colour *fulvus* seems to
be a mixture of red and green, in which sometimes
green predominates, sometimes red. Thus the poet
who was most careful in his choice of words applies
fulvus to an eagle,[1] to jasper,[2] to fur caps,[3] to
gold,[4] to sand,[5] and to a lion;[6] and so Ennius in his
Annals uses *fulvus* of air.[7] *Flavus* on the other
hand seems to be compounded of green and red and
white; thus Virgil speaks of golden hair as *flava*[8]
and applies that adjective also to the leaves of the
olive,[9] which I see surprises some; and thus,
much earlier, Pacuvius called water *flava* and dust
fulvus.[10] I am glad to quote his verses, for they
are most charming:

Give me thy foot, that with the same soft hands
With which oft times I did Ulysses soothe
I may with golden (*flavis*) waters wash away
The tawny (*fulvum*) dust and heal thy weariness.

" Now, *rubidus* is a darker red and with a larger
admixture of black; *luteus*, on the other hand, is
a more diluted red, and from this dilution its name
too seems to be derived. Therefore, my dear
Favorinus," said he, " the shades of red have no
more names in Greek than with us. But neither

---

[7] 454 Vahlen.[2] Ennius has *fulva*; and is so quoted by
Gellius in xiii. 21. 14.
[8] *Aen.* iv. 590.   [9] *Aen.* v. 309.   [10] v. 244, Ribbeck.[3]

17 Sed ne viridis quidem color pluribus a vobis vocabu-
18 lis dicitur, neque non potuit Vergilius, colorem equi
significare viridem volens, 'caerulum' magis dicere
ecum quam 'glaucum,' sed maluit verbo uti notiore
19 Graeco quam inusitato Latino. Nostris autem
veteribus 'caesia' dicta est, quae a Graecis γλαυκῶπις, ut Nigidius ait, de colore caeli, quasi caelia."

20   Postquam haec Fronto dixit, tum Favorinus
scientiam rerum uberem verborumque eius elegantiam exosculatus, "Absque te," inquit, "uno forsitan
lingua profecto Graeca longe anteisset, sed tu, mi
Fronto, quod in versu Homerico est, id facis :

Καί νύ κεν ἢ παρέλασσας ἢ ἀμφήριστον ἔθηκας.

21 Sed cum omnia libens audivi quae peritissime dixisti,
tum maxime quod varietatem flavi coloris enarrasti
fecistique ut intellegerem verba illa ex *Annali*
quarto decimo Ennii amoenissima, quae minime
intellegebam :

Verrunt extemplo placide [1] mare marmore flavo
Caeruleum, spumat sale [2] conferta rate pulsum ;

22 non enim videbatur 'caeruleum' mare cum 'marmore
23 flavo' convenire. Sed cum sit, ita ut dixisti, flavus
color [3] e viridi et albo mixtus, pulcherrime prorsus
spumas virentis maris 'flavom marmor' appellavit."

---

[1] placide, ω ; placidum, *Hertz* (*Parrhasius*).
[2] sale, *Priscian ;* mare, *MSS.*   [3] colore, ω.

---

[1] *Georg.* iii. 82, *honesti spadices glaucique.* We should
use "grey," rather than "green." *Glaucus* was a greyish
green or a greenish grey. Since *caerulus* and *caeruleus* are
not unusual words, Gellius probably means "unusual" as
applied to a horse. Ovid, *Fasti* iv. 446, uses *caeruleus* of the
horses of Pluto, but in the sense of "dark, dusky."
[2] Fr. 72, Swoboda.   [3] *Iliad,* xxiii. 382.

is the colour green expressed by more terms in
your language, and Virgil, when he wished to indicate the green colour of a horse, could perfectly
well have called the horse *caerulus* rather than
glaucus, but he preferred to use a familiar Greek
word, rather than one which was unusual in Latin.[1]
Moreover, our earlier writers used *caesia* as the
equivalent of the Greek γλαυκῶπις, as Nigidius says,[2]
from the colour of the sky, as if it were originally
caelia."

After Fronto had said this, Favorinus, enchanted
with his exhaustive knowledge of the subject and
his elegant diction, said : " Were it not for you, and
perhaps for you alone, the Greek language would
surely have come out far ahead ; but you, my dear
Fronto, exemplify Homer's line : [3]

Thou would'st either have won or made the
result indecisive.

But not only have I listened with pleasure to all
your learned remarks, but in particular in describing
the diversity of the colour *flavus* you have made
me understand these beautiful lines from the fourteenth book of Ennius' *Annals*,[4] which before I did
not in the least comprehend :

The calm sea's golden marble now they skim ;
Ploughed by the thronging craft, the green seas
foam ;

for 'the green seas' did not seem to correspond
with 'golden marble.' But since, as you have said,
flavus is a colour containing an admixture of green
and white, Ennius with the utmost elegance called
the foam of the green sea 'golden marble.'"

[4] v. 384 f., Vahlen [2], who reads *placide* and *sals*.

XXVII

Quid T. Castricius existimarit super Sallustii verbis et Demosthenis, quibus alter Philippum descripsit, alter Sertorium.

1 VERBA sunt haec gravia atque illustria de rege Philippo Demosthenis: Ἑώρων δ' αὐτὸν τὸν Φίλιππον, πρὸς ὃν ἦν ἡμῖν ὁ ἀγών, ὑπὲρ ἀρχῆς καὶ δυναστείας τὸν ὀφθαλμὸν ἐκκεκομμένον, τὴν κλεῖν κατεαγότα, τὴν χεῖρα, τὸ σκέλος πεπηρωμένον, πᾶν ὅτι βουληθείη μέρος ἡ τύχη τοῦ σώματος παρελέσθαι, τοῦτο προϊέμενον, ὥστε 2 τῷ λοιπῷ μετὰ τιμῆς καὶ δόξης ζῆν. Haec aemulari volens Sallustius de Sertorio duce in *Historiis* ita scripsit : "Magna gloria tribunus militum in Hispania T. Didio imperante, magno usui bello Marsico paratu militum et armorum fuit, multaque tum ductu eius iussuque[1] patrata[2] primo per ignobilitatem, deinde per invidiam scriptorum incelebrata[3] sunt, quae vivus facie sua ostentabat aliquot adversis cicatricibus et effosso oculo. Quin ille dehonestamento corporis maxime laetabatur, neque illis anxius,[4] quia reliqua gloriosius retinebat." 3 De utriusque his verbis T. Castricius cum iudicaret, "Nonne," inquit, "ultra naturae humanae modum est, dehonestamento corporis laetari? Siquidem laetitia dicitur exultatio quaedam animi gaudio efferventior eventu rerum expetitarum. 4 Quanto illud sincerius veriusque[5] et humanis magis

---

[1] iussu, *added by Hertz.*   [2] patrata, *Dietsch* ; rapta, *ω.*
[3] celebrata, *ω* ; incelebrata, *J. Gronov* ; celata, *Ciacconi.*
[4] neque illis anxius *before* quin, *Maurenbrecher.*
[5] verius, *an addition suggested by Hosius* ; sinceriusque et, *ω.*

---

[1] *De Cor.* 67.   [2] i. 88, Maurenbrecher.

XXVII

The criticism of Titus Castricius passed upon passages from Sallust and Demosthenes, in which the one described Philip, the other Sertorius.

THIS is Demosthenes' striking and brilliant description of king Philip:[1] "I saw that Philip himself, with whom we were struggling, had in his desire for empire and absolute power had one eye knocked out, his collar-bone broken, his hand and leg maimed, and was ready to resign any part of his body that fortune chose to take from him, provided that with what remained he might live in honour and glory." Sallust, desiring to rival this description, in his *Histories* thus wrote of the leader Sertorius[2]: "He won great glory in Spain, while military tribune under the command of Titus Didius, rendered valuable service in the Marsic war in providing troops and arms; but he got no credit for much that was then done under his direction and orders, at first because of his low birth and afterwards through unfriendly historians; but during his lifetime his appearance bore testimony to these deeds, in many scars on his breast, and in the loss of an eye. Indeed, he rejoiced greatly in his bodily disfigurement, caring nothing for what he had lost, because he kept the rest with greater glory."

In his estimate of these words of the two writers Titus Castricius said: "Is it not beyond the range of human capability to rejoice in bodily disfigurement? For rejoicing is a certain exaltation of spirit, delighting in the realization of something greatly desired. How much truer, more natural, and more

condicionibus [1] conveniens : πᾶν ὅτι ἂν βουληθείη
μέρος ἡ τύχη τοῦ σώματος παρελέσθαι, τοῦτο προϊέμε-
5 νον. Quibus verbis," inquit, " ostenditur Philippus,
non, ut Sertorius, corporis dehonestamento laetus,
quod est," inquit, "insolens et inmodicum, sed prae
studio laudis et honoris iacturarum damnorumque
corporis contemptor, qui singulos artus suos for-
tunae prodigendos daret quaestu atque compendio
gloriarum."

XXVIII

Non esse compertum cui deo rem divinam fieri oporteat, cum terra movet.

1 QUAENAM esse causa videatur quamobrem terrae
tremores fiant, non modo his communibus hominum
sensibus opinionibusque incompertum,[2] sed ne inter
physicas quidem philosophias satis constitit vento-
rumne vi accidant specus hiatusque terrae subeuntium
an aquarum subter in terrarum cavis undantium
pulsibus fluctibusque, ita uti videntur existimasse
antiquissimi Graecorum, qui Neptunum σεισί-
χθονα appellaverunt, an cuius aliae rei causa al-
teriusve dei vi ac numine, nondum etiam, sicuti
2 diximus, pro certo creditum. Propterea veteres
Romani, cum in omnibus aliis vitae officiis, tum in
constituendis religionibus atque in dis inmortalibus
animadvertendis castissimi cautissimique, ubi terram
movisse senserant nuntiatumve erat, ferias eius rei

---

[1] conditionibus, *J. F. Gronov*; communibus, ω.
[2] incompertum, *Skutsch*; compertum, *MSS.*

in accordance with human limitations is this : ' Giving up whatever part of his body fortune chose to take.' In these words," said he, " Philip is shown, not like Sertorius, rejoicing in bodily disfigurement, which," he said, "is unheard of and extravagant, but as a scorner of bodily losses and injuries in his thirst for honour and glory, who in exchange for the fame which he coveted would sacrifice his limbs one by one to the attacks of fortune."

XXVIII

That it is uncertain to which deity sacrifices ought to be offered when there is an earthquake.

WHAT is to be regarded as the cause of earthquakes is not only not obvious to the ordinary understanding and thought of mankind, but it is not agreed even among the natural philosophers whether they are due to the mighty winds that gather in the caverns and hollow places of the earth, or to the ebb and flow of subterranean waters in its hollows, as seems to have been the view of the earliest Greeks, who called Neptune "the Earth Shaker"; or whether they are the result of something else or due to the divine power of some other god—all this, I say, is not yet a matter of certain knowledge. For that reason the Romans of old, who were not only exceedingly scrupulous and careful in discharging all the other obligations of life, but also in fulfilling religious duties and venerating the immortal gods, whenever they felt an earthquake or received report of one, decreed a holy day on that account, but forbore to declare and specify in the decree, as is commonly

causa edicto imperabant, sed dei nomen, ita uti
solet, cui servari ferias oporteret, statuere et edicere
quiescebant, ne alium pro alio nominando falsa
3 religione populum alligarent. Eas ferias si quis
polluisset piaculoque ob hanc rem opus esset,
hostiam " si deo, si deae" immolabant, idque ita ex
decreto pontificum observatum esse M. Varro dicit,
quoniam et qua vi et per quem deorum dearumve
terra tremeret incertum esset.

4   Sed de lunae solisque defectionibus, non minus in
5 eius rei causa reperienda sese exercuerunt.   Quippe
M. Cato, vir in cognoscendis rebus multi studii, in-
certa tamen et incuriose super ea re opinatus est.
6 Verba Catonis ex *Originum* quarto haec sunt : " Non
lubet scribere quod in tabula apud pontificem maximum est, quotiens annona cara, quotiens lunae aut
7 solis lumine caligo aut quid obstiterit." Usque
adeo parvi fecit rationes veras solis et lunae
deficientium vel scire vel dicere.

XXIX

Apologus Aesopi Phrygis memoratu non inutilis

1   AESOPUS ille e Phrygia fabulator haut inmerito
sapiens existimatus est, cum quae utilia monitu sua-
suque erant, non severe neque imperiose praecepit et
censuit, ut philosophis mos est, sed festivos delecta-

---

¹ Fr. 1, p. cliii, Merkel.   ² Fr. 77, Peter.

done, the name of the god in whose honour the holy day was to be observed; for fear that by naming one god instead of another they might involve the people in a false observance. If anyone had desecrated that festival, and expiation was therefore necessary, they used to offer a victim "to either the god or goddess," and Marcus Varro tells us [1] that this usage was established by a decree of the pontiffs, since it was uncertain what force, and which of the gods or goddesses, had caused the earthquake.

But in the case of eclipses of the sun or moon they concerned themselves no less with trying to discover the causes of that phenomenon. However, Marcus Cato, although a man with a great interest in investigation, nevertheless on this point expressed himself indecisively and superficially. His words in the fourth book of his *Origins* are as follows: [2] "I do not care to write what appears on the tablet of the high priest: how often grain was dear, how often darkness, or something else, obscured the light [3] of sun or moon." Of so little importance did he consider it either to know or to tell the true causes of eclipses of the sun and moon.

XXIX

A fable of the Phrygian Aesop, which is well worth telling.

AESOP, the well-known fabulist from Phrygia, has justly been regarded as a wise man, since he taught what it was salutary to call to mind and to recommend, not in an austere and dictatorial manner, as is the way of philosophers, but by inventing witty and

[3] Lumine is the old dat., cf. *II viri iure dicundo* and note 1, p. 153.

bilesque apologos commentus, res salubriter ac pro-
spicienter animadversas in mentes animosque ho-
2 minum cum audiendi quadam inlecebra induit. Velut
haec eius fabula de aviculae nidulo lepide atque
iucunde promonet, spem fiduciamque rerum quas
efficere quis possit haut umquam in alio, sed in se-
3 metipso habendam. "Avicula," inquit, "est parva,
4 nomen est cassita. Habitat nidulaturque in segeti-
bus, id ferme temporis, ut appetat messis pullis iam
5 iam plumantibus. Ea cassita in sementes forte
congesserat tempestiviores; propterea frumentis
flavescentibùs pulli etiam tunc involucres erant.
6 Dum igitur ipsa iret cibum pullis quaesitum, monet
eos ut, si quid ibi rei novae fieret dicereturve,
animadverterent idque uti sibi, ubi redisset, nuntia-
7 rent. Dominus postea segetum illarum filium
adulescentem vocat et 'Videsne,' inquit, 'haec
ematuruisse et manus iam postulare? Idcirco die
crastini, ubi primum diluculabit, fac amicos eas et
roges veniant operamque mutuam dent et messim
8 hanc nobis adiuvent.' Haec ubi ille dixit, et
discessit. Atque ubi redit cassita, pulli tremibundi,
trepiduli circumstrepere orareque matrem ut iam
statim properet inque alium locum sese asportet;
'nam dominus,' inquiunt, 'misit qui amicos roget
9 uti luce oriente veniant et metant.' Mater iubet
eos otioso animo esse: 'Si enim dominus,' inquit,
'messim ad amicos reicit, crastino seges non metetur
10 neque necessum est hodie uti vos auferam.' Die,"

---

[1] A shorter version, of 19 choliambic lines, is given by
Babrius, 88; cf. *Fabulae Aesopiae*, 210 Halm, and Avianus, 21,
(14 elegiac verses).

entertaining fables he put into men's minds and
hearts ideas that were wholesome and carefully
considered, while at the same time he enticed their
attention.   For example, this fable of his[1] about the
little nest of a birdlet with delightful humour warns
us that in the case of things which one can do, hope
and confidence should never be placed in another,
but in one's own self.   "There is a little bird,"
he says, "it is called the lark.   It lives in the
grainfields, and generally builds its nest at such a
time that the harvest is at hand exactly when the
young birds are ready to be fledged.   Such a lark
chanced to have built her nest in a field which had
been sown rather early in the year; therefore when
the grain was turning yellow, the fledglings were
still unable to fly.   Accordingly, when the mother
went off in search of food for her young, she warned
them to notice whether anything unusual was said
or done there, and to tell it to her on her return.
A little later the owner of that grainfield calls his
young son and says: 'Do you not see that this is ripe
and already calls for hands?   To-morrow then, as
soon as it is light, see that you go to our friends and
ask them to come and exchange work with us, and
help us with this harvest.'   So saying, he at once
went away.   And when the lark returned, the chicks,
frightened and trembling, twittered about their
mother and implored her to make haste and at once
carry them off to some other place; 'for,' said they,
'the master has sent to ask his friends to come at
daybreak and reap.'   The mother bids them be easy
in mind.   'For if the master,' said she, 'has turned
the harvesting over to his friends, the field will not
be reaped to-morrow, and I need not take you away

inquit, " postero mater in pabulum volat. Dominus
quos rogaverat opperitur. Sol fervit, et fit nihil ;
11 it [1] dies, et amici nulli eunt. Tum ille rursum ad
filium ' amici isti magnam partem,' inquit, ' cessa-
tores sunt. Quin potius imus et cognatos adfinesque [2] nostros oramus ut assint cras tempori ad
12 metendum ? ' Itidem hoc pulli pavefacti matri
nuntiant. Mater hortatur ut tum quoque sine metu
ac sine cura sint, cognatos adfinesque nullos ferme
tam esse obsequibiles ait, ut ad laborem capessendum
nihil cunctentur et statim dicto oboediant : ' Vos
modo,' inquit, ' advertite, si modo quid denuo
13 dicetur.' Alia luce orta avis in pastum profecta est.
Cognati et adfines opera,[3] quam dare rogati sunt
14 supersederunt. Ad postremum igitur dominus filio :
' Valeant,' inquit, ' amici cum propinquis. Afferes
primo luci [4] falces duas ; unam egomet mihi et tu
tibi capies alteram et frumentum nosmetipsi manibus
15 nostris cras metemus.' Id ubi ex pullis dixisse
dominum mater audivit, ' Tempus,' inquit, ' est
cedendi et abeundi ; fiet nunc dubio procul quod
futurum dixit. In ipso enim iam vertitur cuia res
16 est, non in alio, unde petitur.' Atque ita cassita
nidum migravit, seges a domino demessa est."

17 Haec quidem est Aesopi fabula de amicorum et
18 propinquorum levi plerumque et inani fiducia. Sed
quid aliud sanctiores libri philosophorum monent
19 quam ut in nobis tantum ipsis nitamur, alia autem
omnia quae extra nos extraque nostrum animum sunt
20 neque pro nostris neque pro nobis ducamus ? Hunc

---

[1] it, *J. F. Gronov* ; et, *ω*.
[2] adfines amicosque, *MSS.*
[3] opera, *suggested by Hosius* (*cf.* x. 14. 1) ; operam, *MSS.*
[4] primo luci, *P ;* prima luce, *ω*.

to-day.' On the following day the mother flies off to get food. The master waits for those whom he had summoned. The sun grows hot and nothing is done. The day advances and no friends come. Then he says again to his son : 'Those friends of ours are a lot of slackers. Why not rather go and ask our relatives and kinsfolk to come to reap early to-morrow ?' This, too, the frightened chicks tell their mother. She urges them once again to be without fear and without worry, saying that hardly any relatives and kinsfolk are so obliging as to undertake labour without any delay and to obey a summons at once. 'But do you,' she said, 'observe whether anything more is said.' Next day at dawn the bird left to forage. The relatives and kinsfolk neglected the work which they were asked to do. So finally the owner said to his son : 'Enough of friends and relatives. Bring two scythes at daybreak ; I myself will take one and you yourself the other, and to-morrow we ourselves will reap the grain with our own hands.' When the mother heard from her brood that the farmer had said this, she cried : 'It is time to get out and be off; for this time what he said surely will be done. For now it depends on the very man whose business it is, not on another who is asked to do it.' And so the lark moved her nest, the owner harvested his crop.''

This then is Aesop's fable, showing that trust in friends and relatives is usually idle and vain. But what different warning do the more highly revered books of the philosophers give us, than that we should rely on ourselves alone, and regard everything else that is outside us and beyond our control as helpful neither to our affairs nor to ourselves ? This parable

Aesopi apologum Q. Ennius in *Satiris* scite admodum
et venuste versibus quadratis composuit. Quorum
duo postremi isti sunt, quos habere cordi et memoriae
operae pretium esse hercle puto :

> Hóc erit tibi árgumentum sémper in promptú [1]
> situm :
> Né quid expectés amicos, quód tute agere póssies.

XXX

Quid observatum sit in undarum motibus, quae in mari
alio atque alio modo fiunt austris flantibus aquiloni-
busque.

1 Hoc saepenumero in undarum motu, quas aqui-
lones venti quique ex eadem caeli regione aer fluit,
2 faciunt . . .[2] in mari austri atque Africi. Nam fluctus,
qui flante aquilone maximi et creberrimi excitantur,
simul ac ventus posuit, sternuntur et conflaccescunt
3 et mox fluctus esse desinunt. At non idem fit
flante austro vel Africo ; quibus iam nihil spirantibus
undae tamen factae diutius tument et a vento
quidem iamdudum tranquillae [3] sunt, sed mare est
4 etiam atque etiam undabundum. Eius rei causa
esse haec coniectatur, quod venti a septentrionibus,
ex altiore caeli parte in mare incidentes, deorsum in
aquarum profunda quasi praecipites deferuntur un-
dasque faciunt non prorsus inpulsas, sed imitus
commotas, quae tantisper erutae volvuntur, dum

---

[1] promptu, *T*; promptum, *ω*.
[2] *lacuna indicated by Mommsen, who suggested:* animadversum
est ut diversus sit ab eo quem faciunt, *which is followed in
the translation.*
[3] *Beroaldus ;* tranquilla, *MSS.*

---

[1] vv. 57-58, Vahlen, who reads *in promptum* in the first verse.

of Aesop has been rendered in tetrameter verse by Quintus Ennius in his *Saturae* most cleverly and gracefully.[1] The following are the last two lines of that version, and I surely think it is worth while to remember them and take them to heart:

> This adage ever have in readiness;
> Ask not of friends what you yourself can do.

XXX

An observation on the waves of the sea, which take one form when the wind is from the south, and another when it is from the north.

It has often been observed in the motion of the waves caused by the north winds or by any current of air from that quarter of the heaven [that it is different from that caused by] the south and south-west winds. For the waves raised by the blowing of the north wind are very high and follow hard upon one another, but as soon as the wind has ceased, they flatten out and subside, and soon there are no waves at all. But it is not the same when the wind blows from the south or southwest; for although these have wholly ceased to blow, still the waves that they have caused continue to swell, and though they have long been undisturbed by wind, yet the sea keeps continually surging. The reason of this is inferred to be, that the winds from the north, falling upon the sea from a higher part of the sky, are borne straight down, as it were headlong, into the depths of ocean, making waves that are not driven forward, but are set in motion from within; and these, being turned up from beneath, roll only so long as the force of that wind which blows in

5 illius infusi desuper spiritus vis manet. Austri vero et Africi, ad meridianum orbis circulum et ad partem axis infimam depressi, inferiores et humiles, per suprema aequoris euntes protrudunt magis fluctus quam eruunt, et idcirco non desuper laesae, sed propulsae in adversum aquae, etiam desistente flatu, retinent aliquantisper de pristino pulsu impetum.

6 Id autem ipsum quod dicimus ex illis quoque Homericis versibus, si quis non incuriose legat,

7 adminiculari potest. Nam de austri flatibus ita scripsit:

> Ἔνθα νότος μέγα κῦμα ποτὶ σκαιὸν ῥίον ὠθεῖ,

8 contra autem de borea, quem "aquilonem" nos appellamus, alio dicit modo:

> Καὶ βορέης αἰθρηγενέτης μέγα κῦμα κυλίνδων.

9 Ab aquilonibus enim, qui alti supernique sunt, fluctus excitatos quasi per prona volvi dicit, ab austris autem, his qui humiliores sunt, maiore vi [1]

10 quadam propelli sursum [2] atque subici. Id enim significat verbum ὠθεῖ, sicut alio in loco:

> Λᾶαν ἄνω ὤθεσκε ποτὶ λόφον.

11 Id quoque a peritissimis rerum philosophis observatum est, austris spirantibus mare fieri glaucum et caeruleum, aquilonibus obscurius atriusque. Cuius rei causam, cum Aristotelis libros *Problematorum* praecerperemus, notavi.

---

[1] vi, ς ; ut, ω.   [2] sursum, σ ; rursum, ω.

---

[1] That is, away from, or before, the wind, so that they are flattened and do not rise in surges.
[2] *Odyss.* iii. 295.   [3] *Odyss.* v. 296.
[4] *Odyss.* xi. 596.   [5] xxvi. 37.

from above continues. The south and southwest
winds, on the contrary, forced down to the southern
zone and the lowest part of the heavens, are lower
and flatter, and as they blow over the surface of the
sea, they push forward[1] the waves rather than raise
them up. Therefore the waters are not struck from
above but are forced forward, and even after the
wind has fallen they retain for some time the motion
given by the original impulse. Moreover, this very
suggestion of mine may be supported by the following lines of Homer, if one reads them carefully. For
he wrote thus of the blasts of the south wind : [2]

> Then Notus drives huge waves against the western
> cliff,

but on the other hand he speaks in a different way
of boreas, which we call aquilo : [3]

> And Boreas aetherborn, uprolling a great wave.

For he means that the waves stirred up by the north
winds, which are high and blow from above, are so to
speak rolled downward, but that by the south winds,
which are lower than these, they are driven forward
in an upward direction by a somewhat greater force
and pushed up. For that is the meaning of the
verb ὠθεῖ, as also in another passage : [4]

> The stone toward the hilltop pushed he up.

This also has been observed by the most learned
investigators of nature, that when the south winds
blow, the sea becomes blue and bright, but, under
the north winds, darker and more gloomy. I noted
the cause of this when I was making excerpts from
the *Problems* of Aristotle.[5]

BOOK III

LIBER TERTIUS

I

Quaesitum atque tractatum quam ob causam Sallustius avaritiam dixerit non animum modo virilem, sed corpus quoque
ipsum effeminare.

1 Hieme iam decedente, apud balneas Titias in area
subcalido sole cum Favorino philosopho ambula-
bamus; atque ibi inter ambulandum legebatur *Catilina* Sallustii, quem in manu amici conspectum legi
2 iusserat. Cumque haec verba ex eo libro lecta
essent: "Avaritia pecuniae studium habet, quam
nemo sapiens concupivit; ea quasi venenis malis
imbuta corpus animumque virilem effeminat, semper
infinita et [1] insatiabilis est, neque copia neque inopia
3 minuitur," tum Favorinus me aspiciens "Quo," inquit,
"pacto corpus hominis avaritia effeminat? Quid
enim istuc sit, quod animum virilem ab ea effeminari
dixit, videor ferme assequi, set quonam modo corpus
quoque hominis effeminet nondum reperio." "Et
4 ego," inquam, "longe iamdiu in eo ipse quaerendo
fui ac, nisi tu occupasses, ultro te hoc rogassem."
5 Vix ego haec dixeram cunctabundus, atque inibi
quispiam de sectatoribus Favorini, qui videbatur esse

---

[1] *MSS. of Sall. omit* et.

---

[1] Otherwise unknown. The Baths of Titus were *Thermae*
and the adj. is *Titianae.*

BOOK III

I

A discussion of the question why Sallust said that avarice rendered effeminate, not only a manly soul, but also the very body itself.

WHEN winter was already waning, we were walking with the philosopher Favorinus in the court of the Titian baths,[1] enjoying the mild warmth of the sun; and there, as we walked, Sallust's *Catiline* was being read, a book which Favorinus had seen in the hands of a friend and had asked him to read. The following passage from that book had been recited :[2] " Avarice implies a desire for money, which no wise man covets ; steeped as it were with noxious poisons, it renders the most manly body and soul effeminate ; it is ever unbounded, nor can either plenty or want make it less." Then Favorinus looked at me and said : " How does avarice make a man's body effeminate ? For I seem to grasp in general the meaning of his statement that it has that effect on a manly soul, but how it also makes his body effeminate I do not yet comprehend." " I too," said I, " have for a long time been putting myself that question, and if you had not anticipated me, I should of my own accord have asked you to answer it."

Scarcely had I said this with some hesitation, when one of the disciples of Favorinus, who seemed

[1] xi. 3.

in litteris veterator, " Valerium," inquit, " Probum
audivi haec dicere : usum esse Sallustium circumlocu-
tione quadam poetica et, cum dicere vellet hominem
avaritia corrumpi, corpus et animum dixisse, quae
duae res hominem demonstrarent; namque homo
6 ex anima et corpore est." " Numquam," inquit
Favorinus, " quod equidem scio, tam inportuna
tamque audaci argutia fuit noster Probus, ut Sallustium, vel subtilissimum brevitatis artificem, peri-
phrasis poetarum facere diceret."

7 Erat tum nobiscum in eodem ambulacro homo
8 quispiam sane doctus. Is quoque a Favorino rogatus ecquid haberet super ea re dicere, huiuscemodi
9 verbis usus est : " Quorum," inquit, " avaritia mentem[1] tenuit et corrupit quique sese quaerundae
undique pecuniae dediderunt, eos plerosque tali
genere vitae occupatos videmus, ut sicuti alia in his
omnia prae pecunia, ita labor quoque virilis exer-
10 cendique corporis studium relictui sit. Negotiis
enim se plerumque umbraticis et sellulariis quaesti-
bus intentos habent, in quibus omnis eorum vigor
animi corporisque elanguescit, quod Sallustius ait,
' effeminatur.' "

11 Tum Favorinus legi denuo verba eadem Sallustii
iubet atque, ubi lecta sunt, " Quid igitur," inquit,
" dicimus, quod multos videre est pecuniae cupidos
12 et eosdem tamen corpore esse vegeto ac valenti ? "
Tum ille ita respondit : " Respondes non hercle
inscite. Quisquis," inquit, " est pecuniae cupiens
et corpore tamen est bene habito ac strenuo, aliarum
quoque rerum vel studio vel exercitio eum teneri

---

[1] mentem, *supplied by Dziatzko* ; avaritiam tenuit (ienuit,
V ; avaritia intenuit, *R*), ω.

to be an old hand in the study of literature, broke in : " I once heard Valerius Probus say that Sallust here used a kind of poetic circumlocution, and meaning to say that a man was corrupted by avarice, spoke of his body and soul, the two factors which indicate a man ; for man is made up of body and soul." " Never," replied Favorinus, " at least, so far as I know, was our Probus guilty of such impertinent and bold subtlety as to say that Sallust, a most skilful artist in conciseness, used poetic paraphrases."

There was with us at the time in the same promenade a man of considerable learning. He too, on being asked by Favorinus whether he had anything to say on the subject, answered to this effect : " We observe that almost all those whose minds are possessed and corrupted by avarice and who have devoted themselves to the acquisition of money from any and every source, so regulate their lives, that compared with money they neglect manly toil and attention to bodily exercise, as they do everything else. For they are commonly intent upon indoor and sedentary pursuits, in which all their vigour of mind and body is enfeebled and, as Sallust says, ' rendered effeminate.' "

Then Favorinus asked to have the same words of Sallust read again, and when they had been read, he said : " How then are we to explain the fact, that it is possible to find many men who are greedy for money, but nevertheless have strong and active bodies ? " To this the man replied thus : " Your answer is certainly to the point. Whoever," said he, " is greedy for money, but nevertheless has a body that is strong and in good condition, must necessarily be possessed either by an interest in, or devotion to,

necessum est atque in sese colendo non aeque esse
13 parcum. Nam si avaritia sola summa omnes hominis
partes affectionesque occupet et si ad incuriam usque
corporis grassetur, ut per illam unam neque virtutis
neque virium neque corporis neque animi cura adsit,
tum denique id vere dici potest effeminando esse
et animo et corpori, si[1] qui neque sese neque aliud
14 curent, nisi pecuniam." Tum Favorinus "Aut hoc,"
inquit, "quod dixisti, probabile est, aut Sallustius
odio avaritiae plus quam par fuit[2] eam criminatus
est."

II

Quemnam esse natalem diem M. Varro dicat, qui ante noctis
horam sextam postve eam nati sunt; atque inibi de temporibus terminisque dierum qui civiles nominantur et usque-
quaque gentium varie observantur; et praeterea quid Q.
Mucius scripserit super ea muliere quae a[3] marito non iure
se usurpavisset, quod rationem civilis anni non habuerit.

1 QUAERI solitum est, qui noctis hora tertia quartave
sive qua alia nati sunt, uter dies natalis haberi
appellarique debeat, isne quem nox ea consecuta
2 est, an qui dies noctem consecutus est. M. Varro
in libro *Rerum Humanarum*, quem *De Diebus* scripsit,
"homines," inquit, "qui inde a[4] media nocte ad

---

[1] si, *added by H. J. Müller.*
[2] par fuit, *suggested by Hosius;* potuit, *MSS.*; decuit, *Damsté.*
[3] quae a, *Erbius ;* quia, *ω.*
[4] inde a, *Hertz ;* in, *ω;* ex, *Macr.* i. 2. 3.

---

[1] The reading of the MSS., *potuit*, might perhaps be

other things as well, and cannot be equally niggardly in his care of himself. For if extreme avarice, to the exclusion of everything else, lay hold upon all a man's actions and desires, and if it extend even to neglect of his body, so that because of that one passion he has regard neither for virtue nor physical strength, nor body, nor soul—then, and then only, can that vice truly be said to cause effeminacy both of body and of soul, since such men care neither for themselves nor for anything else except money." Then said Favorinus : "Either what you have said is reasonable, or Sallust, through hatred of avarice, brought against it a heavier charge than he could justify."[1]

II

Which was the birthday, according to Marcus Varro, of those born before the sixth hour of the night, or after it ; and in that connection, concerning the duration and limits of the days that are termed "civil" and are reckoned differently all over the world ; and in addition, what Quintus Mucius wrote about that woman who claimed freedom from her husband's control illegally, because she had not taken account of the civil year.

IT is often inquired which day should be considered and called the birthday of those who are born in the third, the fourth, or any other hour of the night ; that is, whether it is the day that preceded, or the day that followed, that night. Marcus Varro, in that book of his *Human Antiquities* which he wrote *On Days*, says :[2] " Persons who are born during the

supported by such expressions as Catull. lxxvi. 16, *hoc facias, sive id non pote, sive pote.*
[2] xiii. Frag. 2, Mirsch.

proximam mediam noctem in his horis viginti quat-
3 tuor nati sunt, uno die nati dicuntur." Quibus
verbis ita videtur dierum observationem divisisse, ut
qui post solem occasum ante mediam noctem natus
sit, is ei dies natalis sit, a quo die ea nox coeperit ;
contra vero, qui in sex noctis horis posterioribus
nascatur, eo die videri natum, qui post eam noctem
diluxerit.

4   Athenienses autem aliter observare, idem Varro
in eodem libro scripsit, eosque a sole occaso ad solem
iterum occidentem omne id medium tempus unum
5 diem esse dicere. Babylonios porro aliter ; a sole
enim exorto ad exortum eiusdem incipientem[1] totum
6 id spatium unius diei nomine appellare ; multos vero
in terra Umbria unum et eundem diem esse dicere a
meridie ad insequentem meridiem ; "quod quidem,"
inquit, "nimis absurdum est. Nam qui Kalendis
hora sexta apud Umbros natus est, dies eius natalis videri debebit et Kalendarum dimidiarum et
qui est post Kalendas dies ante horam eius diei
sextam."

7   Populum autem Romanum ita, uti Varro dixit,
dies singulos adnumerare a media nocte ad mediam
8 proximam, multis argumentis ostenditur. Sacra sunt
Romana partim diurna, alia nocturna, sed ea quae
inter noctem fiunt diebus addicuntur, non noctibus ;
9 quae igitur sex posterioribus noctis horis fiunt, eo
die fieri dicuntur qui proximus eam noctem in-

[1] insequentem, *Damsté.*

---

[1] xiii. Frag. 3, Mirsch.
[2] That is, according to the Roman reckoning. By the
alleged Umbrian reckoning, the first day of the month would
begin at midday and end at the next midday.

twenty-four hours between one midnight and the next midnight are considered to have been born on one and the same day." From these words it appears that he so apportioned the reckoning of the days, that the birthday of one who is born after sunset, but before midnight, is the day after which that night began ; but that, on the other hand, one who is born during the last six hours of the night is considered to have been born on the day which dawned after that night.

However, Varro also wrote in that same book[1] that the Athenians reckon differently, and that they regard all the intervening time from one sunset to the next as one single day. That the Babylonians counted still differently ; for they called by the name of one day the whole space of time between sunrise and the beginning of the next sunrise ; but that in the land of Umbria many said that from midday to the following midday was one and the same day. "But this," he said, "is too absurd. For the birthday of one who is born among the Umbrians at midday on the first of the month will have to be considered as both half of the first day of the month and that part of the second day which comes before midday."[2]

But it is shown by abundant evidence that the Roman people, as Varro said, reckoned each day from midnight to the next midnight. The religious ceremonies of the Romans are performed in part by day, others by night ; but those which take place by night are appointed for certain days, not for nights ; accordingly, those that take place during the last six hours of the night are said to take place on the day which dawns immediately after that night. More-

10 lucescit. Ad hoc ritus quoque et mos auspicandi
eandem esse observationem docet; nam magistratus,
quando uno die eis auspicandum est et id super
quo auspicaverunt agendum, post[1] mediam noctem
auspicantur et post meridiem sole magno agunt,[2]
auspicatique esse et egisse eodem die dicuntur.

11 Praeterea tribuni plebei, quos nullum diem abesse
Roma licet, cum post mediam noctem proficiscuntur
et post primam facem ante mediam sequentem re-
vertuntur, non videntur afuisse unum diem, quoniam,
ante horam noctis sextam regressi, parte aliqua illius
in urbe Roma sunt.

12 Q.[3] quoque Mucium iureconsultum dicere solitum
legi, non esse usurpatam mulierem, quae, cum Kalendis Ianuariis apud virum matrimonii causa esse coe-
pisset, ante diem IV. Kalendas Ianuarias sequentes

13 usurpatum isset; non enim posse impleri trinoctium,
quod abesse a viro usurpandi causa ex *Duodecim
Tabulis* deberet, quoniam tertiae noctis posterioris
sex horae alterius anni essent, qui inciperet ex
Kalendis.

14 Istaec autem omnia de dierum temporibus et
finibus ad observationem disciplinamque iuris antiqui
pertinentia cum in libris veterum inveniremus, non
dubitabamus quin Vergilius quoque id ipsum osten-

---

[1] cum post, *Puteanus ;* dum post, *Damsté.*
[2] meridiem sole magno agunt, *Hertz ;* meridiem solem
agnum (sole magnum, *V*), ω ; meridionalem solem agunt,
Hosius.
[3] Q. *added by* ς, *Macrob.*

---

[1] Fr. 7, Huschke; *Jur. Civ.* iv. 2, Bremer.
[2] Dec. 27th; December at that time had twenty-nine days.
[3] vi. 4.
[4] *Posterioris* is nom. pl. See Varro *De Ling. Lat.* viii. 66.

over, the ceremony and method of taking the auspices point to the same way of reckoning; for the magistrates, whenever they must take the auspices, and transact the business for which they have taken the auspices, on the same day, take the auspices after midnight and transact the business after midday, when the sun is high, and they are then said to have taken the auspices and acted on the same day. Again, when the tribunes of the commons, who are not allowed to be away from Rome for a whole day, leave the city after midnight and return after the first lighting of the lamps on the following day, but before midnight, they are not considered to have been absent for a whole day, since they returned before the completion of the sixth hour of the night, and were in the city of Rome for some part of that day.

I have read that Quintus Mucius, the jurist, also used to say [1] that a woman did not become her own mistress who, after entering upon marriage relations with a man on the day called the Kalends of January, left him, for the purpose of emancipating herself, on the fourth day before the Kalends of the following January; [2] for the period of three nights, during which the *Twelve Tables* [3] provided that a woman must be separated from her husband for the purpose of gaining her independence, could not be completed, since the last [4] six hours of the third night belonged to the next year, which began on the first of January.

Now since I found all the above details about the duration and limits of days, pertaining to the observance and the system of ancient law, in the works of our early writers, I did not doubt that Virgil also

derit, non exposite atque aperte, sed, ut hominem decuit poeticas res agentem, recondita et quasi operta veteris ritus significatione :

15   Torquet (inquit) medios nox umida cursus
         Et me saevus equis oriens afflavit anhelis.

16 His enim versibus` oblique, sicuti dixi, admonere voluit, diem quem Romani "civilem" appellaverunt a sexta noctis hora oriri.

III

De noscendis explorandisque Plauti comoediis, quoniam promisce verae atque falsae nomine eius inscriptae feruntur ; atque inibi, quod Plautus in pistrino [1] et Naevius in carcere fabulas scriptitarint.

1 VERUM esse comperior quod quosdam bene litteratos homines dicere audivi, qui plerasque Plauti comoedias curiose atque contente lectitarunt, non indicibus Aelii nec Sedigiti nec Claudii nec Aurelii nec Accii nec Manilii super his fabulis quae dicuntur "ambiguae" crediturum, sed ipsi Plauto 2 moribusque ingeni atque linguae eius. Hac enim iudicii norma Varronem quoque usum videmus.
3 Nam praeter illas unam et viginti quae "Varronianae" vocantur, quas idcirco a ceteris segregavit, quoniam dubiosae non erant set consensu omnium Plauti esse censebantur, quasdam item alias probavit

      [1] in pistrinum (pistrino, σ), *added in* ς.

---

    [1] *Aen.* v. 738.
    [2] *Crediturum* seems an archaism for *credituros* ; see i. 7.

indicated the same thing, not directly and openly, but, as became one treating poetic themes, by an indirect and as it were veiled allusion to ancient observance. He says : [1]

> For dewy Night has wheeled her way
> Far past her middle course ; the panting steeds
> Of orient Morn breathe pitiless on me.

For in these lines he wished to remind us covertly, as I have said, that the day which the Romans have called " civil " begins after the completion of the sixth hour of the night.

III

On investigating and identifying the comedies of Plautus, since the genuine and the spurious without distinction are said to have been inscribed with his name ; and further as to the report that Plautus wrote plays in a bakery and Naevius in prison.

I am convinced of the truth of the statement which I have heard made by men well trained in literature, who have read a great many plays of Plautus with care and attention : namely, that with regard to the so-called " doubtful " plays they would [2] trust, not the lists of Aelius or Sedigitus or Claudius or Aurelius or Accius or Manilius, but Plautus himself and the characteristic features of his manner and diction. Indeed, this is the criterion which we find Varro using. For in addition to those one and twenty known as " Varronian," which he set apart from the rest because they were not questioned but by common consent were attributed to Plautus, he accepted also some others, influenced by the style and humour of their language, which was

245

adductus filo atque facetia sermonis Plauto con-
gruentis easque iam nominibus aliorum occupatas
Plauto vindicavit, sicuti istam quam nuperrime lege-
4 bamus, cui est nomen *Boeotia.* Nam cum in illis
una et viginti non sit et esse Aquili dicatur, nihil
tamen Varro dubitavit quin Plauti foret, neque alius
quisquam non infrequens Plauti lector dubitaverit,
si vel hos solos ex ea fabula versus cognoverit, qui
quoniam sunt, ut de illius Plauti more dicam,
Plautinissimi, propterea et meminimus eos et
5 ascripsimus. Parasitus ibi esuriens haec dicit:

Ut illúm di perdant, prímus qui horas répperit,
Quique ádeo primus státuit hic solárium,
Qui míhi comminuit mísero articulatím diem.
Nam unúm[1] me puero vénter erat solárium
Multo ómnium istorum óptimum et veríssimum ;
Ubivís monebat ésse, nisi quom níl erat.
Nunc étiam quod est non éstur, nisi solí libet ;
Itaque ádeo iam oppletum óppidum est soláriis,
Maiór pars populi iam [2] áridi reptánt fame.

6 Favorinus quoque noster, cum *Nervulariam* Plauti
legerem, quae inter incertas habita est, et audisset
ex ea comoedia versum hunc:

Scrattáe, scrupipedae, stríttivillae sórdidae,

---

[1] unum, *added by Hertz.*
[2] iam, *added by Hertz;* ut aridi reptent, *Ritschl.*

---

[1] Fr. v. 21 Götz; ii, p. 38, Ribbeck. Translation by
Thornton and Warner.
[2] Fr. v. 100 Götz; translation by Thornton and Warner.

characteristic of Plautus; and although these had
already been listed under the names of other poets, he
claimed them for Plautus: for example, one that I
was recently reading, called *The Boeotian Woman*.
For although it is not among those one and twenty
and is attributed to Aquilius, still Varro had not the
least doubt that it was Plautine, nor will any
other habitual reader of Plautus doubt it, even if
he knows only the following verses from that play,
which, since they are, to speak in the manner of
that famous poet, most Plautine, I recall and have
noted down. There a hungry parasite speaks as
follows:[1]

> The gods confound the man who first found out
> How to distinguish hours! Confound him, too,
> Who in this place set up a sun-dial
> To cut and hack my days so wretchedly
> Into small portions! When I was a boy,
> My belly was my only sun-dial, one more sure,
> Truer, and more exact than any of them.
> This dial told me when 'twas proper time
> To go to dinner, when I had aught to eat;
> But nowadays, why even when I have,
> I can't fall to unless the sun gives leave.
> The town's so full of these confounded dials
> The greatest part of the inhabitants,
> Shrunk up with hunger, crawl along the streets.

My master Favorinus too, when I was reading the
Nervularia of Plautus, and he had heard this line of
the comedy:[2]

> Old, wheezing, physicky, mere foundered hags
> With dry, parched, painted hides, shrivell'd and
>   shrunk,

delectatus faceta verborum antiquitate, meretricum
vitia atque deformitates significantium, " vel unus
hercle," inquit, " hic versus Plauti esse hanc fabulam
satis potest fidei fecisse."

7 Nos quoque ipsi nuperrime, cum legeremus *Fretum*—nomen est id comoediae quam Plauti esse
quidam non putant,—haut quicquam dubitavimus
quin ea Plauti foret, et omnium quidem maxime
8 genuina. Ex qua duo hos versus exscripsimus, ut
historiam quaereremus oraculi Arretini :

> Nunc íllud est quód respónsum Arreti[1] ludis
> magnis[2] dícitur :
> Períbo, si non fécero, si fáxo, vapulábo.

9 M. tamen Varro in libro *De Comoediis Plautinis*
primo Accii verba haec ponit : " Nam nec *Geminei
Lenones* nec *Condalium* nec *Anus* Plauti, nec *Bis
Compressa* nec *Boeotia* umquam fuit, neque adeo
Agroecus neque *Commorientes* Macci Titi."

10 In eodem libro M. Varronis id quoque scriptum,
et Plautium fuisse quempiam poetam comoediarum.
Quoniam fabulae eae " Plauti " inscriptae forent,
acceptas esse quasi Plautinas, cum essent non a
Plauto Plautinae, sed a Plautio Plautianae.

---

[1] Arretini, ω and *T.L.L.* ; Arreti, *Leo.*   [2] magis, ω.

---

[1] Fr. v. 76, Götz.

[2] Nothing is known of this oracle. The inferior manuscripts and earlier editors read *Arietini* and interpreted it as
that of Jupiter Ammon, because that god is sometimes represented as a ram (*aries*), or with a ram's head. According to
Bücheler, *Thes. Ling. Lat.* ii. 636. 9, the reference is to a
person, not to the town of Arretium. Text and meaning
are most uncertain.

[3] According to Bücheler, *T.L.L.* ii. 636. 9, the reference
is to the *ludi Romani*, Sept. 5–19.

delighted with the wit of the archaic words that describe the ugly defects of harlots, cried : " By heaven! just this one verse is enough to convince one that the play is Plautine."

I myself too a little while ago, when reading the *Fretum*—that is the name of a comedy which some think is not Plautine—had no manner of doubt that it was by Plautus and in fact of all his plays the most authentic. From it I copied these two lines,[1] with the intention of looking up the story of the Arretine oracle :[2]

> Now here we have at the great games[3] the Arretine response :
> I perish if I don't, and if I do, I'm flogged.

Yet Marcus Varro, in the first book of his *Comedies of Plautus*,[4] quotes these words of Accius :[5] " For not the *Twin Panders* nor the *Slave-ring* nor the *Old Woman* were the work of Plautus, nor were ever the *Twice Violated* or the *Boeotian Woman*, nor were the *Clownish Rustic* or the *Partners in Death* the work of Titus Maccius."[6]

In that same book of Varro's we are told also that there was another writer of comedies called Plautius. Since his plays bore the title "Plauti,"[7] they were accepted as Plautine, although in fact they were not Plautine by Plautus, but Plautinian by Plautius.

[4] Fr. p. 193, Bipont.
[5] Didascalica, fr. inc., Müller.
[6] On this passage see Leo, *Plaut. Forsch.*, p. 32, who sees three categories : three plays under the name of Plautus, two under that of Titus Maccius, and two (*Agroecus* and *Boeotia*) anonymous.
[7] The early gen. both of *Plautius* and *Plautus*.

11 Feruntur autem sub Plauti nomine comoediae
12 circiter centum atque triginta; sed homo eruditissi-
mus L. Aelius quinque et viginti eius esse solas
13 existimavit. Neque tamen dubium est quin istaec
quae scriptae a Plauto non videntur et nomini eius
addicuntur, veterum poetarum fuerint et ab eo
retractatae et [1] expolitae sint ac propterea resipiant
14 stilum Plautinum. Sed enim *Saturionem* et *Addictum*
et tertiam quandam, cuius nunc mihi nomen non
subpetit, in pistrino eum scripsisse Varro et plerique
alii memoriae tradiderunt, cum, pecunia omni quam
in operis artificum scaenicorum pepererat, in merca-
tibus perdita, inops Romam redisset et ob quae-
rendum victum ad circumagendas molas quae
" trusatiles " appellantur, operam pistori locasset.
15 Sicuti de Naevio quoque accepimus fabulas eum
in carcere duas scripsisse, *Hariolum* et *Leontem*,
cum ob assiduam maledicentiam et probra in principes
civitatis de Graecorum poetarum more dicta in vin-
cula Romae a triumviris coniectus esset. Unde post
a tribunis plebis exemptus est, cum in his quas supra
dixi fabulis delicta sua et petulantias dictorum quibus
multos ante laeserat diluisset.

[1] et, *added by Carrio.*

---

[1] p. 58. 4, Fun.
[2] A large mill with two handles, which two men, ordinarily
slaves, pushed (*truso,* cf. *trudo*) upon, in order to turn the
mill. Contrasted by Cato (*Agr.* x. 4 and xi. 4) with *molae
asinariae,* which had one handle, to which a horse or an ass
was attached and *drew* the mill around.
This whole account is discredited by Leo. *Plaut., Forsch.,*

Now there are in circulation under the name of Plautus about one hundred and thirty comedies; but that most learned of men Lucius Aelius thought that only twenty-five of them were his.[1] However, there is no doubt that those which do not appear to have been written by Plautus but are attached to his name, were the work of poets of old but were revised and touched up by him, and that is why they savour of the Plautine style. Now Varro and several others have recorded that the *Saturio,* the *Addictus,* and a third comedy, the name of which I do not now recall, were written by Plautus in a bakery, when, after losing in trade all the money which he had earned in employments connected with the stage, he had returned penniless to Rome, and to earn a livelihood had hired himself out to a baker, to turn a mill, of the kind which is called a "push-mill." [2]

So too we are told of Naevius that he wrote two plays in prison, the *Soothsayer* and the *Leon,* when by reason of his constant abuse and insults aimed at the leading men of the city, after the manner of the Greek poets, he had been imprisoned at Rome by the triumvirs.[3] And afterwards he was set free by the tribunes of the commons, when he had apologized for his offences and the saucy language with which he had previously assailed many men.

70 ff., but defended by Marx and others. On this, and on Varro's threefold division of the plays, see Klingelhoefer, *Phil. Quart.* iv., pp. 336 ff.

[3] The *triumviri capitales,* police magistrates, in charge of the public prisons.

ATTIC NIGHTS OF AULUS GELLIUS

IV

Quod P. Africano et aliis tunc viris nobilibus ante aetatem senectam barbam et genas radere mos patrius fuit.

1 In libris quos de vita P. Scipionis Africani compositos legimus, scriptum esse animadvertimus P. Scipioni, Pauli filio, postquam de Poenis triumphaverat censorque fuerat, diem dictum esse ad populum a Claudio Asello tribuno plebis, cui equum in censura ademerat, eumque, cum esset reus, neque barbam desisse radi neque candida veste uti neque fuisse
2 cultu solito reorum. Sed cum in eo tempore Scipionem minorem quadraginta annorum fuisse constaret, quod de barba rasa ita scriptum esset mirabamur.
3 Comperimus autem ceteros quoque in isdem temporibus nobiles viros barbam in eiusmodi aetate rasitavisse, idcircoque plerasque imagines veterum, non admodum senum, sed in medio aetatis, ita factas videmus.

V

Deliciarum vitium et mollities oculorum et corporis ab Arcesila philosopho cuidam obprobrata acerbe simul et festiviter.

1 Plutarchus refert Arcesilaum philosophum vehementi verbo usum esse de quodam nimis delicato

---

[1] This fashion changed with Hadrian.

IV

That it was an inherited custom of Publius Africanus and
other distinguished men of his time to shave their beard
and cheeks.

I FOUND it stated in books which I read dealing
with the life of Publius Scipio Africanus, that
Publius Scipio, the son of Paulus, after he had
celebrated a triumph because of his victory over
the Carthaginians and had been censor, was accused
before the people by Claudius Asellus, tribune of
the commons, whom he had degraded from knight-
hood during his censorship; and that Scipio, although he was under accusation, neither ceased to
shave his beard and to wear white raiment nor
appeared in the usual garb of those under accusation. But since it is certain that at that time
Scipio was less than forty years old, I was surprised
at the statement about shaving his beard. I have
learned, however, that in those same times the
other nobles shaved their beards at that time of
life, and that is why we see many busts of early men
represented in that way, men who were not very
old, but in middle life.[1]

V

How the philosopher Arcesilaus severely yet humorously
taunted a man with the vice of voluptuousness and with
unmanliness of expression and conduct.

PLUTARCH tells us[2] that Arcesilaus the philosopher
used strong language about a certain rich man, who
was too pleasure-loving, but nevertheless had a

[2] *Sympos.* vii. 5.3, *De Tuend. San.* 7.

divite, qui incorruptus tamen et a stupro integer di-
2 cebatur. Nam cum vocem eius infractam capillum-
que arte compositum et oculos ludibundos atque
inlecebrae voluptatisque plenos videret, "Nihil
interest," inquit, "quibus membris cinaedi sitis,
posterioribus an prioribus."

VI

Dе vi atque natura palmae arboris, quod lignum ex ea ponderibus positis renitatur.

1 PER hercle rem mirandam Aristoteles in septimo
Problematorum et Plutarchus in octavo *Symposia-*
2 *corum* dicit. "Si super palmae," inquiunt, "arboris
lignum magna pondera inponas ac tam graviter
urgeas oneresque, ut magnitudo oneris sustineri
non queat, non deorsum palma cedit nec intra flecti-
tur, sed adversus pondus resurgit et sursum nititur
3 recurvaturque"; "propterea," inquit Plutarchus,
"in certaminibus palmam signum esse placuit victoriae, quoniam ingenium ligni eiusmodi est, ut
urgentibus opprimentibusque non cedat."

VII

Historia ex annalibus sumpta de Q. Caedicio tribuno militum;
verbaque ex *Originibus* M. Catonis apposita, quibus Caedici
virtutem cum Spartano Leonida aequiperat.

1 PULCRUM, dii boni, facinus Graecarumque facundi-
arum magniloquentia condignum M. Cato libris

---

[1] Fr. 229, Rose.   [2] 4.5.
[3] Hardly to be taken literally. The same statement is

reputation for uprightness and freedom from sen-
suality. For when he observed the man's affected
speech, his artfully arranged hair, and his wanton
glances, teeming with seduction and voluptuousness,
he said : " It makes no difference with what parts
of your body you debauch yourself, front or rear."

VI

On the natural strength of the palm-tree ; for when weights
are placed upon its wood, it resists their pressure.

A TRULY wonderful fact is stated by Aristotle in
the seventh book of his *Problems*,[1] and by Plutarch
in the eighth of his *Symposiaca*.[2] " If," say they,
" you place heavy weights on the wood of the palm-
tree, and load it so heavily and press it down so
hard that the burden is too great to bear, the
wood does not give way downward, nor is it made
concave, but it rises against the weight and struggles
upward and assumes a convex form.[3] It is for that
reason," says Plutarch, " that the palm has been
chosen as the symbol of victory in contests, since
the nature of its wood is such that it does not
yield to what presses hard upon it and tries to
crush it."

VII

A tale from the annals about Quintus Caedicius, tribune of
the soldiers ; and a passage from the *Origins* of Marcus
Cato, in which he likens the valour of Caedicius to that
of the Spartan Leonidas.

A GLORIOUS deed, by the Gods! and well worthy
of the noble strains of Greek eloquence, is that of

made by Pliny, *N. H.* xvi. 223 ; Theophr. *Enquiry into Plants*,
v. 6 (i. 453, *L.C.L.*) ; Xen. *Cyrop.* vii. 5. 11 (ii. 267, *L.C.L.*)

Originum de Q. Caedicio tribuno militum scriptum reliquit.

2,3 Id profecto est ad hanc ferme sententiam: Imperator Poenus in terra Sicilia, bello Carthaginiensi primo, obviam Romano exercitu progreditur, colles locosque idoneos prior occupat. Milites Romani,

4 uti res nata est, in locum insinuant fraudi et per-
5 niciei obnoxium. Tribunus ad consulem venit, ostendit exitium de loci importunitate et hostium

6 circumstantia maturum. "Censeo," inquit, "si rem servare vis, faciundum ut quadringentos[1] aliquos milites ad verrucam illam," sic enim Cato locum editum asperumque appellat, "ire iubeas, eamque uti occupent imperes horterisque; hostes profecto ubi id viderint, fortissimus quisque et promptissimus ad occursandum pugnandumque in eos praevertentur unoque illo negotio sese alligabunt atque illi omnes

7 quadringenti procul dubio obtruncabuntur. Tunc interea, occupatis in ea caede hostibus, tempus exer-
8 citus ex hoc loco educendi habebis. Alia nisi haec salutis via nulla est." Consul tribuno respondit, consilium quidem istud aeque providens sibi viderier; "sed istos," inquit, "milites quadringentos ad eum locum in hostium cuneos quisnam erit qui

9 ducat?" "Si alium," inquit tribunus, "neminem repperis, me licet ad hoc periculum utare; ego

10 hanc tibi et reipublicae animam do." Consul tribuno
11 gratias laudesque agit. Tribunus et quadringenti
12 ad moriendum proficiscuntur. Hostes eorum audac-

---

[1] trecentos, *Livy and others.*

---

[1] Fr. 83, Peter.

the military tribune Quintus Caedicius, recorded by
Marcus Cato in his *Origins*.[1]

The actual account runs about as follows: In the
first Punic war the Carthaginian general in Sicily
advanced to meet the Roman army and was first
to take possession of the hills and strategic points.
As the result of this, the Roman soldiers made their
way into a place exposed to surprise and extreme
danger.   The tribune went to the consul and pointed
out that destruction was imminent from their unfavourable position and from the fact that the enemy
had surrounded them.   "My advice is," said he, "if
you want to save the day, that you order some four
hundred soldiers to advance to yonder wart"—for
that is Cato's term for a high and rough bit of
ground—"and command and conjure them to hold
it.   When the enemy see that, undoubtedly all
their bravest and most active men will be intent
upon attacking and fighting with them; they will
devote themselves to that one task, and beyond
a doubt all those four hundred will be slaughtered.
Then in the meantime, while the enemy is engaged
in killing them, you will have time to get the army
out of this position.   There is no other way of
safety but this."   The consul replied to the tribune
that the plan seemed to him equally wise; "but
who, pray," said he, "will there be to lead those
four hundred men of yours to that place in the
midst of the enemy's troops?"   "If you find no
one else," answered the tribune, "you may use me
for that dangerous enterprise.   I offer this life of
mine to you and to my country."   The consul
thanked and commended the tribune.   The tribune
and his four hundred marched forth to death.   The

iam demirantur, quorsum ire pergant in expectando
13 sunt. Sed ubi apparuit ad eam[1] verrucam occu-
pandam iter intendere, mittit adversum illos imperator Carthaginiensis peditatum equitatumque quos
14 in exercitu viros habuit strenuissimos. Romani
15 milites circumveniuntur, circumventi repugnant; fit
16 proelium diu anceps. Tandem superat multitudo.
Quadringenti omnes cum tribuno[2] perfossi gladiis
17 aut missilibus operti cadunt. Consul interim, dum
ibi pugnatur, se in locos tutos atque editos subducit.
18 Sed quod illi tribuno, duci militum quadringento-
rum, divinitus in eo proelio usus venit, non iam
19 nostris, sed ipsius Catonis verbis subiecimus: " Dii
inmortales tribuno militum fortunam ex virtute eius
dedere. Nam ita evenit: cum saucius multifariam
ibi factus esset, tamen vulnus capiti nullum evenit,
eumque inter mortuos, defetigatum vulneribus atque
quod sanguen eius defluxerat, cognovere. Eum
sustulere, isque convaluit, saepeque post illa operam
reipublicae fortem atque strenuam praehibuit illoque
facto, quod illos milites subduxit, exercitum ceterum
servavit. Sed idem benefactum quo in loco ponas,
nimium interest. Leonides Laco, qui[3] simile apud
Thermopylas fecit, propter eius virtutes omnis
Graecia gloriam atque gratiam praecipuam claritu-
dinis inclitissimae decoravere monumentis: signis,
statuis, elogiis, historiis aliisque rebus gratissimum
id eius factum habuere; at tribuno militum parva

---

[1] ad eam, *J. F. Gronov;* eadem, *RV.;* eandem, *P.*
[2] cum tribuno, *Mähly;* cum uno (una, *V.*), *ω*; ad unum,
Pricaeus.
[3] quia, *Mommsen.*

---

[1] Cf. Sall. *Cat.* viii.

enemy marvelled at their boldness; they were on tiptoe of expectation to see where they would go. But when it appeared that they were on their way to occupy that hill, the Carthaginian commander sent against them the strongest men in his army, horse and foot. The Roman soldiers were surrounded; though surrounded, they resisted; the battle was long and doubtful. At last numbers triumphed. Every man of the four hundred fell, including the tribune, either run through with swords or overwhelmed with missiles. Meanwhile the consul, while the battle was raging there, withdrew to a safe position on high ground.

But what, by Heaven's help, befell that tribune, the leader of the four hundred soldiers, in the battle, I have added, no longer using my own words, but giving those of Cato himself, who says: "The immortal gods gave the tribune good fortune equal to his valour; for this is what happened. Although he had been wounded in many places during the battle, yet his head was uninjured, and they recognized him among the dead, unconscious from wounds and loss of blood. They bore him off the field, he recovered, and often after that rendered brave and vigorous service to his country; and by that act of leading that forlorn hope he saved the rest of the army. But what a difference it makes where you do the same service!¹ The Laconian Leonidas, who performed a like exploit at Thermopylae, because of his valour won unexampled glory and gratitude from all Greece, and was honoured with memorials of the highest distinction; they showed their appreciation of that deed of his by pictures, statues and honorary inscriptions, in their histories, and in other ways; but the tribune

laus pro factis relicta, qui idem fecerat atque rem
servaverat."

20 Hanc Q. Caedici tribuni virtutem M. Cato tali
21 suo testimonio decoravit. Claudius autem Quadrigarius *Annalis* tertio non Caedicio nomen fuisse ait,
sed Laberio.

VIII

Litterae eximiae consulum C. Fabricii et Q. Aemilii ad regem
Pyrrum, a Q. Claudio scriptore historiarum in memoriam
datae.

1 Cum Pyrrus rex in terra Italia esset et unam atque
alteram pugnas prospere pugnasset satisque agerent
Romani et pleraque Italia ad regem descivisset, tum
Ambraciensis quispiam Timochares,[1] regis Pyrri amicus, ad C. Fabricium consulem furtim venit ac
praemium petivit et, si de praemio conveniret,
promisit regem venenis necare, idque facile esse
factu dixit, quoniam filius suus pocula in convivio
2 regi ministraret. Eam rem Fabricius ad senatum
3 scripsit. Senatus ad regem legatos misit manda-
vitque ut de Timochare nihil proderent, sed mone-
rent uti rex circumspectius ageret atque a proxi-
4 morum insidiis salutem tutaretur. Hoc ita, uti
diximus, in Valeri Antiatis *Historia* scriptum est.
5 Quadrigarius autem in libro tertio non Timocharem,
sed Niciam adisse ad consulem scripsit, neque
legatos a senatu missos, sed a consulibus, et Pyrrum[2]
populo Romano laudes atque gratias scripsisse capti-

---

[1] Demochares, *Amm.* xxx. 1.
[2] Pyrrum, *added by Hertz;* regem. σ.

---

[1] Fr. 42, Peter.   [2] Fr. 21, Peter.   [3] Fr. 40, Peter.

of the soldiers, who had done the same thing and saved an army, gained small glory for his deeds."

With such high personal testimony did Marcus Cato honour this valorous deed of Quintus Caedicius the tribune. But Claudius Quadrigarius, in the third book of his *Annals*,[1] says that the man's name was not Caedicius, but Laberius.

VIII

A fine letter of the consuls Gaius Fabricius and Quintus Aemilius to king Pyrrhus, recorded by the historian Quintus Claudius.

At the time when king Pyrrhus was on Italian soil and had won one or two battles, when the Romans were getting anxious, and the greater part of Italy had gone over to the king, a certain Timochares, an Ambracian and a friend of king Pyrrhus, came stealthily to the consul Gaius Fabricius and asked a reward, promising that if they could come to terms, he would poison the king. This, he said, could easily be done, since his son was the monarch's cup-bearer. Fabricius transmitted this offer to the senate. The senate sent envoys to the king, instructing them not to reveal anything about Timochares, but to warn the king to act with more caution, and be on his guard against the treachery of those nearest to his own person. This, as I have told it, is the version found in the *History* of Valerius Antias.[2] But Quadrigarius, in his third book,[3] says that it was not Timochares, but Nicias, that approached the consul; that the embassy was not sent by the senate, but by the consuls; and that Pyrrhus thanked and complimented the Roman people in a

vosque omnes quos tum habuit vestivisse et reddidisse.

6 Consules tum fuerunt C. Fabricius et Q. Aemilius.

7 Litteras, quas ad regem Pyrrum super ea causa
miserunt, Claudius Quadrigarius scripsit fuisse hoc
exemplo :

8 "Consules Romani salutem dicunt Pyrro regi.

Nos pro tuis iniuriis continuis animo tenus [1] commoti
inimiciter tecum bellare studemus. Sed communis
exempli et fidei ergo visum ut te salvum velimus,
ut esset quem armis vincere possemus. Ad nos
venit Nicias familiaris tuus, qui sibi praemium a
nobis peteret, si te clam interfecisset. Id nos nega-
vimus velle, neve ob eam rem quicquam commodi
expectaret, et simul visum est ut te certiorem face-
remus, ne quid eiusmodi, si accidisset, nostro consilio
civitates putarent factum, et quod nobis non placet
pretio aut praemio aut dolis pugnare. Tu, nisi
caves, iacebis."

IX

Quis et cuiusmodi fuerit qui in proverbio fertur equus
   Seianus ; et qualis color equorum sit qui "spadices"
   vocantur ; deque istius vocabuli ratione.

1 GAVIUS BASSUS in *Commentariis* suis, item Iulius
Modestus in secundo *Quaestionum Confusarum,*
historiam de equo Seiano tradunt dignam memoria

---

[1] tenus, *Bentley;* tenui, ω.

letter, besides clothing and returning all the prisoners that were then in his hands.

The consuls at that time were Gaius Fabricius and Quintus Aemilius.[1] The letter which they sent to king Pyrrhus about that matter, according to Claudius Quadrigarius, ran as follows :

" The Roman consuls greet king Pyrrhus.

We, being greatly disturbed in spirit because of your continued acts of injustice, desire to war with you as an enemy. But as a matter of general precedent and honour, it has seemed to us that we should desire your personal safety, in order that we may have the opportunity of vanquishing you in the field. Your friend Nicias came to us, to ask for a reward if he should secretly slay you. We replied that we had no such wish, and that he could look for no advantage from such an action ; at the same time it seemed proper to inform you, for fear that if anything of the kind should happen, the nations might think that it was done with our connivance, and also because we have no desire to make war by means of bribes or rewards or trickery. As for you, if you do not take heed, you will have a fall."

IX

The characteristics of the horse of Seius, which is mentioned in the proverb ; and as to the colour of the horses which are called *spadices* ; and the explanation of that term.

GAVIUS BASSUS in his *Commentaries*,[2] and Julius Modestus in the second book of his *Miscellaneous Questions*,[3] tell the history of the horse of Seius, a

[1] 282 B.C.   [2] Frag. 4, Fun.   [3] p. 15, Bunte.

2 atque admiratione : Gnaeum Seium quempiam scribam fuisse eumque habuisse equum natum Argis in terra Graecia, de quo fama constans esset tamquam de genere equorum progenitus foret qui Diomedis Thracis fuissent, quos Hercules, Diomede occiso, e

3 Thracia Argos perduxisset. Eum equum fuisse dicunt magnitudine invisitata, cervice ardua, colore poeniceo, flora et comanti iuba, omnibusque aliis equorum laudibus quoque longe praestitisse ; sed eundem equum tali fuisse fato sive fortuna ferunt, ut quisquis haberet eum possideretque, ut is cum omni domo, familia fortunisque omnibus suis ad

4 internecionem deperiret. Itaque primum illum Gnaeum Seium, dominum eius, a M. Antonio, qui postea triumvirum reipublicae constituendae fuit, capitis damnatum, miserando supplicio affectum esse ; eodem tempore Cornelium Dolabellam consulem, in Syriam proficiscentem, fama istius equi adductum Argos devertisse cupidineque habendi eius exarsisse emisseque eum sestertiis centum milibus ; sed ipsum quoque Dolabellam in Syria bello civili obsessum atque interfectum esse ; mox eundem equum, qui Dolabellae fuerat, C. Cassium, qui Dolabellam obse-

5 derat, abduxisse. Eum Cassium postea satis notum est victis partibus fusoque exercitu suo miseram mortem oppetisse, deinde post Antonium, post interitum Cassii parta victoria, equum illum nobilem Cassi requisisse et, cum eo potitus esset, ipsum quoque postea victum atque desertum, detestabili exitio

3 interisse. Hinc proverbium de hominibus calami-

---

¹ *IIIviri reipublicae constituendae* was the formal designation of the powers conferred upon Antony, Octavian and Lepidus in 43 B.C. by the bill of the tribune P. Titius. The so-called " first triumvirate," in 60 B.C., was a private arrangement by Caesar, Pompey and Crassus.

tale wonderful and worthy of record. They say
that there was a clerk called Gnaeus Seius, and that
he had a horse foaled at Argos, in the land of
Greece, about which there was a persistent tradition
that it was sprung from the breed of horses that had
belonged to the Thracian Diomedes, those which
Hercules, after slaying Diomedes, had taken from
Thrace to Argos. They say that this horse was of
extraordinary size, with a lofty neck, bay in colour,
with a thick, glossy mane, and that it was far
superior to all horses in other points of excellence;
but that same horse, they go on to say, was of such a
fate or fortune, that whoever owned and possessed
it came to utter ruin, as well as his whole house, his
family and all his possessions. Thus, to begin with,
that Gnaeus Seius who owned him was condemned
and suffered a cruel death at the hands of Marcus
Antonius, afterwards one of the triumvirs for setting
the State in order.[1] At that same time Cornelius
Dolabella, the consul, on his way to Syria, attracted
by the renown of this horse, turned aside to Argos,
was fired with a desire to own the animal, and
bought it for a hundred thousand sesterces; but
Dolabella in his turn was besieged in Syria during
the civil war, and slain. And soon afterwards Gaius
Cassius, who had besieged Dolabella, carried off this
same horse, which had been Dolabella's. It is
notorious too that this Cassius, after his party had
been vanquished and his army routed, met a wretched
end. Then later, after the death of Cassius, Antonius,
who had defeated him, sought for this famous horse
of Cassius, and after getting possession of it was
himself afterwards defeated and deserted in his turn,
and died an ignominious death. Hence the proverb,

tosis ortum dicique solitum : " Ille homo habet equum Seianum."

7   Eadem sententia est illius quoque veteris proverbii, quod ita dictum accepimus : "aurum Tolosanum." Nam cum oppidum Tolosanum in terra Gallia [1] Quintus Caepio consul diripuisset multumque auri in eius oppidi templis fuisset, quisquis ex ea direptione aurum attigit misero cruciabilique exitu periit.

8   Hunc equum Gavius Bassus vidisse se [2] Argis refert haut credibili pulcritudine vigoreque et colore exuberantissimo.

9   Quem colorem nos, sicuti dixi, poeniceum dicimus, Graeci partim φοίνικα, alii σπάδικα appellant, quoniam palmae termes ex arbore cum fructu avulsus "spadix" dicitur.

X

Quod est quaedam septenarii numeri vis et facultas in multis naturae rebus animadversa, de qua M. Varro in *Hebdomadibus* disserit copiose.

1   M. Varro in primo librorum qui inscribuntur *Hebdomades* vel *De Imaginibus*, septenarii numeri, quem Graece ἑβδομάδα [3] appellant, virtutes po-
2 testatesque multas variasque dicit. " Is namque numerus," inquit, " septentriones maiores minores-

---

    [1] Gallia, *Erasmus* ; Italia, *RV.* ; Italica, *P.*
    [2] se, ς ; *omitted by PRV.*   [3] (h)ebdoma, ω.

---

    [1] See ii. 26. 10. The colour is a purple-red, or reddish purple.
    [2] Fr. p. 255, Bipont. This work, more commonly called *Imagines*, consisted of seven hundred portraits of distinguished men, arranged in seven categories of Greeks and

applied to unfortunate men, arose and is current:
"That man has the horse of Seius."

The meaning is the same of that other old proverb,
which I have heard quoted thus: "the gold of
Tolosa." For when the town of Tolosa in the land
of Gaul was pillaged by the consul Quintus Caepio,
and a quantity of gold was found in the temples of
that town, whoever touched a piece of gold from
that sack died a wretched and agonizing death.

Gavius Bassus reports that he saw this horse at
Argos; that it was of incredible beauty and strength
and of the richest possible colouring.

This colour, as I have said, we call *poeniceus;* the
Greeks sometimes name it φοῖνιξ, at others σπάδιξ,
since the branch of the palm (φοῖνιξ), torn from the
tree with its fruit, is called *spadix.*[1]

X

That in many natural phenomena a certain power and
efficacy of the number seven has been observed, concerning which Marcus Varro discourses at length in his *Hebdomades.*[2]

MARCUS VARRO, in the first book of his work
entitled *Hebdomades* or *On Portraits,* speaks of many
varied excellencies and powers of the number
seven, which the Greeks call ἑβδομάς. "For that
number," he says, "forms the Greater and the Lesser
Bear in the heavens; also the *vergiliae,*[3] which

Romans; besides the fourteen books thus formed there was
an introductory fifteenth. Under each portrait was a
metrical elogium and an account of the personage in
prose. Cf. Plin. *N.H.* xxxv. 11.

[3] So called (from *ver*) because their rising, from April 22 to
May 10, marked the beginning of spring.

que in caelo facit, item vergilias, quas πλειάδας
Graeci vocant, facit etiam stellas quas alii 'erraticas,'
3 P. Nigidius 'errones' appellat." Circulos quoque
ait in caelo circum longitudinem axis septem esse;
ex quis duos minimos, qui axem extimum tangunt,
πόλους appellari dicit; sed eos in sphaera, quae
κρικωτὴ vocatur, propter brevitatem non inesse.
4 Ac neque ipse zodiacus septenario numero caret;
nam in septimo signo fit solstitium a bruma, in
septimo bruma a solstitio, in septimo aequinoctium
5 ab aequinoctio. Dies deinde illos quibus alcyones
hieme anni in aqua nidulantur, eos quoque septem
6 esse dicit. Praeterea scribit lunae curriculum confici
integris quater septenis diebus: "nam die duo-[1]
detricesimo luna," inquit, "ex quo vestigio profecta
est, eodem redit," auctoremque opinionis huius
Aristidem esse Samium; in qua re non id solum
animadverti debere dicit quod quater septenis, id est
octo et viginti, diebus conficeret luna iter suum, sed
quod is numerus septenarius, si ab uno profectus,
dum ad semetipsum progreditur, omnes per quos
progressus est numeros comprehendat ipsumque se
addat, facit numerum octo et viginti, quot[2] dies
7 sunt curriculi lunaris. Ad homines quoque nas-

---

[1] duo, ς, *Hertz*; *omitted by* ω.   [2] quod, ω.

---

[1] Fr. 87, Swoboda. The planets of the ancients were
Mercury, Venus, the Sun, Mars, Saturn and Jupiter, to
which they added the moon.

[2] An arrangement of rings (*armillae*), all circles of a single
sphere, intended to show the relative position of the principal
celestial circles. The sphere of Ptolemy has the earth in the
centre, that of Copernicus the sun. Since the purpose is to
show the apparent motions of the solar system, the former is
the one most used.

[3] That is, seven before, and seven after the winter

the Greeks call πλειάδες; and it is likewise the
number of those stars which some call ' wandering,'
but Publius Nigidius ' wanderers.' " [1]   Varro also says
that there are seven circles in the heavens, perpen-
dicular to its axis.   The two smallest of these, which
touch the ends of the axis, he says are called πόλοι,
or " poles " ; but that because of their small diameter
they cannot be represented on what is termed an
armillary sphere.[2]   And the zodiac itself is not unin-
fluenced by the number seven; for the summer
solstice occurs in the seventh sign from the winter
solstice, and the winter solstice in the seventh after
the summer, and one equinox in the seventh sign
after the other.   Then too those winter days during
which the kingfishers nest on the water he says are
seven in number.[3]   Besides this, he writes that the
course of the moon is completed in four times seven
complete days; " for on the twenty-eighth day," he
says, " the moon returns to the same point from
which it started," and he quotes Aristides [4] of Samos
as his authority for this opinion.   In this case he
says that one should not only take note of the fact
that the moon finishes its journey in four times
seven, that is eight and twenty, days, but also
that this number seven, if, beginning with one and
going on until it reaches itself, it includes the sum
of all the numbers through which it has passed and
then adds itself, makes the number eight and twenty,
which is the number of days of the revolution of the
moon.[5]   He says that the influence of that number

solstice.   During these fourteen " halcyon days " the sea was
supposed to be perfectly calm.
[4] A mistake for Aristarchus.
[5] That is, the sum of the numbers 1 to 7 inclusive is 28.

cendos vim numeri istius porrigi pertinereque ait :
"Nam cum in uterum," inquit, "mulieris genitale
semen datum est, primis septem diebus conglo-
batur, coagulaturque fitque ad capiendam figuram
idoneum. Post deinde quarta hebdomade, quod
eius virile secus futurum est, caput et spina, quae
est in dorso, informatur. Septima autem fere hebdomade, id est nono et quadragesimo die, totus,"
8 inquit, "homo in utero absolvitur." Illam quoque
vim numeri huius observatam refert, quod ante
mensem septimum neque mas neque femina salubriter ac secundum naturam nasci potest, et quod hi
qui iustissime in utero sunt, post ducentos septuaginta tres dies postquam sunt concepti, quadragesima
9 denique hebdomade inita[1] nascuntur. Pericula
quoque vitae fortunarumque omnium, quae " cli-
macteras" Chaldaei appellant, gravissimos quosque
10 fieri septenarios. Praeter hoc, modum esse dicit
summum adolescendi humani corporis septem pedes.
11 Quod esse magis verum arbitramur quam quod
Herodotus, homo fabulator, in primo *Historiarum*
inventum esse sub terra scripsit Oresti corpus cubita
longitudinis habens septem, quae faciunt pedes duodecim et quadrantem, nisi si, ut Homerus opinatus
est, vastiora prolixioraque fuerunt corpora hominum
antiquiorum et nunc, quasi iam mundo senescente,
12 rerum atque hominum decrementa sunt. Dentes

---

[1] inita, *Skutsch* ; ita, ω.

---

[1] i. 68.

extends to and affects also the birth of human beings.
"For," says he, "when the life-giving seed has been
introduced into the female womb, in the first seven
days it is compacted and coagulated and rendered fit to
take shape. Then afterwards in the fourth hebdomad
the rudimentary male organ, the head, and the spine
which is in the back, are formed. But in the seventh
hebdomad, as a rule, that is, by the forty-ninth day,"
says he, "the entire embryo is formed in the womb."
He says that this power also has been observed in
that number, that before the seventh month neither
male nor female child can be born in health and
naturally, and that those which are in the womb the
most regular time are born two hundred and seventy-
three days after conception, that is, not until the
beginning of the fortieth hebdomad. Of the periods
dangerous to the lives and fortunes of all men, which
the Chaldaeans call "climacterics," all the gravest are
combinations of the number seven. Besides this, he
says that the extreme limit of growth of the human
body is seven feet. That, in my opinion, is truer
than the statement of Herodotus, the story-teller, in
the first book of his *History*,[1] that the body of
Orestes was found under ground, and that it was
seven cubits in height, that is, twelve and a quarter
feet; unless, as Homer thought,[2] the men of old
were larger and taller of stature, but now, because
the world is ageing, as it were, men and things are
diminishing in size. The teeth too, he says, appear

[1] *Iliad*, v. 302:

ὁ δὲ χερμάδιον λάβε χειρὶ
Τυδείδης, μέγα ἔργον, ὃ οὐ δύο γ' ἄνδρε φέροιεν,
Οἷοι νῦν βροτοί εἰσ'· ὁ δέ μιν ῥέα πάλλε καὶ οἷος.
xii. 383 ; etc.

quoque et in septem mensibus primis et septenos
ex utraque parte gigni ait et cadere annis septimis
13 et genuinos adnasci annis fere bis septenis. Venas
etiam in hominibus, vel potius arterias, medicos
musicos dicere ait numero moveri septenario, quod
ipsi appellant τὴν διὰ τεσσάρων συμφωνίαν, quae fit
14 in collatione quaternarii numeri. Discrimina etiam
periculorum in morbis maiore vi fieri putat in diebus
qui conficiuntur ex numero septenario, eosque dies
omnium maxime, ita ut medici appellant, κρισίμους
videri[1] primam hebdomadam et secundam et tertiam.
15 Neque non id etiam sumit ad vim facultatesque
eius numeri augendas, quod, quibus inedia mori consilium est, septimo demum die mortem oppetunt.
16   Haec Varro de numero septenario scripsit admodum conquisite. Sed alia quoque ibidem congerit
frigidiuscula : veluti septem opera esse in orbe terrae
miranda et sapientes item veteres septem fuisse et
curricula ludorum circensium sollemnia septem esse
et ad oppugnandas Thebas duces septem delectos.
17 Tum ibi addit, se quoque iam duodecimam annorum
hebdomadam ingressum esse et ad eum diem septuaginta hebdomadas librorum conscripsisse, ex quibus
aliquammultos, cum proscriptus esset, direptis biblio-
thecis suis non comparuisse.

---

[1] videri, ς ; cui videri, ω.

---

[1] That is, by the use of the seven-stringed lyre.
[2] The harmony produced by the striking of four different
strings.
[3] Only 39 titles have come down to us, through Hieronymus, *De Vir. Ill.* 54, whose catalogue is unfinished and also
includes ten *libri singulares* under one head.   Ritschl estimated Varro's publications as 74 works, comprising 620 books.
[4] By Antony in 43 B.C.   Varro was saved from death by

in the first seven months seven at a time in each jaw,
and fall out within seven years, and the back teeth
are added, as a rule, within twice seven years.   He
says that the physicians who use music as a remedy
declare that the veins of men, or rather their arteries,
are set in motion according to the number seven,[1] and
this treatment they call τὴν διὰ τεσσάρων συμφωνίαν,[2]
because it results from the harmony of four tones.
He also believes that the periods of danger in
diseases have greater violence on the days which are
made up of the number seven, and that those days
in particular seem to be, as the physicians call them,
κρισίμοι or " critical " ; namely, the first, second and
third hebdomad.   And Varro does not fail to mention
a fact which adds to the power and influence of
the number seven, namely, that those who resolve
to die of starvation do not meet their end until the
seventh day.

These remarks of Varro about the number seven
show painstaking investigation.   But he has also
brought together in the same place others which
are rather trifling : for example, that there are seven
wonderful works in the world, that the sages of old
were seven, that the usual number of rounds in the
races in the circus is seven, and that seven champions
were chosen to attack Thebes.   Then he adds in that
book the further information that he has entered
upon the twelfth hebdomad of his age, and that
up to that day he has completed seventy hebdomads
of books,[3] of which a considerable number were destroyed when his library was plundered, at the time
of his proscription.[4]

Fufius Calenus, and died in 27 B.C., at the age of nearly
ninety.

XI

Quibus et quam frivolis argumentis Accius in *Didascalicis*
utatur, quibus docere nititur Hesiodum esse quam Homerum natu antiquiorem.

1 SUPER aetate Homeri atque Hesiodi non consen-
2 titur. Alii Homerum quam Hesiodum maiorem
natu fuisse scripserunt, in quis Philochorus et
Xenophanes, alii minorem, in quis L. Accius poeta
3 et Ephorus historiae scriptor. M. autem Varro in
primo *De Imaginibus,* uter prior sit natus parum
constare dicit, sed non esse dubium quin aliquo
tempore eodem vixerint, idque ex epigrammate
ostendi quod in tripode scriptum est, qui in monte
4 Helicone ab Hesiodo positus traditur. Accius
autem in primo *Didascalico* levibus admodum argumentis utitur, per quae ostendi putat, Hesiodum
5 natu priorem : " Quod Homerus," inquit, " cum in
principio carminis Achillem esse filium Pelei diceret,
quis esset Peleus non addidit ; quam rem procul,"
inquit, " dubio dixisset, nisi ab Hesiodo iam dictum
videret. De Cyclope itidem," inquit, " vel maxime
quod unoculus fuit, rem tam insignem non praeter-
isset, nisi aeque prioris Hesiodi carminibus invul-
gatum esset."
6 De patria quoque Homeri multo maxime dissensum est. Alii Colophonium, alii Smyrnaeum, sunt

---

[1] F.H.G. i. 393, Müller.
[2] Poet, Phil. Frag. 13, Diels ; Poesis Ludib. fr. 5, p. 191,
Wachsmuth.   [3] F.H.G. i. 277, Müller.
    [4] See note 2, p. 267.   [5] Fr. p. 258, Bipont.
    [6] Anth. Pal. vii. 53, *Greek Anth. L.C.L.,* ii. 53 :

Ἡσίοδος Μούσαις Ἑλικωνίσι τόνδ' ἀνέθηκα.
ὕμνῳ νικήσας ἐν Χαλκίδι θεῖον Ὅμηρον.

XI

The weak arguments by which Accius in his *Didascalica*
attempts to prove that Hesiod was earlier than Homer.

As to the age of Homer and of Hesiod opinions
differ. Some, among whom are Philochorus[1] and
Xenophanes,[2] have written that Homer was older than
Hesiod; others that he was younger, among them
Lucius Accius the poet and Euphorus the historian.[3]
But Marcus Varro, in the first book of his *Portraits*,[4]
says[5] that it is not at all certain which of the two
was born first, but that there is no doubt that they
lived partly in the same period of time, and that
this is proved by the inscription[6] engraved upon a
tripod which Hesiod is said to have set up on
Mount Helicon. Accius, on the contrary, in the
first book of his *Didascalica*,[7] makes use of very
weak arguments in his attempt to show that Hesiod
was the elder: "Because Homer," he writes, "when
he says at the beginning of his poem[8] that Achilles
was the son of Peleus, does not inform us who
Peleus was; and this he unquestionably would
have done, if he did not know that the information
had already been given by Hesiod.[9] Again, in the
case of Cyclops," says Accius, "he would not have
failed to note such a striking characteristic and to
make particular mention of the fact that he was one-
eyed, were it not that this was equally well known
from the poems of his predecessor Hesiod."[10]

Also as to Homer's native city there is the very
greatest divergence of opinion. Some say that he
was from Colophon, some from Smyrna; others

[7] Fr. 1, Müller; F.P.R. 7, Bährens.
[8] *Iliad.* 1. 1.   [9] Frag. 102, Rzach.   [10] *Theogony*, 14 2.

qui Atheniensem, sunt etiam qui Aegyptium fuisse
7 dicant, Aristoteles tradidit ex insula Io. M. Varro in
libro *De Imaginibus* primo Homeri imagini epigramma hoc apposuit.

Capélla Homeri candida haec tumulum índicat,
Quod hac Ietae mórtuo faciúnt sacra.

XII

Largum atque avidum bibendi a P. Nigidio, doctissimo viro,
nova et prope absurda vocabuli figura "bibosum"
dictum.

1 BIBENDI avidum P. Nigidius in *Commentariis*
2 *Grammaticis* "bibacem" et "bibosum" dicit. "Bibacem" ego, ut "edacem," a plerisque aliis dictum
lego; "bibosum" dictum nondum etiam usquam
repperi nisi apud Laberium, neque aliud est quod
3 simili inclinatu dicatur. Non enim simile est ut
"vinosus" aut "vitiosus" ceteraque quae hoc modo
dicuntur, quoniam a vocabulis, non a verbo, inclinata
4 sunt. Laberius in mimo, qui *Salinator* inscriptus
est, verbo hoc ita utitur :

Nón mammosa, nón annosa, nón bibosa, nón procax.

XIII

Quod Demosthenes etiamtum adulescens, cum Platonis
philosophi discipulus foret, audito forte Callistrato
rhetore in contione populi, destitit a Platone et sectatus
Callistratum est.

1 HERMIPPUS hoc scriptum reliquit, Demosthenen
admodum adulescentem ventitare in Academiam Pla-

---

[1] Frag. 76, Rose.   [2] F.P.R. 1, Bährens.
[3] That is, the inhabitants of Ios.   [4] Fr. 5, Swoboda.

assert that he was an Athenian, still others, an Egyptian; and Aristotle declares [1] that he was from the island of Ios. Marcus Varro, in the first book of his *Portraits,* placed this couplet under the portrait of Homer: [2]

> This snow-white kid the tomb of Homer marks;
> For such the Ietae [3] offer to the dead.

XII

That Publius Nigidius, a man of great learning, applied *bibosus* to one who was given to drinking heavily and greedily, using a new, but hardly rational, word-formation.

Publius Nigidius, in his *Grammatical Notes,* [4] calls one who is fond of drinking *bibax* and *bibosus. Bibax,* like *edax,* I find used by many others; but as yet I have nowhere found an example of *bibosus,* except in Laberius, and there is no other word similarly derived. For *vinosus,* or *vitiosus,* and other formations of the kind, are not parallel, since they are derived from nouns, not from verbs. Laberius, in the mime entitled *Salinator,* uses this word thus: [5]

> Not big of breast, not old, not bibulous, not pert.

XIII

How Demosthenes, while still young and a pupil of the philosopher Plato, happening to hear the orator Callistratus addressing the people, deserted Plato and became a follower of Callistratus.

Hermippus has written [6] that Demosthenes, when quite young, used to frequent the Academy and

---

[5] v. 80, Ribbeck².   [6] Fr. Hist. Gr. iii. 49, Müller.

2 tonemque audire solitum. "Atque is," inquit,
"Demosthenes domo egressus, ut ei mos erat, cum
ad Platonem pergeret complurisque populos con-
currentes videret, percontatur eius rei causam
3 cognoscitque currere eos auditum Callistratum.   Is
Callistratus Athenis orator in republica fuit quos illi
4 δημαγωγούς appellant. Visum est paulum dever-
tere experirique an digna auditio tanto properantium
5 studio foret. Venit," inquit, "atque audit Callistratum nobilem illam τὴν περὶ Ὠρωποῦ δίκην dicentem,
atque ita motus et demultus[1] et captus est ut
Callistratum iam inde sectari coeperit Academiam
cum Platone reliquerit."

XIV

"Dimidium librum legi" aut "dimidiam fabulam audivi"
aliaque huiuscemodi qui dicat, vitiose dicere; eiusque
vitii causas reddere M. Varronem; nec quemquam veterem
hisce verbis ita usum esse.

1   "DIMIDIUM librum legi" aut "dimidiam fabulam
audivi," vel quid aliud huiuscemodi, male ac vitiose
2 dici existumat Varro. "Oportet enim," inquit,
"dicere 'dimidiatum librum,' non 'dimidium,' et
'dimidiatam fabulam,' non 'dimidiam.'   Contra
autem si ex sextario hemina fusa est, non 'dimidiatum' sed 'dimidium,'[2] sextarium fusum dicendum

---

[1] *For* demulctus *from* demulceo.
[2] sed dimidium, *added by Skutsch.*

---

[1] "Leaders of the people."

listen to Plato. "And this Demosthenes," says
he, "when he had left home and, as usual, was
on his way to Plato, saw great throngs of people
running to the same place; he inquired the reason
of this, and learned that they were hurrying to hear
Callistratus. This Callistratus was one of those
orators in the Athenian republic that they call
δημαγωγοί, or ' demagogues.' [1] Demosthenes thought
it best to turn aside for a moment and find out
whether the discourse justified such eager haste.
He came," says Hermippus, "and heard Callistratus
delivering that famous speech of his, ἡ περὶ Ὠρωποῦ
δίκη.[2] He was so moved, so charmed, so captivated,
that he became a follower of Callistratus from that
moment, deserting Plato and the Academy."

XIV

That whoever says *dimidium librum legi*, or *dimidiam
fabulam audivi*, and uses other expressions of that kind,
speaks incorrectly: and that Marcus Varro gives the
explanation of that error: and that no early writer has
used such phraseology.

VARRO believes that *dimidium librum legi* ("I
have read half the book"), or *dimidiam fabulam
legi* ("I have read half the play"), or any other
expression of that kind, is incorrect and faulty usage.
"For," says he,[3] "one ought to say *dimidiatum
librum* ('the halved book'), not *dimidium*, and
dimidiatam fabulam, not *dimidiam*. But, on the contrary, if from a pint a half-pint has been poured,
one should not say that 'a halved pint' has been
poured, but a 'half-pint,' and when one has received

---

[2] The Action about Oropus.   [3] Fr. p. 349, Bipont.

est, et qui ex mille nummum, quod ei debebatur,
quingentos recepit, non 'dimidiatum' recepisse
3 dicemus, sed 'dimidium.' At si scyphus," inquit,
"argenteus mihi cum alio communis in duas partis
disiectus sit, 'dimidiatum' eum esse dicere scyphum
debeo, non 'dimidium,' argenti autem, quod in eo
scypho inest, 'dimidium' meum esse, non 'dimi-
4 diatum'"; disseritque ac dividit subtilissime quid
5 "dimidium" "dimidiato" intersit, et Q. Ennium
scienter hoc in *Annalibus* dixisse ait:

Sicuti si quis ferat vas vini dimidiatum,

sicuti pars quae deest ei vaso non "dimidiata"
dicenda est, sed "dimidia."

6 Omnis autem disputationis eius, quam subtiliter
quidem, sed suboscure explicat, summa haec est:
"dimidiatum" est quasi "dismediatum" et in partis
7 duas pares divisum, "dimidiatum" ergo nisi ipsum
8 quod divisum est dici haut convenit; "dimidium"
vero est, non quod ipsum dimidiatum est, sed quae
9 ex dimidiato pars altera est. Cum igitur partem
dimidiam libri legisse volumus dicere aut partem
dimidiam fabulae audisse, si "dimidiam fabulam"
aut "dimidium librum" dicimus, peccamus; totum
enim ipsum quod dimidiatum atque divisum est
10 "dimidium" dicis. Itaque Lucilius eadem secutus:

Uno oculo (inquit) pedibusque duobus dimidiatus
Ut porcus,

et alio loco:

---

[1] The *sestertium* was the designation of a thousand sesterces,
originally a gen. plur., later a nom. sing. neut.
[2] *Ann.* 536, Vahlen[2], reading *sicut*.

five hundred sesterces out of a thousand that were
owing him, we must say that he has received a half
sestertium,[1] not a halved one.   But if a silver bowl,"
he says, "which I own in common with another
person, has been divided into two parts, I ought
to speak of it as 'halved,' not as 'a half': but my
share of the silver of which the bowl is made is
a 'half,' not 'halved.'"   Thus Varro discusses and
analyzes very acutely the difference between *dimidium* and *dimidiatum,* and he declares that Quintus
Ennius spoke, in his *Annals,* with understanding in
the line:[2]

> As if one brought a halvéd cup of wine,

and similarly the part that is missing from the cup
should be spoken of as "half," not "halved."

Now the point of all this argument, which Varro
sets forth acutely, it is true, but somewhat ob-
scurely, is this: *dimidiatum* is equivalent to *dismediatum,* and means "divided into two parts," and
therefore *dimidiatum* cannot properly be used except
of the thing itself that is divided; *dimidium,* however, is not that which is itself divided, but is one
of the parts of what has been divided.   Accordingly,
when we wish to say that we have read the half
part of a book or heard the half part of a play, if
we say *dimidiam fabulam* or *dimidium librum,* we make
a mistake; for in that case you are using *dimidium*
of the whole thing which has been halved and divided.
Therefore Lucilius, following this same rule, says:[3]

> With one eye and two feet, like halvéd pig,

and in another place:[4]

Quidni ? et scruta quidem ut vendat scrutarius
laudat,
Praefractam strigilem, soleam inprobus dimidiatam.

11 Iam in vicesimo manifestius " dimidiam horam " dicere studiose fugit, sed pro " dimidia " " dimidium "
ponit in hisce versibus :

Tempestate sua atque eodem uno tempore, et
horae
Dimidio et tribus confectis dumtaxat—eandem
Ad quartam.

12 Nam cum obvium proximumque esset dicere : " dimidia et tribus confectis," vigilate atque attente
13 verbum non probum vitavit.   Per quod satis apparet
ne " horam " quidem " dimidiam " recte dici, sed vel
" dimidiatam horam " vel " dimidiam partem horae."
14 Propterea Plautus quoque in *Bacchidibus* dimidium
15 auri dicit, non " dimidiatum aurum "; item in
Aulularia " dimidium obsoni," non " dimidiatum
obsonium," in hoc versu :

Ei ádeo obsoni hic [1] iússit dimidiúm dari ;

16 in *Menaechmis* autem " dimidiatum diem," non " dimidium " in hoc versu :

Diés quidem iam ad úmbilicum dímidiatus mór-
tuust.

[1] hinc, *codd. Plauti.*

---

[1] 570, Marx.
[2] The meaning is very uncertain.   Marx thinks that the
reference is to the quartan ague, " the attacks of which

Why not? To sell his trash the huckster lauds
(The rascal !) half a shoe, a strigil split.

Again in his twentieth book it is clearer still that
Lucilius carefully avoids saying *dimidiam horam,* but
puts *dimidium* in the place of *dimidiam* in the following lines:[1]

At its own season and the self-same time,
The half an hour and three at least elapsed,
At the fourth hour again.[2]

For while it was natural and easy to say "three and
a half elapsed," he watchfully and carefully shunned
an improper term. From this it is quite clear that
not even "half an hour" can properly be said, but
we must say either "a halved hour" or "the half
part of an hour." And so Plautus as well, in the
Bacchides,[3] writes "half of the gold," not "the halved
gold," and in the *Aulularia,*[4] "half of the provisions,"
not "the halved provisions," in this verse:

He bade them give him half of all the meats;

But in the *Menaechmi* he has "the halved day," not
"half," as follows:[5]

Down to the navel now the halvéd day is dead.

regularly subside at the same time (*eandem ad quartam horam*),
after a minimum duration of three hours and a half.'
Lucilius refers, not to the fourth hour of the day (*non diei
horam dicit*), but to every fourth hour of the period of illness
(*totius temporis spatii quo aegrotus cubat febri correptus*). *Dumtaxat* is to be taken with the numeral, as in Plaut. *Truc.* 445.
For *ad quartam* he cites Seneca, *Nat. Quaest.* iii. 16. 2,
quartana ad horam venit, and Suet. *Aug.* lxxxvii. 1, *ad
Kalendas Graecas soluturos.*

[3] 1189.   [4] 291.   [5] 157.

17 M. etiam Cato in libro quem *De Agricultura* conscripsit: "Semen cupressi serito crebrum, ita uti
linum seri solet. Eo cribro terram incernito,
dimidiatum digitum. Iam id bene tabula aut pedi-
18 bus aut manibus complanato." "Dimidiatum,"
inquit, "digitum," non "dimidium." Nam "digiti"
quidem "dimidium," digitum autem ipsum "dimi-
19 diatum" dici oportet. Item M. Cato de Cartha-
giniensibus ita scripsit: "Homines defoderunt in
terram dimidiatos ignemque circumposuerunt, ita
20 interfecerunt." Neque quisquam omnium qui probe
locuti sunt his verbis sequius quam dixi usus est.

XV

Extare in litteris perque hominum memorias traditum, quod
repente multis mortem attulit gaudium ingens inspera-
tum, interclusa anima et vim magni novique motus non
sustinente.

1   Cognito repente insperato gaudio expirasse animam
refert Aristoteles philosophus Polycritam, nobilem
2 feminam Naxo insula. Philippides quoque, comoediarum poeta haut ignobilis, aetate iam edita cum in
certamine poetarum praeter spem vicisset et laetis-
sime gauderet, inter illud gaudium repente mortuus
3 est. De Rodio etiam Diagora celebrata historia est.
Is Diagoras tris filios adulescentes habuit, unum
pugilem, alterum pancratiasten, tertium luctatorem.

---

[1] *De Agr.* 151.   [2] p. 56, fr. 3, Jordan.
[3] Frag. 559, V. Rose.

Marcus Cato, too, in his work *On Farming*, writes:[1]
"Sow cypress seed thick, just as flax is commonly
sown. Over it sift earth from a sieve to the depth
of a halved finger. Then smooth it well with a
board, with the feet, or with the hands." He says
"a halved finger," not "a half." For we ought to
say "half of a finger," but the finger itself should be
said to be "halved." Marcus Cato also wrote this
of the Carthaginians:[2] "They buried the men half-
way down (*dimidiatos*) in the ground and built a fire
around them; thus they destroyed them." In fact,
no one of all those who have spoken correctly has
used these words otherwise than in the way I have
described.

XV

That it is recorded in literature and handed down by tradition, that great and unexpected joy has brought sudden
death to many, since the breath of life was stifled and
could not endure the effects of an unusual and strong
emotion.

ARISTOTLE the philosopher relates[3] that Polycrita,
a woman of high rank in the island of Naxos, on
suddenly and unexpectedly hearing joyful news,
breathed her last. Philippides too, a comic poet
of no little repute, when he had unexpectedly won
the prize in a contest of poets at an advanced age,
and was rejoicing exceedingly, died suddenly in the
midst of his joy. The story also of Diogoras of
Rhodes is widely known. This Diogoras had three
young sons, one a boxer, the second a pancratist,[4]
and the third a wrestler. He saw them all victors

---

[4] The pancratium was a contest including both wrestling
and boxing.

Eos omnis vidit vincere coronarique Olympiae eodem
die et, cum ibi eum tres adulescentes amplexi coronis
suis in caput patris positis saviarentur, cum populus
gratulabundus flores undique in eum iaceret, ibidem
in stadio inspectante populo in osculis atque in
manibus filiorum animam efflavit.

4 Praeterea in nostris annalibus scriptum legimus,
qua tempestate apud Cannas exercitus populi Romani
caesus est, anum matrem, nuntio de morte filii allato,
luctu atque maerore affectam esse; sed is nuntius
non verus fuit, utque [1] is adulescens non diu post ex
ea pugna in urbem redit, anus repente filio viso
copia atque turba et quasi ruina incidentis inopinati
gaudii oppressa exanimataque est.

XVI

Temporis varietas in puerperis mulierum quaenam sit a
medicis et a philosophis tradita; atque inibi poetarum
quoque veterum super eadem re opiniones multaque alia
auditu atque memoratu digna; verbaque ipsa Hippocratis
medici ex libro illius sumpta qui inscriptus est Περὶ Τροφῆς.

1 Et medici et philosophi inlustres de tempore humani
partus quaesiverunt. Multa opinio est, eaque iam
pro vero recepta, postquam mulieris uterum semen
conceperit, gigni hominem septimo rarenter, numquam octavo, saepe nono, saepius numero decimo
mense, eumque esse hominum gignendi summum
finem: decem menses non inceptos, sed exactos.

---

[1] utque, *Petschenig*; atque, *MSS.*

---

and crowned at Olympia on the same day, and when
the three young men were embracing him there,
and having placed their crowns on their father's
head were kissing him, and the people were con-
gratulating him and pelting him from all sides with
flowers, there in the very stadium, before the eyes
of the people, amid the kisses and embraces of his
sons, he passed away.

Moreover, I have read in our annals that at the
time when the army of the Roman people was cut
to pieces at Cannae,[1] an aged mother was overwhelmed with grief and sorrow by a message
announcing the death of her son; but that report
was false, and when not long afterwards the young
man returned from that battle to the city, the aged
mother, upon suddenly seeing her son, was over-
powered by the flood, the shock, and the crash, so
to speak, of unlooked-for joy descending upon her,
and gave up the ghost.

XVI

The variations in the period of gestation reported by physicians and philosophers ; and incidentally the views also
of the ancient poets on that subject and many other noteworthy and interesting particulars ; and the words of the
physician Hippocrates, quoted verbatim from his book
entitled Περὶ Τροφῆς.[2]

BOTH physicians and philosophers of distinction
have investigated the duration of the period of gestation in man. The general opinion, now accepted as
correct, is that after the womb of a woman has
conceived the seed, the child is born rarely in the
seventh month, never in the eighth, often in the
ninth, more often in the tenth in number ; and that
the end of the tenth month, not its beginning, is

ATTIC NIGHTS OF AULUS GELLIUS

2 Idque Plautum, veterem poetam, dicere videmus in comoedia *Cistellaria* his verbis:

> tum illa, quam compresserat,
> Decumó post mense exácto hic peperit fíliam.

3 Hoc idem tradit etiam Menander, poeta vetustior, humanarum opinionum vel peritissimus; versus eius super ea re de fabula *Plocio* posui:

> Γυνὴ κυεῖ δέκα μῆνας.

4 sed noster Caecilius, cum faceret eodem nomine et eiusdem argumenti comoediam ac pleraque a Menandro sumeret, in mensibus tamen genitalibus nominandis non praetermisit octavum, quem praeterierat Menander. Caecilii versus hice sunt:

> Sóletne mulier décimo mense párere?—
> Pol nonó quoque
> Étiam septimo átque octavo.

5 Eam rem Caecilium non inconsiderate dixisse neque temere a Menandro atque a multorum opinionibus
6 descivisse, M. Varro uti credamus facit. Nam mense nonnumquam octavo editum esse partum in libro quarto decimo *Rerum Divinarum* scriptum reliquit; quo in libro etiam undecimo mense aliquando nasci posse hominem dicit, eiusque sententiae tam de octavo quam de undecimo mense Aristotelem auctorem laudat.
7 Sed huius de mense octavo dissensionis

---

[1] 162.   [2] Fr. 413, Kock.   [3] 164, Ribbeck[3].
[4] Fr. 12, Agahd.   [5] *Hist. Anim.* vii. 4.

the extreme limit of human gestation. And this
we find the ancient poet Plautus saying in his
comedy the *Cistellaria*, in these words: [1]

> And then the girl whom he did violate
> Brought forth a daughter when ten months had
>   sped.

That same thing is stated by Menander also, a still
older poet and exceedingly well informed as to
current opinion ; I quote his words on that subject
from the play called *Plocium* or *The Necklace*: [2]

> The woman is ten months with child . . .

But although our countryman Caecilius wrote a play
with the same name and of the same plot, and
borrowed extensively from Menander, yet in naming
the months of delivery he did not omit the eighth,
which Menander had passed by. These are the
lines from Caecilius: [3]

> And may a child in the tenth month be born ?—
> By Pollux ! in the ninth, and seventh, and eighth.

Marcus Varro leads us to believe that Caecilius did
not make this statement thoughtlessly or differ
without reason from Menander and from the opinions
of many men. For in the fourteenth book of his
Divine Antiquities he has left the statement on record
that parturition sometimes takes place in the eighth
month. [4] In this book he also says that sometimes
a child may be born even in the eleventh month,
and he cites Aristotle [5] as authority for his statement in regard both to the eighth and the eleventh
month. Now, the reason for this disagreement as

causa cognosci potest in libro Hippocratis qui inscriptus est Περὶ Τροφῆς, ex quo libro verba haec
8 sunt: Ἔστιν δὲ καὶ οὐκ ἔστιν τὰ ὀκτάμηνα. Id tam obscure atque praecise et [1] tamquam adverse dictum Sabinus medicus, qui Hippocratem commodissime commentatus est, verbis his [2] enarravit: Ἔστιν μέν, φαινόμενα ὡς ζῶα μετὰ τὴν ἔκτρωσιν· οὐκ ἔστιν δέ, θνήσκοντα μετὰ ταῦτα· καὶ ἔστιν οὖν καὶ οὐκ ἔστιν, φαντασίᾳ μὲν παραυτίκα ὄντα, δυνάμει δὲ οὐκέτι.

9 Antiquos autem Romanos Varro dicit non recepisse huiuscemodi quasi monstruosas raritates, sed nono mense aut decimo, neque praeter hos aliis, partionem mulieris secundum naturam fieri existimasse idcircoque eos nomina Fatis tribus fecisse a pari-
10 endo et a nono atque decimo mense. Nam "'Parca,'" inquit, "inmutata una littera, a partu nominata, item 'Nona' et 'Decima' a partus tempestivi tempore."
11 Caesellius autem Vindex in *Lectionibus* suis *Antiquis*: "Tria," inquit, "nomina Parcarum sunt: 'Nona,' 'Decuma,' 'Morta,'" et versum hunc Livii, antiquissimi poetae, ponit ex Ὀδυσσείᾳ:

Quandó diés advéniet quém profáta Mórta est?

Sed homo minime malus Caesellius "Mortam" quasi nomen accepit, cum accipere quasi Moeram deberet.

---

[1] et, *added by Otho.*   [2] his, *added by Hertz.*

---

[1] ii. p. 23, Kühn; vol. 1. p. 356, xlii, *L.C.L.* The text is not the same as that of Gellius, but the meaning is practically the same.

[2] *l.c.*

[3] These are the Roman names of the Fates. The Greek Clotho, Lachesis and Atropos were adopted with the rest of the Greek mythology.

to the eighth month may be found in Hippocrates'
work entitled Περὶ Τροφῆς, or *On Nurture*, from which
these words are taken:[1] "Eighth-month's children
exist and do not exist." This statement, so obscure,
abrupt, and apparently contradictory, is thus explained by the physician Sabinus, who wrote a very
helpful commentary on Hippocrates: "They exist,
since they appear to live after the miscarriage; but
they do not exist, since they die afterwards; they
exist and do not exist therefore, since they live for
the moment in appearance, but not in reality."

But Varro says[2] that the early Romans did not
regard such births as unnatural rarities, but they did
believe that a woman was delivered according to
nature in the ninth or tenth month, and in no others,
and that for this reason they gave to the three Fates
names derived from bringing forth, and from the
ninth and tenth months. "For *Parca*," says he, "is
derived from *partus* with the change of one letter, and
likewise *Nona* and *Decima* from the period of timely
delivery."[3] But Caesellius Vindex in his *Ancient
Readings* says: "The names of the Fates are three:
Nona, Decuma, Morta"; and he quotes this verse
from the *Odyssey* of Livius, the earliest of our
poets,[4]

When will the day be present that Morta has
predicted?

But Caesellius, though a man not without learning,
took *Morta* as a name, when he ought to have taken
it as equivalent to Moera.[5]

[4] Fr. 12, Bährens.
[5] *i.e.* the Greek Μοῖρα, Fate.

12 Praeterea ego de partu humano, praeterquam quae
scripta in libris legi, hoc quoque usu venisse Romae
comperi : feminam bonis atque honestis moribus, non
ambigua pudicitia, in undecimo mense post mariti
mortem peperisse factumque esse negotium propter
rationem temporis, quasi marito mortuo postea conce-
pisset, quoniam decemviri in decem mensibus gigni
hominem, non in undecimo scripsissent ; sed divum
Hadrianum, causa cognita, decrevisse in undecimo
quoque mense partum edi posse ; idque ipsum eius
rei decretum nos legimus.   In eo decreto Hadrianus
id statuere se dicit requisitis veterum philosophorum
et medicorum sententiis.

13 Hodie quoque in satura forte M. Varronis legimus,
quae inscribitur *Testamentum,* verba haec : "Si quis
mihi filius unus pluresve in decem mensibus gignan-
tur, ii si erunt ὄνοι λύρας, exheredes sunto ; quod si
quis undecimo mense, κατ᾽ Ἀριστοτέλην, natus est,

14 Attio idem, quod Tettio, ius esto apud me." Per hoc
vetus proverbium Varro significat, sicuti vulgo dici
solitum erat de rebus nihil inter sese distantibus :
"idem Atti, quod Tetti," ita pari eodemque iure
esse in decem mensibus natos et in undecim.

15 Quod si ita neque ultra decimum mensem fetura
mulierum protolli potest, quaeri oportet cur Homerus
scripserit, Neptunum dixisse puellae a se recens
compressae :

---

¹ XII Tab. iv. 4, Schöll.   The fragment is not extant, but
it is cited also by Ulpian, *Dig.* xxxviii. 16. 3. 11 : post decem
menses mortis natus non admittetur ad legitimam hereditatem.
    ² Fr. 543, Bücheler³.
    ³ That is, " stupid," " half-witted."
    ⁴ *i.e.*, as Aristotle says may happen ; *Hist. Anim.* vii. 4.
    ⁵ Attius and Tettius stand for any names like Smith and
Jones in English.

Furthermore, besides what I have read in books about human gestation, I also heard of the following case, which occurred in Rome: A woman of good and honourable character, of undoubted chastity, gave birth to a child in the eleventh month after her husband's death, and because of the reckoning of the time the accusation was made that she had conceived after the death of her husband, since the decemvirs had written [1] that a child is born in ten months and not in the eleventh month. The deified Hadrian, however, having heard the case, decided that birth might also occur in the eleventh month, and I myself have read the actual decree with regard to the matter. In that decree Hadrian declares that he makes his decision after looking up the views of the ancient philosophers and physicians.

This very day I chanced to read these words in a satire of Marcus Varro's entitled *The Will*: [2] "If one or more sons shall be born to me in ten months, let them be disinherited, if they are asses in music; [3] but if one be born to me in the eleventh month, according to Aristotle, [4] let Attius have the same rights under my will as Tettius." Just as it used commonly to be said of things that did not differ from each other, "let Attius be as Tettius," so Varro means by this old proverb that children born in ten months and in eleven are to have the same and equal rights. [5]

But if it is a fact that gestation cannot be prolonged beyond the tenth month, it is pertinent to ask why Homer wrote that Neptune said to a girl whom he had just violated: [6]

[6] *Odyss.* xi. 248.

Χαῖρε γυνὴ φιλότητι· περιπλομένου δ' ἐνιαυτοῦ
Τέξεις ἀγλαὰ τέκν', ἐπεὶ οὐκ ἀποφώλιοι εὐναὶ
'Αθανάτων.

16 Id cum ego ad complures grammaticos attulissem,
partim eorum disputabant Homeri quoque aetate,
sicuti Romuli, annum fuisse non duodecim mensium,
sed decem; alii convenisse Neptuno maiestatique
eius dicebant, ut longiori tempore fetus ex eo
17 grandesceret; alii alia quaedam nugalia. Sed Favorinus mihi ait περιπλομένου ἐνιαυτοῦ non "confecto"
esse "anno," sed "adfecto."

18 In qua re verbo usus est non vulgariae significa-
19 tionis. "Adfecta" enim, sicuti Marcus Cicero et
veterum elegantissimi locuti sunt, ea proprie dicebantur quae non ad finem ipsum, sed proxime finem
progressa deductave erant. Hoc verbum ad hanc
sententiam Cicero in hac[1] fecit,[2] quam dixit *De
Provinciis Consularibus.*

20 Hippocrates autem in eo libro de quo supra
scripsi, cum et numerum dierum quibus conceptum
in utero coagulum conformatur, et tempus ipsius
partionis nono aut decimo mense definisset neque id
tamen semper eadem esse fini dixisset, sed alias
ocius fieri, alias serius, hisce ad postremum verbis
usus est: Γίνεται δὲ ἐν τούτοις καὶ πλείω καὶ ἐλάσσω
καὶ ὅλον καὶ κατὰ μέρος· οὐ πολλὸν δὲ καὶ πλείω πλείω
καὶ ἐλάσσω ἐλάσσω. Quibus verbis significat, quod

---

[1] oratione, σ; hoc, ω.   [2] fuit, *R.V.*

---

[1] § 19, *bellum adfectum videmus et, vere ut dicam, paene confectum;* cf. § 29.
[2] See note 1, p. 291. Here Gellius' text is followed.

Rejoice, O woman, in this act of love;
A year gone by, fair offspring shall be thine,
For not unfruitful is a god's embrace.

When I had brought this matter to the attention
of several scholars, some of them argued that in
Homer's time, as in that of Romulus, the year consisted, not of twelve months, but of ten; others, that
it was in accord with Neptune and his majesty that
a child by him should develop through a longer
period than usual; and others gave other nonsensical
reasons. But Favorinus tells me that περιπλομένου
ἐνιαυτοῦ does not mean "when the year is ended"
(confectus), but "when it is nearing its end" (adfectus).

In this instance Favorinus did not use the
word adfectus in its popular signification (but yet
correctly); for as it was used by Marcus Cicero and
the most polished of the early writers, it was properly
applied to things which had advanced, or been
carried, not to the very end, but nearly to the end.
Cicero gives the word that meaning in the speech
On the Consular Provinces.[1]

Moreover, Hippocrates, in that book of which I
wrote above, when he mentioned the number of
days within which the embryo conceived in the
womb is given form, and had limited the time of
gestation itself to the ninth or tenth month, but
had said that this nevertheless was not always of
the same duration, but that delivery occurred
sometimes more quickly, sometimes later, finally
used these words: "In these cases there are longer
and shorter periods, both wholly and in part; but
the longer are not much longer or the shorter much
shorter."[2] By this he means that whereas a birth

aliquando ocius fieret, non multo tamen fieri ocius, neque quod serius, multo serius.

21   Memini ego Romae accurate hoc atque sollicite quaesitum, negotio non rei tunc parvae postulante, an octavo mense infans ex utero vivus editus et statim mortuus ius trium liberorum supplevisset, cum abortio quibusdam, non partus, videretur mensis octavi intempestivitas.

22   Sed quoniam de Homerico annuo partu ac de undecimo mense diximus quae cognoveramus, visum est non praetereundum quod in Plinii Secundi libro

23 septimo *Naturalis Historiae* legimus.   Id autem quia extra fidem esse videri potest, verba ipsius Plinii posuimus : "Masurius auctor est, L. Papirium praetorem, secundo herede lege agente, bonorum possessionem contra eum dedisse, cum mater partum se tredecim mensibus tulisse diceret, quoniam nullum certum tempus pariendi statutum ei[1] videretur."

24 In eodem libro Plini Secundi verba haec scripta sunt: "Oscitatio in nixu letalis est, sicut sternuisse a coitu abortivum."

----

[1] ei, *omitted by Pliny.*

----

[1] The fathers of three children were granted certain privileges and immunities.

[2] vii. 40.

[3] Fr. 24, Huschke ; *Memor.* 21, *Jur. Civ.* 31, Bremer.

sometimes takes place more quickly, yet it occurs not much more quickly, and when later, not much later.

I recall that this question was carefully and thoroughly investigated at Rome, an inquiry demanded by a suit at law of no small moment at the time, whether, namely, a child that had been born alive in the eighth month but had died immediately, satisfied the conditions of the *ius trium liberorum*,[1] since it seemed to some that the untimely period of the eighth month made it an abortion and not a birth.

But since I have told what I have learned about a birth after a year in Homer and about the eleventh month, I think I ought not to omit what I read in the seventh book of the *Natural History* of Plinius Secundus. But because that story might seem to be beyond belief, I have quoted Pliny's own words :[2] "Masurius makes the statement[3] that the praetor Lucius Papirius, when an heir in the second degree[4] brought suit for the possession of an inheritance, decided against him, although the mother[5] said that she had been pregnant for thirteen months ; and the reason for his decision was that it seemed to him that no definite period of gestation had been fixed by law." In the same book of Plinius Secundus are these words :[6] "Yawning during childbirth is fatal, just as to sneeze after coition produces abortion."

---

[4] The heir or heirs in the second degree inherited only in case the heirs in the first degree died, or were otherwise incompetent.

[5] That is, the mother of the heir in the first degree.

[6] vii. 42.

XVII

Id quoque esse a gravissimis viris memoriae mandatum, quod tris libros Plato Philolai Pythagorici et Aristoteles pauculos Speusippi philosophi mercati sunt pretiis fidem non capientibus.

1 MEMORIAE mandatum est Platonem philosophum tenui admodum pecunia familiari fuisse atque eum tamen tris Philolai Pythagorici libros decem milibus
2 denarium mercatum. Id ei pretium donasse quidam scripserunt amicum eius Dionem Syracosium.

3 Aristotelem quoque traditum libros pauculos Speusippi philosophi post mortem eius emisse talentis Atticis tribus; ea summa fit nummi nostri sestertia duo et septuaginta milia.

4 Τίμων amarulentus librum maledicentissimum con-
5 scripsit, qui Σίλλος inscribitur. In eo libro Platonem philosophum [1] contumeliose appellat, quod inpenso pretio librum Pythagoricae disciplinae emisset exque eo *Timaeum*, nobilem illum dialogum, concinnasset.
6 Versus super ea re Τίμωνος hi sunt:

Καὶ σύ, Πλάτων, καὶ γάρ σε μαθητείης πόθος ἔσχεν,
Πολλῶν δ' ἀργυρίων ὀλίγην ἠλλάξαο βίβλον,
Ἔνθεν ἀπαρχόμενος τιμαιογραφεῖν ἐδιδάχθης.

---

[1] *after* philosophum *the MSS. repeat* tenui . . . fuisse *from* § 1.

---

[1] These were very high prices. The first book of Martial's *Epigrams*, 700 lines, in an elegant form, cost only five

XVII

The statement of men of the highest authority that Plato
bought three books of Philolaus the Pythagorean, and
that Aristotle purchased a few books of the philosopher
Speusippus, at prices beyond belief.

THE story goes that the philosopher Plato was
a man of very slender means, but that nevertheless
he bought three books of Philolaus the Pythagorean
for ten thousand denarii.[1]   That sum, according to
some writers, was given him by his friend Dion of
Syracuse.

Aristotle too, according to report, bought a very
few books of the philosopher Speusippus, after the
latter's death, for three Attic talents, a sum equivalent
in our money to seventy-two thousand sesterces.[1]

The bitter satirist Timon wrote a highly abusive
work, which he entitled Σίλλος.[2]   In that book he
addresses the philosopher Plato in opprobrious
terms, alleging that he had bought a treatise on the
Pythagorean philosophy at an extravagant figure, and
that from it he had compiled that celebrated
dialogue the *Timaeus*.   Here are Timon's lines on
the subject :[3]

Thou, Plato, since for learning thou didst yearn,
A tiny book for a vast sum did'st buy,
Which taught thee a *Timacus* to compose.

denarii, and cheaper editions could be bought for from six to
ten sesterces.   See Martial, i. 117. 15 ff., and Friedländer,
Roman Life and Manners, Eng. Trans., iii. p. 37.
   [2] Meaning a lampoon, or satirical poem.
   [3] *Poet. Phil. Frag.* 54, Diehls ; *Poesis Ludib.* 26, p 130,
Wachsmuth.

ATTIC NIGHTS OF AULUS GELLIUS

XVIII

Quid sint "pedari senatores" et quam ob causam ita appellati;
quamque habeant originem verba haec ex edicto tralaticio
consulum: "senatores quibusque in senatu sententiam
dicere licet."

1 Non pauci sunt qui opinantur "pedarios senatores"
appellatos, qui sententiam in senatu non verbis
dicerent, sed in alienam sententiam pedibus irent.
2 Quid igitur? cum senatusconsultum per discessionem
fiebat, nonne universi senatores sententiam pedibus
3 ferebant? Atque haec etiam vocabuli istius ratio
dicitur, quam Gavius[1] Bassus in *Commentariis* suis
4 scriptam reliquit. Senatores enim dicit in veterum
aetate, qui curulem magistratum gessissent, curru
solitos honoris gratia in curiam vehi, in quo curru
sella esset super quam considerent, quae ob eam
causam "curulis" appellaretur; sed eos senatores,
qui magistratum curulem nondum ceperant, pedibus
itavisse in curiam: propterea senatores nondum
maioribus honoribus usos[2] "pedarios" nominatos.
5 M. autem Varro in *Satira Menippea*, quae Ἱπποκύων inscripta est, equites quosdam dicit "pedarios"
appellatos, videturque eos significare qui, nondum a
censoribus in senatum lecti, senatores quidem non
erant, sed quia honoribus populi usi erant, in
6 senatum veniebant et sententiae ius habebant. Nam
et curulibus magistratibus functi, si[3] nondum a censo-

---

[1] G., ω.   [2] *suggested by Hertz*; functos, ç.
[3] functi si, *Scioppius*; functis, ω; functi qui, ç.

---

[1] Frag. 7, Fun.
[2] For *currulis*, from *currus*. This derivation is given by
Thurneysen, *T.L.L. s.v.*, with the suggestion that the name,
as well as the seat itself, was of Etruscan origin.

300

XVIII

What is meant by *pedari senatores*, and why they are so called; also the origin of these words in the customary edict of the consuls : " senators and those who are allowed to speak in the senate."

THERE are many who think that those senators were called *pedarii* who did not express their opinion in words, but agreed with the opinion of others by stepping to their side of the House. How then? Whenever a decree of the senate was passed by division, did not all the senators vote in that manner? Also the following explanation of that word is given, which Gavius Bassus has left recorded in his *Commentaries*. For he says[1] that in the time of our forefathers senators who had held a curule magistracy used to ride to the House in a chariot, as a mark of honour; that in that chariot there was a seat on which they sat, which for that reason was called *curulis*[2]; but that those senators who had not yet held a curule magistracy went on foot to the House : and that therefore the senators who had not yet held the higher magistracies were called *pedarii*. Marcus Varro, however, in the *Menippean Satire* entitled Ἱπποκύων, says[3] that some knights were called *pedarii,* and he seems to mean those who, since they had not yet been enrolled in the senate by the censors, were not indeed senators, but because they had held offices by vote of the people, used to come into the senate and had the right of voting. In fact, even those who had filled curule magistracies, if they had not

[3] Frag. 220, Bücheler.

ribus in senatum lecti erant, senatores non erant et,
quia in postremis scripti erant, non rogabantur
sententias sed, quas principes dixerant, in eas
7 discedebant. Hoc significabat edictum quo nunc
quoque consules, cum [1] senatores in curiam vocant,
servandae consuetudinis causa tralaticio utuntur.
8 Verba edicti haec sunt: "Senatores quibusque in
senatu sententiam dicere licet."
9 Versum quoque Laberii, in quo id vocabulum
positum est, notari iussimus, quem legimus in mimo
qui *Stricturae* inscriptus est:

> Caput sine lingua pedari sententia est.

10 Hoc vocabulum a plerisque barbare dici animadvertimus; nam pro "pedariis" "pedaneos"
appellant.

XIX

Qua ratione Gavius Bassus scripserit "parcum" hominem
appellatum et quam esse eius vocabuli causam putarit; et
contra, quem in modum quibusque verbis Favorinus hanc
traditionem eius eluserit.

1 Apud cenam Favorini philosophi cum discubitum
fuerat coeptusque erat apponi cibus, servus assistens
mensae eius legere inceptabat aut Graecarum quid
litterarum aut nostratium; velut eo die quo ego
affui, legebatur Gavii Bassi, eruditi viri, liber *De*
2 *Origine Verborum et Vocabulorum*. In quo ita scriptum fuit: "'Parcus' composito vocabulo est dictus,

---

[1] consules qu(a)e cum, ω; c. usque cum, *Mommsen.*

---

[1] v. 88, Ribbeck[3], who reads: *sine lingua caput pedárii
senténtias,* and gives other versions.

yet been added by the censors to the list of senators,
were not senators, and as their names came among
the last, they were not asked their opinions, but
went to a division on the views given by the leading
members.   That was the meaning of the traditional
proclamation, which even to-day the consuls, for
the sake of following precedent, use in summoning
the senators to the House.   The words of the edict
are these: "Senators and those who have the right
to express their opinion in the senate."

I have had a line of Laberius copied also, in which
that word is used; I read it in a mime entitled
Stricturae: [1]

The aye-man's vote is but a tongueless head.

I have observed that some use a barbarous form of
this word; for instead of *pedarii* they say *pedanii*.

XIX

Why, according to Gavius Bassus, a man is called *parcus*
and what he thought to be the explanation of that word;
and how, on the contrary, Favorinus made fun of that
explanation of his.

AT the dinners of the philosopher Favorinus, after
the guests had taken their places and the serving of
the viands began, a slave commonly stood by his table
and began to read something, either from Grecian
literature or from our own.   For example, one day
when I was present the reading was from the
treatise of the learned Gavius Bassus *On the Origin
of Verbs and Substantives*.   In it this passage occurred: [2] "*Parcus* is a compound word, made up

[2] Frag. 6, Fun.

quasi 'par arcae,' quando, sicut in arca omnia reconduntur eiusque custodia servantur et continentur,
ita homo tenax parvoque contentus omnia custodita
et recondita habet, sicuti arca. Quam ob causam
'parcus' quasi 'pararcus' est nominatus."

3   Tum Favorinus, ubi haec audivit, "superstitiose,"
inquit, " et nimis moleste atque odiose confabricatus
commolitusque magis est originem vocabuli Gavius
4 iste Bassus quam enarravit.   Nam si licet res dicere
commenticias, cur non probabilius videatur ut acci-
piamus 'parcum' ob eam causam dictum, quod
pecuniam consumi atque impendi arceat et pro-
5 hibeat, quasi 'pecuniarcus'?   Quin potius," inquit, "quod simplicius veriusque est, id dicimus?
'Parcus' enim neque ab arca, neque ab arcendo,
sed ab eo, quod est 'parum' et 'parvum,' de-
nominatus est."

---

[1] That is, he is like a strong-box.
[2] It is needless to say that all these derivations are wrong,
and that *parcus* is connected with *parco*, "spare."

of *par arcae*, that is 'like a strong-box;' for just as all valuables are put away in a strong-box and preserved and kept under its protection, just so a man who is close and content to spend little keeps all his property guarded and hidden away, as in a strong-box. For that reason he is called *parcus*, as if it were *par arcus*." [1]

Then Favorinus, on hearing these words, said: "That fellow Gavius Bassus has made up and contrived an origin for that word in an unnatural, altogether laboured and repellent manner, rather than explained it. For if it is permissible to draw on one's imagination, why would it not seem more reasonable to believe that a man is called *parcus* for the reason that he forbids and prevents the spending of money, as if he were *pecuniarcus*. Why not rather," he continued, "adopt an explanation which is simpler and nearer the truth? For *parcus* is derived neither from *arca* nor from *arceo*, but from *parum* and *parvum*." [2]

BOOK IV

LIBER QUARTUS

I

Sermo quidam Favorini philosophi cum grammatico iactantiore factus in Socraticum modum ; atque ibi in sermone dictum quibus verbis "penus" a Q. Scaevola definita sit ; quodque eadem definitio culpata reprehensaque est.

1 In vestibulo aedium Palatinarum omnium fere ordinum multitudo opperientes salutationem Caesaris constiterant ; atque ibi in circulo doctorum hominum, Favorino philosopho praesente, ostentabat quispiam grammaticae rei ditior[1] scholica quaedam nugalia, de generibus et casibus vocabulorum disserens cum arduis superciliis vocisque et vultus gravitate composita, tamquam interpres et arbiter 2 Sibyllae oraculorum. Tum aspiciens ad Favorinum, quamquam ei nondum etiam satis notus esset, "'Penus quoque,'" inquit, "variis generibus dictum et varie declinatum est. Nam et 'hoc penus' et 'haec penus' et 'huius peni' et 'penoris' veteres 3 dictaverunt ; mundum quoque muliebrem Lucilius in *Satirarum* xvi. non virili genere, ut ceteri, sed neutro appellavit his verbis :

---

[1] doct(i)or, *ς* ; scitior, *J. F. Gronov* ; eruditior, peritior, *others.*

---

[1] A store of provisions.
[2] Doubtless Antoninus Pius, since Gellius always refers to *Divus Hadrianus.*

BOOK IV

I

A discourse of the philosopher Favorinus carried on in the Socratic manner with an over-boastful grammarian; and in that discourse we are told how Quintus Scaevola defined *penus*[1]; and that this same definition has been criticized and rejected.

In the entrance hall of the palace on the Palatine a large number of men of almost all ranks had gathered together, waiting an opportunity to pay their respects to Caesar.[2] And there in a group of scholars, in the presence of the philosopher Favorinus, a man who thought himself unusually rich in grammatical lore was airing trifles worthy of the schoolroom, discoursing on the genders and cases of nouns with raised eyebrows and an exaggerated gravity of voice and expression, as if he were the interpreter and sovereign lord of the Sibyl's oracle. Then, looking at Favorinus, although as yet he was hardly acquainted with him, he said: "*Penus* too is used in different genders and is variously declined. For the early writers used to say *hoc penus* and *haec penus,* and in the genitive *peni* and *penoris*; Lucilius in his sixteenth satire also used the word *mundus,* which describes women's ornaments, not in the masculine gender, as other writers do, but in the neuter, in these words:[3]

[3] 519 Marx, who reads in the second line: *quid "mundum" atque penus.*

Legavit quidam uxori mundum omne penumque.[1]
Atqui quid mundum, quid non? quis dividet istuc?"

4 Atque horum omnium et testimoniis et exemplis
constrepebat; cumque nimis odiose blatiret,[2] in-
tercessit placide Favorinus et "Amabo," inquit,
"magister, quicquid est nomen tibi, abunde multa
docuisti quae quidem ignorabamus et scire haud
5 sane postulabamus. Quid enim refert mea eiusque
quicum loquor, quo genere 'penum' dicam aut in
quas extremas litteras declinem, si nemo id non
6 nimis barbare fecerimus?[3] Sed hoc plane indigeo
discere, quid sit 'penus' et qua fini id vocabulum
dicatur, ne rem cotidiani usus, tamquam qui in
venalibus Latine loqui coeptant, alia quam oportet
voce appellem."

7 "Quaeris," inquit, "rem minime obscuram. Quis
adeo ignorat, 'penum' esse vinum et triticum et
oleum et lentim et fabam atque huiuscemodi
8 cetera?" "Etiamne," inquit Favorinus, "milium
et panicum et glans et hordeum 'penus' est? sunt
enim propemodum haec quoque eiusdemmodi";
9 cumque ille reticens haereret, "Nolo," inquit, "hoc
iam labores, an ista, quae dixi, 'penus' appelletur.
Sed potesne mihi non speciem aliquam de penu
dicere, sed definire, genere proposito et differentiis
adpositis, quid sit 'penus'"? "Quod," inquit,

---

[1] atque penumqu(a)e quid, ω.
[2] blatiret, *Hosius;* blateraret, *Bentley*; plateret, *RV*,
placeret *P.*
[3] nemo non . . . fecerit, *Mommsen*; si modo, *Lion*;
fecerim, *RV*.

---

[1] A kind of grass of the genus *Panicum*, a word derived,
not from *panis*, "bread," but from *panus*, "an ear of millet,"
or similar grain (Walde).

A man once willed his wife all ornaments (mundum omne) and stores.

But what are ornaments? Who will determine that?

And he kept bawling out illustrations and examples of all these usages; but while he was prating quite too tiresomely, Favorinus interrupted and quietly said: "Well and good, master, whatever your name is, you have taught us more than enough about many things of which we were indeed ignorant and certainly did not ask to know. For what difference does it make to me and the one with whom I am speaking in what gender I use *penus*, or with what endings I inflect it, provided no one of us does this too barbarously? But this is clearly what I need to know, what *penus* is, and how far that word may be employed, so that I may not call a thing in every-day use by the wrong name, as those do who begin to speak their Latin in the slave-market."

"Your question is not at all difficult," replied the man. "Who indeed does not know that *penus* is wine, wheat, oil, lentils, beans, and the other things of that kind?" "Is not *penus* also," said Favorinus, "millet, panic-grass,[1] acorns and barley? for these too are almost of the same sort;" and when the man hesitated and did not answer, he continued: "I do not want you to trouble yourself further about the question whether those things which I have mentioned are called *penus*. But can you not, instead of telling me some essential part of *penus*, rather define the meaning of the word by stating its genus and adding its species?" "Good Heavens!" said he, "I don't understand

"genus et quas differentias dicas, non hercle in-
10 tellego." "Rem," inquit Favorinus, "plane dictam
postulas, quod difficillimum est, dici planius; nam
hoc quidem pervolgatum est, definitionem omnem
11 ex genere et differentia consistere. Sed si me tibi
praemandere, quod aiunt, postulas, faciam sane id
quoque honoris tui habendi gratia."

12 Ac deinde ita exorsus est: "Si," inquit, "ego
te nunc rogem ut mihi dicas et quasi circumscribas
verbis cuiusmodi 'homo' sit, non, opinor, respondeas
hominem esse te atque me. Hoc enim quis homo
sit ostendere est, non quid homo sit dicere. Sed si,
inquam, peterem ut ipsum illud quod homo est
definires, tu profecto mihi diceres hominem esse
animal mortale, rationis et scientiae capiens, vel
quo alio modo diceres, ut eum a ceteris omnibus
separares. Proinde igitur nunc te rogo ut quid sit
'penus' dicas, non ut aliquid ex penu nomines."

13 Tum ille ostentator, voce iam molli atque demissa,
"philosophias," inquit, "ego non didici neque discere
adpetivi et, si ignoro an hordeum ex 'penu' sit aut
quibus verbis 'penus' definiatur, non ea re litteras
quoque alias nescio."

14 "Scire," inquit ridens iam Favorinus, "quid
'penus' sit, non ex nostra magis est philosophia
15 quam ex grammatica tua. Meministi enim, credo,
quaeri solitum quid Vergilius dixerit, penum struere
vel longam vel longo ordine; utrumque enim pro-
16 fecto scis legi solitum. Sed ut faciam te aequiore
animo ut sis, ne illi quidem veteres iuris magistri,

---

[1] *Aen.* i. 704 f.: *Quinquaginta intus famulae, quibus
ordine longo cura penum struere et flammis adolere Penates.*
The MSS. and Servius have *longo*; Charisius, *longam.*

what you mean by genus and species." "You ask," replied Favorinus, "to have a matter which has been stated clearly stated still more clearly, which is very difficult; for it is surely a matter of common knowledge that every definition consists of genus and species. But if you ask me to pre-digest it for you, as they say, I will certainly do that too, for the sake of showing you honour."

And then Favorinus began in this wise: "If," said he, "I should now ask you to tell me, and as it were to define in words, what a man is, you would not, I suppose, reply that you and I are men. For that is to show who is a man, not to tell what a man is. But if, I say, I should ask you to define exactly what a man is, you would undoubtedly tell me that a man is a mortal living being, endowed with reason and knowledge, or you would define him in some other manner which would differentiate him from all other animals. Similarly, then, I now ask you to tell what *penus* is, not to name some example of *penus*." Then that boaster, now in humble and subdued tones, said: "I have never learned philo-sophy, nor desired to learn it, and if I do not know whether barley is included under *penus*, or in what words *penus* is defined, I am not on that account ignorant also of other branches of learning."

"To know what *penus* is," said Favorinus, who was now laughing, "is not more a part of my philosophy than of your grammar. For you re-member, I suppose, that it is often inquired whether Virgil said *penum struere longam* or *longo ordine*;[1] for you surely know that both readings are current. But to make you feel easier in mind, let me say that not even those old masters of the law who

qui 'sapientes' appellati sunt, definisse satis recte
17 existimantur, quid sit 'penus.' Nam Quintum
Scaevolam ad demonstrandam penum his verbis
usum audio : ' Penus est,' inquit, ' quod esculentum
aut posculentum est, quod ipsius patrisfamilias aut
matris familias¹ aut liberum patrisfamilias aut
familiae¹ eius, quae circum eum aut liberos eius est
et opus non² facit, causa paratum est. . . ., ut
Mucius ait, " penus " videri debet. Nam quae ad
edendum bibendumque in dies singulos prandii aut
cenae causa parantur, "penus " non sunt ; sed ea
potius, quae huiusce generis longae usionis gratia
contrahuntur et reconduntur, ex eo, quod non in
promptu est, sed intus et penitus habeatur, "penus "
18 dicta est.' Haec ego," inquit, "cum philosophiae
me dedissem, non insuper tamen habui discere ;
quoniam civibus Romanis Latine loquentibus rem
non suo³ vocabulo demonstrare non minus turpe est
quam hominem non suo nomine appellare."
19 Sic Favorinus sermones id genus communes a
rebus parvis et frigidis abducebat ad ea quae magis
utile esset audire ac discere, non allata extrinsecus,
non per ostentationem, sed indidem nata acceptaque.
20 Praeterea de penu adscribendum hoc etiam putavi,

¹ aut m.f. *and* aut. f., *added by Hertz.*
² eorum, *Lambecius.*   ³ suo, *added in σ.*

---

¹ *Jur. Civ.* fr. 1, Huschke ; II. 5a, Bremer.
² If the reading is correct, *opus* must mean *field-work*, the reference being to the *household* servants of the *pater familias* and his children.
³ There is a lacuna in the text.
⁴ *Penitus*, like *Penates*, is connected with *penus* in the sense of an inner chamber. *Penus* is derived by some from the root *pa-* of *pasco, pabulum*, etc. ; by others it is con-

were called ' wise men ' are thought to have defined
penus with sufficient accuracy. For I hear that
Quintus Scaevola used the following words to explain *penus*[1]: '*Penus*,' said he, 'is what is to be
eaten or drunk, which is prepared for the use of the
father of the family himself, or the mother of the
family, or the children of the father, or the household which he has about him or his children and
which is not engaged in work[2] . . . as[3] Mucius
says ought to be regarded as *penus*. For articles
which are prepared for eating and drinking day
by day, for luncheon or dinner, are not *penus*; but
rather the articles of that kind which are collected
and stored up for use during a long period are
called *penus*, because they are not ready at hand,
but are kept in the innermost part of the house.'[4]
This information," said Favorinus, " although I had
devoted myself to philosophy, I yet did not neglect
to acquire; since for Roman citizens speaking Latin
it is no less disgraceful not to designate a thing by
its proper word than it is to call a man out of his
own name."

Thus Favorinus used to lead ordinary conversations of this kind from insignificant and trivial
topics to those which were better worth hearing
and knowing, topics not lugged in irrelevantly, nor
by way of display, but springing from and suggested
by the conversations themselves.

Besides what Favorinus said, I think this too
ought to be added to our consideration of *penus*,

nected with πένομαι and πόνος, as the fruit of labour. Walde,
Lat. Etym. Wörterb. s.v., separates *penus*, an inner chamber,
from *penus*, a store of provisions, connecting the latter with
pasco, the former with *penes*, *penetro* and *Penates*.

Servium Sulpicium *In Reprehensis Scaevolae Capitibus*
scripsisse Cato Aelio placuisse, non quae esui et
potui forent, sed thus quoque et cereos in penu esse,
quod esset eius ferme rei causa comparatum.
21 Masurius autem Sabinus in *Iuris Civilis* secundo,
etiam quod iumentorum causa apparatum esset qui-
22 bus dominus uteretur, penori attributum dicit. Ligna
quoque et virgas et carbones, quibus conficeretur
23 penus, quibusdam ait videri esse in penu. Ex his
autem quae promercalia et usuaria isdem in locis
essent,[1] esse ea sola penoris putat quae satis sint usu
annuo.

II

Morbus et vitium quid differat et quam vim habeant vocabula ista in edicto aedilium ; et an eunuchus et steriles
mulieres redhiberi possint ; diversaeque super ea re
sententiae.

1 In *Edicto Aedilium Curulium*, qua parte de mancipiis
vendundis cautum est, scriptum sic fuit : "Titulus
servorum[2] singulorum scriptus sit curato ita, ut

---

[1] essent, *added by Mommsen.*
[2] servorum, ς ; scriptorum, ω ; *omitted by Hertz* ; gypsato-
rum, *Damsté.*

---

[1] Fr. 4, Huschke ; 3, Bremer.
[2] Fr. 1, Huschke, and Bremer.
[3] Fr. 1, Huschke ; 38, Bremer.
[4] Rufi *resp.* 1b, p. 44, Mucii *Jur. Civ.* fr. 7a, Bremer.

that Servius Sulpicius, in his *Criticism of the Chapters of Scaevola*, wrote[1] that Aelius Catus believed[2] that not only articles for eating and drinking, but also incense and wax tapers were included under the head of *penus*, since they were provided for practically the same purpose. But Masurius Sabinus, in the second book of his *Civil Law*, declares[3] that whatever was prepared for the beasts of burden which the owner of a house used was also *penus*. He adds that some[4] have thought that the term likewise included wood, faggots and charcoal, by means of which the *penus* was made ready for use. But of articles kept in the same place, for use or for purposes of trade, he thinks that only the amount which was sufficient for a year's needs was to be regarded as *penus*.

II

On the difference between a disease and a defect, and the force of those terms in the aediles' edict; also whether eunuchs and barren women can be returned, and the various views as to that question.

THE edict of the curule aediles,[5] in the section containing stipulations about the purchase of slaves, reads as follows:[6] "See to it that the sale ticket of each slave be so written that it can be known

---

[5] The aediles, and some other magistrates, issued an edict, or proclamation, at the beginning of their term of office, relating to the matters over which they had jurisdiction. When successive officials adopted and announced the same body of rules (*edictum tralaticium*), the edict assumed a more or less permanent form and became practically a code of laws.

[6] *F.J.R.* p. 214; cf. Hor. *Epist.* ii. 2. 1 ff.

intellegi recte possit quid morbi vitiive cuique sit,
quis fugitivus errove sit noxave solutus non sit."

2   Propterea quaesierunt iure consulti veteres, quod
"mancipium morbosum" quodve "vitiosum" recte
diceretur quantumque "morbus" a "vitio" differret.

3 Caelius Sabinus in libro, quem *De Edicto Aedilium
Curulium* composuit, Labeonem refert quid esset
"morbus" hisce verbis definisse : "Morbus est habitus cuiusque corporis contra naturam, qui usum eius

4 facit deteriorem." Sed "morbum" alias in
toto corpore accidere dicit, alias in parte corporis. Totius
corporis "morbum" esse, veluti sit phthisis aut
febris, partis autem, veluti sit caecitas aut pedis de-

5 bilitas.   "Balbus autem," inquit, "et atypus vitiosi
magis quam morbosi sunt, et equus mordax aut
calcitro vitiosus, non morbosus est. Sed cui morbus
est, idem etiam vitiosus est. Neque id tamen
contra fit ; potest enim qui vitiosus est non morbosus
esse. Quamobrem, cum de homine morboso agetur,
aeque,"[1] inquit, "ita dicetur : 'quanto ob id vitium
minoris erit.'"

6   De eunucho quidem quaesitum est an contra edictum aedilium videretur venundatus, si ignorasset

7 emptor eum eunuchum esse. Labeonem respondisse

8 aiunt redhiberi posse quasi morbosum ; sues etiam
feminae si sterilae essent et venum issent, ex edicto

9 aedilium posse agi Labeonem scripsisse. De sterila
autem muliere, si nativa sterilitate sit, Trebatium

---

[1] aeque, *Huschke* ; neque, ω.

---

[1] III. p. 510, Bremer.
[2] Fr. 1, Huschke; 2, Bremer.
[3] *Ad. Ed. Aed.* fr. 27, Huschke ; 1, Bremer.
[4] *Ad. Ed. Aed.* fr. 28, Huschke ; 12, Bremer.

exactly what disease or defect each one has, which one is a runaway or a vagabond, or is still under condemnation for some offence."

Therefore the jurists of old raised the question [1] of the proper meaning of a "diseased slave" and one that was "defective," and to what degree a disease differed from a defect. Caelius Sabinus, in the book which he wrote [2] *On the Edict of the Curule Aediles*, quotes Labeo, [3] as defining a disease in these terms: "Disease is an unnatural condition of any body, which impairs its usefulness." But he adds that disease affects sometimes the whole body and at other times a part of the body. That a disease of the whole body is, for example, consumption or fever, but of a part of the body anything like blindness or lameness. "But," he continues, "one who stutters or stammers is defective rather than diseased, and a horse which bites or kicks has faults rather than a disease. But one who has a disease is also at the same time defective. However, the converse is not also true; for one may have defects and yet not be diseased. Therefore in the case of a man who is diseased," says he, "it will be just and fair to state to what extent 'the price will be less on account of that defect.'"

With regard to a eunuch in particular it has been inquired whether he would seem to have been sold contrary to the aediles' edict, if the purchaser did not know that he was a eunuch. They say that Labeo ruled [4] that he could be returned as diseased; and that Labeo also wrote that if sows were sterile and had been sold, action could be brought on the basis of the edict of the aediles. But in the case of a barren woman, if the barrenness were

10 contra Labeonem respondisse dicunt. Nam cum redhiberi eam Labeo, quasi minus sanam, putasset, negasse aiunt Trebatium ex edicto agi posse, si ea mulier a principio genitali sterilitate esset. At si valitudo eius offendisset exque ea vitium factum esset ut concipere fetus non posset, tum sanam non

11 videri et esse in causa redhibitionis. De myope quoque, qui "luscitiosus" Latine appellatur, dissensum est; alii enim redhiberi omnimodo debere, alii contra, nisi id vitium morbo contractum esset.

12 Eum vero cui dens deesset, Servius redhiberi posse respondit, Labeo in causa esse redhibendi negavit; vit; "Nam et magna," inquit, "pars dente aliquo carent, neque eo magis plerique homines morbosi sunt, et absurdum admodum est dicere non sanos nasci homines, quoniam cum infantibus non simul dentes gignuntur."

13 Non praetereundum est id quoque in libris veterum iurisperitorum scriptum esse, "morbum" et "vitium" distare, quod "vitium" perpetuum,

14 "morbus" cum accessu decessuque sit. Sed hoc si ita est, neque caecus neque eunuchus morbosus est, contra Labeonis quam supra dixi sententiam.

15 Verba Masuri Sabini apposui ex libro *Iuris civilis* secundo: "Furiosus mutusve cuive quod membrum lacerum laesumque est aut obest quo ipse minus

---

[1] Fr. 28 ; Huschke ; 3, Bremer.
[2] Fr. 10, Huschke ; *Resp.* 24. Bremer.
[3] Fr. 17, Huschke ; *Resp.* 108, Bremer.
[4] Fr. 29, Huschke ; 2, Bremer.
[5] Cael. Sab. *ad. ed.* fr. 1 ff., Bremer.
[6] Fr. 5. Huschke ; 173 ff., Bremer.

congenital they say that Trebatius gave a ruling opposed to that of Labeo. For while Labeo thought [1] that she could be returned as unsound, they quote Trebatius as declaring [2] that no action could be taken on the basis of the edict, if the woman had been born barren. But if her health had failed, and in consequence such a defect had resulted that she could not conceive, in that case she appeared to be unsound and there was ground for returning her. With regard to a short-sighted person too, one whom we call in Latin *luscitiosus*, there is disagreement; for some maintain that such a person should be returned in all cases, while others on the contrary hold that he can be returned only if that defect was the result of disease. Servius indeed ruled [3] that one who lacked a tooth could be returned, but Labeo said [4] that such a defect was not sufficient ground for a return: " For," says he, " many men lack some one tooth, and most of them are no more diseased on that account, and it would be altogether absurd to say that men are not born sound, because infants come into the world unprovided with teeth."

I must not omit to say that this also is stated in the works of the early jurists, [5] that the difference between a disease and a defect is that the latter is lasting, while the former comes and goes. But if this be so, contrary to the opinion of Labeo, which I quoted above, neither a blind man nor a eunuch is diseased.

I have added a passage from the second book of Masurius Sabinus *On Civil Law*: [6] " A madman or a mute, or one who has a broken or crippled limb, or any defect which impairs his usefulness, is

aptus sit, morbosi sunt. Qui natura longe minus
videt tam sanus est quam qui tardius currit."

III

Quod nullae fuerunt rei uxoriae actiones in urbe Roma ante
Carvilianum divortium ; atque inibi, quid sit proprie
paelex quaeque eius vocabuli ratio sit.

1 MEMORIAE traditum est quingentis fere annis post
Romam conditam nullas rei uxoriae neque actiones
neque cautiones in urbe Roma aut in Latio fuisse,
quoniam profecto nihil desiderabantur, nullis etiam-
2 tunc matrimoniis divertentibus. Servius quoque
Sulpicius in libro, quem composuit *De Dotibus,* tum
primum cautiones rei uxoriae necessarias esse visas
scripsit, cum Spurius Carvilius, cui Ruga cognomentum fuit, vir nobilis, divortium cum uxore fecit,
quia liberi ex eá corporis vitio non gignerentur, anno
urbis conditae quingentesimo vicesimo tertio M.
Atilio, P. Valerio consulibus. Atque is Carvilius
traditur uxorem quam dimisit egregie dilexisse
carissimamque morum eius gratia habuisse, set[1]
iurisiurandi religionem animo atque amori praever-
tisse quod iurare a censoribus coactus erat, uxorem
se liberum quaerundum gratia habiturum.

[1] sed, *Carrio*; et, ω.

---

[1] That is, the repayment of the dowry in case of a divorce
was not secured. A *cautio* was a verbal or written promise,
sometimes confirmed by an oath, as in Suet. *Aug.* xcviii. 2,
ius iurandum et cautionem exegit.

[2] Fr. 1, Huschke; p. 227, Bremer.   [3] 231 B.C.

[4] An oath was regularly required by the censors that a man

diseased. But one who is by nature near-sighted is as sound as one who runs more slowly than others."

III

That before the divorce of Carvilius there were no lawsuits about a wife's dowry in the city of Rome; further, the proper meaning of the word paelex and its derivation.

It is on record that for nearly five hundred years after the founding of Rome there were no lawsuits and no warranties[1] in connection with a wife's dowry in the city of Rome or in Latium, since of course nothing of that kind was called for, inasmuch as no marriages were annulled during that period. Servius Sulpicius too, in the book which he compiled *On Dowries,* wrote[2] that security for a wife's dower seemed to have become necessary for the first time when Spurius Carvilius, who was surnamed Ruga, a man of rank, put away his wife because, owing to some physical defect, no children were born from her; and that this happened in the five hundred and twenty-third year after the founding of the city, in the consulship of Marcus Atilius and Publius Valerius.[3] And it is reported that this Carvilius dearly loved the wife whom he divorced, and held her in strong affection because of her character, but that above his devotion and his love he set his regard for the oath which the censors had compelled him to take,[4] that he would marry a wife for the purpose of begetting children.

married for the purpose of begetting legal heirs (*liberorum quaerendorum causa*); cf. Suet. *Jul.* lii. 3.

3   " Paelicem " autem appellatam probrosamque
habitam, quae iuncta consuetaque esset cum eo in
cuius manu mancipioque alia matrimonii causa foret,
hac antiquissima lege ostenditur, quam Numae regis
fuisse accepimus : " Paelex aedem [1] Iunonis ne
tangito ; si tangit, Iunoni crinibus demissis agnum
feminam caedito."

" Paelex " autem quasi πάλλαξ, id est quasi
παλλακίς. Ut pleraque alia, ita hoc quoque vocabulum de Graeco flexum est.

IV

Quid Servius Sulpicius, in libro qui est *De Dotibus*, scripserit
de iure atque more veterum sponsaliorum.

1   SPONSALIA in ea parte Italiae quae Latium appellatur hoc more atque iure solita fieri scripsit Servius
Sulpicius in libro quem inscripsit [2] *De Dotibus* :
2   " Qui uxorem," inquit, " ducturus erat, ab eo unde
ducenda erat stipulabatur, eam in matrimonium
datum [3] iri. Qui ducturus erat, id [4] itidem spondebat.
Is contractus stipulationum sponsionumque dicebatur ' sponsalia.' Tunc, quae promissa erat
' sponsa ' appellabatur, qui spoponderat ducturum,
' sponsus.' Sed si post eas stipulationis uxor non

----

[1] aram, *Paulus* ; aedem (edem), *MSS.*
[2] inscripsit, *Huschke* ; scripsit, ω.
[3] ducturum iri. Cui, ω.
[4] id, *suggested by Hosius.*

----

[1] *F.J.R.*, p. 8, fr. 2 ; I, p. 135, Bremer.
[2] Walde, *Lat. Etym. Wörterb. s.v.*, regards *paelex* and the
Greek πάλλαξ and παλλακίς, the former in the sense of a

Moreover, a woman was called *paelex*, or " concubine," and regarded as infamous, if she lived on
terms of intimacy with a man who had another
woman under his legal control in a state of matrimony, as is evident from this very ancient law, which
we are told was one of king Numa's :[1] " Let no concubine touch the temple of Juno ; if she touch it,
let her, with hair unbound, offer up a ewe lamb to
Juno."

Now *paelex* is the equivalent of πάλλαξ, that is
to say, of παλλακίς.[2] Like many other words of ours,
this one too is derived from the Greek.

IV

What Servius Sulpicius wrote in his work *On Dowries* about
the law and usage of betrothals in early times.

In the book to which he gave the title *On Dowries*
Servius Sulpicius wrote [3] that in the part of Italy
known as Latium betrothals were regularly contracted
according to the following customary and legal practice. " One who wished to take a wife," says he,
" demanded of him from whom she was to be received a formal promise that she would be given in
marriage. The man who was to take the woman to
wife made a corresponding promise. That contract,
based upon pledges given and received, was called
sponsalia, or ' betrothal.' Thereafter, she who had
been promised was called *sponsa*, and he who had
asked her in marriage, *sponsus*. But if, after such

young slave, as loan words from the Phoenician-Hebrew
pillegesh, "concubine." The spelling *pellex* is due to popular
etymology, which associated the word with *pellicio*, "entice."
[3] Fr. 2, Huschke ; p. 226, Bremer.

dabatur aut non ducebatur, qui stipulabatur aut qui spoponderat[1] ex sponsu agebat. Iudices cognoscebant. Iudex quamobrem data acceptave non esset uxor quaerebat. Si nihil iustae causae videbatur, litem pecunia aestimabat, quantique interfuerat eam uxorem accipi aut dari, eum qui spoponderat aut[2] qui stipulatus erat, condemnabat."

3 Hoc ius sponsaliorum observatum dicit Servius ad id tempus quo civitas universo Latio lege Iulia
4 data est. Haec eadem Neratius scripsit in libro quem *De Nuptiis* composuit.

V

Historia narrata de perfidia aruspicum Etruscorum ; quodque ob eam rem versus hic a pueris Romae urbe tota cantatus est: "Malum consilium consultori pessimum est."

1 STATUA Romae in comitio posita Horatii Coclitis,
2 fortissimi viri, de caelo tacta est. Ob id fulgur piaculis luendum aruspices ex Etruria acciti, inimico atque hostili in populum Romanum animo, institue-
3 rant eam rem contrariis religionibus procurare, atque

---

[1] aut . . . spoponderat, *Gronov.*
[2] aut, *added in* σ; ei, *Cramer*

---

[1] 90 B.C.   [2] Fr. 1, Bremer.
[3] The Comitium, or place of assembly (*com-*, *eo*), was a *templum*, or inaugurated plot of ground, orientated according

an interchange of pledges, the bride to be was not given in marriage, or was not received, then he who had asked for her hand, or he who had promised her, brought suit on the ground of breach of contract. The court took cognizance of the case. The judge inquired why the woman was not given in marriage, or why she was not accepted. If no good and sufficient reason appeared, the judge then assigned a money value to the advantage to be derived from receiving or giving the woman in marriage, and condemned the one who had made the promise, or the one who had asked for it, to pay a fine of that amount."

Servius Sulpicius says that this law of betrothal was observed up to the time when citizenship was given to all Latium by the Julian law.[1] The same account as the above was given also by Neratius in the book which he wrote *On Marriage.*[2]

V

A story which is told of the treachery of Etruscan diviners; and how because of that circumstance the boys at Rome chanted this verse all over the city : "Bad counsel to the giver is most ruinous."

THE statue of that bravest of men, Horatius Cocles, which stood in the Comitium[3] at Rome, was struck by lightning. To make expiatory offerings because of that thunderbolt, diviners were summoned from Etruria. These, through personal and national hatred of the Romans, had made up their minds to give false directions for the performance of that rite.

to the points of the compass, at the north-western corner of the Forum Romanum.

illam statuam suaserunt in inferiorem locum perperam transponi, quem sol oppositu circum undique [1]
4 altarum [2] aedium numquam illustraret. Quod cum
ita fieri persuasissent, delati ad populum proditique
sunt et, cum de perfidia confessi essent, necati sunt,
constrtitque, eam statuam, proinde ut verae rationes
post compertae monebant, in locum editum sub-
ducendam atque ita in area Volcani sublimiore loco
statuendam ; ex quo res bene ac prospere populo
5 Romano cessit. Tum igitur, quod in Etruscos
aruspices male consulentis animadversum vindica-
tumque fuerat, versus hic scite factus cantatusque
esse a pueris urbe tota fertur :

Malúm consilium cónsultori péssimum est.

6   Ea historia de aruspicibus ac de versu isto senario
scripta est in *Annalibus Maximis,* libro undecimo,
et in Verri Flacci libro primo *Rerum Memoria Digna-*
7 *rum.* Videtur autem versus hic de Graeco illo
Hesiodi versu expressus :

Ἡ δὲ κακὴ βουλὴ τῷ βουλεύσαντι κακίστη.

---

[1] undique montis aliarumque, *P* ; monetae, *Mommsen.*
[2] altarum, *Jahn* ; aliarum, *RV* ; aliarumque *P, Mommsen.*

---

[1] On the lower slope of the Capitoline Hill, at the north-
west corner of the Forum.
[2] p. 37, Bährens, who needlessly changes the reading.
[3] The *senarius* was an iambic trimeter, consisting of six

They accordingly gave the misleading advice that
the statue in question should be moved to a lower
position, on which the sun never shone, being cut off
by the high buildings which surrounded the place on
every side. When they had induced the Romans to
take that course, they were betrayed and brought to
trial before the people, and having confessed their
duplicity, were put to death. And it became evident,
in exact accord with what were later found to be the
proper directions, that the statue ought to be taken
to an elevated place and set up in a more command-
ing position in the area of Vulcan;[1] and after that
was done, the matter turned out happily and suc-
cessfully for the Romans. At that time, then, because the evil counsel of the Etruscan diviners had
been detected and punished, this clever line is said
to have been composed, and chanted by the boys all
over the city:[2]

> Bad counsel to the giver is most ruinous.

This story about the diviners and that *senarius*[3]
is found in the *Annales Maximi*, in the eleventh
book,[4] and in Verrius Flaccus' first book of *Things
Worth Remembering*.[5] But the verse appears to be
a translation of the Greek poet Hesiod's familiar line:[6]

> And evil counsel aye most evil is
> To him who gives it.

iambic feet, or three dipodies. The early Roman dramatic
poets allowed substitutions (the tribrach, irrational spondee,
irrational anapaest, cyclic dactyl, and proceleusmatic) in
every foot except the last; others conformed more closely to
the Greek models.

[4] Fr. 3, Peter.   [5] p. xiii, Müller.
[6] *Works and Days*, 166.

VI

Verba veteris senatusconsulti posita, quo decretum est
hostiis maioribus expiandum, quod in sacrario hastae
Martiae movissent ; atque ibi enarratum quid sint "hostiae succidaneae," quid item " porca praecidanea " ; et
quod Capito Ateius ferias "praecidaneas" appellavit.

1 Ut "terram movisse " nuntiari solet eaque res
procuratur, ita in veteribus memoriis scriptum legimus nuntiatum esse senatui in sacrario in regia
2 "hastas Martias movisse." Eius rei causa senatusconsultum factum est M. Antonio A. Postumio
consulibus, eiusque exemplum hoc est : "Quod C.
Iulius, L. filius, pontifex nuntiavit in sacrario in [1]
regia hastas Martias movisse, de ea re ita censuerunt,
uti M. Antonius consul hostiis maioribus Iovi et
Marti procuraret et ceteris dis, quibus videretur,
lactantibus. Ibus [2] uti procurasset satis habendum
censuerunt. Si quid succidaneis opus esset, robiis
succideret.
3 Quod "succidaneas " hostias senatus appellavit,
4 quaeri solet quid verbum id significet. In Plauti

---

[1] in, *added in σ.*   [2] ibus, *added by Scioppius.*

---

[1] The spears sacred to Mars and the sacred shields
(*ancilia*) were said to move of their own accord when danger
threatened. According to Dio, xliv. 17, they shook violently
before the death of Caesar.
[2] A building in the Roman Forum, near the temple of
Vesta, the official headquarters of the *pontifex maximus*.
According to tradition, it was built and dwelt in by Numa.
It contained a sanctuary of Mars, in which the sacred spears
and shields (*ancilia*) were sometimes kept. Dio, however,

VI

A quotation from an early decree of the senate, which provided that sacrifice should be made with full-grown victims
because the spears of Mars had moved in the sanctuary ;
also an explanation of the meaning of *hostiae succidaneae*
and likewise of *porca praecidanea* ; and further, that Ateius
Capito called certain holidays *praecidaneae*.

NOT only was an earthquake regularly reported,
and expiatory offerings made on that account, but I
also find it mentioned in early records, that report
was made to the senate when the spears of Mars [1] had
moved in the sanctuary in the Regia.[2]   Because of
such an occurrence, a decree of the senate was
passed in the consulship of Marcus Antonius and
Aulus Postumius,[3] of which this is a copy : " Whereas Gaius Julius, son of Lucius, the pontifex, has
reported that the spears of Mars have moved in the
sanctuary in the Regia, the senate has therefore
decreed with reference to that matter, that Marcus
Antonius the consul should make expiation to
Jupiter and Mars with full-grown victims, and with
unweaned victims to such of the other gods as he
thought proper.   They decided that it should be
regarded as sufficient for him to have sacrificed with
these.   If there should be any need of additional
victims, the additional offerings should be made with
red victims."

Inasmuch as the senate called some victims *succidaneae,* it is often inquired what that word means.

xliv. 17, tells us that at the time of Caesar's death they were
in his house, *i.e.* the *domus publica* (see Suet. *Jul.* xlvi.).
    [3] 99 B.C.

quoque comoedia quae *Epidicus* inscripta est, super
eodem ipso verbo requiri audio in his versibus :

Mén piaculárem oportet fíeri ob stultitiám tuam,
Ut meum tergum tuaé stultitiae súbdas succi-
dáneum ?

5 "Succidaneae" autem "hostiae" dicuntur, *ae*
littera per morem compositi vocabuli in *i* [1] litteram
6 tramutata [2] quasi "succaedaneae," appellatae, quoniam, si primis hostiis litatum non erat, aliae post
easdem ductae hostiae caedebantur ; quae quia,[3]
prioribus iam caesis, luendi piaculi gratia subdebantur
et succidebantur, "succidaneae" nominatae, littera *i* [1]
scilicet tractim pronuntiata ; audio enim quosdam
eam litteram in hac voce barbare corripere.
7 Eadem autem ratione verbi "praecidaneae" quoque hostiae dicuntur quae ante sacrificia sollemnia
8 pridie caeduntur. "Porca" etiam "praecidanea"
appellata quam piaculi gratia ante fruges novas
captas immolare Cereri mos fuit, si qui familiam
funestam aut non purgaverant, aut aliter eam rem,
quam oportuerat, procuraverant.
9 Sed porcam et hostias quasdam "praecidaneas,"
sicuti dixi, appellari, vulgo notum est, ferias "praeci-
10 daneas" dici, id, opinor, a volgo remotum est.
Propterea verba Atei Capitonis, ex quinto librorum
quos *De Pontificio Iure* composuit, scripsi : "Tib.

---

[1] i, *added in σ.*   [2] tramutata, *Mommsen* ; nam, ω.
[3] quae quia, *Otho* ; due qua (quas, *R*), ω.

---

[1] 139 f.   [2] From *sub* and *caedo.*
[3] From *prae* and *caedo*, "slay beforehand."
[4] Fr. 8, Huschke ; 1, Bremer.

Also in the comedy of Plautus which is entitled
Epidicus I hear that inquiry is made about that same
word, which occurs in these verses : [1]

> Should I the victim of your folly be
> And let you sacrifice my back to it,
> As substitute for yours ?

Now it is said that the victims were called *succidaneae*
—which is equivalent to *succaedaneae*, the diphthong
ae, according to the custom in compound words, being
changed to *i*—because if the expiation was not effected
by the first victims, other victims were brought and
killed after them ; and since these, after the first
had already been offered, were substituted for the
sake of making atonement and were "slain in succes-
sion to" the others, they were called *succidaneae*,[2] the
letter *i*, of course, being pronounced long ; for I hear
that some barbarously shorten that letter in this
word.

Moreover, it is on the same linguistic principle
that *praecidanea* is applied to those victims which
are offered on the day before the regular sacrifices.
Also the sow is called *praecidanea* [3] which it was
usual to offer up to Ceres before the harvesting of
the new crops, for the sake of expiation in case any
had failed to purify a defiled household, or had
performed that rite in an improper manner.

But that a sow and certain victims are called
praecidaneae, as I have said, is a matter of common
knowledge ; that some festivals are called *praecidaneae* is a fact I think that is not known to the
general public. Therefore I have quoted a passage
from the fifth book of the treatise which Ateius
Capito compiled *On Pontifical Law* : [4] "Tiberius

333

Coruncanio pontifici maximo feriae praecidaneae in
atrum diem inauguratae sunt. Collegium decrevit
non habendum religioni, quin eo die feriae praecidaneae essent."

VII

De epistula Valerii Probi grammatici ad Marcellum scripta
super accentu nominum quorundam Poenicorum.

1 VALERIUS PROBUS grammaticus inter suam aeta-
2 tem praestanti scientia fuit. Is " Hannibalem" et
" Hasdrubalem" et " Hamilcarem" ita pronuntiabat
ut paenultimam circumflecteret, et est [1] epistula
eius scripta *Ad Marcellum,* in qua Plautum et
Ennium multosque alios veteres eo modo pronun-
3 tiasse affirmat, solius tamen Ennii versum unum
ponit ex libro, qui *Scipio* inscribitur.
4 Eum versum quadrato numero factum subiecimus,
in quo, nisi tertia syllaba de Hannibalis nomine
5 circumflexe promatur, numerus clausurus est. Versus
Ennii quem dixit, ita est:

Quáque [2] propter Hánnibalis cópias consíderat.

[1] et est, *Lion;* ut est, ω; teste, *J. F. Gronov.*
[2] quaque, *Hertz, Vahlen;* si qua, *Boücheler;* qua, ω.

---

[1] So little is known about the *feriae praecidaneae* that it is
not easy to tell whether this vote was for that occasion only
(" on that day ") or was general (" on such a day "). Since
Gellius, v. 17. 2, quotes Verrius Flaccus as saying that no
sacrifice could properly be made on a *dies ater,* the former
seems the more probable. In any case, the action of
Coruncanius was evidently criticized, and his colleagues
came to his rescue. Possibly *preliminary* sacrifices might be
offered on such a day, or *praecidaneae* as applied to *feriae*
may not have involved sacrifices. The statement in Smith's
Dict. of Antiq. 3rd ed., ii. p. 839, that *feriae praecidaneae*
were " often " *dies atri,* and were " on certain occasions "

Coruncanius, the pontifex maximus, appointed *feriae praecidaneae,* or "a preparatory festival," for a day of ill-omen. The college of pontiffs voted that there need be no religious scruple against celebrating the *feriae praecidaneae* on that day."[1]

VII

On a letter of the grammarian Valerius Probus, written to Marcellus, regarding the accent of certain Punic names.

VALERIUS PROBUS the grammarian was conspicuous among the men of his time for his learning. He pronounced Hannibalem and Hasdrubalem and Hamilcarem with a circumflex accent on the penult, and there is a letter addressed *To Marcellus,* in which he asserts that Plautus,[2] and Ennius and many other early writers pronounced in that way; but he quotes a single line of Ennius alone, from the book entitled *Scipio.*

That verse, composed in octonarii,[3] I have appended; in it, unless the third syllable of Hannibal's name is circumflexed,[4] the metre will halt. The verse of Ennius to which I referred reads thus :[5]

And where near Hannibal's forces he had camped.[6]

---

inaugurated by the chief pontiff, does not seem warranted by this passage, which is the only one in which the phrase occurs.

[2] Frag. inc. xlii. Götz.

[3] The term *octonarius* is applied both to a trochaic tetrameter acatalectic (as here in the Latin verse) or to an iambic tetrameter acatalectic. It consisted of eight trochaic or iambic feet. Substitutions were allowed in every foot except the last. See note on *senarius,* p. 329.

[4] In the Latin line the ictus falls on the penult *Hánnibális,* but the ordinary pronunciation was *Hannibalis.*

[5] Varia, 13, Vahlen[2], who reads *quaque.*

[6] Vahlen and the T.L.L. take *considerat* from *consido,* Weiss from *considero.*

VIII

Quid C. Fabricius de Cornelio Rufino homine avaro dixerit,
quem, cum odisset inimicusque esset, designandum tamen
consulem curavit.

1 FABRICIUS LUSCINUS magna gloria vir magnisque
2 rebus gestis fuit. P. Cornelius Rufinus manu quidem
strenuus et bellator bonus militarisque disciplinae
peritus admodum fuit, sed furax homo et avaritia
3 acri erat. Hunc Fabricius non probabat neque
amico utebatur osusque eum morum causa fuit.
4 Sed cum in temporibus rei publicae[1] difficillimis
consules creandi forent et is Rufinus peteret consulatum competitoresque eius essent inbelles quidam
et futtiles, summa ope adnixus est Fabricius uti
5 Rufino consulatus deferretur. Eam rem plerisque
admirantibus, quod hominem avarum cui esset ini-
6 micissimus, creari consulem vellet, "Malo," inquit,
"civis me[2] compilet, quam hostis vendat."
7 Hunc Rufinum postea, bis consulatu et dictatura
functum, censor Fabricius senatu movit ob luxuriae
notam, quod decem pondo libras argenti facti
8 haberet.[3] Id autem quod supra scripsi, Fabricium
de Cornelio Rufino ita, uti in pleraque historia
scriptum est, dixisse, M. Cicero non aliis a Fabricio,
sed ipsi Rufino, gratias agenti quod ope[4] eius
designatus esset, dictum esse refert in libro secundo
De Oratore.

---

[1] publicae, σ, *Damsté.* [2] consulem . . . me, *not in MSS.*
[3] facti haberet, *Scioppius;* factitaret, ω.
[4] ope, *added by Hertz.*

---

[1] This was in 290 B.C. at the beginning of the last Samnite
war. Rufinus was consul again in 277 B.C.

VIII

What Gaius Fabricius said of Cornelius Rufinus, an avaricious man, whose election to the consulship he supported, although he hated him and was his personal enemy.

FABRICIUS LUSCINUS was a man of great renown and great achievements. Publius Cornelius Rufinus was, to be sure, a man energetic in action, a good warrior, and a master of military tactics, but thievish and keen for money. This man Fabricius neither respected nor treated as a friend, but hated him because of his character. Yet when consuls were to be chosen at a highly critical period for the State, and that Rufinus was a candidate while his competitors were without military experience and untrustworthy, Fabricius used every effort to have the office given to Rufinus.[1] When many men expressed surprise at his attitude, in wishing an avaricious man, towards whom he felt bitter personal enmity, to be elected consul, he said : " I would rather be robbed by a fellow-citizen than sold [2] by the enemy."

This Rufinus afterwards, when he had been dictator and twice consul, Fabricius in his censorship expelled from the senate [3] on the charge of extravagance, because he possessed ten pounds weight of silver plate. That remark of Fabricius about Rufinus I gave above in the form in which it appears in most historians; but Marcus Cicero, in the second book of the *De Oratore*, says[4] that it was not made by Fabricius to others, but to Rufinus himself, when he was thanking Fabricius because he had been elected consul through his help.

---

[2] That is, sold into slavery by a victorious foe.
[3] In 275 B.C.   [4] § 268.

IX

Quid significet proprie "religiosus"; et in quae diverticula
significatio istius vocabuli flexa sit; et verba Nigidii
Figuli ex *Commentariis* eius super ea re sumpta.

1 NIGIDIUS FIGULUS, homo, ut ego arbitror, iuxta
M. Varronem doctissimus, in undecimo *Commentariorum Grammaticorum* versum ex antiquo carmine
refert memoria hercle dignum:

Religentem esse oportet, religiosus ne fuas,

2 cuius autem id carmen sit non scribit. Atque in
eodem loco Nigidius: "Hoc," inquit, "inclinamentum
semper huiuscemodi verborum, ut 'vinosus,' 'mulierosus,' 'religiosus,' significat copiam quandam in-
modicam rei super qua dicitur. Quocirca 'religiosus' is appellabatur, qui nimia et superstitiosa
religione sese alligaverat, eaque res vitio assigna-
batur."

3 Sed praeter ista quae Nigidius dicit, alio quodam
diverticulo significationis "religiosus" pro casto
atque observanti cohibentique sese certis legibus
4 finibusque dici coeptus. Simili autem modo illa
quoque vocabula, ab eadem profecta origine, diversum significare videntur, "religiosi dies" et
5 "religiosa delubra." "Religiosi" enim "dies"
dicuntur tristi omine infames inpeditique, in quibus
et res divinas facere et rem quampiam novam exor-
diri temperandum est, quos multitudo imperitorum
6 prave et perperam "nefastos" appellat. Itaque

---

[1] Fr. 4, Swoboda.
[2] p. 297, Ribbeck[3], who reads: *réligentem esse <téd>
oportet, réligiosus né fuas*, following Fleckeisen.

IX

On the proper meaning of *religiosus*; and what changes the meaning of that word has undergone; and remarks of Nigidius Figulus on that subject, drawn from his *Commentaries*.

NIGIDIUS FIGULUS, in my opinion the most learned of men next to Marcus Varro, in the eleventh book of his *Grammatical Commentaries*, quotes[1] a truly remarkable line from an early poet:[2]

Best it is to be religious, lest one superstitious be ;

but he does not name the author of the poem. And in the same connection Nigidius adds : " The suffix *osus* in words of this kind, such as *vinosus, mulierosus, religiosus,* always indicates an excessive amount of the quality in question. Therefore *religiosus* is applied to one who has involved himself in an extreme and superstitious devotion, which was regarded as a fault."

But in addition to what Nigidius says, by another shift in meaning *religiosus* began to be used of an upright and conscientious man, who regulates his conduct by definite laws and limits. Similarly too the following terms, which have the same origin, appear to have acquired different meanings ; namely, *religiosus dies* and *religiosa delubra*. For those days are called *religiosi* which are of ill-fame and are hampered by an evil omen, so that on them one must refrain from offering sacrifice or beginning any new business whatever ; they are, namely, the days that the ignorant multitude falsely and improperly call *nefasti*.[3] Thus Marcus Cicero, in the ninth

---

[3] On *nefasti dies* it was impious for legal business to be carried on, or assemblies held.

M. Cicero in libro *Epistularum* nono *Ad Atticum*,
" Maiores," inquit, " nostri funestiorem diem esse
voluerunt Alliensis pugnae quam urbis captae,
quod hoc malum ex illo. Itaque alter religiosus
7 etiamnunc dies, alter in volgus ignotus." Idem
tamen M. Tullius in oratione *De Accusatore Constituendo* "religiosa delubra" dicit non ominosa
nec tristia, sed maiestatis venerationisque plena.
8 Masurius autem Sabinus in *Commentariis* quos *De
Indigenis* composuit, "Religiosum," inquit, "est
quod propter sanctitatem aliquam remotum ac
sepositum a nobis est, verbum a 'reliquendo' dic-
9 tum, tamquam 'caerimoniae' a 'carendo.'" Secundum hanc Sabini interpretationem templa quidem
ac delubra—quia horum cumulus in vituperationem
non cadit, ut illorum quorum laus in modo extat[1]—,
quae non volgo ac temere, sed cum castitate caeri-
moniaque adeundum, et reverenda et reformidanda
10 sunt magis quam involganda; sed dies "religiosi"
dicti, quos ex contraria causa, propter ominis diri-
11 tatem, relinquimus. Et Terentius :

Tum, quód dem "recte" est. Nám, nihil esse
míhi, religio est dícere.

---

[1] quia . . . extat, *omitted by Madvig.*

---

[1] ix. 5. 2.   [2] *Div. in Caec.* 3.
[3] Fr. 13, Huschke ; p. 366, Bremer.
[4] The sense of *relinquo* as= "avoid " is shown below (§ 10);
that of *careo* is explained by Paul. Fest. (pp. 62 and 298,
Lindsay, *s.v. denariae* and *purimenstrio*) as referring to doing
without, or refraining from, certain things on ceremonial
days. Some Roman etymologists derived *caerimonia* from
the town of Caere, others from *caritas* ; see Paul. Fest.
p. 38, Linds. The origin of the word is uncertain. For

book of his *Letters to Atticus*, writes:[1] "Our fore-fathers maintained that the day of the battle at the Allia was more calamitous than that on which the city was taken; because the latter disaster was the result of the former. Therefore the one day is even now *religiosus,* while the other is unknown to the general public." Yet the same Marcus Tullius, in his speech *On Appointing a Prosecutor,*[2] uses the term *religiosa delubra* of shrines which are not ill-omened and gloomy, but full of majesty and sacredness. Masurius Sabinus too, in his *Notes on Native Words,* says:[3] "*Religiosus* is that which because of some sacred quality is removed and withdrawn from us; the word is derived from *relinquo,* as is *caerimonia* from *careo.*"[4] According to this explanation of Sabinus, temples indeed and shrines—since an accumulation of these does not give rise to censure, as in case of things which are praised for their moderate use—since they are to be approached, not unceremoniously and thoughtlessly, but after purification and in due form, must be both revered and feared, rather than profaned; but those days are called *religiosi* which for the opposite reason, because they are of dire omen, we avoid.[5] And Terence says:[6]

Then too I give her nothing, except to say "All right;"
For I avoid confessing my impecunious plight.

---

religio some accept Cicero's derivation from *relegere* (*Nat. Deor.* ii. 72), others that of Lactantius (iv. 28) from *religare.*

[5] That is, we avoid doing business, or undertaking any enterprise, on such days.

[6] *Heaut.* 228; Dziatzko reads: *tum quód dem ei "recte" est; nám nil esse míhi religiost dícere.*

12 Quod si, ut ait Nigidius, omnia istiusmodi in-
clinamenta nimium ac praeter modum significant et
idcirco in culpas cadunt, ut " vinosus," " mulierosus,"
" morosus," " verbosus," " famosus," cur " ingeniosus " et " formosus " et " officiosus " et " speciosus,"
quae pariter ab ingenio et forma et officio et specie,[1]
inclinata sunt, cur etiam " disciplinosus," " consiliosus," " victoriosus," quae M. Cato ita affiguravit,
cur item " facundiosa," quod Sempronius Asellio XIII
Rerum Gestarum ita scripsit : facta sua spectare
oportere, non dicta, si minus facundiosa essent—
cur, inquam, ista omnia numquam in culpam, sed
in laudem dicuntur, quamquam haec item[2] incre-
mentum sui nimium demonstrent? an propterea,
quia illis quidem, quae supra posui, adhibendus
13 est modus quidam necessarius ? Nam et gratia, si
nimia atque inmodica, et mores, si multi atque
varii, et verba, si perpetua atque infinita et obtun-
dentia, et fama, si magna et inquieta et invidiosa sit,
14 neque laudabilia neque utilia sunt ; ingenium autem
et officium et forma et disciplina et consilium et
victoria et facundia sicut ipsae virtutum amplitu-

----

[1] et specie, *suggested by Hosius; Damsté would omit*
speciosus.
[2] haec item, *Hosius;* haec cum, *ω* ; quamquam aecum,
Hertz.

----

[1] The meaning " full of " or " abounding in " does not suit
all these words, although it is related to their meaning.
Thus a habit (*mos*) easily becomes a whim, and one who is
morosus is likely to be peevish ; for a somewhat different idea
see Cicero, *Tusc. Disp.* iv. 54, *bene igitur nostri, cum omnia
essent in moribus vitia, quod nullum erat iracundia foedius,
iracundos solos morosos nominaverunt.* It should be noted
too that *famosus* is used also in a good sense.

But if, as Nigidius says, all derivatives of that kind indicate an excessive and immoderate degree, and therefore have a bad sense, as do *vinosus* (" fond of wine "), *mulierosus* (" fond of women "), *morosus* (" whimsical "), *verbosus* (" wordy "), *famosus* (" notorious "),[1] why are *ingeniosus* (" talented "), *formosus* (" beautiful "), *officiosus* (" dutiful "), and *speciosus* (" showy "),[2] which are formed in the same way from *ingenium, forma, officium,* and *species,* why too are *disciplinosus* (" well-trained "), *consiliosus* (" full of wisdom "), *victoriosus* (" victorious "), words coined by Marcus Cato,[3] why too *facundiosus*—for Sempronius Asellio in the thirteenth book of his *History* wrote,[4] " one should regard his deeds, not his words if they are less eloquent (*facundiosa*)"—why, I say, are all these adjectives used, not in a bad, but in a good sense, although they too indicate an excessive amount of the quality which they signify? Is it because a certain necessary limit must be set for the qualities indicated by those words which I first cited? For favour if it is excessive and without limit,[5] and habits if they are too many and varied, and words if they are unceasing, endless and deafening, and fame if it should be great and restless and begetting envy; all these are neither praiseworthy nor useful; but talent, duty, beauty, training, wisdom, victory and eloquence, being in them-

---

[2] Since *speciosus* is used also in a bad sense, it should perhaps be omitted (see crit. note) ; but cf. *famosus*, in the preceding list.

[3] Fr. inc. 42, Jordan.   [4] Fr. 10, Peter.

[5] As would be indicated by *gratiosus*, which, however, Gellius has not mentioned among " the words which he first cited."

dines nullis finibus cohibentur, sed quanto maiora
auctioraque sunt, multo etiam tanto laudatiora sunt.

X

Quid observatum de ordine rogandarum in senatu sententiarum ; iurgiumque in senatu C. Caesaris consulis et
M. Catonis, diem dicendo eximentis.

1 ANTE legem quae nunc de senatu habendo ob-
2 servatur, ordo rogandi sententias varius fuit.   Alias
primus rogabatur qui princeps a censoribus in senatum lectus fuerat, alias qui designati consules erant ;
3 quidam e consulibus, studio aut necessitudine aliqua
adducti, quem is visum erat honoris gratia extra
4 ordinem sententiam primum rogabant.   Observatum
tamen est, cum extra ordinem fieret, ne quis quemquam ex alio quam ex consulari loco sententiam
5 primum rogaret.   C. Caesar in consulatu, quem cum
M. Bibulo gessit, quattuor solos extra ordinem
rogasse sententiam dicitur.   Ex his quattuor prin-
cipem rogabat M. Crassum ; sed, postquam filiam
Cn. Pompeio desponderat, primum coeperat Pom-
peium rogare.
6   Eius rei rationem reddidisse eum senatui Tiro
Tullius, M. Ciceronis libertus, refert, itaque se ex
7 patrono suo audisse scribit.   Id ipsum Capito Ateius
in libro quem De Officio Senatorio composuit, scriptum reliquit.

---

[1] In 59 B.C.
[2] See Suet. *Jul.* xxi., who adds the information that it
was the custom for the consul to maintain throughout the
year the order with which he had begun on the first of
January.

selves great virtues, are confined within no limits, but the greater and more extensive they are, the more are they deserving of praise.

X

The order observed in calling upon senators for their opinions ; and the altercation in the senate between Gaius Caesar, when consul, and Marcus Cato, who tried to use up the whole day in talk.

BEFORE the passage of the law which is now observed in the proceedings of the senate, the order in calling for opinions varied. Sometimes the man was first called upon whom the censors had first enrolled in the senate, sometimes the consuls elect ; some of the consuls, influenced by friendship or some personal relationship, used to call first upon anyone they pleased, as a compliment, contrary to the regular order. However, when the usual order was not followed, the rule was observed of not calling first upon any but a man of consular rank. It is said that Gaius Caesar, when he was consul with Marcus Bibulus,[1] called upon only four senators out of order. The first of these was Marcus Crassus, but after Caesar had betrothed his daughter to Gnaeus Pompeius, he began to call upon Pompeius first.[2]

Caesar gave the senate his reason for this procedure, according to the testimony of Tullius Tiro, Cicero's freedman, who writes [3] that he had the information from his patron. Ateius Capito has made the same statement in his work *On Senatorial Conduct*.[4]

[3] Fr. 1, Peter ; p. 6, Lion.
[4] Fr. 18, Huschke ; 1, Bremer.

8   In eodem libro Capitonis id quoque scriptum
est : " C.," inquit, " Caesar consul M. Catonem
sententiam rogavit.   Cato rem quae consulebatur,
quoniam non e republica videbatur, perfici nolebat.
Eius rei ducendae gratia longa oratione utebatur
eximebatque dicendo diem.   Erat enim ius sena-
tori, ut sententiam rogatus diceret ante quicquid
vellet aliae rei et quoad vellet.   Caesar consul
viatorem vocavit eumque, cum finem non faceret,
prendi loquentem et in carcerem duci iussit.
Senatus consurrexit et prosequebatur Catonem in
carcerem.   Hac," inquit, " invidia facta Caesar
destitit et mitti Catonem iussit."

XI

Quae qualiaque sint quae Aristoxenus quasi magis comperta
de Pythagora memoriae mandavit ; et quae item Plutarchus
in eundem modum de eodem Pythagora scripserit.

1   OPINIO vetus falsa occupavit et convaluit, Pythagoram philosophum non esitavisse ex animalibus,
item abstinuisse fabulo, quem Graeci κύαμον
2 appellant.   Ex hac opinione Callimachus poeta
scripsit :

Καὶ κυάμων ἄπο χεῖρας ἔχειν, ἀνιῶντος ἐδεστοῦ,
Κἀγώ, Πυθαγόρας ὡς ἐκέλευε, λέγω.

3 Ex eadem item opinione M. Cicero in libro *De
Divinatione* primo haec verba posuit : " Iubet igitur

---

[1] Fr. 18, Huschke ; 2, Bremer.
[2] According to Suet. *Jul.* xx. 4, it was a lictor.
[3] Fr. 128, Schn.   [4] § 62 ; see Pease, ad loc.

In the same treatise of Capito is this passage:[1]
"The consul Gaius Caesar called upon Marcus Cato
for his opinion. Cato did not wish to have the
motion before the house carried, since he did not
think it for the public good. For the purpose of
delaying action, he made a long speech and tried
to use up the whole day in talking. For it was
a senator's right, when asked his opinion, to speak
beforehand on any other subject he wished, and as
long as he wished. Caesar, in his capacity as consul,
summoned an attendant,[2] and since Cato would not
stop, ordered him to be arrested in the full tide of
his speech and taken to prison. The senate arose
in a body and attended Cato to the prison. But
this," he says, "aroused such indignation, that Caesar
yielded and ordered Cato's release."

XI

*The nature of the information which Aristoxenus has
handed down about Pythagoras on the ground that it was
more authoritative; and also what Plutarch wrote in the
same vein about that same Pythagoras.*

An erroneous belief of long standing has established
itself and become current, that the philosopher
Pythagoras did not eat of animals: also that he
abstained from the bean, which the Greeks call
κύαμος. In accordance with that belief the poet
Callimachus wrote:[3]

I tell you too, as did Pythagoras,
Withhold your hands from beans, a hurtful food.

Also, as the result of the same belief, Marcus Cicero
wrote these words in the first book of his work
On Divination:[4] "Plato therefore bids us go to our

Plato sic ad somnum proficisci corporibus affectis,
ut nihil sit quod errorem animis perturbationemque
afferat. Ex quo etiam Pythagoreis[1] interdictum
putatur ne faba vescerentur, quae res habet inflationem magnam,[2] tranquillitatem mentis quae-
rentibus contrariam."

4 Haec quidem M. Cicero. Sed Aristoxenus
musicus, vir litterarum veterum diligentissimus,
Aristoteli philosophi auditor, in libro quem De
Pythagora reliquit, nullo saepius legumento Pythagoram dicit usum quam fabis, quoniam is cibus
5 subduceret sensim alvum et levigaret. Verba ipsa
Aristoxeni subscripsi: Πυθαγόρας δὲ τῶν ὀσπρίων
μάλιστα τὸν κύαμον ἐδοκίμασεν· λειαντικόν τε γὰρ
εἶναι καὶ διαχωρητικόν· διὸ καὶ μάλιστα κέχρηται αὐτῷ.
6 Porculis quoque minusculis et haedis teneribus
7 victitasse, idem Aristoxenus refert. Quam rem
videtur cognovisse e Xenophilo Pythagorico familiari suo, et ex quibusdam aliis natu maioribus, qui
8 ab aetate Pythagorae minus diu aberant.[3] Ac de
animalibus Alexis etiam poeta in comoedia, quae
9 Πυθαγορίζουσα inscribitur, docet. Videtur autem
de κυάμῳ non esitato causam erroris fuisse, quia in
Empedocli carmine, qui disciplinas Pythagorae
secutus est, versus hic invenitur:

Δειλοί, πάνδειλοι, κυάμων ἄπο χεῖρας ἔχεσθαι.

10 Opinati enim sunt plerique κυάμους legumentum

---

[1] Pythagoricis, Cic.
[2] magnam is cibus t. m. q. constat esse contrariam, ω;
corrected by J. F. Gronov; quod habet inflationem magnam
is cibus tranquillitati mentis quaerenti(s) vera contrariam,
Cic.
[3] minus . . . aberant, added by Hertz.

sleep in such bodily condition that there may be
nothing to cause delusion and disturbance in our
minds. It is thought to be for that reason too that
the Pythagoreans were forbidden to eat beans, a
food that produces great flatulency, which is disturbing
to those who seek mental calm.''

So then Cicero. But Aristoxenus the musician, a
man thoroughly versed in early literature, a pupil
of the philosopher Aristotle, in the book *On Pytha-*
goras which he has left us, says that Pythagoras
used no vegetable more often than beans, since that
food gently loosened the bowels and relieved them.
I add Aristoxenus' own words : [1] " Pythagoras among
vegetables especially recommended the bean, saying
that it was both digestible and loosening ; and
therefore he most frequently made use of it."

Aristoxenus also relates that Pythagoras ate very
young pigs and tender kids. This fact he seems to
have learned from his intimate friend Xenophilus
the Pythagorean and from some other older men,
who lived not long after the time of Pythagoras.
And the same information about animal food is
given by the poet Alexis, in the comedy entitled
" The Pythagorean Bluestocking." [2] Furthermore,
the reason for the mistaken idea about abstaining
from beans seems to be, that in a poem of Empedocles, who was a follower of Pythagoras, this line
is found : [3]

O wretches, utter wretches, from beans withhold
    your hands.

For most men thought that κυάμους meant the

[1] *F.H.G.* ii. 273.   [2] Fr. 199, Kock.
[3] Fr. 141, Diehls.

dici, ut a vulgo dicitur. Sed qui diligentius scitiusque carmina Empedocli arbitrati sunt, κυάμους hoc in loco testiculos significare dicunt, eosque more Pythagorae operte atque symbolice κυάμους appellatos, quod sint αἴτιοι τοῦ κυεῖν et geniturae humanae vim praebeant; idcircoque Empedoclen versu isto non a fabulo edendo, sed a rei veneriae prolubio[1] voluisse homines deducere.

11   Plutarchus quoque, homo in disciplinis gravi auctoritate, in primo librorum quos *De Homero* composuit, Aristotelem philosophum scripsit eadem ipsa de Pythagoricis scripsisse, quod non abstinuerint edundis animalibus, nisi pauca carne quadam.

12 Verba ipsa Plutarchi, quoniam res inopinata est, subscripsi: Ἀριστοτέλης δὲ μήτρας καὶ καρδίας καὶ ἀκαλήφης καὶ τοιούτων τινῶν ἄλλων ἀπέχεσθαί φησιν

13 τοὺς Πυθαγορικούς· χρῆσθαι δὲ τοῖς ἄλλοις. Ἀκαλήφη autem est animal marinum, quod "urtica" appellatur. Sed et piscibus mullis[2] abstinere Pythagoricos, Plutarchus in *Symposiacis* dicit.

4   Pythagoram vero ipsum, sicuti celebre est Euphorbum primo fuisse dictasse, ita[3] haec remotiora sunt his quae Clearchus et Dicaearchus memoriae tradiderunt, fuisse eum postea Pyrrum Pyranthium, deinde Aethaliden, deinde feminam pulcra facie meretricem, cui nomen fuerat Alco.

---

[1] proluvio, ω, *Hertz.*
[2] mullis, *omitted by Hertz;* multis, *Mommsen.*
[3] dictasse. Ita, ω.

vegetable, according to the common use of the
word. But those who have studied the poems of
Empedocles with greater care and knowledge say
that here κυάμους refers to the testicles, and that
after the Pythagorean manner they were called in
a covert and symbolic way κύαμοι, because they are
the cause of pregnancy and furnish the power for
human generation :[1] and that therefore Empedocles
in that verse desired to keep men, not from eating
beans, but from excess in venery.

Plutarch too, a man of weight in scientific matters,
in the first book of his work *On Homer* wrote that
Aristotle[2] gave the same account of the Pythagoreans :
namely, that except for a few parts of the flesh they
did not abstain from eating animals. Since the statement is contrary to the general belief, I have appended
Plutarch's own words :[3] "Aristotle says that the
Pythagoreans abstained from the matrix, the heart,
the ἀκαλήφη and some other such things, but used
all other animal food." Now the ἀκαλήφη is a marine
creature which is called the sea-nettle. But Plutarch
in his *Table Talk* says[4] that the Pythagoreans also
abstained from mullets.

But as to Pythagoras himself, while it is well
known that he declared that he had come into
the world as Euphorbus, what Cleanthes[5] and
Dicaearchus[6] have recorded is less familiar—that he
was afterwards Pyrrhus Pyranthius, then Aethalides,
and then a beautiful courtesan, whose name was Alco.

---

[1] Associating κύαμος with κυεῖν " to conceive."
[2] Fr. 194, Rose.   [3] vii., p. 100, Bern.
[4] viii. 8.   [5] *F.H.G.* ii. 317.
[6] *F.H.G.* ii. 244.

XII

Notae et animadversiones censoriae in veteribus monumentis
repertae memoria dignae.

1 Si quis agrum suum passus fuerat sordescere
eumque indiligenter curabat ac neque araverat neque purgaverat, sive quis arborem suam vineamque
habuerat derelictui, non id sine poena fuit, sed erat
opus censorium censoresque aerarium faciebant.
2 Item, si quis[1] eques Romanus equum habere graci-
lentum aut parum nitidum visus erat, "inpolitiae"
notabatur; id verbum significat quasi tu dicas
3 "incuriae." Cuius rei utriusque auctoritates sunt
et M. Cato id saepenumero adtestatus est.

XIII

Quod incentiones quaedam tibiarum certo modo factae
ischiacis mederi possunt.

1 Creditum hoc a plerisque esse[2] et memoriae
mandatum, ischia cum maxime doleant, tum, si
2 modulis lenibus tibicen incinat, minui dolores, ego
nuperrime in libro Theophrasti Περὶ Ἐνθουσιασμοῦ[3]
3 scriptum inveni. Viperarum morsibus tibicinium
scite modulateque adhibitum mederi, refert etiam

---

[1] si quis, σ ; quis, ω ; qui, *Vogel ;* quisquis, *C. F. W.
Müller.*
[2] esse, *Hertz ;* est, ω.   [3] *title added by Hosius.*

---

[1] Made him an *aerarius,* originally a citizen who owned
no land, but paid a tax (*aes*) based on such property as he
had. The *aerarii* had no political rights until about the

XII

Instances of disgrace and punishment inflicted by the censors, found in ancient records and worthy of notice.

IF anyone had allowed his land to run to waste and was not giving it sufficient attention, if he had neither ploughed nor weeded it, or if anyone had neglected his orchard or vineyard, such conduct did not go unpunished, but it was taken up by the censors, who reduced such a man to the lowest class of citizens.[1]   So too, any Roman knight, if his horse seemed to be skinny or not well groomed, was charged with *inpolitiae*, a word which means the same thing as negligence.[2]   There are authorities for both these punishments, and Marcus Cato has cited frequent instances.[3]

XIII

On the possibility of curing gout by certain melodies played in a special way on the flute.

I RAN across the statement very recently in the book of Theophrastus *On Inspiration*[4] that many men have believed and put their belief on record, that when gouty pains in the hips are most severe, they are relieved if a flute-player plays soothing measures.   That snake-bites are cured by the music of the flute, when played skilfully and melodiously, is also stated in a book of Democritus, entitled *On*

middle of the fifth century B.C., when they were enrolled in the four city tribes.   See Mommsen, *Staatsr.* ii. 392 ff.

[2] More literally, *inpolitia* is "lack of neatness," from *in-*, negative, and *polio*, "polish," from which *pulcher* also is derived.

[3] Fr. 2, p. 52, Jordan.   [4] Fr. 87, Wimmer.

Democriti liber, qui inscribitur Περὶ Λοιμῶν,[1] in quo docet plurimis hominum morbidis medicinae fuisse
4 incentiones tibiarum. Tanta prosus adfinitas est corporibus hominum mentibusque et propterea vitiis quoque aut medellis animorum et corporum.

XIV

Narratur historia de Hostilio Mancino aedili cur.[2] et Manilia meretrice; verbaque decreti tribunorum ad quos a Manilia provocatum est.

1 Cum librum IX.[3] Atei Capitonis *Coniectaneorum* legeremus, qui inscriptus est *De Iudiciis Publicis*, decretum tribunorum visum est gravitatis antiquae
2 plenum. Propterea id meminimus, idque ob hanc causam et in hanc sententiam scriptum est: Aulus
3 Hostilius Mancinus aedilis curulis fuit. Is Maniliae meretrici diem ad populum dixit, quod e tabulato eius noctu lapide ictus esset, vulnusque ex eo lapide
4 ostendebat. Manilia ad tribunos plebi provocavit.
5 Apud eos dixit comessatorem Mancinum ad aedes suas venisse; eum sibi recipere non fuisse e re[4] sua,
6 sed cum vi inrumperet, lapidibus depulsum. Tribuni decreverunt aedilem ex eo loco iure deiectum quo eum venire cum corollario non decuisset; propterea, ne cum populo aedilis ageret intercesserunt

---

[1] *title added by Hertz.*
[2] aedili cur., *suggested by Hosius;* aedilium, ω.
[3] VIII, *Scioppius.*
[4] e re, *Bentley;* ede, ω.

---

[1] Fr. 1, Huschke; 1, Bremer.   [2] The date is uncertain.
[3] That is, as a reveller coming from a drinking-bout. An

Deadly Infections, in which he shows that the music of the flute is medicine for many ills that flesh is heir to. So very close is the connection between the bodies and the minds of men, and therefore between physical and mental ailments and their remedies.

XIV

A story told of Hostilius Mancinus, a curule aedile, and the courtesan Manilia; and the words of the decree of the tribunes to whom Manilia appealed.

As I was reading the ninth book of the *Miscellany* of Ateius Capito, entitled *On Public Decisions*,[1] one decree of the tribunes seemed to me full of old-time dignity. For that reason I remember it, and it was rendered for this reason and to this purport. Aulus Hostilius Mancinus was a curule aedile.[2] He brought suit before the people against a courtesan called Manilia, because he said that he had been struck with a stone thrown from her apartment by night, and he exhibited the wound made by the stone. Manilia appealed to the tribunes of the commons. Before them she declared that Mancinus had come to her house in the garb of a reveller; that it would not have been to her advantage to admit him, and that when he tried to break in by force, he had been driven off with stones. The tribunes decided that the aedile had rightly been refused admission to a place to which it had not been seemly for him to go with a garland on his head;[3] therefore they forbade the aedile to bring an action before the people.

aedile might visit such a place officially in the course of his duty of regulating taverns and brothels.

XV

Defensa a culpa sententia ex historia Sallustii, quam iniqui
eius cum insectatione maligni reprehenderint.

1 ELEGANTIA orationis Sallustii verborumque fingendi
et novandi studium cum multa prorsus invidia fuit,
multique non mediocri ingenio viri conati sunt re-
prehendere pleraque et obtrectare.   In quibus plura
inscite aut maligne vellicant.   Nonnulla tamen videri possunt non indigna reprehensione; quale illud
in *Catilinae Historia* repertum est, quod habeat eam
speciem, quasi parum adtente dictum.   Verba Sal-
2 lustii haec sunt: "Ac mihi quidem, tametsi hautquaquam par gloria sequitur scriptorem et auctorem
rerum, tamen inprimis arduum videtur res gestas
scribere; primum, quod facta dictis exaequanda
sunt; dein, quia plerique quae delicta reprehenderis[1]
malivolentia et invidia dicta putant.   Ubi de magna
virtute atque gloria bonorum memores, quae sibi
quisque facilia factu putat, aequo animo accipit;
3 supra ea,[2] veluti ficta, pro falsis ducit" "Proposuit,"
inquiunt, "dicturum causas quamobrem videatur
esse 'arduum,' 'res gestas scribere'; atque ibi cum
primam causam dixerit, dein non alteram causam,[3]
4 sed querellas dicit.   Non enim causa videri debet
cur historiae opus 'arduum' sit, quod hi qui legunt

---

[1] reprehenderis, *Sall.*; deprehenderis, ω.
[2] supra ea, *Sall.*; supra, ω.
[3] dixerit . . . causam *added by Hertz, who reads* primum
causam aliquam dixerit . . . causam.

---

[1] iii. 2.

XV

The defence of a passage in the historical works of Sallust, which his enemies attacked in a spirit of malicious criticism.

THE elegance of Sallust's style and his passion for coining and introducing new words was met with exceeding great hostility, and many men of no mean ability tried to criticize and decry much in his writings. Many of the attacks on him were ignorant or malicious. Yet there are some things that may be regarded as deserving of censure, as for example the following passage in the *History of Catiline*,[1] which has the appearance of being written somewhat carelessly. Sallust's words are these : " And for myself, although I am well aware that by no means equal repute attends the narrator and the doer of deeds, yet I regard the writing of history as one of the hardest of tasks ; first because the style and diction must be equal to the deeds recorded ; and in the second place, because such criticisms as you make of others' shortcomings are thought by most men to be due to malice and envy. Furthermore, when you commemorate the distinguished merit and fame of good men, while everyone is quite ready to believe you when you tell of things which he thinks he could easily do himself, everything beyond that he regards as fictitious, if not false." The critics say : " He declared that he would give the reasons why it appears to be ' hard ' ' to write history ' ; and then, after mentioning the first reason, he does not give a second, but gives utterance to complaints. For it ought not to be regarded as a reason why the work of history is ' hard,' that the reader either mis-

aut inique interpretantur quae scripta sunt aut vera
5 esse non credunt." Obnoxiam quippe et obiectam
falsis existimationibus eam rem dicendam aiunt
quam "arduam"; quia quod est "arduum" sui
operis difficultate est arduum, non opinionis alienae
erroribus.

6 Haec illi malivoli reprehensores dicunt. Sed
"arduum" Sallustius non pro difficili tantum, sed
pro eo quoque ponit quod Graeci χαλεπὸν appellant, quod est cum difficile, tum molestum quoque
et incommodum et intractabile. Quorum verborum
significatio a sententia Sallustii supra scripta non
abhorret.

XVI

De vocabulis quibusdam a Varrone et Nigidio contra cotidiani sermonis consuetudinem declinatis ; atque inibi id
genus quaedam cum exemplis veterum relata.

1 M. Varronem et P. Nigidium, viros Romani generis doctissimos, comperimus non aliter elocutos
esse et scripsisse quam "senatuis" et "domuis" et
"fluctuis," qui est patrius casus ab eo quod est
"senatus," "domus" "fluctus";[1] huic "senatui,"
"domui"[1] "fluctui" ceteraque is consimilia pariter
2 dixisse. Terentii quoque comici versus in libris
veteribus itidem scriptus est :

Eius ánuis causa, opínor, quae est emórtua.[2]

3 Hanc eorum auctoritatem quidam e veteribus grammaticis ratione etiam firmare voluerunt, quod omnis

---

[1] (et) fluctus *and* domui, *added in* σ.
[2] erat mortua, *Ter.*

---

[1] Fr. 63, Swoboda.　　　　[2] *Heaut.* 287.

interprets what is written or does not believe it to
be true." They maintain that he ought to say that
such work is exposed and subject to misjudgments,
rather than "hard"; for that which is "hard" is hard
because of the difficulty of its accomplishment, not
because of the mistaken opinions of other men.

That is what those ill-natured critics say. But
Sallust does not use *arduus* merely in the sense
of "hard," but as the equivalent of the Greek word
χαλεπός, that is, both difficult and also troublesome,
disagreeable and intractable. And the meaning of
these words is not inconsistent with that of the
passage which was just quoted from Sallust.

XVI

On the inflection of certain words by Varro and Nigidius
contrary to everyday usage; and also a quotation of some
instances of the same kind from the early writers, with
examples.

I LEARN that Marcus Varro and Publius Nigidius,[1]
the most learned of all the Romans, always said and
wrote *senatuis, domuis* and *fluctuis* as the genitive case
of the words *senatus, domus* and *fluctus,* and used
senatui, domui, fluctui, and other similar words, with
the corresponding dative ending. There is also a
line of the comic poet Terence, which in the old
manuscripts is written as follows:[2]

Because, I think, of that old dame (*anuis*) who
died.

Some of the early grammarians wished to give this
authority of theirs[3] the sanction of a rule; namely,

---

[3] That is, of Varro, Nigidius, and Terence.

dativus singularis "i" littera finitus, si non similis est
genetivi singularis, s littera addita genetivum singu-
larem facit, ut " patri patris," "duci ducis," "caedi
4 caedis." " Cum igitur" inquiunt " in casu dandi
' huic senatui' dicamus, genetivus ex eo singularis
' senatuis' est, non ' senatus.' "

5   Set[1] non omnes concedunt in casu dativo "sena-
6 tui" magis dicendum quam " senatu." Sicuti
Lucilius in eodem casu " victu " et "anu " dicit, non
" victui " nec " anui," in hisce versibus :

> Quod sumptum atque epulas victu praeponis
> honesto

et alio in loco :

> Anu noceo (inquit).

7 Vergilius quoque in casu dandi "aspectu " dicit, non
" aspectui " :

> Teque aspectu ne subtrahe nostro

et in *Georgicis :*

> Quod nec concubitu indulgent.

8   C. etiam Caesar, gravis auctor linguae Latinae, in
Anticatone, " unius," inquit, " arrogantiae, superbiae
dominatuque." Item *In Dolabellam actionis I. lib. I.*:
" Isti, quorum in aedibus fanisque posita et honori
9 erant et ornatu." In libris quoque analogicis omnia
istiusmodi sine "i " littera dicenda censet.

---

[1] sed, σ ; et, ω.

---

[1] Dative singulars ending in *i* and having the same form as
the genitive singular occur only in the fifth declension (*diei,
rei,* etc.), except for the archaic forms of the first declension
in -*ai.*

[2] 1288, Marx.   [3] 280, Marx.
[4] *Aen.* vi. 465.   [5] iv. 198.

that every dative singular ending in *i*, if it has not the same form as the genitive singular,[1] makes the genitive singular by adding *s*, as *patri patris, duci ducis, caedi caedis.* " Therefore," they say, " since we use *senatui* as the dative case, the genitive singular of that word is *senatuis*, not *senatus*."

But all are not agreed that we should use *senatui* in the dative case rather than *senatu*. For example, Lucilius in that same case uses *victu* and *anu*, and not *victui* and *anui*, in these verses :[2]

Since you to honest fare (*victu*) do waste and feasts prefer,

and in another place :[3]

I'm doing harm to the old girl (*anu*).

Vergil also in the dative case writes *aspectu* and not *aspectui* :[4]

Withdraw not from our view (*aspectu*)

and in the *Georgics* :[5]

Nor give themselves to love's embrace (*concubitu*).

Gaius Caesar too, a high authority on the Latin language, says in his *Speech against Cato* :[6] " owing to the arrogance, haughtiness and tyranny (*dominatu*) of one man." Also in the *First Action against Dolabella*, Book I :[7] " Those in whose temples and shrines they had been placed for an honour and an adornment (*ornatu*)."[8] Also, in his books on analogy he decides that *i* should be omitted in all such forms.

[6] ii. p. 136, Dinter.
[7] ii. p. 121, Dinter ; *O.R.F.*[2], p. 410.
[8] ii. p. 129, Dinter.

XVII

De natura quarundam particularum quae praepositae verbis
intendi atque produci barbare et inscite videntur, exemplis
rationibusque plusculis disceptatum.

1 LUCILII ex XI. versus sunt :

Scipiadae magno improbus obiciebat Asellus,
Lustrum illo censore malum infelixque fuisse.

"Obiciebat" "o" littera producta multos legere
2 audio, idque eo facere dicunt ut ratio numeri salva
sit. Idem infra :

Conicere in versus dictum praeconis volebam
Grani.

In hac quoque primi verbi praepositione "o"[1] ob
3 eandem causam producunt. Item XV. :

Subicit huic humilem et suffercitus posteriorem,

"subicit" "u" littera longa legunt, quia primam
4 syllabam brevem esse in versu heroico non convenit.
Item apud Plautum in *Epidico* "con" syllabam
productam pronuntiant :

Age núnciam orna te, Epidice, et pallíolum in
collum cónice.

5 Apud Vergilium quoque "subicit" verbum produci
a plerisque audio :

[1] o, *added by Mommsen.*

---

[1] 394, Marx.
[2] The point is, that the *syllable ob*, being a closed syllable,
is long, while the *vowel o* is short. Hence *o* is pronounced
short, but the first three syllables of *obiciebat* form a dactyl
(– ᴗ ᴗ). Gellius' explanation in §§ 7–8 is correct, although not
so clear as it might be.

XVII

A discussion of the natural quantity of certain particles, the long pronunciation of which, when prefixed to verbs, seems to be barbarous and ignorant; with several examples and explanations.

In the eleventh book of Lucilius are these lines :[1]

> Thus base Asellus did great Scipio taunt :
> Unlucky was his censorship and bad.

I hear that many read *obiciebat* with a long *o,* and they say that they do this in order to preserve the metre.[2]   Again farther on he says :[3]

> I'd versify the words the herald Granius spoke.

In this passage also they lengthen the prefix of the first word for the same reason.   Again in the fifteenth book :[4]

> Subicit huic humilem et suffercitus posteriorem,[5]

they read *subicit* with a long *u,* because it is not proper for the first syllable to be short in heroic verse.   Likewise in the *Epidicus* of Plautus[6] they lengthen the syllable *con* in

> Haste now, Epidicus, prepare yourself,
> And throw (*conice*) your mantle round about your
>   neck.

In Virgil too I hear that some lengthen the verb *subicit* in :[7]

---

[3] 411, Marx.
[4] 509, Marx, who reads *suffert citus,* following Lion.
[5] The reading is uncertain and the meaning doubtful. The line is an hexameter, since final *s* (as in *suffercitus*) did not make position in early Latin.
[6] 194.   [7] *Georg.* ii. 18.

> etiam Parnasia laurus
> Parva sub ingenti matris se subicit umbra.

6 Sed neque "ob" neque "sub" praepositio produ-
cendi habet naturam, neque item "con,"[1] nisi cum
eam litterae secuntur quae in verbis "constituit" et
"confecit" secundum eam primae sunt, vel cum
eliditur ex ea "n"[2] littera, sicut Sallustius: "faenori-
7 bus," inquit, "copertus." In his autem quae supra
posui et metrum esse integrum potest et praepositiones istae possunt non barbare protendi ; secunda
enim littera in his verbis per duo "i," non per unum
8 scribenda est. Nam verbum ipsum, cui supradictae
particulae praepositae sunt, non est "icio," sed
"iacio" et praeteritum non "icit" facit, sed "iecit."
Id ubi compositum est, "a"[3] littera in "i"[4] mutatur,
sicuti fit in verbis "insilio" et "incipio," atque "i"[5]
ita vim consonantis capit, et idcirco ea syllaba pro-
ductius latiusque paulo pronuntiata priorem syllabam
brevem esse non patitur, sed reddit eam positu
longam, proptereaque et numerus in versu et ratio in
pronuntiatu manet.

9   Haec quae diximus eo etiam conducunt, ut quod[6]
apud Vergilium in sexto positum invenimus :

> Eripe me his, invicte, malis, aut tu mihi terram
> Inice,

[1] con, *added in* σ.   [2] ex ea n, σ ; ea non, ω.
[3] a, *Lion* ; ex a, ω.   [4] i, *added in* σ.
[5] i, *added in* σ.   [6] quod, *added in* σ.

---

[1] *Cf.* ii. 17.

[2] "Loaded with debt," Hist. fr. iv. 52, Maur. ; see note
on ii. 17. 11, p. 168. *Copertus* is from *co-* (not *con-*) *opertus*,
and there is no loss of *n*.

[3] Gellius is partly right. As *in+capio* and *in+salio* became

364

Parnassian laurel too
Lifts (*subicit*) 'neath large mother-shade its infant
stem.

But neither the preposition *ob* nor *sub* is long by
nature, nor is *con* long either, except when it is
followed by the letters which come directly after it
in *constituit* and *confecit*,[1] or when its *n* is lost, as in
Sallust's *faenoribus copertus*.[2] But in those instances
which I have mentioned above the metre may be preserved without barbarously lengthening the prefixes ;
for the following letter in those words should be
written with two *i*'s, not with one. For the simple
verb to which the above-mentioned particles are
prefixed, is not *icio*, but *iacio*, and the perfect is not
icit, but *iecit*. When that word is used in compounds,
the letter *a* is changed into *i*, as happens in the
verbs *insilio* and *incipio*, and thus the first *i* acquires
consonantal force.[3] Accordingly, that syllable, being
pronounced a little longer and fuller, does not allow
the first syllable to be short, but makes it long by
position, and thus the rhythm of the verse and the
correct pronunciation are preserved.

What I have said leads also to a knowledge of
this, that in the line which we find in the sixth book
of Virgil :[4]

Unconquered chieftain, save me from these ills;
Or do thou earth cast on (*inice*) me,

incipio and *insilio*, so *ob + iacio* became *obiicio*. As the
Romans disliked the combination *ii*, only one *i* was written,
but both were pronounced, and the syllable *ob* was thus long
" by position." In the early Latin dramatists the scansion
ăbicio indicates that the *i* was syncopated and the semi-vowel
changed to a vowel. See Sommer, *Lat. Laut- und Formen-
lehre*, p. 522.   [4] *Aen.* vi. 365.

sic esse "iniice," ut supra dixi, et scribendum et legendum sciamus, nisi quis tam indocilis est, ut[1] in hoc quoque verbo "in" praepositionem metri gratia protendat.

10   Quaerimus igitur in "obicibus" "o" littera qua ratione intendatur, cum id vocabulum factum sit a verbo "obiicio" et nequaquam simile sit quod a

11 verbo "moveo" "motus" "o" littera longa dicitur. Equidem memini Sulpicium Apollinarem, virum praestanti litterarum scientia, "obices" et "obicibus" "o" littera correpta dicere, in Vergilio quoque sic eum legere :

> qua vi maria alta tumescant
> Obicibus ruptis ;

12 sed ita ut diximus, "i" litteram, quae in hoc[2] vocabulo quoque gemina esse debet, paulo uberius largiusque pronuntiabat.

13   Congruens igitur est ut "subices" etiam, quod proinde ut "obices" compositum est, "u" littera

14 brevi dici oporteat. Ennius in tragoedia quae *Achilles* inscribitur, "subices" pro aere alto ponit qui caelo subiectus est, in his versibus :

> per ego déum sublimas súbices
> Húmidas, unde óritur imber sónitu saevo et
> spíritu ;[3]

plerosque omnes tamen legere audias "u" littera

15 producta. Id ipsum autem verbum M. Cato sub alia praepositione dicit in oratione quam *De Consulatu Suo* habuit : "Ita hos,"[4] inquit, "fert ventus ad pri-

---

[1] ut, *added in σ*.   [2] hoc, *added by Hertz*.
[3] spiritu, *Festus* ; strepitu, *ω*.
[4] nos, *H. Meyer* ; Italos, *Falster*.

iniice is to be written and pronounced as I have
indicated above, unless anyone is so ignorant as to
lengthen the preposition *in* in this word too for the
sake of the metre.

We ask then for what reason the letter *o* in
obicibus is lengthened, since this word is derived from
the verb *obiicio*, and is not at all analogous to *motus*,
which is from *moveo* and is pronounced with a long *o*.
I myself recall that Sulpicius Apollinaris, a man
eminent for his knowledge of literature, pronounced
obices and *obicibus* with a short *o*, and that in Virgil
too he read in the same way the lines : [1]

> And by what force the oceans fathomless
> Rise, bursting all their bounds (*obicibus*) ;

but, as I have indicated, he gave the letter *i*, which
in that word also should be doubled, a somewhat
fuller and longer sound.

It is consistent therefore that *subices* also, which is
formed exactly like *obices*, should be pronounced with
the letter *u* short. Ennius, in his tragedy which is
entitled *Achilles*, uses *subices* for the upper air which
is directly below the heavens, in these lines : [2]

> By lofty, humid regions (*subices*) of the gods I
>   swear,
> Whence comes the storm with savage roaring
>   wind ;

yet, in spite of what I have said, you may hear almost
everyone read *subices* with a long *u*. But Marcus
Cato uses that very verb with another prefix in the
speech which he delivered *On his Consulship* : [3] "So
the wind bears them to the beginning of the

---

[1] *Georg.* iii. 479.   [2] 2, Ribbeck [3].
[3] i. 9, Jordan, who reads *nos* for *hos*.

morem Pyrenaeum, quo proicit in altum." Et
Pacuvius item in *Chryse* :

Idae [1] promúnturium, cuius língua in altum próicit.

XVIII

De P. Africano superiore sumpta quaedam ex annalibus
memoratu dignissima.

1 Scipio Africanus antiquior quanta virtutum gloria
praestiterit et quam fuerit altus animi atque magni-
ficus et qua sui conscientia subnixus, plurimis rebus
2 quae dixit quaeque fecit declaratum est. Ex quibus
sunt haec duo exempla eius fiduciae atque exuper-
antiae ingentis.
3 Cum M. Naevius tribunus plebis accusaret eum ad
populum diceretque accepisse a rege Antiocho pecuniam, ut condicionibus gratiosis et mollibus pax cum
eo populi Romani nomine fieret, et quaedam item alia
crimini daret indigna tali viro, tum Scipio pauca
praefatus quae dignitas vitae suae atque gloria
postulabat, "Memoria," inquit, "Quirites, repeto,
diem esse hodiernum quo Hannibalem Poenum
imperio vestro inimicissimum magno proelio vici in
terra Africa pacemque et victoriam vobis peperi
spectabilem.[2] Non igitur simus adversum deos
ingrati et, censeo, relinquamus nebulonem hunc,
eamus hinc protinus Iovi optimo maximo gratulatum."
4 Id cum dixisset, avertit et ire ad Capitolium coepit.

[1] Idae, *Voss* ; id, *ω*.
[2] spectabilem, *Scioppius* ; inspectabilem, *ω*.

---

[1] 94, Ribbeck [3].   [2] In 185 B.C.

Pyrenees' range, where it extends (*proicit*) into the deep." And so too Pacuvius in the *Chryses*: [1]

> High Ida's cape, whose tongue into the deep
>   extends (*proicit*).

XVIII

Some stories of the elder Publius Africanus, taken from the annals and well worth relating.

How greatly the earlier Scipio Africanus excelled in the splendour of his merits, how lofty and noble of spirit he was, and to what an extent he was upheld by consciousness of his own rectitude, is evident from many of his words and acts. Among these are the following two instances of his extreme self-confidence and sense of superiority.

When Marcus Naevius, tribune of the commons, accused him before the people [2] and declared that he had received money from king Antiochus to make peace with him in the name of the Roman people on favourable and easy terms, and when the tribune added sundry other charges which were unworthy of so great a man, then Scipio, after a few preliminary remarks such as were called for by the dignity and renown of his life, said : " I recall, fellow citizens, that this is the day on which in Africa in a mighty battle I conquered Hannibal the Carthaginian, the most bitter enemy of your power, and won for you a splendid peace and a glorious victory. Let us then not be ungrateful to the gods, but, I suggest, let us leave this worthless fellow, and go at once to render thanks to Jupiter, greatest and best of gods." So saying, he turned away and set out for the Capitol. Thereupon the whole assembly, which

5 Tum contio universa, quae ad sententiam de Scipione
ferendam convenerat, relicto tribuno, Scipionem
in Capitolium comitata atque inde ad aedes eius
cum laetitia et gratulatione sollemni prosecuta est.
6 Fertur etiam oratio quae videtur habita eo die a
Scipione, et qui dicunt eam non veram, non eunt
infitias quin haec quidem verba fuerint, quae dixi,
Scipionis.

7   Item aliud est factum eius praeclarum. Petilii
quidam tribuni plebis a M., ut aiunt, Catone,
inimico Scipionis, comparati in eum atque inmissi,
desiderabant in senatu instantissime ut pecuniae
Antiochinae praedaeque in eo bello captae rationem
8 redderet; fuerat enim L. Scipioni Asiatico, fratri
9 suo, imperatori in ea provincia legatus. Ibi Scipio
exurgit et, prolato e sinu togae libro, rationes in eo
10 scriptas esse dixit omnis pecuniae omnisque praedae;
illatum, ut palam recitaretur et ad aerarium defer-
11 retur. "Sed enim id iam non faciam," inquit, "nec
12 me ipse afficiam contumelia," eumque librum statim
coram discidit suis manibus et concerpsit, aegre
passus quod cui salus imperii ac reipublicae accepta
ferri deberet rationem pecuniae praedatae posceretur.

---

[1] *O. R. F.*, p. 6, Meyer [2].

[2] Probably in 187 B.C., but the details of these attacks on
Scipio are confused and uncertain.

had gathered to pass judgment on Scipio, left the
tribune, accompanied Scipio to the Capitol, and then
escorted him to his home with the joy and expressions of gratitude suited to a festal occasion. The
very speech is in circulation which is believed to
have been delivered that day by Scipio,[1] and those
who deny its authenticity at least admit that these
words which I have quoted were spoken by Scipio.

There is also another celebrated act of his. Certain Petilii, tribunes of the commons, influenced they
say by Marcus Cato, Scipio's personal enemy, and
instigated to appear against him, insisted most vigor-
ously in the senate [2] on his rendering an account of
the money of Antiochus and of the booty taken in
that war; for he had been deputy to his brother
Lucius Scipio Asiaticus, the commander in that cam-
paign. Thereupon Scipio arose, and taking a roll
from the fold of his toga, said that it contained an
account of all the money and all the booty; that he
had brought it to be publicly read and deposited in
the treasury. "But that," said he, "I shall not do
now, nor will I so degrade myself." And at once,
before them all, he tore the roll across with his own
hands and rent it into bits, indignant that an account
of money taken in war should be required of him, to
whose account the salvation of the Roman State and
its power ought to be credited.[3]

[3] *Accepta ferri* is a technical term of book-keeping, "to
enter as received" or "on the credit side"; the opposite is
ferre expensum, i. 16. 5, "to enter as paid out" or "on the
debit side."

XIX

Quid M. Varro in *Logistorico* [1] scripserit de moderando victu
puerorum inpubium.

1   PUEROS inpubes compertum est, si plurimo cibo
nimioque somno uterentur, hebetiores fieri ad veterni
usque aut eluci tarditatem, corporaque eorum inpro-
2 cera fieri minusque adolescere.   Idem plerique alii
medicorum philosophorumque et M. Varro in *Logistorico* [2] scripsit, quae inscripta est *Catus aut De
Liberis Educandis.*

XX

Notati a censoribus qui audientibus iis dixerant ioca quaedam intempestiviter ; ac de eius [3] quoque nota deliberatum qui steterat forte apud eos oscitabundus.

1   INTER censorum severitates tria haec exempla in
2 litteris sunt castigatissimae disciplinae.   Unum est
3 huiuscemodi : Censor agebat de uxoribus sollemne
iusiurandum ; verba erant ita concepta : " Ut tu ex
animi tui sententia uxorem habes?" Qui iurabat
cavillator quidam et canicula [4] et nimis ridicularius
4 fuit.   Is locum esse sibi ioci dicundi ratus, cum ita
uti mos erat censor dixisset, " Ut tu ex animi tui
5 sententia uxorem habes ? " " Habeo equidem,"
inquit, "uxorem, sed non hercle ex animi mei

___

¹ longi historia, ω.   ² longa (h)istoria, ω.
³ ac de, *s* ; accede, ω ; atque de, *Lion* ; ac quod de,
suggested by Hosius ; aeque de, *Damsté.*
⁴ canalicola, *Lipsius.*

___

¹ Fr. 17, Riese.

XIX

What Marcus Varro wrote in his *Philosophical-historical Treatise* on restricting the diet of immature children.

It has been found that if immature children eat a great deal and sleep too much, they become so sluggish as to have the dulness of a sufferer from insomnia or lethargy; and their bodies are stunted and under-developed. This is stated by numerous other physicians and philosophers and also by Marcus Varro in that section of his *Philosophical-historical Treatise* which is entitled *Catus, or On Bringing up Children*.[1]

XX

On the punishment by the censors of men who had made untimely jokes in their hearing; also a deliberation as to the punishment of a man who had happened to yawn when standing before them.

Among the severities of the censors these three examples of the extreme strictness of their discipline are recorded in literature. The first is of this sort: The censor was administering the usual oath regarding wives, which was worded as follows: " Have you, to the best of your knowledge and belief, a wife? " The man who was to take the oath was a jester, a sarcastic dog,[2] and too much given to buffoonery. Thinking that he had a chance to crack a joke, when the censor asked him, as was customary, " Have you, to the best of your knowledge and belief, a wife? " he replied: " I indeed have a wife,

---

[2] *Canicula* is used of a biting woman by Plaut. *Curc.* 598, and of Diogenes by Tertullian, *adv. Marc.* 1. 1.

6 sententia." Tum censor eum, quod intempestive
lascivisset, in aerarios rettulit, causamque hanc ioci
scurrilis apud se dicti subscripsit.

7 Altera severitas eiusdem sectae disciplinaeque est.

8 Deliberatum est de nota eius qui ad censores ab
amico advocatus est et in iure stans clare nimis et
sonore oscitavit; atque inibi ut plecteretur fuit, tamquam illud indicium esset vagi animi et alucinantis

9 et fluxae atque apertae securitatis. .Sed cum ille
deiurasset invitissimum sese ac repugnantem osci-
tatione victum tenerique eo vitio quod "oscedo"
appellatur, tum notae iam destinatae exemptus est.

10 Publius Scipio Africanus, Pauli filius, utramque
historiam posuit in oratione quam dixit in censura,
cum ad maiorum mores populum hortaretur.

11 Item aliud refert Sabinus Masurius in septimo
Memoriali severe factum : " Censores," inquit, " Publius Scipio Nasica et Marcus Popilius cum equitum
censum agerent, equum nimis strigosum et male
habitum, sed equitem eius uberrimum et habitis-
simum viderunt et 'cur,'" inquiunt, "'ita est, ut tu
sis quam equus curatior?' 'Quoniam,' inquit,
'ego me curo, equum Statius nihili servos.' Visum
est parum esse reverens responsum relatusque in
aerarios, ut mos est."

---

[1] The joke, which seems untranslatable, is of course on the
double meaning of *ex sententia*, "according to your opinion"
and "according to your wish."

[2] Made him one of the *aerarii* ; see note 1, p. 352.

[3] *O. R. F.*², p. 179.

but not, by Heaven! such a one as I could desire."[1]
Then the censor reduced him to a commoner for his
untimely quip,[2] and added that the reason for his
action was a scurrilous joke made in his presence.

Here is another instance of the sternness of the
same officials. The censors deliberated about the
punishment of a man who had been brought before
them by a friend as his advocate, and who had
yawned in court very clearly and loudly. He was
on the point of being condemned for his lapse, on
the ground that it was an indication of a wandering
and trifling mind and of wanton and undisguised
indifference. But when the man had sworn that the
yawn had overcome him much against his will and
in spite of his resistance, and that he was afflicted
with the disorder known as *oscedo*, or a tendency to
yawning, he was excused from the penalty which
had already been determined upon. Publius Scipio
Africanus, son of Paulus, included both these stories
in a speech which he made when censor, urging the
people to follow the customs of their forefathers.[3]

Sabinus Masurius too in the seventh book of his
Memoirs relates a third instance of severity. He
says: "When the censors Publius Scipio Nasica and
Marcus Popilius were holding a review of the
knights, they saw a horse that was very thin and
ill-kept, while its rider was plump and in the best of
condition. 'Why is it,' said they, 'that you are
better cared for than your mount?' 'Because,' he
replied, 'I take care of myself, but Statius, a
worthless slave, takes care of the horse.' This
answer did not seem sufficiently respectful, and the
man was reduced to a commoner, according to
custom."

12   "Statius" autem servile nomen fuit. Plerique
13 apud veteres servi eo nomine fuerunt. Caecilius
quoque, ille comoediarum poeta inclutus, servus fuit
et propterea nomen habuit "Statius." Sed postea
versum est quasi in cognomentum, appellatusque est
"Caecilius Statius."

---

[1] This was regular in the case of freedmen, who took the
forename and gentile name of their patron, or former master,

Now *Statius* was a slave-name. In old times there
were many slaves of that name. Caecilius too,
the famous comic poet, was a slave and as such
called *Statius*. But afterwards this was made into a
kind of surname and he was called *Caecilius Statius.*[1]

and added their slave-name as a cognomen ; *e.g.* M. Tullius
Tiro. The forename of the Caecilius to whom Statius
belonged is not known.

BOOK V

LIBER QUINTUS

I

Quod Musonius philosophus reprehendit inprobavitque
laudari philosophum disserentem a vociferantibus et in
laudando gestientibus.

1   *** [1] Musonium philosophum solitum [2] accepimus.
"Cum philosophus," inquit, "hortatur, monet, suadet,
obiurgat aliudve quid disciplinarum disserit, tum qui
audiunt si de summo et soluto pectore obvias vulga-
tasque laudes effutiunt, si clamitant etiam, si gestiunt,
si vocum eius festivitatibus, si modulis verborum, si
quibusdam quasi fritamentis [3] orationis moventur,
exagitantur et gestiunt, tum scias et qui dicit et
qui audiunt frustra esse, neque illi philosophum
2 loqui, sed tibicinem canere. Animus," inquit,
"audientis philosophum, dum [4] quae dicuntur utilia
ac salubria sunt et errorum atque vitiorum medicinas
ferunt, laxamentum atque otium prolixe profuseque
laudandi non habet. Quisquis ille est qui audit, nisi
3 ille est plane deperditus, inter ipsam philosophi
orationem et perhorrescat necesse est et pudeat

---

[1] *Lacuna suggested by Hertz.*   [2] solitum dicere, σ.
[3] fretamentis, ω : *corr. by Heraeus ; cf. C.G.L. ii. 580, 42 ;*
v. 23. 3 ; v. 70. 21
[4] dum, *added by Hertz.*

---

[1] p. 130, Hense.

BOOK V

I

That the philosopher Musonius criticized and rebuked those
who expressed approval of a philosopher's discourse by
loud shouts and extravagant demonstrations of praise.

I HAVE heard that the philosopher Musonius [1] was
accustomed. . . .[2]   " When a philosopher," he says,
" is uttering words of encouragement, of warning,
of persuasion, or of rebuke, or is discussing any other
philosophical theme, then if his hearers utter trite
and commonplace expressions of praise without re-
flection or restraint, if they shout too, if they gesti-
culate, if they are stirred and swayed and impassioned
by the charm of his utterance, by the rhythm of his
words, and by certain musical notes,[3] as it were,
then you may know that speaker and hearers are
wasting their time, and that they are not hearing a
philosopher's lecture, but a fluteplayer's recital.   The
mind," said he, " of one who is listening to a philosopher, so long as what is said is helpful and salutary,
and furnishes a cure for faults and vices, has no time
or leisure for continued and extravagant applause.
Whoever the hearer may be, unless he is wholly lost,
during the course of the philosopher's address he
must necessarily shudder and feel secret shame and

[2] There seems to be a lacuna in the text ; see crit. note.
[3] Heraeus suggests *fritamenta* in i. 11, 12.

4 tacitus et paeniteat et gaudeat et admiretur, varios
adeo vultus disparilesque sensus gerat, proinde ut
eum conscientiamque eius adfecerit utrarumque
animi partium, aut sincerarum aut aegrarum, philosophi pertractatio."

5 Praeterea dicebat magnam laudem non abesse ab
admiratione, admirationem autem quae maxima est
6 non verba parere, sed silentium. " Idcirco," inquit,
".poetarum sapientissimus auditores illos Ulixi,
labores suos inlustrissime narrantis, ubi loquendi
finis factus, non exultare nec strepere nec vociferari
facit, sed consiluisse universos dicit, quasi attonitos
et obstupidos, delenimentis aurium ad origines usque
vocis permanantibus :

"Ὡς φάτο· τοὶ δ᾽ ἄρα πάντες ἀκὴν ἐγένοντο σιωπῇ,
Κηληθμῷ δ᾽ ἔσχοντο κατὰ μέγαρα σκιόεντα.

II

Super equo Alexandri regis, qui Bucephalas appellatus est.

1 Equus Alexandri regis et capite et nomine " Buce-
2 phalas " fuit. Emptum Chares scripsit talentis
tredecim et regi Philippo donatum ; hoc autem aeris
3 nostri summa est sestertia trecenta duodecim. Super
hoc equo dignum memoria visum, quod, ubi ornatus
erat armatusque ad proelium, haud umquam inscendi
4 sese ab alio nisi ab rege passus sit. Id etiam de
isto equo memoratum est, quod, cum insidens in eo
Alexander bello Indico et facinora faciens fortia, in

---

[1] Odyss. xiii. 1. Odysseus (Ulysses) had just finished
telling his story to Alcinous, king of the Phaeacians, and his
court.

repentance, or rejoice or wonder, and even show changes of countenance and betray varying emotions, according as the philosopher's discourse has affected him and his consciousness of the different tendencies of his mind, whether noble or base."

He added that great applause is not inconsistent with admiration, but that the greatest admiration gives rise, not to words, but to silence. "Therefore," said he, "the wisest of all poets does not represent those who heard Ulysses' splendid account of his hardships as leaping up, when he ceased speaking, with shouts and noisy demonstrations, but he says they were one and all silent, as if amazed and confounded, since the gratification of their ears even affected their power of utterance.

Thus he; but they in silence all were hushed
And held in rapture through the shadowy hall.[1]

II

About the horse of king Alexander, called Bucephalas.

THE horse of king Alexander was called *Bucephalas* because of the shape of his head.[2] Chares wrote[3] that he was bought for thirteen talents and given to king Philip; that amount in Roman money is three hundred and twelve thousand sesterces. It seemed a noteworthy characteristic of this horse that when he was armed and equipped for battle, he would never allow himself to be mounted by any other than the king.[4] It is also related that Alexander in the war against India, mounted upon that horse and doing

---

[2] Bucephalas in Greek means "ox-headed."
[3] Fr. 14, p. 117, Müller.   [4] *Cf.* Suet. *Jul.* lxi.

hostium cuneum non satis sibi providens inmisisset,
coniectisque undique in Alexandrum telis, vulneribus
altis in cervice atque in latere equus perfossus esset,
moribundus tamen ac prope iam exanguis e mediis
hostibus regem vivacissimo cursu retulit atque, ubi
eum extra tela extulerat, ilico concidit et, domini
iam superstitis securus, quasi cum sensus humani
5 solacio animam expiravit. Tum rex Alexander,
parta eius belli victoria, oppidum in isdem locis
condidit idque ob equi honores "Bucephalon"
appellavit.

III

Quae causa quodque initium fuisse dicatur Protagorae ad
philosophiae litteras adeundi.

1 Protagoram, virum in studiis doctrinarum egre-
gium, cuius nomen Plato libro suo illi incluto inscripsit, adulescentem aiunt victus quaerendi gratia
in mercedem missum vecturasque onerum corpore
2 suo factitavisse, quod genus Graeci ἀχθοφόρους
3 vocant, Latine "baiulos" appellamus. Is de proximo rure Abdera in oppidum, cuius popularis fuit,
caudices ligni plurimos funiculo brevi circumdatos
4 portabat. Tum forte Democritus, civitatis eiusdem
civis, homo ante alios virtutis et philosophiae gratia
venerandus, cum egrederetur extra urbem, videt
eum cum illo genere oneris tam impedito ac tam
incohibili facile atque expedite incedentem, et prope

valorous deeds, had driven him, with disregard of his own safety, too far into the enemies' ranks. The horse had suffered deep wounds in his neck and side from the weapons hurled from every hand at Alexander, but though dying and almost exhausted from loss of blood, he yet in swiftest course bore the king from the midst of the foe; but when he had taken him out of range of the weapons, the horse at once fell, and satisfied with having saved his master breathed his last, with indications of relief that were almost human. Then king Alexander, after winning the victory in that war, founded a city in that region and in honour of his horse called it *Bucephalon*.

III

The reason and the occasion which are said to have introduced Protagoras to the study of philosophical literature.

THEY say that Protagoras, a man eminent in the pursuit of learning, whose name Plato gave to that famous dialogue of his, in his youth earned his living as a hired labourer and often carried heavy burdens on his back, being one of that class of men which the Greeks call ἀχθοφόροι and we Latins *baiuli*, or porters. He was once carrying a great number of blocks of wood, bound together with a short rope, from the neighbouring countryside into his native town of Abdera. It chanced at the time that Democritus, a citizen of that same city, a man esteemed before all others for his fine character and his knowledge of philosophy, as he was going out of the city, saw Protagoras walking along easily and rapidly with that burden, of a kind so awkward and so difficult to hold together. Democritus drew near, and

accedit et iuncturam posituramque ligni scite peri-
teque factam considerat petitque ut paullulum ad-
5 quiescat. Quod ubi Protagoras, ut erat petitum,
fecit atque itidem Democritus acervum illum et
quasi orbem caudicum, brevi vinculo comprehensum,
ratione quadam quasi geometrica librari continerique
animadvertit, interrogavit quis id lignum ita com-
posuisset, et cum ille a se compositum dixisset,
desideravit uti solveret ac denuo in modum eundem
6 collocaret. At postquam ille solvit ac similiter composuit, tum Democritus, animi aciem sollertiamque
hominis non docti demiratus, "Mi adulescens,"
inquit, "cum ingenium bene faciendi habeas, sunt
maiora melioraque quae facere mecum possis,"
abduxitque eum statim secumque habuit et sumptum
ministravit et philosophias docuit et esse eum fecit
quantus postea fuit.
7   Is tamen Protagoras insincerus quidem philosophus, sed acerrimus sophistarum fuit ; pecuniam
quippe ingentem cum a discipulis acciperet annuam,
pollicebatur se id docere quanam verborum industria
causa infirmior fieret fortior, quam rem Graece ita
dicebat : τὸν ἥττω λόγον κρείττω ποιεῖν.

IV

De verbo "duovicesimo," quod vulgo incognitum est, a viris
doctis multifariam in libris scriptum est.

1   Apud Sigillaria forte in libraria ego et Iulius
Paulus poeta, vir memoria nostra doctissimus, consi-

noticing with what skill and judgment the wood was arranged and tied, asked the man to stop and rest awhile. When Protagoras did as he was asked, and Democritus again observed that the almost circular heap of blocks was bound with a short rope, and was balanced and held together with all but geometrical accuracy, he asked who had put the wood together in that way. When Protagoras replied that he had done it himself, Democritus asked him to untie the bundle and arrange it again in the same way. But after he had done so, then Democritus, astonished at the keen intellect and cleverness of this uneducated man, said : " My dear young man, since you have a talent for doing things well, there are greater and better employments which you can follow with me "; and he at once took him away, kept him at his own house, supplied him with money, taught him philosophy, and made him the great man that he afterwards became.

Yet this Protagoras was not a true philosopher, but the cleverest of sophists; for in consideration of the payment of a huge annual fee, he used to promise his pupils that he would teach them by what verbal dexterity the weaker cause could be made the stronger, a process which he called in Greek : τὸν ἥττω λόγον κρείττω ποιεῖν, or " making the worse appear the better reason."

IV

On the word *duovicesimus*, which is unknown to the general public, but occurs frequently in the writings of the learned.

I CHANCED to be sitting in a bookshop in the Sigillaria[1] with the poet Julius Paulus, the most

[1] See note 2, p. 128.

deramus ; atque ibi expositi erant Fabii *Annales,*
bonae atque sincerae vetustatis libri, quos venditor
2 sine mendis esse contendebat. Grammaticus autem
quispiam de nobilioribus, ab emptore ad spectandos
libros adhibitus, repperisse se [1] unum in libro mendum dicebat ; sed contra librarius in quodvis pignus
vocabat, si in una uspiam littera delictum esset.
3 Ostendebat grammaticus ita scriptum in libro quarto :
" Quapropter tum primum ex plebe alter consul
factus est, duovicesimo anno postquam Romam Galli
4 ceperunt." " Non," inquit, " duovicesimo, sed
5 ' duo et vicesimo ' scribi oportuit. Quid enim est
duovicesimo ? " *** Varro *Humanarum Rerum* lib.
XVI ; [2] hic ita scripsit : Mortuus est anno duovicesimo ; rex fuit annos XXI.***

V

Cuiusmodi ioco incavillatus sit Antiochum regem Poenus
Hannibal.

1 IN libris veterum memoriarum scriptum est,
Hannibalem Carthaginiensem apud regem Antiochum facetissime cavillatum esse. Ea cavillatio

---

[1] se, *added by Hertz.*
[2] Varro . . . xvi, *from* Nonius II., p. 100, 9.

---

[1] Quintus Fabius Pictor, who was sent as an envoy to
Delphi after the battle of Cannae (216 B.C.), wrote a history
of Rome from the coming of Aeneas to his own time. He

learned man within my memory; and there was on
sale there the *Annals* of Fabius[1] in a copy of good
and undoubted age, which the dealer maintained
was without errors. But one of the better known
grammarians, who had been called in by a purchaser
to inspect the book, said that he had found in it one
error; but the bookseller for his part offered to
wager any amount whatever that there was not a
mistake even in a single letter. The grammarian
pointed out the following passage in the fourth
book:[2] "Therefore it was then that for the first
time one of the two consuls was chosen from the
plebeians, in the twenty-second (*duovicesimo*) year
after the Gauls captured Rome." "It ought," said
he, "to read, not *duovicesimo,* but *duodevicesimo* or
twenty-second; for what is the meaning of *duovicesimo*?" . . . Varro[3] in the sixteenth book of his
Antiquities of Man; there he wrote as follows:[4]
"He died in the twenty-second year[5] (*duovicesimo*);
he was king for twenty-one years." . . .

V

How the Carthaginian Hannibal jested at the expense of
king Antiochus.

In collections of old tales it is recorded that
Hannibal the Carthaginian made a highly witty jest
when at the court of king Antiochus. The jest was

wrote in Greek, but a Latin version is mentioned also by
Quintilian (i. 6. 12) and was used by Varro and by Cicero.
   [2] Fr. 6, Peter.
   [3] There is a lacuna in the text which might be filled by
"This question might be answered by."
   [4] Fr. 1, Mirsch.   [5] Of his reign.

2 huiuscemodi fuit : ostendebat ei Antiochus in campo
copias ingentis quas bellum populo Romano facturus
comparaverat, convertebatque exercitum insignibus
3 argenteis et aureis florentem; inducebat etiam
currus cum falcibus et elephantos cum turribus
equitatumque frenis, ephippiis, monilibus, phaleris
4 praefulgentem. Atque ibi rex, contemplatione tanti
ac tam ornati exercitus gloriabundus, Hannibalem
aspicit et " Putasne," inquit, " conferri posse ac satis
5 esse [1] Romanis haec omnia ? " Tum Poenus, eludens
ignaviam inbelliamque militum eius pretiose arma-
torum : " Satis, plane satis esse credo Romanis haec
6 omnia, etiamsi avarissimi sunt." Nihil prorsum
neque tam lepide neque tam acerbe dici potest;
7 rex de numero exercitus sui ac de aestimanda
aequiperatione quaesiverat, respondit Hannibal de
praeda.

VI

De coronis militaribus; quae sit earum triumphalis, quae
obsidionalis, quae civica, quae muralis, quae castrensis,
quae navalis, quae ovalis, quae oleaginea.

1 MILITARES coronae multae et [2] variae sunt.
2 Quarum quae nobilissimae sunt, has ferme esse
accepimus : " triumphalem, obsidionalem, civicam,
3 muralem, castrensem, navalem "; est ea quoque
corona quae " ovalis " dicitur, est item postrema
4 " oleaginea," qua uti solent qui in proelio non
fuerunt sed triumphum procurant.

[1] esse, *Macrob.* ii. 2. 2 ; esse credo, ω.   [2] et, *added by Lion.*

this : Antiochus was displaying to him on the plain the gigantic forces which he had mustered to make war on the Roman people, and was manœuvring his army glittering with gold and silver ornaments. He also brought up chariots with scythes, elephants with turrets, and horsemen with brilliant bridles, saddle-cloths, neck-chains and trappings. And then the king, filled with vainglory at the sight of an army so great and so well-equipped, turned to Hannibal and said : " Do you think that all this can be equalled and that it is enough for the Romans ? " Then the Carthaginian, deriding the worthlessness and inefficiency of the king's troops in their costly armour, replied : " I think all this will be enough, yes, quite enough, for the Romans, even though they are most avaricious." Absolutely nothing could equal this remark for wit and sarcasm ; the king had inquired about the size of his army and asked for a comparative estimate ; Hannibal in his reply referred to it as booty.

VI

On military crowns, with a description of the triumphal, siege, civic, mural, camp, naval, ovation, and olive crowns.

MILITARY crowns are many and varied. Of these the most highly esteemed I find to be in general the following : the " triumphal, siege, civic, mural, camp and naval crowns." There is besides the so-called " ovation " crown, and lastly also the " olive " crown, which is regularly worn by those who have not taken part in a battle, but nevertheless are awarded a triumph.

5 "Triumphales" coronae sunt aureae, quae im-
6 peratoribus ob honorem triumphi mittuntur. Id
7 vulgo dicitur "aurum coronarium." Haec antiquitus
e lauru erant, post fieri ex auro coeptae.

8 "Obsidionalis" est, quam ii qui liberati obsidione
9 sunt dant ei duci qui liberavit. Ea corona graminea
est, observarique solitum ut fieret e gramine quod
in eo loco gnatum esset intra quem clausi erant qui
10 obsidebantur. Hanc coronam gramineam senatus
populusque Romanus Q. Fabio Maximo dedit bello
Poenorum secundo, quod urbem Romam obsidione
hostium liberasset.

11 "Civica" corona appellatur, quam civis civi a quo
in proelio servatus est testem vitae salutisque per-
12 ceptae dat. Ea fit e fronde quernea, quoniam cibus
victusque antiquissimus quercus[1] capi solitus; fuit
etiam ex ilice, quod genus superiori proximum est,
sicuti scriptum est in quadam comoedia Caecilii:

† "Advehuntur,"[2] (inquit), "cum ilignea corona
et chlamyde; di vostram fidem!"

13 Masurius autem Sabinus, in undecimo *Librorum
Memorialium,* civicam coronam tum dari solitam
dicit, cum is qui civem servaverat eodem tempore
etiam hostem occiderat neque locum in ea pugna
reliquerat; aliter ius civicae coronae negat conces-
14 sum. Tiberium tamen Caesarem consultum an

---

[1] *perhaps* querceus *or* querneus.
[2] advehitur cum iligna, *Fleckeisen* ; advehunt Eum, *C. W. F. Müller.*

---

[1] v. 269, Ribbeck[3].   [2] Fr. 17, Huschke; 8, Bremer.

"Triumphal" crowns are of gold and are presented to a commander in recognition of the honour of a triumph. This in common parlance is "gold for a crown." This crown in ancient times was of laurel, but later they began to make them of gold.

The "siege" crown is the one which those who have been delivered from a state of siege present to the general who delivered them. That crown is of grass, and custom requires that it be made of grass which grew in the place within which the besieged were confined. This crown of grass the Roman senate and people presented to Quintus Fabius Maximus in the second Punic war, because he had freed the city of Rome from siege by the enemy.

The crown is called "civic" which one citizen gives to another who has saved his life in battle, in recognition of the preservation of his life and safety. It is made of the leaves of the esculent oak, because the earliest food and means of supporting life were furnished by that oak; it was formerly made also from the holm oak, because that is the species which is most nearly related to the esculent; this we learn from a comedy of Caecilius, who says:[1]

> They pass with cloaks and crowns of holm; ye Gods!

But Masurius Sabinus,[2] in the eleventh book of his *Memoirs*, says that it was the custom to award the civic crown only when the man who had saved the life of a fellow citizen had at the same time slain the enemy who threatened him, and had not given ground in that battle; under other conditions he says that the honour of the civic crown was not granted. He adds, however, that Tiberius Caesar

civicam coronam capere posset qui civem in proelio
servasset et hostes ibidem duos interfecisset, sed
locum in quo pugnabat non retinuisset eoque loco
hostes potiti essent, rescripsisse dicit eum quoque
civica dignum videri, quod appareret e tam iniquo
loco civem ab eo servatum, ut etiam a fortiter pug-
15 nantibus retineri non quiverit. Hac corona civica
L. Gellius, vir censorius, in senatu Ciceronem consulem donari a republica censuit, quod eius opera
esset atrocissima illa Catilinae coniuratio detecta
vindicataque.

16   " Muralis " est corona, qua donatur ab imperatore
qui primus murum subiit inque oppidum hostium
per vim ascendit ; idcirco quasi muri pinnis decorata
17 est.   " Castrensis " est corona, qua donat imperator
eum qui primus hostium castra pugnans introivit;
18 ea corona insigne valli habet.   " Navalis " est, qua
donari solet maritimo proelio qui primus in hostium
navem [1] armatus transiluit ; ea quasi navium rostris
19 insignita est.   Et " muralis " autem et " castrensis "
et " navalis " fieri ex auro solent.

20, 21   " Ovalis "   corona   murtea   est ; ea   utebantur
imperatores qui ovantes urbem introibant.

Ovandi ac non triumphandi causa est, cum aut
bella non rite indicta neque cum iusto hoste gesta
sunt, aut hostium nomen humile et non idoneum est,
ut servorum piratarumque, aut, deditione repente

[1] vi *after* navem, *ω* ; *cf.* Paul. Fest. *p.* 157. 7, *Lindsay.*

was once asked to decide whether a soldier might receive the civic crown who had saved a citizen in battle and killed two of the enemy, yet had not held the position in which he was fighting, but the enemy had occupied it. The emperor ruled that the soldier seemed to be among those who deserved the civic crown, since it was clear that he had rescued a fellow citizen from a place so perilous that it could not be held even by valiant warriors. It was this civic crown that Lucius Gellius, an ex-censor, proposed in the senate that his country should award to Cicero in his consulship, because it was through his efforts that the frightful conspiracy of Catiline had been detected and punished.

The " mural " crown is that which is awarded by a commander to the man who is first to mount the wall and force his way into an enemy's town ; therefore it is ornamented with representations of the battlements of a wall. A " camp " crown is presented by a general to the soldier who is first to fight his way into a hostile camp ; that crown represents a palisade. The " naval " crown is commonly awarded to the armed man who has been the first to board an enemy ship in a sea-fight ; it is decorated with representations of the beaks of ships. Now the " mural," " camp," and " naval " crowns are regularly made of gold.

The " ovation " crown is of myrtle ; it was worn by generals who entered the city in an ovation.

The occasion for awarding an ovation, and not a triumph, is that wars have not been declared in due form and so have not been waged with a legitimate enemy, or that the adversaries' character is low or unworthy, as in the case of slaves or pirates, or that,

facta, "inpulverea," ut dici solet, incruentaque
22 victoria obvenit. Cui facilitati aptam esse Veneris
frondem crediderunt, quod non Martius, sed quasi
23 Venerius quidam triumphus foret. Ac murteam
coronam M. Crassus, cum bello fugitivorum confecto
ovans rediret, insolenter aspernatus est senatusque
consultum faciundum per gratiam curavit, ut lauro,
non murto, coronaretur.
24 Marcus Cato obicit M. Fulvio Nobiliori quod milites
per ambitum coronis de levissimis causis donasset.
25 De qua re verba ipsa apposui Catonis: "Iam principio
quis vidit corona donari quemquam, cum oppidum
captum non esset aut castra hostium non incensa
26 essent?" Fulvius autem, in quem hoc a Catone
dictum est, coronis donaverat milites qui[1] vallum
curaverant aut qui puteum strenue foderant.
27 Praetereundum non est quod ad ovationes attinet,
super quo dissensisse veteres scriptores accipio.
Partim enim scripserunt qui ovaret introire solitum
equo vehentem; set Sabinus Masurius pedibus ingredi ovantes dicit, sequentibus eos non militibus,
sed universo senatu.

[1] qui, *Lion*; quia, ω.

---

[1] 'Ακονιτί ("dustless") was proverbial in Greek for "without an effort," as in Thuc. iv. 73; Xen. *Ages.* 6. 3. *Cf.* Hor.
Epist. i. 1. 54, *cui sit condicio dulcis sine pulvere palma.*
[2] Nobilior was consul in 189 B.C. Cicero, *Tusc. Disp.* i. 2. 3,
says that Cato criticized him also for taking Ennius with him
to his province of Aetolia.

because of a quick surrender, a victory was won
which was "dustless," as the saying is,[1] and bloodless.
For such an easy victory they believed that the
leaves sacred to Venus were appropriate, on the
ground that it was a triumph, not of Mars, but as it
were of Venus. And Marcus Crassus, when he
returned after ending the Servile war and entered
the city in an ovation, disdainfully rejected the
myrtle crown and used his influence to have a decree
passed by the senate, that he should be crowned with
laurel, not with myrtle.

Marcus Cato charges Marcus Fulvius Nobilior[2] with
having awarded crowns to his soldiers for the most
trifling reasons possible, for the sake of popularity.
On that subject I give you Cato's own words :[3]
"Now to begin with, who ever saw anyone presented
with a crown, when a town had not been taken or an
enemy's camp burned ?" But Fulvius, against whom
Cato brought that charge, had bestowed crowns on
his soldiers for industry in building a rampart or in
digging a well.

I must not pass over a point relating to ovations,
about which I learn that the ancient writers dis-
agreed. For some of them have stated that the man
who celebrated an ovation was accustomed to enter
the city on horseback : but Masurius Sabinus says[4]
that they entered on foot, followed, not by their
soldiers, but by the senate in a body.

[3] xiv. 1, Jordan.   [4] Fr. 26, Huschke ; *memor.* 15, Bremer.

VII

" Personae " vocabulum quam lepide interpretatus sit quamque esse vocis eius originem dixerit Gavius Bassus.

1 LEPIDE, mi hercules, et scite Gavius Bassus in libris, quos *De Origine Vocabulorum* composuit, unde appellata " persona " sit interpretatur ; a personando
2 enim id vocabulum factum esse coniectat. " Nam caput," inquit, " et os coperimento personae tectum undique unaque tantum vocis emittendae via pervium, quoniam non vaga neque diffusa est, set[1] in unum tantummodo exitum collectam coactamque vocem ciet, magis claros canorosque sonitus facit. Quoniam igitur indumentum illud oris clarescere et resonare vocem facit, ob eam causam ' persona ' dicta est, ' o ' littera propter vocabuli formam productiore."

VIII

Defensus error a Vergilii versibus, quos arguerat Iulius Hyginus grammaticus ; et ibidem, quid sit lituus; deque ἐτυμολογίᾳ vocis eius.

1 IPSE Quirinali lituo parvaque sedebat
Subcinctus trabea laevaque ancile gerebat.

In his versibus errasse Hyginus Vergilium scripsit, tamquam non animadverterit deesse aliquid hisce verbis :

Ipse Quirinali lituo.

---

[1] set, *added by Mommsen.*

VII

How cleverly Gavius Bassus explained the word persona, *and what he said to be the origin of that word.*

CLEVERLY, by Heaven ! and wittily, in my opinion, does Gavius Bassus explain the derivation of the word *persona*, in the work that he composed *On the Origin of Words;* for he suggests that that word is formed from *personare.* " For," he says,[1] " the head and the face are shut in on all sides by the covering of the *persona*, or mask, and only one passage is left for the issue of the voice ; and since this opening is neither free nor broad, but sends forth the voice after it has been concentrated and forced into one single means of egress, it makes the sound clearer and more resonant.   Since then that covering of the face gives clearness and resonance to the voice, it is for that reason called *persona*, the *o* being lengthened because of the formation of the word."

VIII

A defence of some lines of Virgil, in which the grammarian Julius Hyginus alleged that there was a mistake ; and also the meaning of lituus ; *and on the etymology of that word.*

> HERE, wielding his Quirinal augur-staff,
> Girt with scant shift and bearing on his left
> The sacred shield, Picus appeared enthroned.

In these verses [2] Hyginus wrote [3] that Virgil was in error, alleging that he did not notice that the words *ipse Quirinali lituo* lacked something.   " For," said

---

[1] Frag. 8, Fun.   [2] *Aen.* vii. 187.
[3] Frag. 5, Fun.

2 "Nam si nihil," inquit, "deesse animadverterimus, videtur ita dictum ut fiat 'lituo et trabea subcinctus,' quod est," inquit, "absurdissimum; quippe cum 'lituus' sit virga brevis, in parte qua robustior est incurva, qua augures utuntur, quonam modo 'subcinctus lituo' videri potest?"

3 Immo ipse Hyginus parum animadvertit sic hoc esse dictum, ut pleraque dici per defectionem solent.

4 Veluti cum dicitur "M. Cicero homo magna eloquentia" et "Q. Roscius histrio summa venustate," non plenum hoc utrumque neque perfectum est, sed

5 enim pro pleno atque perfecto auditur. Ut Vergilius alio in loco:

> Victorem Buten inmani corpore,

id est corpus inmane habentem, et item alibi:

> In medium geminos inmani pondere caestus
> Proiecit,

ac similiter:

> Domus sanie dapibusque cruentis,
> Intus opaca, ingens,

6 sic igitur id quoque videri dictum debet: "Picus Quirinali lituo erat," sicuti dicimus: "statua grandi

7 capite erat." Et "est" autem et "erat" et "fuit" plerumque absunt cum elegantia sine detrimento sententiae.

8 Et, quoniam facta "litui" mentio est, non praetermittendum est quod posse quaeri animadvertimus, utrum lituus auguralis a tuba quae "lituus" appel-

---

[1] *Aen.* v. 372.   [2] *Aen.* v. 401.   [3] *Aen.* iii. 618.
[4] This explanation of *Quirinali lituo* as an ablative of quality is of course wrong; we simply have zeugma in *subcinctus*, "equipped with" and "girt with.'

he, " if we have not observed that something is lacking, the sentence seems to read ' girt with staff and scant shift,' which," says he, " is utterly absurd ; for since the *lituus* is a short wand, curved at its thicker end, such as the augurs use, how on earth can one be looked upon as ' girt with a *lituus* ? ' "

As a matter of fact, it was Hyginus himself who failed to notice that this expression, like very many others, contains an ellipsis. For example, when we say " Marcus Cicero, a man of great eloquence " and " Quintus Roscius, an actor of consummate grace," neither of these phrases is full and complete, but to the hearer they seem full and complete. As Vergil wrote in another place : [1]

Victorious Butes of huge bulk,

that is, having huge bulk, and also in another passage : [2]

Into the ring he hurled gauntlets ot giant weight,

and similarly : [3]

A house of gore and cruel feasts, dark, huge within,

so then it would seem that the phrase in question ought to be interpreted as " Picus was with the Quirinal staff," just as we say " the statue was with a large head," and in fact *est, erat* and *fuit* are often omitted, with elegant effect and without any loss of meaning.[4]

And since mention has been made of the *lituus*, I must not pass over a question which obviously may be asked, whether the augurs' *lituus* is called after the trumpet of the same name, or whether the

latur, an tuba a lituo augurum " lituus " dicta sit;
9 utrumque enim pari forma et pariter incurvum est
10 Sed si, ut quidam putant, tuba a sonitu " lituus "
appellata est ex illo Homerico verbo :

$$\Lambda i \gamma \xi \epsilon \ \beta \iota \acute{o} s,$$

necesse est ita accipi, ut virga auguralis a tubae
11 similitudine "lituus" vocetur. Utitur autem vocabulo
isto Vergilius et pro tuba :

Et lituo pugnas insignis obibat et hasta.

IX

Historia de Croesi filio muto,[1] ex Herodoti libris.

1   FILIUS Croesi regis, cum iam fari per aetatem
posset, infans erat et, cum iam multum adolevisset,
item nihil fari quibat. Mutus adeo et elinguis diu
2 habitus est.   Cum in patrem eius, bello magno
victum et urbe in qua erat capta, hostis gladio
educto,[2] regem esse ignorans, invaderet, diduxit
adulescens os, clamare nitens, eoque nisu atque
impetu spiritus vitium nodumque linguae rupit
planeque et articulate elocutus est, clamans in
3 hostem ne rex Croesus occideretur. Tum et hostis
gladium reduxit et rex vita donatus est et adulescens

---

[1] filio muto, *Hertz*; filium tam, *ω*.
[2] educto, *J. F. Gronov* ; deducto, *MSS.*; destricto, *Lion*.

---

[1] The trumpet called *lituus* was slightly curved at the end,
differing from the *tuba*, which was straight, and the spiral
cornu. The augur's staff was like a crook with a short handle.

trumpet derived its name *lituus* from the augurs'
staff; for both have the same form and both alike
are curved.[1] But if, as some think, the trumpet
was called *lituus* from its sound, because of the
Homeric expression λίγξε βιός,[2]

> The bow twanged,

it must be concluded that the augural staff was
called *lituus* from its resemblance to the trumpet.
And Virgil uses that word also as synonymous with
tuba :[3]

> He even faced the fray
> Conspicuous both with clarion (*lituo*) and with spear.

IX

The story of Croesus' dumb son, from the books of Herodotus.

THE son of king Croesus, when he was already old
enough to speak, was dumb, and after he had become
a well-grown youth, he was still unable to utter a
word. Hence he was for a long time regarded as
mute and tongue-tied. When his father had been
vanquished in a great war, the city in which he
lived had been taken, and one of the enemy was
rushing upon him with drawn sword, unaware that
he was the king, then the young man opened his
mouth in an attempt to cry out. And by that
effort and the force of his breath he broke the
impediment and the bond upon his tongue, and
spoke plainly and clearly, shouting to the enemy not
to kill king Croesus. Then the foeman withheld
his sword, the king's life was saved, and from that

---

[2] *Iliad* iv. 125.   *Aen.* vi. 167.

4 loqui prorsum deinceps incepit. Herodotus in
Historiis huius memoriae scriptor est eiusque verba
sunt, quae prima dixisse filium Croesi refert: Ἄνθρωπε, μὴ κτεῖνε Κροῖσον.

5 Sed et quispiam Samius athleta, nomen illi fuit
Ἐχεκλοῦς, cum antea non loquens fuisset, ob similem

6 dicitur causam loqui coepisse. Nam cum in sacro
certamine sortitio inter ipsos et adversarios non bona
fide fieret et sortem nominis falsam subici animad-
vertisset, repente in eum qui id faciebat, videre sese
quid faceret, magnum inclamavit. Atque is oris
vinclo solutus per omne inde vitae tempus non
turbide neque adhaese locutus est.

X

De argumentis quae Graece ἀντιστρέφοντα appellantur, a
nobis " reciproca " dici possunt.

1 INTER vitia argumentorum longe maximum esse
vitium videtur quae ἀντιστρέφοντα Graeci dicunt.

2 Ea quidam e nostris non hercle nimis absurde

3 " reciproca " appellaverunt. Id autem vitium accidit
hoc modo, cum argumentum propositum referri contra
convertique in eum potest a quo dictum est, et
utrimque pariter valet; quale est pervolgatum illud
quo Protagoram, sophistarum acerrimum, usum esse
ferunt adversus Euathlum, discipulum suum.

---

[1] i. 85.
[2] Valerius Maximus, i. 8. ext. 4 says: cum ei victoriae
quam adeptus erat titulus et praemium eriperetur, indigna-
tione accensus vocalis evasit. Just how he was cheated in
the story told by Gellius is not clear, unless the lots were

time on the youth began to speak. Herodotus in his *Histories* [1] is the chronicler of that event, and the words which he says the son of Croesus first spoke are : " Man, do not kill Croesus."

But also an athlete of Samos—his name was Echeklous—although he had previously been speechless, is said to have begun to speak for a similar reason. For when in a sacred contest the casting of lots between the Samians and their opponents was not being done fairly, and he had noticed that a lot with a false name was being slipped in, he suddenly shouted in a loud voice to the man who was doing it that he saw what he was up to. And he too was freed from the check upon his speech and for all the remaining time of his life spoke without stammering or lack of clearness. [2]

X

On the arguments which by the Greeks are called ἀντιστρέφον- τα, and in Latin may be termed *reciproca*.

AMONG fallacious arguments the one which the Greeks call ἀντιστρέφον seems to be by far the most fallacious. Such arguments some of our own philosophers have rather appropriately termed *reciproca*, or " convertible." The fallacy arises from the fact that the argument that is presented may be turned in the opposite direction and used against the one who has offered it, and is equally strong for both sides of the question. An example is the well-known argument which Protagoras, the keenest of all sophists, is said to have used against his pupil Euathlus.

cast to determine which of the contestants should be matched together, and he was matched against an unsuitable opponent.

4 Lis namque inter eos et controversia super pacta
5 mercede haec fuit. Euathlus, adulescens dives, eloquentiae discendae causarumque orandi cupiens fuit.
6 Is in disciplinam Protagorae sese dedit daturumque
promisit mercedem grandem pecuniam, quantam
Protagoras petiverat, dimidiumque eius dedit iam
tunc statim priusquam disceret, pepigitque ut re-
liquum dimidium daret quo primo die causam apud
7 iudices orasset et vicisset. Postea cum diutule
auditor adsectatorque Protagorae fuisset et[1] in studio
quidem facundiae abunde promovisset, causas tamen
non reciperet tempusque iam longum transcurreret
et facere id videretur, ne relicum mercedis daret,
8 capit consilium Protagoras, ut tum existimabat,
astutum ; petere institit ex pacto mercedem, litem
cum Euathlo contestatur.
9 Et cum ad iudices coniciendae consistendaeque
causae gratia venissent, tum Protagoras sic exorsus
est : " Disce," inquit, " stultissime adulescens, utroque id modo fore uti reddas quod peto, sive contra
10 te pronuntiatum erit sive pro te. Nam si contra te
lis data erit, merces mihi ex sententia debebitur,
quia ego vicero ; sin vero secundum te iudicatum
erit, merces mihi ex pacto debebitur, quia tu
viceris."
11 Ad ea respondit Euathlus : " Potui," inquit, " huic
tuae tam ancipiti captioni isse obviam, si verba non
12 ipse facerem atque alio patrono uterer. Sed maius

---

[1] et, *added in σ.*

For a dispute arose between them and an altercation as to the fee which had been agreed upon, as follows : Euathlus, a wealthy young man, was desirous of instruction in oratory and the pleading of causes. He became a pupil of Protagoras and promised to pay him a large sum of money, as much as Protagoras had demanded. He paid half of the amount at once, before beginning his lessons, and agreed to pay the remaining half on the day when he first pleaded before jurors and won his case. Afterwards, when he had been for some little time a pupil and follower of Protagoras, and had in fact made considerable progress in the study of oratory, he nevertheless did not undertake any cases. And when the time was already getting long, and he seemed to be acting thus in order not to pay the rest of the fee, Protagoras formed what seemed to him at the time a wily scheme ; he determined to demand his pay according to the contract, and brought suit against Euathlus.

And when they had appeared before the jurors to bring forward and to contest the case, Protagoras began as follows : " Let me tell you, most foolish of youths, that in either event you will have to pay what I am demanding, whether judgment be pronounced for or against you. For if the case goes against you, the money will be due me in accordance with the verdict, because I have won ; but if the decision be in your favour, the money will be due me according to our contract, since you will have won a case."

To this Euathlus replied : " I might have met this sophism of yours, tricky as it is, by not pleading my own cause but employing another as my advocate. But I take greater satisfaction in a victory in which

mihi in ista victoria prolubium est, cum te non in
causa tantum, sed in argumento quoque isto vinco.
13 Disce igitur tu quoque, magister sapientissime,
utroque modo fore uti non reddam quod petis, sive
14 contra me pronuntiatum fuerit sive pro me. Nam
si iudices pro causa mea senserint, nihil tibi ex
sententia debebitur, quia ego vicero ; sin contra me
pronuntiaverint, nihil tibi ex pacto debebo, quia non
vicero.''

15 Tum iudices, dubiosum hoc inexplicabileque esse
quod utrimque dicebatur rati, ne sententia sua,
utramcumque in partem dicta esset, ipsa sese re-
scinderet, rem iniudicatam reliquerunt causamque in
16 diem longissimam distulerunt. Sic ab adulescente
discipulo magister eloquentiae inclutus suo sibi
argumento confutatus est et captionis versute ex-
cogitatae frustratus fuit.

XI

Biantis de re uxoria syllogismum non posse videri ἀντιστρέφειν.

1 EXISTIMANT quidam etiam illud Biantis, viri sa-
pientis ac nobilis, responsum consimile esse atque
est Protagorion illud de quo dixi modo, ἀντι-
2 στρέφον. Nam cum rogatus esset a quodam Bias,
deberetne uxorem ducere an vitam vivere caelibem,
Ἤτοι, inquit, καλὴν ἄξεις ἢ αἰσχράν· καὶ εἰ καλήν,
ἕξεις κοινήν, εἰ δὲ αἰσχράν, ἕξεις ποινήν· ἑκάτερον δὲ οὐ
ληπτέον· οὐ γαμητέον ἄρα.

---

[1] The ''convertible'' argument described in x.
[2] In the Greek there is a word play on κοινή and

I defeat you, not only in the suit, but also in this argument of yours. So let me tell you in turn, wisest of masters, that in either event I shall not have to pay what you demand, whether judgment be pronounced for or against me. For if the jurors decide in my favour, according to their verdict nothing will be due you, because I have won; but if they give judgment against me, by the terms of our contract I shall owe you nothing, because I have not won a case."

Then the jurors, thinking that the plea on both sides was uncertain and insoluble, for fear that their decision, for whichever side it was rendered, might annul itself, left the matter undecided and postponed the case to a distant day. Thus a celebrated master of oratory was refuted by his youthful pupil with his own argument, and his cleverly devised sophism failed.

XI

The impossibility of regarding Bias' syllogism on marriage as an example of ἀντιστρέφον.

SOME think that the famous answer of the wise and noble Bias, like that of Protagoras of which I have just spoken, was ἀντιστρέφον.[1] For Bias, being asked by a certain man whether he should marry or lead a single life, said: "You are sure to marry a woman either beautiful or ugly; and if beautiful, you will share her with others, but if ugly, she will be a punishment.[2] But neither of these things is desirable; therefore do not marry."

ποινή, which it does not seem possible to reproduce in English. Perhaps, a flirt or a hurt, or, a harlot or a hard lot.

ATTIC NIGHTS OF AULUS GELLIUS

3 Sic autem hoc rursum convertunt: Εἰ μὲν καλὴν
ἄξω, οὐχ ἕξω ποινήν· εἰ δὲ αἰσχράν, οὐχ ἕξω κοινήν·
4 γαμητέον ἄρα. Sed minime hoc esse videtur ἀντιστρέφον, quoniam ex altero latere conversum frigidius
5 est infirmiusque. Nam Bias proposuit non esse ducendam uxorem propter alterutrum incommodum,
6 quod necessario patiendum erit ei qui duxerit. Qui
convertit autem, non ab eo se defendit incommodo
quod adest, sed carere se altero dicit quod non
7 adest. Satis est autem tuendae sententiae quam
Bias dixit, quod eum qui duxit uxorem pati necesse
est ex duobus incommodis alterum; ut aut κοινὴν
habeat aut ποινήν.

8 Sed Favorinus noster, cum facta esset forte mentio
syllogismi istius quo Bias usus est, cuius prima πρό-
τασις est, ἤτοι καλὴν ἄξεις ἢ αἰσχράν, non ratum id
neque iustum diiunctivum esse ait, quoniam non
necessum sit alterum ex duobus quae diiunguntur
9 verum esse, quod in proloquio diiunctivo necessarium
est. Eminentia enim quadam significari formarum
10 turpes et pulcrae videntur. "Est autem," inquit,
"tertium quoque inter duo ista quae diiunguntur,
11 cuius rationem prospectumque Bias non habuit. Inter
enim pulcherrimam feminam et deformissimam media
forma quaedam est, quae et a nimiae pulcritudinis

---

[1] That is, in Bias' syllogism.

410

Now, they turn this argument about in this way.
" If I marry a beautiful woman, she will not be
a punishment; but if an ugly one, I shall be her
sole possessor; therefore marry." But this syllogism
does not seem to be in the least convertible, since
it appears somewhat weaker and less convincing
when turned into the second form. For Bias
maintained that one should not marry because of
one of two disadvantages which must necessarily be
suffered by one who took a wife. But he who
converts the proposition does not defend himself
against the inconvenience which is mentioned, but
says that he is free from another which is not
mentioned. But to maintain the opinion that Bias
expressed, it is enough that a man who has taken a
wife must necessarily suffer one or the other of two
disadvantages, of having a wife that is unfaithful, or
a punishment.

But our countryman Favorinus, when that syllogism which Bias had employed happened to be
mentioned, of which the first premise is : " You will
marry either a beautiful or an ugly woman," declared that this was not a fact, and that it was not a
fair antithesis, since it was not inevitable that one
of the two opposites be true, which must be the case
in a disjunctive proposition. For obviously certain
outstanding extremes of appearance are postulated,
ugliness and beauty.[1] " But there is," said he, " a
third possibility also, lying between those two
opposites, and that possibility Bias did not observe or
regard. For between a very beautiful and a very
ugly woman there is a mean in appearance, which
is free from the danger to which an excess of beauty
is exposed, and also from the feeling of repulsion

12 periculo et a summae deformitatis odio vacat; qualis
a Quinto Ennio in *Melanippa* perquam eleganti
vocabulo 'stata' dicitur, quae neque κοινὴ futura sit
13 neque ποινή." Quam formam modicam et modestam
14 Favorinus non, mi hercule, inscite appellabat "uxo-
riam." Ennius autem in ista quam dixi tragoedia,
eas fere feminas ait incolumi pudicitia esse quae stata
forma forent.

XII

De nominibus deorum populi Romani Diovis et Vediovis.

1 IN antiquis precationibus nomina haec deorum
2 inesse animadvertimus: "Diovis" et "Vediovis";
est autem etiam aedes Vediovis Romae inter Arcem
3 et Capitolium. Eorum nominum rationem esse hanc
4 comperi: "Iovem" Latini veteres a "iuvando" ap-
pellavere, eundemque alio vocabulo iuncto "patrem"
5 dixerunt. Nam quod est, elisis aut inmutatis quibusdam litteris, "Iupiter," id plenum atque integrum
est "Iovispater." Sic et "Neptunuspater" con-
iuncte dictus est et "Saturnuspater" et "Ianuspater"
et "Marspater"—hoc enim est "Marspiter"—
itemque Iovis "Diespiter" appellatus, id est diei et
6 lucis pater. Idcircoque simili nomine Iovis[1] "Diovis"
dictus est et "Lucetius," quod nos die et luce quasi
7 vita ipsa afficeret et iuvaret. "Lucetium" autem
Iovem Cn. Naevius in libris *Belli Poenici* appellat.

---

[1] Iovis, *added by Hertz.*

---

[1] 253, Ribbeck[3].
[2] The two summits of the Capitoline Hill.
[3] The correct spelling in Latin is *Iuppiter*.
[4] Fr. 55, Bährens.

inspired by extreme ugliness. A woman of that kind is called by Quintus Ennius in the *Melanippa*[1] by the very elegant term 'normal,' and such a woman will be neither unfaithful nor a punishment." This moderate and modest beauty Favorinus, to my mind most sagaciously, called "conjugal." Moreover Ennius, in the tragedy which I mentioned, says that those women as a rule are of unblemished chastity who possess normal beauty.

XII

On the names of the gods of the Roman people called *Diovis* and *Vediovis*.

IN ancient prayers we have observed that these names of deities appear : *Diovis* and *Vediovis* ; furthermore, there is also a temple of Vediovis at Rome, between the Citadel and the Capitolium.[2] The explanation of these names I have found to be this : the ancient Latins derived *Iovis* from *iuvare* (help), and called that same god "father," thus adding a second word. For *Iovispater* is the full and complete form, which becomes *Iupiter*[3] by the syncope or change of some of the letters. So also *Neptunuspater* is used as a compound, and *Saturnuspater* and *Ianuspater* and *Marspater*—for that is the original form of *Marspiter*—and Jove also was called *Diespiter*, that is, the father of day and of light. And therefore by a name of similar origin Jove is called *Diovis* and also *Lucetius*, because he blesses and helps us by means of the day and the light, which are equivalent to life itself. And *Lucetius* is applied to Jove by Gnaeus Naevius in his poem *On the Punic War*.[4]

8 Cum Iovem igitur et Diovem a iuvando nomi-
nassent, eum contra deum, qui non iuvandi potestatem, sed vim nocendi haberet—nam deos quosdam,
ut prodessent, celebrabant, quosdam, ut ne obessent,
placabant—"Vediovem"appellaverunt, dempta atque
9 detracta iuvandi facultate. " Ve " enim particula,
quae in aliis atque aliis vocabulis varia, tum per has
duas litteras, tum " a " littera media inmissa dicitur,
duplicem significatum eundemque inter sese diversum
10 capit. Nam et augendae rei et minuendae valet,
sicuti aliae particulae plurimae ; propter quod accidit
ut quaedam vocabula quibus particula ista praeponitur
ambigua sint et utroqueversum dicantur, veluti
" vescum," " vemens " et " vegrande," de quibus alio
in loco, uberiore tractatu facto, admonuimus ; " ve-
sani" autem et " vecordes " ex una tantum parte
dicti, quae privativa est, quam Graeci κατὰ στέρησιν dicunt.

11 Simulacrum igitur dei Vediovis, quod est in aede
de qua supra dixi, sagittas tenet, quae sunt videlicet
12 partae ad nocendum. Quapropter eum deum plerumque Apollinem esse dixerunt ; immolaturque ritu

---

[1] That is, it is uncertain what force *ve-* has in these
words ; but see the next note.

[2] Gellius is wrong in supposing that *ve-* strengthened the
force of a word ; it means " without, apart from." Nonius
cites Lucilius for *vegrandis* in the sense of " very great," but
wrongly ; see Marx on Lucil. 631. *Vescus* means "small,"
or, in an active sense, "make small " (Lucr. i. 326) ; Walde
derives it from *vescor* in the sense of " eating away, corroding "
(Lucr. i. 326) and from *ve-escus* in the sense of " small."
Vemens, for *vehemens,* is probably a participle (*vehemenos*)
from *veho.*

[3] xvi. 5. 6.

[4] Vediovis, or Veiovis, was the opposite of Jupiter, *ve-*
having its negative force. He was a god of the nether world

Accordingly, when they had given the names *Iovis* and *Diovis* from *iuvare* (help), they applied a name of the contrary meaning to that god who had, not the power to help, but the force to do harm— for some gods they worshipped in order to gain their favour, others they propitiated in order to avert their hostility ; and they called him *Vediovis*, thus taking away and denying his power to give help. For the particle *ve* which appears in different forms in different words, now being spelled with these two letters and now with an *a* inserted between the two, has two meanings which also differ from each other. For *ve*, like very many other particles, has the effect either of weakening or of strengthening the force of a word ; and it therefore happens that some words to which that particle is prefixed are ambiguous [1] and may be used with either force, such as *vescus* (small), *vemens* (mighty), and *vegrandis* (very small),[2] a point which I have discussed elsewhere [3] in greater detail. But *vesanus* and *vecordes* are used with only one of the meanings of *ve*, namely, the privative or negative force, which the Greeks call κατὰ στέρησιν.

It is for this reason that the statue of the god Vediovis, which is in the temple of which I spoke above, holds arrows, which, as everyone knows, are devised to inflict harm. For that reason it has often been said that that god is Apollo ; and a she-goat is sacrificed to him in the customary fashion,[4]

and of death ; hence the arrows and the she-goat, which was an animal connected with the lower world (see Gell. x. 15. 12, and Wissowa *Religion und Kultus*, p. 237). Some regarded the god as a youthful (little) Jupiter and the she-goat as the one which suckled him in his infancy ; others as Apollo, because of the arrows, but the she-goat has no connection with Apollo.

humano[1] capra eiusque animalis figmentum iuxta simulacrum stat.

13 Propterea Vergilium quoque aiunt, multae antiquitatis hominem sine ostentationis studio[2] peritum, numina laeva in *Georgicis* deprecari, significantem vim quandam esse huiuscemodi deorum in laedendo magis quam in iuvando potentem. Versus Vergilii sunt:

> In tenui labor; at tenuis non gloria, si quem
> Numina laeva sinunt auditque vocatus Apollo.

14 In istis autem diis quos placari oportet, uti mala a nobis vel a frugibus natis amoliantur, Auruncus quoque habetur et Robigus.

XIII

De officiorum gradu atque ordine moribus populi Romani observato.

1 SENIORUM hominum et Romae nobilium atque in morum disciplinarumque veterum doctrina memoriaque praestantium disceptatio quaedam fuit, praesente et audiente me, de gradu atque ordine officiorum. Cumque quaereretur quibus nos ea prioribus potioribusque facere oporteret, si necesse esset in opera danda faciendoque officio alios aliis anteferre, non

---

[1] humano, ω; Romano *Thysius*.
[2] studio, *Cornelissen from* v. 14. 3; odio, ω.

---

[1] *Georg.* iv. 6.
[2] Commonly called *Averruncus*, although the glosses give also the form *Auruncus*. From *averrunco*, "to avert."

and a representation of that animal stands near his statue.

It was for this reason, they say, that Virgil, a man deeply versed in antiquarian lore, but never making a display of his knowledge, prays to the unpropitious gods in the *Georgics*, thus intimating that in gods of that kind there is a power capable of injuring rather than aiding. The verses of Vergil are these : [1]

A task of narrow span, but no small praise,
If unpropitious powers bar not my way
And favouring Phoebus grant a poet's prayer.

And among those gods which ought to be placated in order to avert evil influences from ourselves or our harvests are reckoned Auruncus [2] and Robigus. [3]

XIII

On the rank and order of obligations established by the usage of the Roman people.

THERE was once a discussion, in my presence and hearing, of the rank and order of obligations, carried on by a company of men of advanced age and high position at Rome, who were also eminent for their knowledge and command of ancient usage and conduct. And when the question was asked to whom we ought first and foremost to discharge those obligations, in case it should be necessary to prefer some to others in giving assistance or showing attention, there was a difference of opinion. But it

[3] Also called *Robigo* (f.), the god or goddess who averted mildew from the grain.

2 consentiebatur.[1]   Conveniebat autem facile con-
stabatque, ex moribus populi Romani primum iuxta
parentes locum tenere pupillos debere, fidei tutelaeque
nostrae creditos; secundum eos proximum locum
clientes habere, qui sese itidem in fidem patro-
ciniumque nostrum dediderunt; tum in tertio loco
esse hospites; postea esse cognatos adfinesque.

3   Huius moris observationisque multa sunt testimonia
atque documenta in antiquitatibus perscripta, ex
quibus unum hoc interim de clientibus cognatisque,

4 quod prae manibus est, ponemus.   M. Cato in
oratione, quam dixit apud censores *In Lentulum*, ita
scripsit: " Quod maiores sanctius habuere, defendi
pupillos quam clientem non fallere.   Adversus
cognatos pro cliente testatur, testimonium adversus
clientem nemo dicit.   Patrem primum, postea patro-
num proximum nomen habuere."

5   Masurius autem Sabinus in libro *Iuris Civilis*
tertio antiquiorem locum hospiti tribuit quam clienti.
Verba ex eo libro haec sunt: " In officiis apud
maiores ita observatum est, primum tutelae, deinde
hospiti, deinde clienti, tum cognato, postea adfini.
Aequa[2] causa feminae viris potiores habitae pupil-
larisque tutela muliebri praelata.   Etiam adversus
quem adfuissent, eius filiis tutores relicti, in eadem
causa pupillo aderant."

6   Firmum atque clarum isti rei testimonium per-

---

[1] consentiebatur, *Hosius, comparing* iii. 11. 1, *etc.*; con-
stituebat (confatuebat, R), ω.
[2] aequa, *Boot*; de qua, ω.

---

[1] xli. 1, Jordan.
[2] Fr. 6, Huschke; 2 Bremer.

was readily agreed and accepted, that in accordance
with the usage of the Roman people the place next
after parents should be held by wards entrusted to
our honour and protection; that second to them
came clients, who also had committed themselves to
our honour and guardianship; that then in the third
place were guests; and finally relations by blood and
by marriage.

Of this custom and practice there are numerous
proofs and illustrations in the ancient records, of
which, because it is now at hand, I will cite only
this one at present, relating to clients and kindred.
Marcus Cato in the speech which he delivered
before the censors *Against Lentulus* wrote thus :[1]
" Our forefathers regarded it as a more sacred
obligation to defend their wards than not to deceive
a client. One testifies in a client's behalf against
one's relatives; testimony against a client is given
by no one. A father held the first position of
honour; next after him a patron."

Masurius Sabinus, however, in the third book of
his *Civil Law* assigns a higher place to a guest than
to a client. The passage from that book is this :[2]
" In the matter of obligations our forefathers observed the following order : first to a ward, then
to a guest, then to a client, next to a blood relation,
finally to a relation by marriage. Other things
being equal, women were given preference to men,
but a ward who was under age took precedence of
one who was a grown woman. Also those who were
appointed by will to be guardians of the sons of
a man against whom they had appeared in court,
appeared for the ward in the same case."

Very clear and strong testimony on this subject

hibet auctoritas C. Caesaris pontificis maximi, qui
in oratione quam *Pro Bithynis* dixit hoc principio
usus est : "Vel pro hospitio regis Nicomedis vel pro
horum necessitate quorum res [1] agitur, refugere hoc
munus, M. Iunce, non potui. Nam neque hominum
morte memoria deleri debet quin a proximis retine-
atur, neque clientes sine summa infamia deseri
possunt, quibus etiam a propinquis nostris opem
ferre instituimus."

XIV

Quod Apion, doctus homo, qui Plistonices appellatus est,
vidisse se Romae scripsit recognitionem inter sese mutuam
ex vetere notitia hominis et leonis.

1 APION, qui Plistonices appellatus est, litteris homo
multis praeditus rerumque Graecarum plurima atque
2 varia scientia fuit. Eius libri non incelebres feruntur,
quibus omnium ferme quae mirifica in Aegypto
3 visuntur audiunturque historia comprehenditur. Sed
in his quae vel audisse vel legisse sese dicit, fortas-
sean vitio studioque ostentationis sit loquacior—est
enim sane quam in praedicandis doctrinis sui [2] ven-
4 ditator—hoc autem, quod in libro *Aegyptiacorum*
quinto scripsit, neque audisse neque legisse, sed
ipsum sese in urbe Roma vidisse oculis suis confirmat.

---

[1] res, *s* ; re, *ω* ; de re, *Hertz.*   [2] sui, *Eussner* ; suis, *ω.*

---

[1] ii. p. 123, Dinter ; *O.R.F.*[2] p. 419.

is furnished by the authority of Gaius Caesar, when he was high priest; for in the speech which he delivered *In Defence of the Bithynians* he made use of this preamble:[1] "In consideration either of my guest-friendship with king Nicomedes or my relationship to those whose case is on trial, O Marcus Iuncus, I could not refuse this duty. For the remembrance of men ought not to be so obliterated by their death as not to be retained by those nearest to them, and without the height of disgrace we cannot forsake clients to whom we are bound to render aid even against our kinsfolk."

XIV

The account of Apion, a learned man who was surnamed Plistonices, of the mutual recognition, due to old acquaintance, that he had seen at Rome between a man and a lion.

Apion, who was called Plistonices, was a man widely versed in letters, and possessing an extensive and varied knowledge of things Greek. In his works, which are recognized as of no little repute, is contained an account of almost all the remarkable things which are to be seen and heard in Egypt. Now, in his account of what he professes either to have heard or read he is perhaps too verbose through a reprehensible love of display—for he is a great self-advertiser in parading his learning; but this incident, which he describes in the fifth book of his *Wonders of Egypt*,[2] he declares that he neither heard nor read, but saw himself with his own eyes in the city of Rome.

[2] *F.H.G.* iii. 510.

5 "In Circo Maximo," inquit, "venationis amplis-
6 simae pugna populo dabatur. Eius rei, Romae cum
7 forte essem, spectator," inquit, "fui. Multae ibi
saevientes ferae, magnitudines bestiarum excellentes
omniumque invisitata aut forma erat aut ferocia.
8 Sed praeter alia omnia leonum," inquit, "immanitas
9 admirationi fuit praeterque omnis ceteros unus. Is
unus leo corporis impetu et vastitudine terrificoque
fremitu et sonoro, toris comisque cervicum fluctuanti-
bus, animos oculosque omnium in sese converterat.
10 Introductus erat inter compluris ceteros ad pugnam
bestiarum datos [1] servus viri consularis; ei servo
11 Androclus nomen fuit. Hunc ille leo ubi vidit
procul, repente," inquit, "quasi admirans stetit ac
deinde sensim atque placide, tamquam noscitabundus,
12 ad hominem accedit. Tum caudam more atque ritu
adulantium canum clementer et blande movet
hominisque se corpori adiungit cruraque eius et
manus, prope iam exanimati metu, lingua leniter
13 demulcet. Homo Androclus inter illa tam atrocis
ferae blandimenta amissum animum recuperat, paul-
14 atim oculos ad contuendum leonem refert. Tum
quasi mutua recognitione facta laetos," inquit, "et
gratulabundos videres hominem et leonem."
15 Ea re prorsus tam admirabili maximos populi
clamores excitatos dicit, accersitumque a C. [2] Caesare
Androclum quaesitamque causam cur illi [3] atrocis-
16 simus leo uni parsisset. Ibi Androclus rem mirifi-

---

[1] datos, *Hertz*; datus, *ω*.
[2] C. *added by L. Müller.*
[3] illi, *John of Salisbury*; ille, *ω*.

"In the Great Circus," he says, "a battle with wild beasts on a grand scale was being exhibited to the people. Of that spectacle, since I chanced to be in Rome, I was," he says, "an eye-witness. There were there many savage wild beasts, brutes remarkable for their huge size, and all of uncommon appearance or unusual ferocity. But beyond all others," says he, "did the vast size of the lions excite wonder, and one of these in particular surpassed all the rest. This one lion had drawn to himself the attention and eyes of all because of the activity and huge size of his body, his terrific and deep roar, the development of his muscles, and the mane streaming over his shoulders. There was brought in, among many others who had been condemned to fight with the wild beasts, the slave of an ex-consul; the slave's name was Androclus. When that lion saw him from a distance," says Apion, "he stopped short as if in amazement, and then approached the man slowly and quietly, as if he recognized him. Then, wagging his tail in a mild and caressing way, after the manner and fashion of fawning dogs, he came close to the man, who was now half dead from fright, and gently licked his feet and hands. The man Androclus, while submitting to the caresses of so fierce a beast, regained his lost courage and gradually turned his eyes to look at the lion. Then," says Apion, "you might have seen man and lion exchange joyful greetings, as if they had recognized each other."

He says that at this sight, so truly astonishing, the people broke out into mighty shouts; and Gaius Caesar called Androclus to him and inquired the reason why that fiercest of lions had spared him alone. Then Androclus related a strange and

17 cam narrat atque admirandam. "Cum provinciam,"
inquit, "Africam proconsulari imperio meus dominus
obtineret, ego ibi iniquis eius et cotidianis verberibus
ad fugam sum coactus et, ut mihi a domino, terrae
illius praeside, tutiores latebrae forent, in camporum
et arenarum solitudines concessi ac, si defuisset
cibus, consilium fuit mortem aliquo pacto quaerere.
18 Tum sole medio," inquit, "rabido et flagranti specum
quandam nanctus remotam latebrosamque, in eam
19 me penetro et recondo. Neque multo post ad
eandem specum venit hic leo, debili uno et cruento
pede, gemitus edens et murmura, dolorem cruciatum-
20 que vulneris commiserantia." Atque illic primo
quidem conspectu advenientis leonis territum sibi et
21 pavefactum animum dixit. "Sed postquam intro-
gressus," inquit, "leo, uti re ipsa apparuit, in habita-
culum illud suum, videt me procul delitescentem,
mitis et mansues accessit et sublatum pedem ostendere mihi et porgere quasi opis petendae gratia visus
22 est. Ibi," inquit, "ego stirpem ingentem, vestigio
pedis eius haerentem, revelli conceptamque saniem
volnere intimo expressi accuratiusque sine magna
iam formidine siccavi penitus atque detersi cruorem.
23 Illa tunc mea opera et medella levatus, pede in
manibus meis posito, recubuit et quievit atque ex eo
24 die triennium totum ego et leo in eadem specu
25 eodemque et victu viximus. Nam, quas venabatur
feras, membra opimiora ad specum mihi subgerebat,
quae ego, ignis copiam non habens, meridiano sole
26 torrens edebam. Sed ubi me," inquit, "vitae illius

surprising story. " My master," said he, " was governing Africa with proconsular authority. While there, I was forced by his undeserved and daily floggings to run away, and that my hiding-places might be safer from my master, the ruler of that country, I took refuge in lonely plains and deserts, intending, if food should fail me, to seek death in some form. Then," said he, " when the midday sun was fierce and scorching, finding a remote and secluded cavern, I entered it, and hid myself. Not long afterwards this lion came to the same cave with one paw lame and bleeding, making known by groans and moans the torturing pain of his wound." And then, at the first sight of the approaching lion, Androclus said that his mind was overwhelmed with fear and dread. " But when the lion," said he, " had entered what was evidently his own lair, and saw me cowering at a distance, he approached me mildly and gently, and lifting up his foot, was evidently showing it to me and holding it out as if to ask for help. Then," said he, " I drew out a huge splinter that was embedded in the sole of the foot, squeezed out the pus that had formed in the interior of the wound, wiped away the blood, and dried it thoroughly, being now free from any great feeling of fear. Then, relieved by that attention and treatment of mine, the lion, putting his paw in my hand, lay down and went to sleep, and for three whole years from that day the lion and I lived in the same cave, and on the same food as well. For he used to bring for me to the cave the choicest parts of the game which he took in hunting, which I, having no means of making a fire, dried in the noonday sun and ate. But," said he, " after I had finally grown tired of that wild

ferinae iam pertaesum est, leone in venatum profecto, reliqui specum et viam ferme tridui permensus
a militibus visus adprehensusque sum et ad dominum
27 ex Africa Romam deductus. Is me statim rei capi-
talis damnandum dandumque ad bestias curavit.
28 Intellego autem," inquit, " hunc quoque leonem, me
tunc separato captum, gratiam mihi nunc beneficii et
medicinae referre."

29 Haec Apion dixisse Androclum tradit, eaque
omnia scripta circumlataque tabula populo declarata,
atque ideo cunctis petentibus dimissum Androclum
et poena solutum leonemque ei suffragiis populi
30 donatum. " Postea," inquit, " videbamus Androclum
et leonem, loro tenui revinctum, urbe tota circum
tabernas ire, donari aere Androclum, floribus spargi
leonem, omnes ubique obvios dicere : ' Hic est leo
hospes hominis, hic est homo medicus leonis.' "

XV

Corpusne sit vox an ἀσώματον varias esse philosophorum
sententias.

1 VETUS atque perpetua quaestio inter nobilissimos
philosophorum agitata est, corpusne sit vox an incor-
2 poreum. Hoc enim vocabulum quidam finxerunt
3 proinde quod Graece dicitur ἀσώματον. Corpus
autem est quod aut efficiens est aut patiens ; id
4 Graece definitur τὸ ἤτοι ποιοῦν ἢ πάσχον. Quam

life, I left the cave when the lion had gone off to hunt, and after travelling nearly three days, I was seen and caught by some soldiers and taken from Africa to Rome to my master. He at once had me condemned to death by being thrown to the wild beasts. But," said he, " I perceive that this lion was also captured, after I left him, and that he is now requiting me for my kindness and my cure of him."

Apion records that Androclus told this story, and that when it had been made known to the people by being written out in full on a tablet and carried about the Circus, at the request of all Androclus was freed, acquitted and presented with the lion by vote of the people. " Afterwards," said he, " we used to see Androclus with the lion, attached to a slender leash, making the rounds of the shops throughout the city ; Androclus was given money, the lion was sprinkled with flowers, and everyone who met them anywhere exclaimed : ' This is the lion that was a man's friend, this is the man who was physician to a lion.' "

XV

That it is a disputed question among philosophers whether voice is corporeal or incorporeal.

A question that has been argued long and continuously by the most famous philosophers is whether voice has body or is incorporeal ; for the word *incorporeus* has been coined by some of them, corresponding exactly to the Greek ἀσώματος. Now a body is that which is either active or passive : this in Greek is defined as τὸ ἤτοι ποιοῦν ἢ πάσχον, or " that which either acts or is acted upon." Wishing

427

definitionem significare volens, Lucretius poeta ita scripsit :

> Tangere enim aut [1] tangi, nisi corpus, nulla potest res.

5 Alio quoque modo corpus esse Graeci dicunt τὸ τριχῇ
6 διάστατον. Sed vocem Stoici corpus esse contendunt
7 eamque esse dicunt ictum aera, Plato autem non esse vocem corpus putat : "Non enim percussus," inquit, "aer, sed plaga ipsa atque percussio, id vox est."
8 Democritus ac deinde Epicurus ex individuis corporibus vocem constare dicunt eamque, ut ipsis eorum
9 verbis utar, ῥεῦμα ἀτόμων appellant. Hos aliosque talis argutae delectabilisque desidiae aculeos cum audiremus vel lectitaremus neque in his scrupulis aut emolumentum aliquod solidum ad rationem vitae pertinens aut finem ullum quaerendi videremus, Ennianum Neoptolemum probabamus, qui profecto ita ait :

> Philósophandum est paúcis; nam omnino haút placet.

XVI

De vi oculorum deque videndi rationibus.

1 DE videndi ratione deque cernendi natura diversas
2 esse opiniones philosophorum animadvertimus. Stoici causas esse videndi dicunt radiorum ex oculis in ea quae videri queunt emissionem aerisque simul inten-

---

[1] et, *Lucr.*

---

[1] i. 304.   [2] II. 141, Arn.
[3] *Timaeus*, p. 67, B.   [4] p. 353, Usener.

to reproduce this definition the poet Lucretius wrote : [1]

Naught save a body can be touched or touch.

The Greeks also define body in another way, as τὸ τριχῆ διάστατον, or "that which has three dimensions." But the Stoics maintain [2] that voice is a body, and say that it is air which has been struck ; Plato, however, thinks that voice is not corporeal : "for," says he,[3] "not the air which is struck, but the stroke and the blow themselves are voice." Democritus, and following him Epicurus, declare that voice consists of individual particles, and they call it, to use their own words, ῥεῦμα ἀτόμων,[4] or "a stream of atoms." When I heard of these and other sophistries, the result of a self-satisfied cleverness combined with lack of employment, and saw in these subtleties no real advantage affecting the conduct of life, and no end to the inquiry, I agreed with Ennius' Neoptolemus, who rightly says : [5]

Philosophizing there must be, but by the few ;
Since for all men it's not to be desired.

XVI

On the function of the eye and the process of vision.

I HAVE observed that the philosophers have varying opinions about the method of seeing and the nature of vision. The Stoics say [6] that the causes of sight are the emission of rays from the eyes to those objects which can be seen, and the simultaneous

---

[5] 340, Ribbeck[3].   [6] II. 871, Arn.

3 tionem. Epicurus afluere semper ex omnibus corporibus simulacra quaedam corporum ipsorum eaque
sese in oculos inferre atque ita fieri sensum videndi
4 putat. Plato existimat, genus quoddam ignis lucis-
que de oculis exire idque, coniunctum continuatumque
vel cum luce solis vel cum alterius ignis lumine, sua
vi et externa nixum efficere ut quaecumque offen-
5 derit inlustraveritque cernamus. Set hic aeque[1]
non diutius muginandum, eiusdemque illius Enniani
Neoptolemi, de quo supra scripsimus, consilio utendum est, qui " degustandum " ex philosophia censet,
" non in eam ingurgitandum."

XVII

1 VERRIUS FLACCUS, in quarto *De Verborum Significatu*,
dies qui sunt postridie Kalendas, Nonas, Idus, quos
vulgus imperite " nefastos " dicit, propter hanc
causam dictos habitosque " atros " esse scribit.
2 " Urbe," inquit, " a Gallis Senonibus recuperata,
L. Atilius in senatu verba fecit, Q. Sulpicium
tribunum militum, ad Alliam adversus Gallos pugna-
turum, rem divinam dimicandi gratia postridie Idus
fecisse; tum exercitum populi Romani occidione
occisum et post diem tertium eius diei urbem praeter

---

[1] aeque, *Petschenig*; eaque, ω; quoque, *Madvig*.

---

[1] 319, Usener.   [2] *Timaeus*, p. 45, B.   [3] xv. 9.
         [4] p. xiv. Müller.   [5] In 390 B.C.

expansion of the air. Epicurus believes[1] that there is a constant flow from all bodies of images of those bodies themselves, and that these impinge upon the eyes and hence the sensation of seeing arises. Plato is of the opinion[2] that a kind of fire or light issues from the eyes, and that this, being united and joined either with the light of the sun or with that of some other fire, by means of its own and the external force makes us see whatever it has struck and illumined. But here too we must not dally longer, but follow the advice of that Neoptolemus in Ennius, of whom I have just written,[3] who advises having a "taste" of philosophy, but not "gorging oneself with it."

XVII

Why the first days after the Kalends, Nones and Ides are considered unlucky; and why many avoid also the fourth day before the Kalends, Nones or Ides, on the ground that it is ill-omened.

VERRIUS FLACCUS, in the fourth book of his work *On the Meaning of Words*, writes[4] that the days immediately following the Kalends, Nones and Ides, which the common people ignorantly call "holidays," are properly called, and considered, "ill-omened," for this reason:—"When the city," he says, "had been recovered from the Senonian Gauls, Lucius Atilius stated in the senate that Quintus Sulpicius, tribune of the soldiers, when on the eve of fighting against the Gauls at the Allia,[5] offered sacrifice in anticipation of that battle on the day after the Ides; that the army of the Roman people was thereupon cut to pieces, and three days later the whole

Capitolium captam esse : compluresque alii senatores recordari sese dixerunt, quotiens belli gerendi gratia res divina postridie Kalendas, Nonas, Idus a magistratu populi Romani facta esset, eius belli proximo deinceps proelio rem publicam male gestam esse. Tum senatus eam rem ad pontifices reiecit, ut ipsi quod videretur statuerent. Pontifices decreverunt nullum his diebus sacrificium recte futurum.''

3 Ante diem quoque quartum Kalendas vel Nonas vel Idus tamquam inominalem[1] diem plerique vitant. 4 Eius observationis an religio ulla sit tradita, quaeri 5 solet. Nihil nos super ea re scriptum invenimus, nisi quod Q. Claudius *Annalium* quinto cladem illam pugnae Cannensis vastissimam factam dicit ante diem quartum Nonas Sextiles.

XVIII

In quid et quantum differat historia ab annalibus ; superque ea re verba posita ex libro *Rerum Gestarum* Sempronii Asellionis primo.

1 HISTORIAM ab annalibus quidam differre eo putant, quod, cum utrumque sit rerum gestarum narratio, earum tamen proprie rerum sit historia, quibus rebus 2 gerendis interfuerit is qui narret ; eamque esse opinionem quorundam, Verrius Flaccus refert in libro *De Significatu Verborum* quarto. Ac se quidem dubitare super ea re dicit, posse autem videri putat nonnihil esse rationis in ea opinione, quod ἱστορία

---

[1] nominalem, *P* ; ominalem, *Salmasius.*

city, except the Capitol, was taken. Also many other senators said that they remembered that whenever with a view to waging war a magistrate of the Roman people had sacrificed on the day after the Kalends, Nones or Ides, in the very next battle of that war the State had suffered disaster. Then the senate referred the matter to the pontiffs, that they might take what action they saw fit. The pontiffs decreed that no offering would properly be made on those days."

Many also avoid the fourth day before the Kalends, Nones and Ides, as ill-omened. It is often inquired whether any religious reason for that observance is recorded. I myself have found nothing in literature pertaining to that matter, except that Quintus Claudius Quadrigarius, in the fifth book of his *Annals*, says that the prodigious slaughter of the battle of Cannae occurred on the fourth day before the Nones of August.[1]

XVIII

In what respect, and how far, history differs from annals ; and a quotation on that subject from the first book of the *Histories* of Sempronius Asellio.

SOME think that history differs from annals in this particular, that while each is a narrative of events, yet history is properly an account of events in which the narrator took part ; and that this is the opinion of some men is stated by Verrius Flaccus in the fourth book of his treatise *On the Meaning of Words*.[2] He adds that he for his part has doubts about the matter, but he thinks that the view may have some appearance of reason, since ἱστορία in Greek means a

---

[1] August 2, 216 B.C.   [2] p. xiv. Müller.

Graece significet rerum cognitionem praesentium.
3 Sed nos audire soliti sumus annales omnino id esse
4 quod historiae sint; historias non omnino esse id
5 quod annales sint: sicuti, quod est homo, id necessario animal esse; quod est animal, non id necesse est
hominem esse.

6 Ita historias quidem esse aiunt rerum gestarum
vel expositionem vel demonstrationem vel quo alio
nomine id dicendum est; annales vero esse, cum res
gestae plurium annorum, observato cuiusque anni
7 ordine, deinceps componuntur. Cum vero non per
annos, sed per dies singulos res gestae scribuntur,
ea historia Graeco vocabulo ἐφημερὶς dicitur, cuius
Latinum interpretamentum scriptum est in libro
Semproni Asellionis primo, ex quo libro plura verba
ascripsimus, ut simul ibidem quid ipse inter res
gestas et annales esse dixerit ostenderemus.

8 "Verum inter eos," inquit, "qui annales relin-
quere voluissent, et eos qui res gestas a Romanis
perscribere conati essent, omnium rerum hoc interfuit. Annales libri tantummodo quod factum quoque anno gestum sit, ea demonstrabant, id est
quasi qui diarium scribunt, quam Graeci ἐφημερίδα
vocant. Nobis non modo satis esse video, quod
factum esset, id pronuntiare, sed etiam quo consilio
9 quaque ratione gesta essent demonstrare." Paulo
post idem Asellio in eodem libro: "Nam neque
alacriores," inquit, "ad rempublicam defendundam,
neque segniores ad rem perperam faciundam annales
libri commovere quicquam possunt. Scribere autem
bellum initum quo consule et quo confectum sit et
quis triumphans introierit ex eo, et eo[1] libro quae

---

[1] et eo, *added by Hertz.*

knowledge of current events. But we often hear it said that annals are exactly the same as histories, but that histories are not exactly the same as annals; just as a man is necessarily an animal, but an animal is not necessarily a man.

Thus they say that history is the setting forth of events or their description, or whatever term may be used; but that annals set down the events of many years successively, with observance of the chronological order. When, however, events are recorded, not year by year, but day by day, such a history is called in Greek ἐφημερίς, or "a diary," a term of which the Latin interpretation is found in the first book of Sempronius Asellio. I have quoted a passage of some length from that book, in order at the same time to show what his opinion is of the difference between history and chronicle.

"But between those," he says,[1] "who have desired to leave us annals, and those who have tried to write the history of the Roman people, there was this essential difference. The books of annals merely made known what happened and in what year it happened, which is like writing a diary, which the Greeks call ἐφημερίς. For my part, I realize that it is not enough to make known what has been done, but that one should also show with what purpose and for what reason things were done." A little later in the same book Asellio writes:[2] "For annals cannot in any way make men more eager to defend their country, or more reluctant to do wrong. Furthermore, to write over and over again in whose consulship a war was begun and ended, and who in consequence entered the city in a triumph, and in that

---

[1] Fr. 1, Peter.   [2] Fr. 2, Peter.

in bello gesta sint[1] non praedicare aut interea quid
senatus decreverit aut quae lex rogatiove lata sit
neque quibus consiliis ea gesta sint iterare: id
fabulas pueris est narrare, non historias scribere."

XIX

Quid sit adoptatio, quid item sit adrogatio, quantumque haec
inter se differant ; verbaque eius quae qualiaque sint, qui
in liberis adrogandis super ea re populum rogat.

1 CUM in alienam familiam inque liberorum locum
extranei sumuntur, aut per praetorem fit aut per po-
2 pulum. Quod per praetorem fit, " adoptatio " dicitur,
3 quod per populum, " arrogatio." Adoptantur autem,
cum a parente in cuius potestate sunt tertia manci-
patione in iure ceduntur atque ab eo qui adoptat
apud eum apud quem legis actio est vindicantur ;
4 adrogantur hi qui, cum sui iuris sunt, in alienam
sese potestatem tradunt eiusque rei ipsi auctores fiunt.
5 Sed adrogationes non temere nec inexplorate commit-
6 tuntur ; nam comitia arbitris pontificibus praeben-
tur, quae " curiata " appellantur, aetasque eius qui
adrogare vult, an liberis potius gignundis idonea sit,
bonaque eius qui adrogatur ne insidiose adpetita sint

---

[1] sint enarrare, *Nipperdey* ; sint blaterare, *Machly* ; sint
iterare id fabulas non praedicare aut, *ω* (from line 3).

---

[1] This was a symbolic sale, made by thrice touching a
balance with a penny, in the presence of a praetor ; see Suet.,
Aug. lxiv.

[2] The assembly of the *curiae*, the thirty divisions into
which the Roman citizens were divided, ten for each of the
original three tribes. It was superseded at an early period
by the *comitia centuriata*, and its action was confined to
formalities. See xv. 27. 5.

book not to state what happened in the course of the war, what decrees the senate made during that time, or what law or bill was passed, and with what motives these things were done—that is to tell stories to children, not to write history."

XIX

The meaning of *adoptatio* and also of *adrogatio*, and how they differ ; and the formula used by the official who, when children are adopted, brings the business before the people.

WHEN outsiders are taken into another's family and given the relationship of children, it is done either through a praetor or through the people. If done by a praetor, the process is called *adoptatio* ; if through the people, *arrogatio*. Now, we have *adoptatio*, when those who are adopted are surrendered in court through a thrice repeated sale [1] by the father under whose control they are, and are claimed by the one who adopts them in the presence of the official before whom the legal action takes place. The process is called *adrogatio*, when persons who are their own masters deliver themselves into the control of another, and are themselves responsible for the act. But arrogations are not made without due consideration and investigation ; for the so-called *comitia curiata* [2] are summoned under the authority of the pontiffs, and it is inquired whether the age of the one who wishes to adopt is not rather suited to begetting children of his own ; precaution is taken that the property of the one who is being adopted is not being sought under false pretences ; and an oath is administered which is said

437

consideratur, iusque iurandum a Q. Mucio pontifice
maximo conceptum dicitur, quod in adrogando
7 iuraretur. Sed adrogari non potest nisi iam vesti-
8 ceps. "Adrogatio" autem dicta, quia genus hoc in
alienam familiam transitus per populi rogationem fit.
9 Eius rogationis verba haec sunt : "Velitis, iubea-
tis, uti L. Valerius L. Titio tam iure legeque filius
siet, quam si ex eo patre matreque familias eius
natus esset, utique ei vitae necisque in eum potestas
siet, uti patri endo filio est. Haec ita uti dixi, ita
vos, Quirites, rogo."
10 Neque pupillus autem neque mulier quae in paren-
tis potestate non est adrogari possunt ; quoniam et
cum feminis nulla comitiorum communio est et tuto-
ribus in pupillos tantam esse auctoritatem potesta-
temque fas non est, ut caput liberum fidei suae com-
11 missum alienae dicioni[1] subiciant. Libertinos vero
ab ingenuis adoptari quidem iure posse, Masurius
12 Sabinus scripsit. Sed id neque permitti dicit, neque
permittendum esse umquam putat, ut homines liber-
tini ordinis per adoptiones in iura ingenuorum inva-
13 dant. "Alioquin," inquit, "si iuris ista antiquitas
servetur, etiam servus a[2] domino per praetorem
14 dari in adoptionem potest." Idque ait plerosque
iuris veteris auctores posse fieri scripsisse.
15 Animadvertimus in oratione P. Scipionis, quam

---

[1] condicioni (-ditioni, P), ω.   [2] a, *omitted by Skutsch.*

---

[1] Fr. 13, Huschke ; I. p. 58 and p. 80, Bremer.
[2] Fr. 27, Huschke ; *Jus. Civ.* 60, Bremer.
[3] Cato, Fr. 4a, I. p. 21, Bremer.

to have been formulated for use in that ceremony by Quintus Mucius,[1] when he was pontifex maximus. But no one may be adopted by *adrogatio* who is not yet ready to assume the gown of manhood. The name *adrogatio* is due to the fact that this kind of transfer to another's family is accomplished through a *rogatio* or " request," put to the people.

The language of this request is as follows : " Express your desire and ordain that Lucius Valerius be the son of Lucius Titius as justly and lawfully as if he had been born of that father and the mother of his family, and that Titius have that power of life and death over Valerius which a father has over a son. This, just as I have stated it, I thus ask of you, fellow Romans."

Neither a ward nor a woman who is not under the control of her father may be adopted by *adrogatio* ; since women have no part in the comitia, and it is not right that guardians should have so much authority and power over their wards as to be able to subject to the control of another a free person who has been committed to their protection. Freedmen, however, may legally be adopted in that way by freeborn citizens, according to Masurius Sabinus.[2] But he adds that it is not allowed, and he thinks it never ought to be allowed, that men of the condition of freedmen should by process of adoption usurp the privileges of the freeborn. " Furthermore," says he, " if that ancient law be maintained, even a slave may be surrendered by his master for adoption through the agency of a praetor." And he declares that several authorities[3] on ancient law have written that this can be done.

I have observed in a speech of Publius Scipio *On*

censor habuit ad populum *De Moribus,* inter ea quae
reprehendebat, quod contra maiorum instituta
fierent, id etiam eum culpavisse, quod filius adop-
tivos patri adoptatori inter praemia patrum
16 prodesset. Verba ex ea oratione haec sunt : " In
alia tribu patrem, in alia filium suffragium ferre,
filium adoptivum tam procedere quam si se natum
habeat ; absentis censeri iubere, ut ad censum
nemini necessus sit venire."

XX

Quod vocabulum **Latinum** soloecismo fecerit Capito Sinnius,
quid autem id ipsum appellaverint veteres Latini ; quibusque verbis soloecismum definierit idem Capito Sinnius.

1 " Soloecismus," Latino vocabulo a Sinnio Capitone
eiusdemque aetatis aliis " inparilitas " appellatus,
vetustioribus Latinis " stribiligo " dicebatur, a versura
videlicet et pravitate tortuosae orationis, tamquam
2 " strobiligo " quaedam. Quod vitium Sinnius Capito
in litteris, quas ad Clodium Tuscum dedit, hisce
verbis definit : " ' Soloecismus ' est," inquit, " im-
par atque inconveniens compositura partium orationis."
3 Cum Graecum autem vocabulum sit " soloecismus,"
an Attici homines qui elegantius locuti sunt usi eo

---

[1] That is, the privileges and exemptions conferred upon
the fathers of children, later comprised under the *ius trium
liberorum* ; see ii. 15. 3 ff.

[2] *O.R.F.*[2] p. 180.

[3] The meaning is that a man who had been adopted would

Morais, which he made to the people in his censorship, that among the things that he criticized, on
the ground that they were done contrary to the
usage of our forefathers, he also found fault with
this, that an adopted son was of profit to his adoptive
father in gaining the rewards for paternity.[1] The
passage in that speech is as follows:[2] "A father
votes in one tribe, the son in another,[3] an adopted
son is of as much advantage as if one had a son of his
own; orders are given to take the census of ab-
sentees, and hence it is not necessary for anyone to
appear in person at the census."

XX

The Latin word coined by Sinnius Capito for "solecism,"
and what the early writers of Latin called that same fault;
and also Sinnius Capito's definition of a solecism.

A SOLECISM, which by Sinnius Capito and other
men of his time was called in Latin *inparilitas,* or
"inequality," the earlier Latin writers termed *stribiligo,*[4] evidently meaning the improper use of an
inverted form of expression, a sort of twist as it
were. This kind of fault is thus defined by Sinnius
Capito, in a letter which he wrote to Clodius Tuscus:
"A solecism," he says,[5] "is an irregular and incon-
gruous joining together of the parts of speech."

Since "soloecismus" is a Greek word, the question
is often asked, whether it was used by the men of

vote in the tribe of his adoptive father, which might be
different from that of his own father.

[4] This word, which seems to occur only here and in
Arnobius i. 36, apparently means "twisted, awry."

[5] Fr. 2, Huschke.

4 sint quaeri solet. Sed nos neque "soloecismum"
neque "barbarismum" apud Graecorum idoneos
5 adhuc invenimus; nam sicut βάρβαρον, ita σόλοικον
6 dixerunt. Nostri quoque antiquiores "soloecum"
facile, "soloecismum" haut scio an umquam, dix-
7 erunt. Quod si ita est, neque in Graeca neque
in Latina lingua "soloecismus" probe dicitur.

XXI

"Pluria" qui dicat et "compluria" et "compluriens" non
barbare dicere, sed Latine.

1 "PLURIA" forte quis dixit sermocinans vir adprime
doctus, meus amicus, non hercle studio se [1] ferens
ostentandi neque quo "plura" non dicendum putaret.
2 Est enim doctrina homo seria et ad vitae officia
3 devincta ac nihil de verbis laborante. Sed, opinor,
assidua veterum scriptorum tractatione inoleverat
linguae illius vox quam in libris saepe offenderat.
4 Aderat, cum ille hoc dicit, reprehensor audaculus
verborum, qui perpauca eademque a volgo protrita
legerat habebatque nonnullas disciplinae grammaticae
inauditiunculas, partim rudes inchoatasque, partim
non probas, easque quasi pulverem ob oculos, cum
5 adortus quemque fuerat, adspergebat. Sicut tunc
amico nostro "Barbare," inquit, "dixisti 'pluria';

---

[1] se, *added by Hertz.*

---

[1] These words were applied to any impropriety in the use
of language.
[2] Both words have the general meaning of "foreign";
according to some, σόλοικος was derived from Soloi, a town
of Cilicia, whose inhabitants spoke a perverted Attic

Attica who spoke most elegantly. But I have as yet found neither *soloecismus* nor *barbarismus* [1] in good Greek writers; for just as they used βάρβαρος, so they used σόλοικος.[2] So too our earlier writers used *soloecus* regularly, *soloecismus* never, I think. But if that be so, *soloecismus* is proper usage neither in Greek nor in Latin.

XXI

One who says *pluria*, *compluria* and *compluriens* speaks good Latin, and not incorrectly.

An extremely learned man, a friend of mine, chanced in the course of conversation to use the word *pluria*, not at all with a desire to show off, or because he thought that *plura* ought not to be used. For he is a man of serious scholarship and devoted to the duties of life, and not at all meticulous in the use of words. But, I think, from constant perusal of the early writers a word which he had often met in books had become second nature to his tongue.

There was present when he said this a very audacious critic of language, who had read very little and that of the most ordinary sort; this fellow had some trifling instruction in the art of grammar, which was partly ill-digested and confused and partly false, and this he used to cast like dust into the eyes of any with whom he had entered into discussion. Thus on that occasion he said to my friend: "You were incorrect in saying *pluria*; for that form has

dialect. This derivation seems to be accepted to-day. *Barbarus* is regarded as an onomatopoeic word, representing stammering; *cf. balbus*.

nam neque rationem verbum hoc neque auctoritates
6 habet." Ibi ille amicus ridens, " Amabo te," inquit,
" vir bone, quia nunc mihi a magis seriis rebus otium
est, velim doceas nos cur ' pluria ' sive ' compluria,'
nihil enim differt, non Latine sed barbare dixerint M.
Cato, Q. Claudius, Valerius Antias, L. Aelius, P.
Nigidius, M. Varro, quos subscriptores approbator-
esque huius verbi habemus praeter poetarum orator-
7 umque veterum multam copiam." Atque ille nimis
arroganter " Tibi," inquit, " habeas auctoritates istas,
ex Faunorum et Aboriginum saeculo repetitas, atque
8 huic rationi respondeas. Nullum enim vocabulum
neutrum comparativum numero plurativo, recto casu,
ante extremum ' a ' habet ' i ' litteram, sicuti 'meliora,
maiora, graviora.' Proinde igitur ' plura,' non
' pluria,' dici convenit, ne contra formam perpetuam
in comparativo ' i ' littera sit ante extremum ' a '."
9 Tum ille amicus noster, cum hominem confidentem
pluribus verbis non dignum existimaret, " Sinni," inquit, " Capitonis, doctissimi viri, epistulae sunt uno
in libro multae positae, opinor, in templo Pacis.
10 Prima epistula scripta est ad Pacuvium Labeonem,
cui titulus praescriptus est ' Pluria, non plura dici
11 debere.' In ea epistula rationes grammaticas
posuit per quas docet ' pluria ' Latinum esse,
' plura ' barbarum. Ad Capitonem igitur te dimit-
12 timus. Ex eo id quoque simul disces, si modo asse-
13 qui poteris quod in ea epistula scriptum est, ' pluria '
sive ' plura ' absolutum esse et simplex, non, ut tibi
videtur, comparativum."
14 Huius opinionis Sinnianae id quoque adiumen-

---

[1] Fr. 24, Peter.	[2] Fr. 90, Peter.
[3] Fr. 65, Peter.	[4] Fr. 48, Fun.
[5] Frag. 64, Swoboda.	[6] Fr. 1, Huschke.

neither justification nor authorities." Thereupon
that friend of mine rejoined with a smile: " My
good sir, since I now have leisure from more serious
affairs, I wish you would please explain to me why
pluria and *compluria*—for they do not differ—are
used barbarously and incorrectly by Marcus Cato,[1]
Quintus Claudius,[2] Valerius Antias,[3] Lucius Aelius,[4]
Publius Nigidius,[5] and Marcus Varro, whom we have
as endorsers and sanctioners of this form, to say
nothing of a great number of the early poets and
orators." And the fellow answered with excessive
arrogance : " You are welcome to those authorities of
yours, dug up from the age of the Fauns and Aborigines, but what is your answer to this rule ? No
neuter comparative in the nominative plural has an *i*
before its final *a*; for example, *meliora, maiora,
graviora.* Accordingly, then, it is proper to say *plura*,
not *pluria*, in order that there be no *i* before final *a* in
a comparative, contrary to the invariable rule."

Then that friend of mine, thinking that the self-
confident fellow deserved few words, said: " There
are numerous letters of Sinnius Capito, a very learned
man, collected in a single volume and deposited, I
think, in the Temple of Peace. The first letter is
addressed to Pacuvius Labeo, and it is prefixed by
the title, ' *Pluria*, not *plura*, should be used.' [6] In
that letter he has collected the grammatical rules
to show that *pluria*, and not *plura*, is good Latin.
Therefore I refer you to Capito. From him you will
learn at the same time, provided you can comprehend
what is written in that letter, that *pluria*, or *plura*,
is the positive and simple form, not, as it seems to
you, a comparative."

It also confirms that view of Sinnius, that when

tum est, quod "complures" cum dicimus, non compa-
15 rative dicimus.   Ab eo autem quod est "compluria"
16 adverbium est factum "compluriens."   Id quoniam
minus usitatum est, versum Plauti subscripsi ex comoedia quae *Persa* inscribitur :

> Quíd metuis ?—Metuo hércle vero ; sénsi ego[1]
> complúriens.

17 Item M. Cato in IV. *Originum* eodem in loco ter
hoc verbum posuit : " Compluriens eorum milites
mercennarii inter se multi alteri alteros in castris [2]
occidere, compluriens multi simul ad hostis trans-
fugere, compluriens in imperatorem impetum
facere."

[1] ego iam, *Plaut.*
[2] in castris, *Nonius*, ii, p. 124. 13, *Lindsay* ; *omitted by* ω.

we say *complures* or " several," we are not using a comparative. Moreover, from the word *compluria* is derived the adverb *compluriens*, " often." Since this is not a common word, I have added a verse of Plautus, from the comedy entitled *The Persian* :[1]

What do you fear ?—By Heaven ! I am afraid ;
I've had the feeling many a time and oft (*compluriens*).

Marcus Cato too, in the fourth book of his *Origins*, has used this word three times in the same passage :[2] " Often (*compluriens*) did their mercenary soldiers kill one another in large numbers in the camp ; often (*compluriens*) did many together desert to the enemy ; often (*compluriens*) did they attack their general."

---

[1] v. 534.   [2] Fr. 79, Peter.

INDEX [1]

ABDERA, a town on the southern coast of Thrace.

Aborigines, a name applied to the primitive inhabitants of Italy.

Academia, the grove near Athens in which Plato taught.

Accius, L., an early Roman poet (170–86 B.C.), famous for his tragedies [2] and for a history of the drama (*Didascalica* [3]).

Achaei, inhabitants of Achaea in the northern part of the Peloponnesus; also a general term for the Greeks.

Achilles, the famous hero of the Greeks before Troy; the name of a tragedy by Ennius. *Achilles Romanus*, applied to L. Sicinius Dentatus.

Aegina, an island in the Saronic Gulf, near Athens.

Aegyptiaci libri, a work of Apion.

Aelius Catus (Sex.),[4] a celebrated Roman jurist, consul in 189 B.C.

Aelius Stilo, L.,[5] one of the earliest and most famous of Roman grammarians, the teacher of Varro and Cicero.

Aelius Tubero, Q., a Roman jurist of the time of the Gracchi, one of the speakers in Cicero's *De Republica*.

Aemilia lex, *see* note 1, p. 207.

Aemilius Papus, Q., consul in 278 B.C. and censor in 275, with C. Fabricius.

Aemilius Paulus, L., surnamed Macedonicus because of his victory at Pydna in 168 B.C.

Aeschines, an Athenian orator (389–314 B.C.), a political opponent and personal enemy of Demosthenes.

Aesopus, a Greek writer of fables of the sixth century B.C. According to Herodotus (ii. 134) he was a slave of Iadmon of Samos; according to others, a Phrygian.

Africus ventus, the south-west wind, blowing from the direction of Africa.

Alba Longa, an ancient city of Latium in the Alban hills south-east of Rome.

Alcibiades, a brilliant but unprincipled Athenian, a friend of Socrates; he lived from about 450 to 404 B.C.

Alexander Magnus, Alexander the Great, King of Macedon from 356 to 323 B.C.

---

[1] In this Index a brief explanation is given of some of the proper names occurring in Volume I, titles of books being in italics. A complete Index, with references to the places where the names occur, will be given at the end of Volume III. The footnotes refer to the editions of the fragments of those writers whose works have survived only in that form. The parts of the titles used in the references are italicized.

[2] Tragicorum Romanorum Fragmenta, O. *Ribbeck*[3], Leipzig, 1897.

[3] O. Lucili Saturarum Reliquiae, L. *Müller*. Accedunt Acci praeter scaenica . . . Reliquiae, Leipzig, 1872.

E. *Bährens*, Fragmenta Poetarum Romanorum, Leipzig, 1886 (*F.P.R.*).

[4] Iurisprudentiae Anteiustinianae quae supersunt[5], P. E. *Huschke*, Leipzig, 1886. Iurisprudentiae Antehadrianae, F. P. *Bremer*, Leipzig, 1896– (three vols.).

[5] H. *Funaioli*, Gramm. Rom. Frag. vol. I; Leipzig 1907.

INDEX

Alexis,[6] a Greek writer of the New Comedy, uncle of Menander. He was born at Thurii in Magna Graecia about 394 B.C. and lived to the age of 106.

Allia, a tributary of the Tiber a few miles north of Rome, the scene of the defeat of the Romans by the Gauls in 390 B.C.

Alyattes, an early king of Lydia. He came to the throne in 617 B.C. and was succeeded by his son Croesus.

Amata, the name applied to a Vestal virgin during the ceremony of *captio*; see note 3, p. 65.

Ambraciensis, *adj.* from Ambracia, a town in south-western Epirus.

Analogia, De, a grammatical work of Julius Caesar. For the fragments *see* Julius Caesar.

Annaeus Cornutus, (L.), a Greek philosopher from Leptis in Africa, a freedman of the Annaei at Rome. He taught at Rome in the time of Nero and was the author of commentaries on Aristotle and on Virgil.

Annales Maximi,[7] early records kept by the *pontifex maximus* at Rome, collected and published in eighty books by P. Mucius Scaevola about 120 B.C.

Antia lex, *see* note 2, p. 207.

Antias, *see* Valerius.

Anticato, one of two speeches of Julius Caesar against Cato Uticensis.

Antiquitates Rerum Divinarum et Humanarum, a work of M. Terentius Varro. For the fragments *see* Terentius Varro.

Antiochus Magnus, a king of Syria, defeated in 190 B.C. by the Romans under the command of Scipio Asiaticus and his brother, the elder Scipio Africanus, who were charged with misappropriating the money and booty taken from the king.

Antistius Labeo,[8] a celebrated Roman jurist, the founder of a school of jurisprudence at Rome. He was a contemporary of Julius Caesar and one of the conspirators against his life.

Antonius, L., brother of Mark Antony, consul in 41 B.C.

Antonius M., consul in 99 B.C.

Antonius, M., Mark Antony, the triumvir.

Antonius Iulianus, a rhetorician, one of the teachers of Gellius.

Apion Pleistonices,[8] a rhetorician and grammarian of Egyptian origin, who taught in Rome in the time of Tiberius and Claudius.

Apollinaris, *see* Sulpicius.

Apollo, son of Zeus (Jupiter) and Leto (Latona), god of light.

Apollodorus, a Greek writer of the New Comedy, born at Charystus in Euboea; he lived in the early part of the third century B.C.

Apuli, the people of Apulia in south-eastern Italy.

Aquilius,[10] a Roman writer of *palliatae*, or comedies based on Greek models; he was a contemporary of Caecilius Statius and Terence.

Arcesilaus or Arcesilas, an Athenian philosopher from Pitane in Aeolia, who lived from 315 to 241 B.C.

Area Capitolina, *see* note 5, p. 171.

Area Volcani, also called Volcanol, a raised place at the north-west corner of the Forum Romanum.

Argi or Argos, the famous city in Argolis in the north-eastern part of the Peloponnesus.

Aristarchus, a celebrated Alexandrian grammarian, a native of Samothrace, who lived from about 155 to 83 B.C.

Aristarchus, an astronomer of Samos, who flourished about 250 B.C. wrongly cited by Gellius as Aristides.

---

[6] Th. *Kock*, Comicorum Atticorum Fragmenta, Leipzig, 1880–.

[7] H. *Peter*, Historicorum Romanorum Fragmenta, Leipzig, 1883.

[8] See note 4, above; also R. *Peter*, Quaestionum Pontificalium Specimen, Strassburg, 1886.

[9] C. *Müller*, Fragmenta Historicorum Graecorum, Paris, 1841–.

[10] O. *Ribbeck*[2], Comicorum Romanorum Fragmenta, Leipzig, 1898.

INDEX

Aristides, *see* Aristarchus of Samos.

Aristophanes, the famous Attic writer of the Old Comedy, who lived from 444 to 388 B.C.

Aristoteles,[11] the celebrated philosopher of the Lyceum at Athens (384–322 B.C.), born at Stageira in Thrace.

Aristoxenus,[9] a Greek philosopher from Tarentum, a pupil of Aristotle; he flourished about 330 B.C., and was celebrated for his writings on music.

Arretinum oraculum, *see* note 2, p. 249.

Arrianus (Flavius), a pupil of Epictetus and a native of Nicomedia in Bithynia, eminent as an historian. He was consul at Rome under Antoninus Pius and archon at Athens in A.D. 147. He published a handbook of Epictetus and eight books of his lectures (edition by H. Schenkl, Leipzig, 1894).

Asellus, *see* Claudius.

Asinius Pollio, C., a Roman historian, orator and writer of tragedies, born in 75 B.C. and died in A.D. 4. He was consul in 40 B.C. and he founded the first public library in Rome.

Atabulus, *see* note 1, p. 191.

Ateius Capito, C.,[4] a Roman jurist of the time of Augustus and Tiberius, consul in A.D. 5. He founded a school of jurisprudence opposed to that of Antistius Labeo.

Atilius Regulus, M., consul in 227 B.C. with P. Valerius Flaccus.

Attica, the south-eastern part of central Greece.

Atticus, *see* Herodes.

Attius, *see* note 5, p. 293.

Augustus, Caesar,[12] the first emperor of Rome, from 31 B.C. to A.D. 14.

Aurelius Opilius,[13] a freedman who taught philosophy, rhetoric and grammar at Rome. In 92 B.C. he followed Rutilius Rufus to Smyrna and died there.

Aurunci, an ancient people of Campania.

Auruncus, a Roman god; *see* note 2, p. 14.

BABYLONII, the inhabitants of Babylon, the famous city of Babylonia, on the Euphrates river, south of Mesopotamia.

Bassus, *see* Gavius.

Bias, a Greek philosopher of the early part of the sixth century B.C. One of the " Seven Sages "; *see* note 2, p. 11.

Bibulus, *see* Calpurnius.

Bithyni, the people of Bithynia, in the north-western part of Asia Minor.

Boeotia, the name of a comedy attributed by some to Plautus by others to Aquilius.

Bucephalas, the horse of Alexander the Great, so called from the breadth of his forehead.

Bucephalon, a city on the Hydaspes river in northern India.

Busiris, a king of Egypt, slain by Hercules.

Butes, one of the Argonauts, renowned as a boxer.

CAECILIUS METELLUS NUMIDICUS,[14] Q., consul in 109 B.C., commander-in-chief against Jugurtha from 109 to 107. *See* note 1, p. 31.

Caecilius Statius,[10] a celebrated Roman writer of *palliatae*, by birth an Insubrian Gaul. An older contemporary of Terence and a friend of Ennius.

Caedicius, Q., a Roman military tribune.

Caelius, M., a tribune of the commons in the time of Cato the Censor.

Caelius Sabinus,[4] a Roman legal writer of the time of Vespasian (A.D. 69–79).

Caepio, *see* Servilius.

Caesar, a general term for the emperor of Rome; *see* also Augustus, Iulius and Καῖσαρ.

---

[11] V. *Rose*, Aristotelis qui ferebantur librorum fragmenta, Leipzig, 1886.

[12] M. A. *Weichert*, Imperatoris Caesaris Augusti Reliquiae, Grima, 1846.

[13] Cf. No. 5.

[14] H. *Meyer*³, Oratorum Romanorum Fragmenta, Zurich, 1842 (*O.R.F.*).

INDEX

Caesellius Vindex, a Roman grammarian of the time of Hadrian (A.D. 117–138).

Callimachus,[15] a celebrated poet of the Alexandrine period. He also composed several encyclopaedic works in prose and was curator of the Alexandrian Library from 260 to about 240 B.C.

Callistratus, an Athenian orator of the latter part of the fourth century B.C.

Calpurnius Bibulus, M., Caesar's colleague in his first consulship, 59 B.C.

Calvisius Taurus, a philosopher of the time of Gellius.

Campanus, -a, -um, adj. from Campania, the division of Italy south of Latium.

Cannae, a town in Apulia on the river Aufidus, where the Romans were defeated by Hannibal in 216 B.C.

Capito, see Ateius and Sinnius.

Capitolinus, -a, -um, adj. from Capitolium; see also Area Capitolina.

Capitolium, the temple of Jupiter, Juno and Minerva, on the Capitoline Hill at Rome; also applied to the southern summit of that hill, on which the temple stood.

Carvilius Ruga, Sp., consul in 234 and 228 B.C.

Cassius Longinus, C., leader with Brutus of the conspiracy against Caesar's life.

Castricius, T., a Roman rhetorician, contemporary with Gellius.

Catilina, L. Sergius, the leader of the notorious conspiracy; he died in battle in 62 B.C.

Cato, see Porcius.

Catulus, see Lutatius.

Catus, see Aelius.

Cebes, a Theban, a disciple of Socrates.

Cephisia, a deme of Attica, near the source of the river Cephissus; also the name of a villa of Herodes Atticus near that place.

Ceres, an Italic goddess of agriculture, identified by the Romans with the Greek Demeter.

Chaldaei, the people of Chaldaea in the southern part of Babylonia; see note, 2, p. 47.

Chares,[16] a native of Mitylene in Lesbos, master of ceremonies to Alexander the Great.

Chilo, a Lacedaemonian of the sixth century B.C.; see note 2, p. 11.

Chryses, the name of a tragedy of Pacuvius.

Chrysippus,[17] see Χρύσιππος.

Cicero, see Tullius.

Circenses ludi, games held in the Circus Maximus at Rome.

Circus Maximus, the Great Circus at Rome, situated in the valley between the Palatine and Aventine hills.

Claudius Asellus, Ti., tribune of the commons at Rome in 139 B.C.

Claudius Quadrigarius, Q., a Roman annalist who flourished between 120 and 78 B.C. His Annals, in at least twenty-three books, began immediately after the destruction of Rome by the Gauls and came down to the time of Sulla, or thereabouts.

Cleanthes, see Κλεάνθης.

Clearchus,[9] a native of Soli in Cilicia and a pupil of Aristotle. He was the author of learned works on various subjects.

Cleopatra, the celebrated Egyptian queen, defeated, with Mark Antony, by Octavian at Actium in 31 B.C.

Clodius, P., the notorious tribune, the enemy of Cicero.

Cocles, see Horatius.

Colophonius, adj. from Colophon, a city on the coast of Lydia, near Ephesus.

Corinthius, -a, -um, adj. from Corinthus, the well-known city near the Isthmus of Corinth, in the northeastern part of the Peloponnesus.

---

[15] O. Schneider, Callimachea, Leipzig, 1870–.

[16] C. Müller, Scriptores Rerum Alex. Magni, Paris, 1846.

[17] J. von Arnim. Stoicorum veterum Frag., Leipzig, 1905–24.

INDEX

Cornelius, Dolabella, Cn., perhaps the same as P. Cornelius Dolabella; Valerius Maximus has P.

Cornelius Dollabella, (P.), consul in 44 B.C., Cicero's son-in-law.

Cornelius Fronto, M., the famous rhetorician and teacher of Marcus Aurelius, consul in A.D. 143.

Cornelius Rufinus, P., consul in 290 and 277 B.C.

Cornelius Scipio, P., father of the elder Scipio Africanus.

Cornelius Scipio Africanus maior, P., the conqueror of Hannibal, consul in 205 and 194 B.C., censor in 199.

Cornelius Scipio Africanus minor, P.,[14] son of L. Aemilius Paulus, adopted by the son of the elder Africanus; consul in 147, censor in 142 B.C.

Cornelius Scipio Asiaticus, L., brother of Scipio Africanus the elder.

Cornelius Scipio Nasica, P., consul in 191 B.C.

Cornelius Sisenna, L., praetor in 78 B.C. His History in from fourteen to nineteen books, contained an account of his own times.

Cornelius Sulla, P., the first to bear the surname Sulla.

Cornelius Sulla, P., consul in 66 B.C.

Cornelius Sulla Felix, L.,[7] the dictator; he lived from 138 to 78 B.C.

Cornutus, see Annaeus.

Coruncanius, Ti., consul in 280 B.C. The first plebeian to be elected pontifex maximus.

Crassus, see Licinius.

Crates, a celebrated grammarian, a native of Mallos in Cilicia, who founded the Pergamene school. He introduced the study of grammar to the Romans in 155 B.C.

Creta, a large island south-east of Greece.

Croesus, king of Lydia from 560 to 546 B.C., proverbial for his wealth.

Curius, M'., one of the heroes of early Rome, consul in 290 B.C. and for the third time in 275; victor over the Samnites and Pyrrhus.

Cyclops, originally one of three giants, having a single eye in the middle of their foreheads, who forged thunderbolts for Zeus. Later, a race of giants of the same descrip-

tion, located by Virgi near Mt. Etna.

Cynicae saturae, another name for the Menippean satires of M. Terentius Varro.

Cynicus, see Diogenes.

DEMOCRITUS ,a celebrated philosopher, born at Abdera about 360 B.C., an expounder of the atomic theory.

Demosthenes, the great Athenian orator, who lived from about 383 to 322 B.C.

Dentatus, see Sicinius.

Dialis, adj. to Iuppiter (cf. Diespiter); flamen Dialis, the special priest of Jupiter.

Diana, an ancient Italic goddess, identified by the Romans with the Greek Artemis.

Dicaearchus,[9] a native of Messana in Sicily, a pupil of Aristotle. He wrote on philosophy and geography, in particular the βίος Ἑλλάδος, an account of the geography, history and customs of the Greeks.

Didius, T., a Roman general of the time of Sertorius.

Diespiter, an earlier form of Iuppiter.

Dio Syracosius, a Syracusan, a friend and disciple of Plato. He drove the younger Dionysius from the throne and ruled for a brief time in his place. He was assassinated in 354 B.C.

Diogenes Cynicus, a native of Sinope in Paphlagonia, born about 412 B.C. Many stories of his eccentricities are told.

Diogenes Stoicus, born at Seleucia in Babylonia, a pupil of Chrysippus and Zeno. He was one of the envoys sent to Rome in 155 B.C.

Diomedes, next to Achilles the bravest of the Greeks before Troy.

Diomedes Thrax, king of the Bistones in Thrace. He was a son of Ares and possessed mares that were fed upon human flesh. He was slain by Heracles.

Diovis, an old Italic name for Iuppiter.

Dolabella, see Cornelius.

Dorici, the Dorian Greeks.

Dulichiae rates, the ships of Odysseus (Ulysses), so called from Dulichium,

453

INDEX

an island near Ithaca belonging to his kingdom.

ELIDENSIS, a native of Elis, a district in the north-western part of the Peloponnesus.

Empedocles,[18] a philosopher of Agrigentum in southern Sicily, who flourished about 450 B.C.

Ennius, Q.,[19] the "father of Roman poetry," who lived from 239 to 169 B.C. He wrote an epic called *Annales*, numerous tragedies, *saturae*, and other works.

Ephesus, a city on the western coast of Asia Minor, in Lydia.

Ephorus,[9] a Greek historian of Cyme in Aeolis, contemporary with Philip of Macedon and Alexander the Great.

Epicharmius, -a, -um, *adj.* from Epicharmus,[20] of Syracuse, the earliest writer of comedies. He produced his first play about 500 B.C.

Epictetus, a Greek philosopher of the Stoic school. He was for a time the slave at Rome of Epaphroditus, Nero's freedman, and was one of the philosophers banished by Domitian in A.D. 94.

Epicurus,[21] a celebrated Greek philosopher, born in 341 B.C. on the island of Samos, founder of the Epicurean school.

Epidicus, a comedy of Plautus and the chief character in that play.

Etruria, the district of Italy lying north of Latium.

Euander, *see* note 1, p. 51.

Euphorbus, a Trojan warrior, slain by Menelaus.

Eupolis,[6] an Athenian writer of the Old Comedy, born about 446 B.C., a contemporary of Aristophanes.

Euripides, the famous Athenian writer of tragedy, who lived from 480 to 406 B.C.

Eurystheus, a king o Mycenae, who imposed the Twelve Labours upon Heracles.

FABIUS MAXIMUS, Q., the famous *Cunctator*, the opponent of Hannibal.

Fabius Maximus, Q., son of the above, consul in 213 B.C.

Fabius Pictor, Q.,[7] the first Roman writer of history, born about 254 B.C.; *see* note 1, p. 389.

Fabricius Luscinus, C., one of the heroes of early Rome, consul in 282, 278 and 273 B.C. Victor over the Samnites and Pyrrhus.

Fannia lex, a sumptuary law, proposed by the consul C. Fannius in 161 B.C.

Fannius Strabo, C., consul in 161 B.C.

Fata, the Fates; *see* note 3, p. 291.

Fauni, mythological creatures, attendants on the rustic god Faunus. They are sometimes represented with the horns and feet of goats, or merely with pointed ears like those of an animal.

Favorinus,[22] a philosopher of the time of Gellius, born at Arelate in Gaul. He wrote and lectured as a rule in Greek. He was greatly admired by Gellius and had a strong influence upon him.

Fidus, *see* Optatus.

Figulus, *see* Nigidius.

Flaccus, *see* Verrius.

Fronto, *see* Cornelius.

Fulvius (Flaccus) Nobilior, M., consul in 189 B.C.

GALBA, *see* Sulpicius.

Gavius Bassus,[23] governor of Pontus under Trajan, noted for his knowledge of history and literature.

Gellius, L., *see* Introd. p. xii.

Gracchus, *see* Sempronius.

HADRIANUS, DIVUS,[14] emperor of Rome from A. D. 117 to 138.

---

[18] H. *Diehls*, Poetarum Philosophorum Fragmenta, Berlin, 1901.

[19] J. *Vahlen*[2], Ennianae Poesis Reliquiae, Leipzig, 1903. See also No. 2.

[20] G. *Kaibel*, Comicorum Graecorum Fragmenta, Berlin, 1899.

[21] H. *Usener*, Epicurea, Leipzig, 1887.

[22] J. L. *Marres*, De Favorini Arelatensis Vita, Studiis, Scriptis, Utrecht, 1853.

[23] Cf. No. 5.

INDEX

Hannibal, the famous Carthaginian general, 247 to 183 B.C.

Hebdomades, see *Imaginibus, De.*

Helicon, a mountain in Boeotia, the fabled abode of the Muses.

(Heraclitus),[24] a philosopher of Ephesus who flourished from about 535 to about 475 B.C.

Hercules, the Latin name of the Greek deified hero Heracles.

Hermippus,[9] a philosopher of Smyrna, who flourished about 200 B.C. He was the author of a biographical work called βίοι, containing the *Pinakes* of his teacher Callimachus.

Herodes Atticus, Tiberius Claudius, a famous Greek rhetorician, born at Marathon about A.D. 104, consul at Rome in 143. He spent a considerable part of his great wealth in the adornment of Athens.

Herodotus, the "father of History," born at Halicarnassus in Caria in 484 B.C., died about 425.

Hesiodus, the celebrated poet of Ascra in Boeotia. He seems to have flourished towards the end of the eighth century B.C.

Hiberus, a river, modern Ebro, in the north eastern part of Spain.

Hippocrates,[25] a famous Greek physician, born at Cos about 460 B.C.

Historia Naturalis, the name of a work of the elder Pliny.

Homerus, the great Greek epic poet.

Horatii, three Roman brothers who overcame the three Alban *Curiatii* in the time of Tullus Hostilius.

Horatius Cocles, one of the heroes of early Rome. He defended the bridge over the Tiber against the Etruscan army under Lars Porsena.

Hortensius (Hortalus), Q., a celebrated Roman orator, an older contemporary of Cicero. He lived from 114 to 42 B.C.

Hostilius Mancinus, A., a Roman aedile of uncertain date.

(Hostilius) Tubulus, (L.), *see* note 1, p. 147.

Hyginus, *see* Iulius.

IANUS, an old Italic deity, represented with two faces fronting in opposite directions; also his temple and the district in which it stood; *see* note 6, p. 81. Also called Ianuspater.

Ianuspater, *see* Ianus.

Iapyx, *adj.* from Iapygia, a district n south-eastern Italy; Iapyx ventus, a wind blowing from that quarter.

Ida, a mountain in north-western Asia Minor, near Troy.

Idus, the fifteenth of March, May, July and October; and the thirteenth of the other months.

Ietae, the people of the island of Ios, in the Aegean Sea.

Imaginibus, De, see note 2, p. 267.

Indicum bellum, the war in India, waged by Alexander the Great in 327 B.C.

Iocus, Mirth, personified as a minor deity.

Ios, one of the Cyclades; *see* Ietae.

Iovispater, *see* Iuppiter.

Iugurtha, Jugurtha, a Numidian prince with whom the Romans waged war from 112 to 106 B.C.

Iulianus, *see* Antonius.

Iulius, C., pontifex maximus in 99 B.C.

(Iulius), L., father of C. Iulius.

Iulius Caesar, C.,[26] the dictator.

Iulius Caesar (Octavianus), C., *see* Augustus Caesar.

Iulius Hyginus, C.,[27] a freedman of Augustus of Spanish birth, in charge of the Palatine Library, author of a commentary on Virgil and other works.

Iulius Modestus,[28] a freedman of Julius Hyginus, also eminent as a grammarian.

Iulius Paulus, a poet contemporary with Gellius.

---

[24] H. *Diels* Heracleitos von Ephesus, Berlin, 1901, die Frag. der vorsokratiken, id. 1903.

[25] *Kühn*, Medicorum Graecorum Opera, Leipzig, 1821–1830.

[26] Complete edition, with the fragments, by B. *Dinter*, Leipzig, 1876. For the speeches see also No. 14.

[27] B. *Bunte*, De C. Iulii Hygini vita et scriptis, Marburg, 1846. Cf. also No. 5.

[28] See No. 27.

INDEX

Iuno, the Roman goddess identified by the Romans with the Greek Hera.

Iuppiter, king of the gods, identified by the Romans with Zeus.

KALENDAE, the first day of the month.

LABEO, see Antistius and Pacuvius.

Laberius, D.,[10] a Roman knight, a writer of mimes, or farces, contemporary with Julius Caesar.

Lacedaemonii, the people of Lacedaemon, or Sparta, the principal city of Laconia in the southeastern part of the Peloponnesus.

Laco, Laconian, see Lacedaemonii.

Laconicus, adj. from Laconia; see Lacedaemonii.

Laelius (Sapiens), C., the intimate friend of Scipio Africanus the younger, consul in 140 B.C. The principal speaker in Cicero's De Amicitia and one of the speakers in the De Senectute and De Republica.

Laevius, see note 2, p. 205.

Latina, Lingua, De, a work of M. Terentius Varro, dedicated to Cicero; of its twenty-five books about five have survived.

Latium, the district of Italy in which Rome is situated.

Lavinia, daughter of Latinus, an early king in Latium, and wife of Aeneas.

Leonides, another form of Leonidas, the king of Sparta who fell in the defence of Thermopylae in 480 B.C.

Leucae, a town near Phocaea, in north-western Lydia.

Licinia lex, a sumptuary law of uncertain date.

Licinius, a freedman of Lutatius Catulus, formerly a slave of C. Gracchus. He probably took his name from Licinia, the wife of Gracchus.

(Licinius) Crassus, M., triumvir with Caesar and Pompey.

(Licinius) Crassus Mucianus, P., consul and pontifex maximus in 131 B.C.

Lingua Latina, De, see Latina Lingua.

Livius Andronicus,[3] the earliest recorded writer of Graeco-Roman literature, brought to Rome from Tarentum in 272 B.C.

Logistorici,[29] a work of M. Terentius Varro.

Longa Alba, see Alba Longa.

Longinus, see Cassius.

Lucani, the people of Lucania, the district south of Campania in south-western Italy.

Lucetius, a name, or epithet, of Jupiter.

Lucilius, C.,[30] a writer of saturae, a native of Suessa Aurunca in Campania, 167(?) to 103 B.C.

Lucretius, the great Roman didactic poet, author of the De Rerum Natura. He lived from about 95 to about 55 B.C.

Luscinus, see Fabricius.

Lutatius Catulus, Q., consul in 102 B.C., victor over the Cimbri.

Lutatius Catulus, Q., son of the above, consul in 78 B.C.

Lycurgus, an early Spartan legislator, probably of the latter part of the ninth century B.C.

Lydia, a country in the western part of Asia Minor.

Lysias, a famous Athenian orator, who lived from about 485 to about 378 B.C.

MACCIUS PLAUTUS, T., the great Roman writer of comedies; his literary activity extended from 221 to 184 B.C.; see p. 251.

Mancinus, see Hostilius.

Manliana imperia, see note 1, p. 69.

Marcellum, Epistula ad, a work of Valerius Probus.

---

[29] A. Riese, M. Terentii Varronis Sat. Menip. Reliquiae, Leipzig, 1865.

[30] See No. 3, but especially Fr. Marx, Lucilii Carminum Reliquiae, Leipzig, 1904–5.

INDEX

Mars, an important Italic deity, identified by the Romans with the Greek Ares, but of quite a different character.

Marsi, an Italic people, dwelling in the south-eastern part of the Sabine territory, around Lake Fucinus.

Marsicum bellum, the Social war of 90–89 B.C., in which the Marsi took a leading part.

Marspater and Marspiter, another name for Mars.

Martius, -a, -um, adj. from Mars; hastae, see notes 1 and 2, p. 331.

Masurius Sabinus,[4] a Roman jurist of the time of Tiberius, author of important legal treatises.

Maximus, see Fabius.

Megalensia (sc. sacra), see note 3, p. 203.

Melanippa, the name of a tragedy by Ennius.

Menander,[6] the greatest of the Athenian writers of New Comedy (342–290 B.C.).

Menippeae saturae,[31] see note, p. 84.

Menippus, a Greek philosopher of Gadara in Syria, who flourished in the third century B.C.

Messala, see Valerius.

Metellus, see Caecilius.

Milesii, the people of Miletus, a city in the north-western part of Caria in Asia Minor.

Milone, pro, an oration of Cicero in defence of T. Annius Milo.

Minerva, the Roman goddess of wisdom, identified by them with the Greek Athena.

Modestus, see Iulius.

Moera, the Greek name for one of the Fates.

Morta, a Latin equivalent for Moera.

Mucianus, see Licinius.

Mucius (Scaevola), Q.,[4] an eminent Roman jurist, consul in 95 B.C., and pontifex maximus; he was the first to give a comprehensive treatment of the Roman Civil Law.

(Munatius) Plancus, L., a native of Tibur, consul at Rome in 42 B.C.; see note 6, p. 103.

Musa, originally a fountain-nymph; then one of nine goddesses of music, arts and sciences.

Musonius,[32] a celebrated Stoic philosopher of the first century A.D.

NAEVIUS, Cn.,[3] an early Roman epic and dramatic poet, who produced his first play in 235 B.C.

Naevius, M., tribune of the commons at Rome in 185 B.C.

Naxos, the largest of the Cyclades islands in the Aegean Sea.

Neoptolemus, the name of a tragedy of Ennius; also of its principal character, the son of Achilles.

Neptunus, the Italic god of the waters, identified by the Romans with the Greek Poseidon.

Neptunuspater, another name for Neptunus.

Neratius (Priscus), a Roman jurist of the time of Trajan and Hadrian.

Nicomedes, Nicomedes III, king of Bithynia from 91 to 74 B.C.

Nigidius Figulus, P.,[33] a learned Roman grammarian, contemporary with Cicero and Varro.

Nobilior, see Fulvius.

Nonae, the seventh of March, May, July and October, and the fifth of the other months.

Numa, the second king of Rome.

Numantia, a city in the north central part of Spain.

Numeri, Numbers, personified.

Officio Mariti, De, one of the Menippean Satires of M. Terentius Varro.

Olympia, the famous city of Elis, in the north-western part of the Peloponnesus.

Olympius, adj. from Olympus, the mountain on the borders of Thessaly and Macedonia regarded as the

---

[31] F. *Bücheler*, Petronii Saturae[4], Berlin, 1904.

[32] O. Hense, C. Musonii Rufi Reliquiae, Leipzig, 1905.

[3] (*F.P.R.*)

[33] A. *Swoboda*, P. Nigidii Figuli operum Reliquiae, Vienna, 1889.

INDEX

abode of the gods; an epithet of
Jupiter.

Opilius, *see* Aurelius.

Optatus, Fidus, a Roman grammarian
contemporary with Gellius.

Orchus, the Lower World; also the
god of the Lower World.

Orestes, son of Agamemnon and
Clytemnestra.

PACUVIUS,[1] M., a Roman writer of
tragedies, a native of Brundisium
and nephew of Ennius.

Pacuvius Labeo, a Roman jurist,
father of Antistius Labeo.

Palatinae aedes, the Palace of the
Caesars on the Palatine Hill at
Rome.

Papia lex, *see* note 1, p. 63.

Papus, *see* Aemilius.

Parnasia laurus, referring to Mt.
Parnasus or Parnassus in Phocis,
sacred to Apollo and the Muses.

Pax, Peace, personified as a goddess;
Pacis templum, the temple of Peace
in the Forum of Vespasian, begun
by Vespasian in A.D. 71 and finished
by Domitian.

Paulus, *see* Aemilius and Iulius.

Pelasgi, a name applied to prehistoric
inhabitants of Greece and Italy.

Peleus, a Thessalian king who married
Thetis and became the father of
Achilles.

Peloponnesiacum bellum, the war between Athens and the Peloponnesian
allies from 431 to 404 B.C.

Pericles, the great Athenian statesman, whose career extended from
469 to 429 B.C.

Peripateticus (sc. *philosophus*), a
member of the school, or sect,
founded by Aristotle, so called
because the master gave his instruction while walking about (περιπατέω)
in the Lyceum.

Petilii, tribunes of the commons at
Rome in 187 B.C.

Phaedon, a Greek philosopher, born
in Elis but brought to Athens as a
prisoner of war, where he became
a follower of Socrates.

Philippides, a writer of the Attic New
Comedy, who flourished about 323
B.C.

Philippus, Philip II of Macedon,
father of Alexander the Great; he
reigned from 359 to 336 B.C.

Philochorus,[9] a Greek historian who
lived in Athens from 306 to 260 B.C.
and wrote a history of that city.

Philolaus, a Pythagorean philosopher,
contemporary with Socrates.

Phrygia, a country of Asia Minor,
east of Mysia, Lydia and the
northern part of Caria.

Paryx, a native of Phrygia.

Pictor, *see* Fabius.

Picus, an early Italic deity and hero,
the earliest king of Latium, changed
by Circe into a woodpecker (*picus*).

Piraeus, the chief seaport of Athens,
about five miles south-west of the
city.

Pisae, more commonly Pisa, a city
of Elis near Olympia.

Piso, *see* Calpurnius and Pupius.

Plancius, Cn., a Roman defended
by Cicero against a charge of
sodalicium, or improper aid from
societies, in securing his election
as curule aedile in 54 B.C.

Plancio, pro, an oration of Cicero; *see*
Plancius.

Plancus, *see* Munatius.

Plato, the great Athenian philosopher
(428–347 B.C.).

Plautius, a conjectured Roman poet,
whose plays were attributed to
Plautus.

Plautus, *see* Maccius.

Plinius Secundus, C., the elder Pliny,
born at Novum Comum in 23, died
in the eruption of Mt. Vesuvius,
A.D. 79. Author of the *Natural
History* in thirty-seven books.

Plistonices, *see* Apion.

Plocium, The Necklace, a comedy of
Menander, the source of a comedy
of the same name by Caecilius
Statius.

Plutarchus, the celebrated Greek
philosopher- and biographer of
Chaeronea in Boeotia; he lived
from about A.D. 46 to 120.

Poeni, a name applied to the Carthaginians because of their Phoenician
origin.

Poeniceus color, the so-called " purple," varying from violet to scarlet,

458

INDEX

according to the strength of the dye and the number of times the cloth was dipped in it.

Pollio, see Asinius.

Pompeius Magnus, Cn., Pompey the Great, triumvir with Caesar and Crassus in 60 B.C., victor over the pirates and Mithridates.

Pontius, C., a Samnite general who defeated the Romans at the Caudine Forks in 321 B.C.

Popilius, M., censor in 159 B.C.

Porcius Cato Censorinus, M.,[34] a native of Tusculum, consul at Rome in 195 B.C., censor in 184. Eminent as an orator, statesman and writer.

Porcius Cato Uticensis, M., great-grandson of the Censor, born in 95 B.C.; he committed suicide at Utica after the battle of Thapsus in 46 B.C.

Posidippus, a writer of the New Comedy at Athens, born at Cassandrea in Macedonia. He produced his first play in 289 B.C.

Postumiana imperia, see note 1, p. 69.

Postumius, A., consul in 99 B.C.

Postumus, see Silvius.

Pratum, the title of works of Suetonius and others.

Problemata, the title of works of Aristotle and others.

Probus, see Valerius.

Protagoras, a celebrated sophist from Abdera, who lived from about 480 to 411 B.C.

Pyrenaeus, the Pyrenees, a range of mountains between France and Spain.

Pyrrus or Pyrrhus, son of Achilles, also called Neoptolemus.

Pyrrus or Phyrrus, a king of Epirus who warred with the Romans from 280 to 274 B.C.

Pythagoras, the celebrated Greek philosopher of the latter part of the sixth century B.C. He was a native of Samos, but was most influential at Crotona in southern Italy.

Pythagoricus, *adj.* from Pythagoras; as subst., a follower of Pythagoras.

QUADRIGARIUS, see Claudius.

Quinquatrus, see note 2, p. 181.

Quirinalis, *flamen*, the special priest of Quirinus, the deified Romulus.

Quirites, the designation of the Roman people as citizens.

REGULUS, see Atilius.

Robigus, the Italic deity that protected the grain from blight (*robigo*).

Rodii or Rhodii, the people of Rhodes, an island south of Caria in Asia Minor.

Romulus, the reputed founder of Rome in 753 B.C., and its first king. After his death deified as Quirinus.

Roscius, Q., a celebrated Roman actor of comedy of the time of Cicero; he died in 62 B.C.

Rufinus, see Cornelius.

Ruga, see Carvilius.

SABINUS, a physician of the end of the first century B.C.

Sabinus, see Caelius and Masurius.

Salernum, a city of Campania.

Salius, one of a very early college of priests at Rome, who worshipped Mars with processions and a war-dance in the month of March; see also note 5, p. 61.

Sallustius (Crispus), C.,[35] the celebrated Roman historian (86–34 B.C.).

Samius, *adj.* from Samos, an island near Ephesus, in south-western Lydia.

Samnites, an Italic nation of central Italy, with which the Romans waged war for the sovereignty of the peninsular from 343 to 290 B.C.

Saturio, a lost comedy of Plautus.

Saturnalia, see note 5, p. 203.

Saturnuspater, another name for Saturnus, a mythical Italic king and deity, identified by the Romans with the Greek Cronos.

---

[34] H. *Jordan*, M. Catonis praeter librum De Re Rustica quae extant, Leipzig, 1860. See also No. 7.

[35] B. *Maurenbrecher*, C. Sallusti Crispi Historiarum Reliquiae, Leipzig, 1891–3.

INDEX

---

[36] M. *Hertz,* Sinnius Capito, Berlin, 1844.

[37] R. *Agahd,* M. Terentii Varronis Antiquitatum . . . Divinarum libri, Fleckeisen's Jahrb. Suppl. xxiv. 1, Leipzig, 1898.

P. *Mirsch,* De M. Ter. Varr. Antiq. . . . Humanarum lib i, Leipzig. Studien, v. 1, Leipzig, 1882.

O. *Goetz* & F. *Schoch,* M. Terr. Varr. de Ling. Lat.; aecedunt fragmenta Leipzig, 1910.

INDEX

Tettius, *see* note 5, p. 293.

Thebae, the principal city of Boeotia in central Greece.

Theognis, an elegiac and gnomic poet of Megara, who flourished about 548 B.C.

Theophrastus, a Greek philosopher, a native of Eresos in Lesbos. At Athens he was a pupil of Aristotle, who designated him as his successor as the head of the Lyceum.

Thermopylae, the pass leading from Thessaly into Locris between Mt. Oeta and the shore of the Malic Gulf.

Thersites, an ugly and impudent Greek at Troy, slain by Achilles.

Thracia, a country north of the Aegean and west of the Euxine (Black) Sea.

Thrax, a native of Thrace.

Thucydides, the famous Athenian historian, who lived from about 455 to 400 B.C. He wrote a history of the Peloponnesian War.

Tiberius Caesar, emperor of Rome from A.D. 14 to 37.

Timaeus, a dialogue of Plato.

Tiro, *see* Tullius.

Titiae balneae, *see* note 1, p. 235.

Titius, L., used as a general, or indefinite, name.

Tolosanus, -a, -um, *adj.* from Tolosa, a city in the western part of Gallia Narbonensis, the modern Toulouse.

Trebatius, C., a Roman jurist, a friend of Cicero.

Tubero, *see* Aelius.

Tubulus, *see* Hostilius.

Tullius Cicero, M.,[38] the famous Roman orator, statesman and writer (106 to 43 B.C.).

Tullius Tiro,[39] M., *see* note 2, p. 35.

Tusculanum fundum, an estate at Tusculum, a town of Latium about ten miles south-east of Rome.

Tuscus, *see* Clodius.

ULIXES, a Latin form of the Greek Ὀδυσσεύς (dialectic Ὀλυσσεύς, Quint. i. 4, 16). The hero of the Odyssey.

Umbria, a district of Italy east of Etruria and north-east of Rome.

Usus, Experience, personified.

VALERIUS, L., used as a general, or indefinite, name.

Valerius Antias,[7] a Roman historian from Antium, who flourished about 80 B.C. He wrote a *History of Rome,* in at least seventy-five books, from the earliest times to those of Sulla.

Valerius (Flaccus), P., consul in 231 B.C.

Valerius Messala, M., consul in 161 B.C.

Valerius Probus, a celebrated Roman grammarian, born in Berytus in Syria, who flourished in the second half of the first century A.D.

Valerius Soranus, Q., a grammarian of Varro's time.

Varro, *see* Terentius.

Vediovis, a Roman deity.

Venus, the Italic goddess identified by the Romans with the Greek Aphrodite.

Vergiliae, the constellation of the Pleiades; *see* note 3, p. 267.

Vergilius Maro, P., the famous Roman poet (70–19 B.C.).

Verrem, in, an oration of Cicero.

Verrius Flaccus,[40] M., a Roman grammarian of the Augustan age: *see* Suetonius, *De Gramm.* xvii. He made the first Latin lexicon, existing only in the fragments of an abridgment by Festus, and a further abridgment by Paulus Diaconus.

Vesta, an ancient Italic goddess of the hearth and hearth-fire.

Vindex, *see* Caesellius.

---

[38] For the fragments see the edition of *Orelli*[2], vol. iv, Zurich, 1861.

[39] A. *Lion*, Tironiana et Maecenatiana, Göttingen, 1846.

[40] See preface of C. O. Müller, Festus, Leipzig, 1839.

INDEX

Volcacius Sedigitus, a Roman poet who lived about 130 B.C.
Volcani area, *see* Area Volcani.

XANTHIPPE, the wife of Socrates.
Xenophanes, a philosopher born at Colophon in 556 B.C., founder of the Eleatic school of philosophy.

Xenophilus, a Pythagorean philosopher, a teacher of Aristoxenus.

ZENO, founder of the Stoic school of philosophy; he was born at Citium in Cyprus about 362 and died in 264 B.C.

GREEK INDEX

Ἀγαμέμνων, Agamemnon, king of Mycenae in Argolis, and leader of the Greeks at Troy.

Ἀθηνᾶ, Athena, the Greek goddess of wisdom.

Αἰγυπτιακά, see Ἑλλάνικος.

Ἀμάλθεια, Amalthea, a Cretan nymph who nourished the infant Zeus with the milk of a goat. When the goat broke off one of its horns, Amalthea filled it with fruits and flowers and offered it to Zeus. The god transported both the goat and the "horn of plenty" to the heavens.

ἅμαξα, the Greek name for the constellation of the Great Bear.

Ἀπόλλων, see Apollo.

Ἀργεῖοι, the Argives, inhabitants of Argos; also a general term for the Greeks.

Ἀριστοτέλης, see Aristoteles.

Ἀχαῖοι, see Achaei.

Βοώτης, the constellation near the Great Bear.

Διδασκαλικά, see Accius.

Διογένης, see Diogenes Stoicus.

Ἑλλάνικος, a writer of history and chronicles, born in Mitylene in Lesbos and contemporary with Herodotus and Thucydides. Author of an Egyptian history (Αἰγυπτιακά).

Ἕλλην, = Graecus.

Εὐκλείδης, the celebrated mathematician of Alexandria in the time of Ptolemaeus Lagi.

Ἐχεκλῆς, an athlete of Samos.

Ἠθική, ἡ, the Ethics of Diogenes Stoicus.

Ἰαπυγία, Iapygia, see Iapyx.

Ἰλιόθεν, from Ilium, or Troy.

Ἱπποκύων, the title of one of the Menippean Satires of M. Terentius Varro, dealing with the dog-world of Diogenes the Cynic.

Ἱστωρία Παντοδαπή, a work of Favorinus; see note 2, p. ix.

Καῖσαρ, see Caesar, as a general term.

Κίκωνες, a Thracian people, living near the Hebrus river.

Κλεάνθης, a Greek philosopher, born at Assos in the Troad about 300 B.C. He was a pupil of Zeno and became head of the Stoic school.

Κορίνθιος, see Corinthius.

Κόρινθος, see Corinthus.

Κρωβύλη, a character in the Plocium of Menander.

Κροῖσος, see Croesus.

Λακεδαιμόνιοι, see Lacedaemonii.

Λάμια, an ogress.

Λοίμων, περί, a work of Democritus.

Μοῦσαι, see Musa.

Ξενιάδης, a Greek philosopher of Corinth, whose date is uncertain.

Ὀδύσσεια, the Latin version of the Odyssey in Saturnian verse made by Livius Andronicus.

Ὀλύμπιος, see Olympius.

Πλάτων, see Plato.

Πλειάδες, the constellation of the Pleiades, originally the seven daughters of Atlas and Pleione; see Vergiliae.

Πυθαγόρας, see Pythagoras.

Πυθαγορικοί, see Pythagoricus.

GREEK INDEX

Πυθαγορίζουσα, the title of a comedy by Alexis.

Σεισίχθων, Earth-shaker, an epithet of Poseidon, the Greek god of the sea; *see* Neptunus.

Τίμων, a Greek writer of Phlius, in the north-eastern part of the Peloponnesus, author of tragedies, satyr-dramas, and satiric poems in hexameter verse called Σίλλοι.

Φίλιππος, *see* Philippus.

Χείλων, *see* Chilo.

Χρύσιππος, a Greek philosopher from Soli in Cilicia, of about 280 B.C. A disciple of Carneades the Stoic.

Ὠρωπός, a town in the north-eastern part of Attica, near the Boeotian frontier.

Printed in Great Britain by Richard Clay (The Chaucer Press), Ltd., Bungay, Suffolk

THE LOEB CLASSICAL LIBRARY

VOLUMES ALREADY PUBLISHED

Latin Authors

AMMIANUS MARCELLINUS. Translated by J. C. Rolfe. 3 Vols.

APULEIUS: THE GOLDEN ASS (METAMORPHOSES). W. Adlington (1566). Revised by S. Gaselee.

ST. AUGUSTINE: CITY OF GOD. 7 Vols. Vol. I. G. E. McCracken. Vols. II and VII. W. M. Green. Vol. III. D. Wiesen. Vol. IV. P. Levine. Vol. V. E. M. Sanford and W. M. Green. Vol. VI. W. C. Greene.

ST. AUGUSTINE, CONFESSIONS OF. W. Watts (1631). 2 Vols.

ST. AUGUSTINE, SELECT LETTERS. J. H. Baxter.

AUSONIUS. H. G. Evelyn White. 2 Vols.

BEDE. J. E. King. 2 Vols.

BOETHIUS: TRACTS and DE CONSOLATIONE PHILOSOPHIAE. Rev. H. F. Stewart and E. K. Rand. Revised by S. J. Tester.

CAESAR: ALEXANDRIAN, AFRICAN and SPANISH WARS. A. G. Way.

CAESAR: CIVIL WARS. A. G. Peskett.

CAESAR: GALLIC WAR. H. J. Edwards.

CATO: DE RE RUSTICA. VARRO: DE RE RUSTICA. H. B. Ash and W. D. Hooper.

CATULLUS. F. W. Cornish. TIBULLUS. J. B. Postgate. PERVIGILIUM VENERIS. J. W. Mackail.

CELSUS: DE MEDICINA. W. G. Spencer. 3 Vols.

CICERO: BRUTUS and ORATOR. G. L. Hendrickson and H. M. Hubbell.

[CICERO]: AD HERENNIUM. H. Caplan.

CICERO: DE ORATORE, etc. 2 Vols. Vol. I. DE ORATORE, Books I and II. E. W. Sutton and H. Rackham. Vol. II. DE ORATORE, Book III. DE FATO; PARADOXA STOICORUM; DE PARTITIONE ORATORIA. H. Rackham.

CICERO: DE FINIBUS. H. Rackham.

CICERO: DE INVENTIONE, etc. H. M. Hubbell.

CICERO: DE NATURA DEORUM and ACADEMICA. H. Rackham.

CICERO: DE OFFICIIS. Walter Miller.

CICERO: DE REPUBLICA and DE LEGIBUS. Clinton W. Keyes.

CICERO: DE SENECTUTE, DE AMICITIA, DE DIVINATIONE. W. A. Falconer.
CICERO: IN CATILINAM, PRO FLACCO, PRO MURENA, PRO SULLA. New version by C. Macdonald.
CICERO: LETTERS TO ATTICUS. E. O. Winstedt. 3 Vols.
CICERO: LETTERS TO HIS FRIENDS. W. Glynn Williams, M. Cary, M. Henderson. 4 Vols.
CICERO: PHILIPPICS. W. C. A. Ker.
CICERO: PRO ARCHIA, POST REDITUM, DE DOMO, DE HARUS-PICUM RESPONSIS, PRO PLANCIO. N. H. Watts.
CICERO: PRO CAECINA, PRO LEGE MANILIA, PRO CLUENTIO, PRO RABIRIO. H. Grose Hodge.
CICERO: PRO CAELIO, DE PROVINCIIS CONSULARIBUS, PRO BALBO. R. Gardner.
CICERO: PRO MILONE, IN PISONEM, PRO SCAURO, PRO FONTEIO, PRO RABIRIO POSTUMO, PRO MARCELLO, PRO LIGARIO, PRO REGE DEIOTARO. N. H. Watts.
CICERO: PRO QUINCTIO, PRO ROSCIO AMERINO, PRO ROSCIO COMOEDO, CONTRA RULLUM. J. H. Freese.
CICERO: PRO SESTIO, IN VATINIUM. R. Gardner.
CICERO: TUSCULAN DISPUTATIONS. J. E. King.
CICERO: VERRINE ORATIONS. L. H. G. Greenwood. 2 Vols.
CLAUDIAN. M. Platnauer. 2 Vols.
COLUMELLA: DE RE RUSTICA. DE ARBORIBUS. H. B. Ash, E. S. Forster and E. Heffner. 3 Vols.
CURTIUS, Q.: HISTORY OF ALEXANDER. J. C. Rolfe. 2 Vols.
FLORUS. E. S. Forster. CORNELIUS NEPOS. J. C. Rolfe.
FRONTINUS: STRATAGEMS and AQUEDUCTS. C. E. Bennett and M. B. McElwain.
FRONTO: CORRESPONDENCE. C. R. Haines. 2 Vols.
GELLIUS. J. C. Rolfe. 3 Vols.
HORACE: ODES and EPODES. C. E. Bennett.
HORACE: SATIRES, EPISTLES, ARS POETICA. H. R. Fairclough.
JEROME: SELECTED LETTERS. F. A. Wright.
JUVENAL and PERSIUS. G. G. Ramsay.
LIVY. B. O. Foster, F. G. Moore, Evan T. Sage, and A. C. Schlesinger and R. M. Geer (General Index). 14 Vols.
LUCAN. J. D. Duff.
LUCRETIUS. W. H. D. Rouse. Revised by M. F. Smith.
MANILIUS. G. P. Goold.
MARTIAL. W. C. A. Ker. 2 Vols. Revised by E. H. Warmington.
MINOR LATIN POETS: from PUBLILIUS SYRUS to RUTILIUS NAMATIANUS, including GRATTIUS, CALPURNIUS SICULUS, NEMESIANUS, AVIANUS and others, with " Aetna " and the " Phoenix." J. Wight Duff and Arnold M. Duff. 2 Vols.

2

Minucius Felix. Cf. Tertullian.

Ovid: The Art of Love and Other Poems. J. H. Mosley. Revised by G. P. Goold.

Ovid: Fasti. Sir James G. Frazer

Ovid: Heroides and Amores. Grant Showerman. Revised by G. P. Goold

Ovid: Metamorphoses. F. J. Miller. 2 Vols. Vol. 1 revised by G. P. Goold.

Ovid: Tristia and Ex Ponto. A. L. Wheeler.

Persius. Cf. Juvenal.

Pervigilium Veneris. Cf. Catullus.

Petronius. M. Heseltine. Seneca: Apocolocyntosis. W. H. D. Rouse. Revised by E. H. Warmington.

Phaedrus and Babrius (Greek). B. E. Perry.

Plautus. Paul Nixon. 5 Vols.

Pliny: Letters, Panegyricus. Betty Radice. 2 Vols.

Pliny: Natural History. 10 Vols. Vols. I–V and IX. H. Rackham. VI.–VIII. W. H. S. Jones. X. D. E. Eichholz.

Propertius. H. E. Butler.

Prudentius. H. J. Thomson. 2 Vols.

Quintilian. H. E. Butler. 4 Vols.

Remains of Old Latin. E. H. Warmington. 4 Vols. Vol. I. (Ennius and Caecilius) Vol. II. (Livius, Naevius Pacuvius, Accius) Vol. III. (Lucilius and Laws of XII Tables) Vol. IV. (Archaic Inscriptions)

Res Gestae Divi Augusti. Cf. Velleius Paterculus.

Sallust. J. C. Rolfe.

Scriptores Historiae Augustae. D. Magie. 3 Vols.

Seneca, The Elder: Controversiae, Suasoriae. M. Winterbottom. 2 Vols.

Seneca: Apocolocyntosis. Cf. Petronius.

Seneca: Epistulae Morales. R. M. Gummere. 3 Vols.

Seneca: Moral Essays. J. W. Basore. 3 Vols.

Seneca: Tragedies. F. J. Miller. 2 Vols.

Seneca: Naturales Quaestiones. T. H. Corcoran. 2 Vols.

Sidonius: Poems and Letters. W. B. Anderson. 2 Vols.

Silius Italicus. J. D. Duff. 2 Vols.

Statius. J. H. Mozley. 2 Vols.

Suetonius. J. C. Rolfe. 2 Vols.

Tacitus: Dialogus. Sir Wm. Peterson. Agricola and Germania. Maurice Hutton. Revised by M. Winterbottom, R. M. Ogilvie, E. H. Warmington.

Tacitus: Histories and Annals. C. H. Moore and J. Jackson. 4 Vols.

TERENCE. John Sargeaunt. 2 Vols.

TERTULLIAN: APOLOGIA and DE SPECTACULIS. T. R. Glover. MINUCIUS FELIX. G. H. Rendall.

TIBULLUS. Cf. CATULLUS.

VALERIUS FLACCUS. J. H. Mozley.

VARRO: DE LINGUA LATINA. R. G. Kent. 2 Vols.

VELLEIUS PATERCULUS and RES GESTAE DIVI AUGUSTI. F. W. Shipley.

VIRGIL. H. R. Fairclough. 2 Vols.

VITRUVIUS: DE ARCHITECTURA. F. Granger. 2 Vols.

Greek Authors

ACHILLES TATIUS. S. Gaselee.

AELIAN: ON THE NATURE OF ANIMALS. A. F. Scholfield. 3 Vols.

AENEAS TACTICUS. ASCLEPIODOTUS and ONASANDER. The Illinois Greek Club.

AESCHINES. C. D. Adams.

AESCHYLUS. H. Weir Smyth. 2 Vols.

ALCIPHRON, AELIAN, PHILOSTRATUS: LETTERS. A. R. Benner and F. H. Fobes.

ANDOCIDES, ANTIPHON. Cf. MINOR ATTIC ORATORS.

APOLLODORUS. Sir James G. Frazer. 2 Vols.

APOLLONIUS RHODIUS. R. C. Seaton.

APOSTOLIC FATHERS. Kirsopp Lake. 2 Vols.

APPIAN: ROMAN HISTORY. Horace White. 4 Vols.

ARATUS. Cf. CALLIMACHUS.

ARISTIDES: ORATIONS. C. A. Behr. Vol. I.

ARISTOPHANES. Benjamin Bickley Rogers. 3 Vols. Verse trans.

ARISTOTLE: ART OF RHETORIC. J. H. Freese.

ARISTOTLE: ATHENIAN CONSTITUTION, EUDEMIAN ETHICS, VICES AND VIRTUES. H. Rackham.

ARISTOTLE: GENERATION OF ANIMALS. A. L. Peck.

ARISTOTLE: HISTORIA ANIMALIUM. A. L. Peck. Vols. I.–II.

ARISTOTLE: METAPHYSICS. H. Tredennick. 2 Vols.

ARISTOTLE: METEOROLOGICA. H. D. P. Lee.

ARISTOTLE: MINOR WORKS. W. S. Hett. On Colours, On Things Heard, On Physiognomies, On Plants, On Marvellous Things Heard, Mechanical Problems, On Indivisible Lines, On Situations and Names of Winds, On Melissus, Xenophanes, and Gorgias.

ARISTOTLE: NICOMACHEAN ETHICS. H. Rackham.

ARISTOTLE: OECONOMICA and MAGNA MORALIA. G. C. Armstrong (with METAPHYSICS, Vol. II).

ARISTOTLE: ON THE HEAVENS. W. K. C. Guthrie.

ARISTOTLE: ON THE SOUL, PARVA NATURALIA, ON BREATH. W. S. Hett.

ARISTOTLE: CATEGORIES, ON INTERPRETATION, PRIOR ANALYTICS. H. P. Cooke and H. Tredennick.

ARISTOTLE: POSTERIOR ANALYTICS, TOPICS. H. Tredennick and E. S. Forster.

ARISTOTLE: ON SOPHISTICAL REFUTATIONS.
On Coming to be and Passing Away, On the Cosmos. E. S. Forster and D. J. Furley.

ARISTOTLE: PARTS OF ANIMALS. A. L. Peck; MOTION AND PROGRESSION OF ANIMALS. E. S. Forster.

ARISTOTLE: PHYSICS. Rev. P. Wicksteed and F. M. Cornford. 2 Vols.

ARISTOTLE: POETICS and LONGINUS. W. Hamilton Fyfe; DEMETRIUS ON STYLE. W. Rhys Roberts.

ARISTOTLE: POLITICS. H. Rackham.

ARISTOTLE: PROBLEMS. W. S. Hett. 2 Vols.

ARISTOTLE: RHETORICA AD ALEXANDRUM (with PROBLEMS. Vol. II). H. Rackham.

ARRIAN: HISTORY OF ALEXANDER and INDICA. Rev. E. Iliffe Robson. 2 Vols. New version P. Brunt.

ATHENAEUS: DEIPNOSOPHISTAE. C. B. Gulick. 7 Vols.

BABRIUS AND PHAEDRUS (Latin). B. E. Perry.

ST. BASIL: LETTERS. R. J. Deferrari. 4 Vols.

CALLIMACHUS: FRAGMENTS. C. A. Trypanis. MUSAEUS: HERO AND LEANDER. T. Gelzer and C. Whitman.

CALLIMACHUS, Hymns and Epigrams, and LYCOPHRON. A. W. Mair; ARATUS. G. R. Mair.

CLEMENT OF ALEXANDRIA. Rev. G. W. Butterworth.

COLLUTHUS. Cf. OPPIAN.

DAPHNIS AND CHLOE. Thornley's Translation revised by J. M. Edmonds: and PARTHENIUS. S. Gaselee.

DEMOSTHENES I.: OLYNTHIACS, PHILIPPICS and MINOR ORATIONS I.–XVII. AND XX. J. H. Vince.

DEMOSTHENES II.: DE CORONA and DE FALSA LEGATIONE. C. A. Vince and J. H. Vince.

DEMOSTHENES III.: MEIDIAS, ANDROTION, ARISTOCRATES, TIMOCRATES and ARISTOGEITON I. and II. J. H. Vince.

DEMOSTHENES IV.–VI: PRIVATE ORATIONS and IN NEAERAM. A. T. Murray.

DEMOSTHENES VII: FUNERAL SPEECH, EROTIC ESSAY, EXORDIA and LETTERS. N. W. and N. J. DeWitt.

DIO CASSIUS: ROMAN HISTORY. E. Cary. 9 Vols.

5

DIO CHRYSOSTOM. J. W. Cohoon and H. Lamar Crosby. 5 Vols.

DIODORUS SICULUS. 12 Vols. Vols. I.–VI. C. H. Oldfather. Vol. VII. C. L. Sherman. Vol. VIII. C. B. Welles. Vols. IX. and X. R. M. Geer. Vol. XI. F. Walton. Vol. XII. F. Walton. General Index. R. M. Geer.

DIOGENES LAERTIUS. R. D. Hicks. 2 Vols. New Introduction by H. S. Long.

DIONYSIUS OF HALICARNASSUS: ROMAN ANTIQUITIES. Spelman's translation revised by E. Cary. 7 Vols.

DIONYSIUS OF HALICARNASSUS: CRITICAL ESSAYS. S. Usher. 2 Vols. Vol. I.

EPICTETUS. W. A. Oldfather. 2 Vols.

EURIPIDES. A. S. Way. 4 Vols. Verse trans.

EUSEBIUS: ECCLESIASTICAL HISTORY. Kirsopp Lake and J. E. L. Oulton. 2 Vols.

GALEN: ON THE NATURAL FACULTIES. A. J. Brock.

GREEK ANTHOLOGY. W. R. Paton. 5 Vols.

GREEK BUCOLIC POETS (THEOCRITUS, BION, MOSCHUS). J. M Edmonds.

GREEK ELEGY AND IAMBUS with the ANACREONTEA. J. M. Edmonds. 2 Vols.

GREEK LYRIC. D. A. Campbell. 4 Vols. Vol. I.

GREEK MATHEMATICAL WORKS. Ivor Thomas. 2 Vols.

HERODES. Cf. THEOPHRASTUS: CHARACTERS.

HERODIAN. C. R. Whittaker. 2 Vols.

HERODOTUS. A. D. Godley. 4 Vols.

HESIOD AND THE HOMERIC HYMNS. H. G. Evelyn White.

HIPPOCRATES and the FRAGMENTS OF HERACLEITUS. W. H. S. Jones and E. T. Withington. 4 Vols.

HOMER: ILIAD. A. T. Murray. 2 Vols.

HOMER: ODYSSEY. A. T. Murray. 2 Vols.

ISAEUS. E. W. Forster.

ISOCRATES. George Norlin and LaRue Van Hook. 3 Vols.

[ST. JOHN DAMASCENE]: BARLAAM AND IOASAPH. Rev. G. R. Woodward, Harold Mattingly and D. M. Lang.

JOSEPHUS. 10 Vols. Vols. I.–IV. H. Thackeray. Vol. V. H. Thackeray and R. Marcus. Vols. VI.–VII. R. Marcus. Vol. VIII. R. Marcus and Allen Wikgren. Vols. IX.–X. L. H. Feldman.

JULIAN. Wilmer Cave Wright. 3 Vols.

LIBANIUS. A. F. Norman. 3 Vols. Vols. I.–II.

LUCIAN. 8 Vols. Vols. I.–V. A. M. Harmon. Vol. VI. K. Kilburn. Vols. VII.–VIII. M. D. Macleod.

LYCOPHRON. Cf. CALLIMACHUS.

Lyra Graeca, J. M. Edmonds. 2 Vols.

Lysias. W. R. M. Lamb.

Manetho. W. G. Waddell.

Marcus Aurelius. C. R. Haines.

Menander. W. G. Arnott. 3 Vols. Vol. I.

Minor Attic Orators (Antiphon, Andocides, Lycurgus, Demades, Dinarchus, Hyperides). K. J. Maidment and J. O. Burtt. 2 Vols.

Musaeus: Hero and Leander. Cf. Callimachus.

Nonnos: Dionysiaca. W. H. D. Rouse. 3 Vols.

Oppian, Colluthus, Tryphiodorus. A. W. Mair.

Papyri. Non-Literary Selections. A. S. Hunt and C. C. Edgar. 2 Vols. Literary Selections (Poetry). D. L. Page.

Parthenius. Cf. Daphnis and Chloe.

Pausanias: Description of Greece. W. H. S. Jones. 4 Vols. and Companion Vol. arranged by R. E. Wycherley.

Philo. 10 Vols. Vols. I.–V. F. H. Colson and Rev. G. H. Whitaker. Vols. VI.–IX. F. H. Colson. Vol. X. F. H. Colson and the Rev. J. W. Earp.

Philo: two supplementary Vols. (*Translation only.*) Ralph Marcus.

Philostratus: The Life of Apollonius of Tyana. F. C. Conybeare. 2 Vols.

Philostratus: Imagines; Callistratus: Descriptions. A. Fairbanks.

Philostratus and Eunapius: Lives of the Sophists. Wilmer Cave Wright.

Pindar. Sir J. E. Sandys.

Plato: Charmides, Alcibiades, Hipparchus, The Lovers, Theages, Minos and Epinomis. W. R. M. Lamb.

Plato: Cratylus, Parmenides, Greater Hippias, Lesser Hippias. H. N. Fowler.

Plato: Euthyphro, Apology, Crito, Phaedo, Phaedrus, H. N. Fowler.

Plato: Laches, Protagoras, Meno, Euthydemus. W. R. M. Lamb.

Plato: Laws. Rev. R. G. Bury. 2 Vols.

Plato: Lysis, Symposium, Gorgias. W. R. M. Lamb.

Plato: Republic. Paul Shorey. 2 Vols.

Plato: Statesman, Philebus. H. N. Fowler; Ion. W. R. M. Lamb.

Plato: Theaetetus and Sophist. H. N. Fowler.

Plato: Timaeus, Critias, Clitopho, Menexenus, Epistulae. Rev. R. G. Bury.

Plotinus: A. H. Armstrong. 7 Vols. Vols. I.–III.

PLUTARCH: MORALIA. 16 Vols. Vols I.–V. F. C. Babbitt. Vol. VI. W. C. Helmbold. Vols. VII. and XIV. P. H. De Lacy and B. Einarson. Vol. VIII. P. A. Clement and H. B. Hoffleit. Vol. IX. E. L. Minar, Jr., F. H. Sandbach, W. C. Helmbold. Vol. X. H. N. Fowler. Vol. XI. L. Pearson and F. H. Sandbach. Vol. XII. H. Cherniss and W. C. Helmbold. Vol. XIII 1–2. H. Cherniss. Vol. XV. F. H. Sandbach.

PLUTARCH: THE PARALLEL LIVES. B. Perrin. 11 Vols.

POLYBIUS. W. R. Paton. 6 Vols.

PROCOPIUS. H. B. Dewing. 7 Vols.

PTOLEMY: TETRABIBLOS. F. E. Robbins.

QUINTUS SMYRNAEUS. A. S. Way. Verse trans.

SEXTUS EMPIRICUS. Rev. R. G. Bury. 4 Vols.

SOPHOCLES. F. Storr. 2 Vols. Verse trans.

STRABO: GEOGRAPHY. Horace L. Jones. 8 Vols.

THEOCRITUS. Cf. GREEK BUCOLIC POETS.

THEOPHRASTUS: CHARACTERS. J. M. Edmonds. HERODES, etc. A. D. Knox.

THEOPHRASTUS: ENQUIRY INTO PLANTS. Sir Arthur Hort, Bart. 2 Vols.

THEOPHRASTUS: DE CAUSIS PLANTARUM. G. K. K. Link and B. Einarson. 3 Vols. Vol. I.

THUCYDIDES. C. F. Smith. 4 Vols.

TRYPHIODORUS. Cf. OPPIAN.

XENOPHON: CYROPAEDIA. Walter Miller. 2 Vols.

XENOPHON: HELLENCIA. C. L. Brownson. 2 Vols.

XENOPHON: ANABASIS. C. L. Brownson.

XENOPHON: MEMORABILIA AND OECONOMICUS. E. C. Marchant. SYMPOSIUM AND APOLOGY. O. J. Todd.

XENOPHON: SCRIPTA MINORA. E. C. Marchant. CONSTITUTION OF THE ATHENIANS. G. W. Bowersock.

7.